Investment Appraisal

Uwe Götze · Deryl Northcott · Peter Schuster

Investment Appraisal

Methods and Models

Springer

Prof. Dr. Uwe Götze
TU Chemnitz
Fakultät für Wirtschaftswissenschaften
Thüringer Weg 7
09107 Chemnitz
Germany
u.goetze@wirtschaft.tu-chemnitz.de

Prof. Deryl Northcott
School of Business
The Auckland University of Technology
42 Wakefield Street
Auckland 1142
New Zealand
deryl.northcott@aut.ac.nz

Prof. Dr. Peter Schuster
Schmalkalden University
of Applied Sciences
Faculty of Business and Economics
P.O.Box 10 04 52
98564 Schmalkalden
Germany

and

St. Mary's University
Bill Greehey School of Business
Graduate Faculty
One Camino Santa Maria
San Antonio, Texas 78228-8607
USA
schuster@fh-schmalkalden.de

ISBN 978-3-540-39968-1 e-ISBN 978-3-540-39969-8

DOI 10.1007/978-3-540-39969-8

Library of Congress Control Number: 2007937123

Production: LE-TEX Jelonek, Schmidt & Vöckler GbR, Leipzig
Coverdesign: WMX Design GmbH, Heidelberg

Printed on acid-free paper

9 8 7 6 5 4 3 2 1

springer.com

Preface

Investment decisions are of vital importance to all companies, since they determine both their potential to succeed and their ultimate cost structure. Investments usually entail high initial cash outflows and thus tie up substantial funds. Sound investment decisions are important, therefore. Yet, due to a highly complex and rapidly changing business environment they remain a challenging management task.

Effective appraisal methods are valuable tools to support investment decisions. They have been the subject of discussion for several decades, particularly in the 1960s and 1970s. During this period, different approaches were examined, developed and refined to support aspects of investment appraisal such as multi-criteria or simultaneous decision-making and the consideration of uncertainty. In the last decade these methods have been advanced further by insights from capital market theory, such as options pricing and risk-return models.

A number of methods are included in this book, some of which – while examined in research journals – are not widely known, or at least not widely described in other textbooks. Investment appraisal methods are an important part of an academic management accounting education, yet they are sometimes neglected in books and university curricula. Due to its growing importance for companies, however, this rapidly developing area of expertise has become increasingly relevant for potential management accountants.

This book derives from a long-standing tradition in Germany and builds on a successful German textbook by one of the authors (Götze, U. 2006. *Investitionsrechnung*. 5 ed. Berlin et al.: Springer). It describes a wide range of investment appraisal methods to support capital budgeting decisions and evaluates their use, assumptions and limitations using illustrative examples and calculations.

The authors would like to express their gratitude to several people who made valuable contributions to this book: Prof. Jürgen Bloech for his substantial input on investments and their assessment; Dr. Fadi Alkaraan (Aleppo University) for his contribution to the discussion of strategic analysis tools in Chapter 1; Dr. Necia France (Auckland University of Technology) for her careful proofreading; as well as Susann Butze, Dietlind Scholz and Anja Wappler (Chemnitz University of Technology) for their editorial assistance.

Chemnitz, Auckland and Schmalkalden, July 2007

Uwe Götze
Deryl Northcott
Peter Schuster

Guided Tour of the Book

This book is split into five main parts organised into nine chapters. After an introductory part about capital budgeting and investment decisions, Part Two describes the basic methods of investment appraisal. They can be classified into *static methods* (analysing an average period) and the most widely used *discounted cash flow methods*. Part Three then moves beyond the basic techniques to introduce *compounded cash flow methods* and illustrates *specific applications* of discounted and compounded cash flow methods.

Part Four deals with *multi-criteria methods* and the application of *selected methods for simultaneous investment and financing or production decisions*. Methods and models for the consideration of uncertainty form the concluding Part Five of the book. These are divided between methods and models applied to single investment projects and those useful for investment programmes.

Each of the sections is organised in the same way, with a sequence consisting of the *Description* of the model or method, an *Example* providing ample illustration and practice in performing the investment appraisal calculation and the *Assessment* of the model or method. Additionally, *Key Concepts* are highlighted throughout the text. Finally, end of chapter *Exercises* are provided to reinforce and extend relevant concepts, with *Solutions* to the exercises given at the end of the book. The suggested *Further Readings* offer additional sources for readers who wish to research a topic in greater depth.

The main target audience for this book is students of management, business and, specifically, management accounting. However, the book will also interest business practitioners concerned with investment decision-making and students engaged in higher professional education. The instructional approach of the book combines the delivery of overviews, as bases of understanding, with a detailed description and discussion of relevant models and techniques, supported by extensive examples and exercises. This combination of features aims to meet the needs of university students around the world and provide all readers with a thorough insight into the different investment appraisal methods, their uses, assumptions and limitations.

Contents

List of Figures .... **XIII**

Part I Introduction **1**

1 Capital Budgeting and Investment Decisions 3
1.1 Characteristics and Classification of Investment Projects 3
1.2 Investment Planning and Investment Decisions 6
1.2.1 Investment Planning as Part of the Management Process 7
1.2.2 Investment Planning as Part of the Capital Investment Decision-Making Process 8
1.2.3 Strategic Analysis Tools Supporting the Capital Investment Decision-Making Process 20
1.3 Investment Appraisal Methods as Tools for Investment Planning 24

Further Reading 27

Part II Basic methods of investment appraisal **29**

2 Static Methods 31
2.1 Cost Comparison Method 32
2.2 Profit Comparison Method 39
2.3 Average Rate of Return Method 41
2.4 Static Payback Period Method 44
Assessment Material 47

3 Discounted Cash Flow Methods 51
3.1 Introduction 51
3.2 Net Present Value Method 54
3.3 Annuity Method 65
3.4 Internal Rate of Return Method 67
3.5 Dynamic Payback Period Method 75
3.6 Data Collection 77
Assessment Material 84

Further Reading 87

Part III Advanced Methods and Applications of Investment Appraisal..........91

4 Compounded Cash Flow Methods....93
4.1 Compound Value Method....93
4.2 Critical Debt Interest Rate Method....98
4.3 Visualisation of Financial Implications (VoFI) Method....100
Assessment Material....109

5 Selected Further Applications of Investment Appraisal Methods....111
5.1 Income Taxes and Investment Decisions....111
5.1.1 Taxes and the Net Present Value Method....111
5.1.2 Taxes and the Visualisation of Financial Implications (VoFI) Method....116
5.2 The Assessment of Foreign Direct Investments....118
5.2.1 Special Characteristics of Foreign Direct Investments....118
5.2.2 Net Present Value Model and the Assessment of Foreign Direct Investments....122
5.2.3 The Visualisation of Financial Implications (VoFI) Method and the Assessment of Foreign Investments....127
5.3 Models for Economic Life and Replacement Time Decisions....131
5.3.1 Overview....131
5.3.2 Optimum Economic Life without Subsequent Projects....133
5.3.3 Optimum Economic Life with a Limited Number of Identical Subsequent Projects....137
5.3.4 Optimum Economic Life with an Unlimited Number of Identical Subsequent Projects....141
5.3.5 Optimum Replacement Time with an Unlimited Number of Identical Subsequent Projects....144
5.3.6 Optimum Replacement Time with a Limited Number of Non-Identical Subsequent Projects....148
5.4 Models to Determine Optimum Investment Timing....151
Assessment Material....161

Further Reading....167

Part IV Multi-Criteria Methods and Simultaneous Decision-Making 169

6 Multi-Criteria Methods 171
6.1 Introduction 171
6.2 Utility Value Analysis 175
6.3 Analytic Hierarchy Process 179
6.4 Multi-Attribute Utility Theory 193
6.5 PROMETHEE 203
Assessment Material 215

7 Simultaneous Decision-Making Models 221
7.1 Static Model for Simultaneous Investment and Financing Decisions (DEAN Model) 221
7.2 Multi-Tier Model of Simultaneous Investment and Financing Decisions (HAX and WEINGARTNER Model) 228
7.3 Multi-Tier model of Simultaneous Investment and Production Decisions (Extended FÖRSTNER and HENN Model) 238
Assessment Material 248

Further Reading 255

Part V Methods and Models that Incorporate Uncertainty 259

8 Methods and Models for Appraising Investment Projects under Uncertainty ... 261
8.1 Decision Theory 262
8.2 Risk-Adjusted Analysis 268
8.3 Sensitivity Analysis 274
8.4 Risk Analysis 280
8.5 Decision-Tree Method 286
8.6 Options Pricing Models 296
Assessment Material 308

9 Analysing Investment Programmes under Uncertainty 317
9.1 Overview 317
9.2 Portfolio Selection 320
9.3 Flexible Planning 329

Further Reading 337

Solutions......341

References......369

Index......383

List of Figures

1-1 Classification of investments ... 4
1-2 Phases of the management process in companies ... 7
1-3 The capital investment decision-making process ... 10
1-4 Characteristics of decision models ... 25
1-5 Structure of the book ... 26

2-1 Capital tie-up for investment project A (with zero liquidation value) ... 35
2-2 Capital tie-up of investment project B (with positive liquidation value) .. 36

3-1 Dynamic investment appraisal methods ... 53
3-2 Discounting net cash flows for the net present value method ... 55
3-3 The NPV of isolated investment projects as a function of the uniform discount rate ... 69
3-4 Interpolation to determine the internal rate of return ... 71

4-1 Dynamic investment appraisal methods ... 93
4-2 The VoFI table ... 102
4-3 VoFI plan for investment project A ... 104
4-4 VoFI plan for investment project B ... 105

5-1 VoFI plan for investment project A considering taxes ... 117
5-2 Separate calculations to determine the tax effects of investment project A ... 117
5-3 VoFI table of a daughter company ... 128
5-4 VoFI table of a mother company ... 130
5-5 Number and types of subsequent projects in economic life and replacement time models ... 133
5-6 Temporal linkage between projects in a two-project investment chain ... 138
5-7 Annuities for a chain of identical investment projects as a function of economic life ... 142
5-8 Marginal profit criterion and the optimum economic life ... 143
5-9 Replacement criterion for an unlimited chain of identical projects ... 146

6-1 MADM methods according to the type of information ... 174
6-2 Hierarchy of targets ... 177

6-3 Transformation function for the criterion 'size of land' 178
6-4 SAATY's nine-point scale for pair comparisons 181
6-5 Average values of indices of consistency 185
6-6 Decision hierarchy 187
6-7 Pair comparison assessments for the alternatives and their evaluation 190
6-8 Pair comparison assessments for the target criteria and sub-targets, and their evaluation 191
6-9 Utility measurement by attribute comparison 195
6-10 Determination of an individual utility function 196
6-11 Indifference curves 197
6-12 Individual utility function for the attribute 'size of land' 200
6-13 Generalised criteria with PROMETHEE 205
6-14 Generalised criteria and preference functions in the example 210
6-15 The outranking relationship 211
6-16 The partial pre-order 212
6-17 Graphical presentation of the partial pre-order 212

7-1 Graphical solution using the DEAN model 226
7-2 Relationships between the model endogenous compounding factors and the model endogenous interest rates 234
7-3 Production structure in the basic model for a production programme decision 239
7-4 Temporal structure of the liquidity, capacity and sales restrictions and the objective function 244

8-1 Decision matrix 262
8-2 Changes in the net present value with variations in individual input measures 276
8-3 Critical values of individual input measures 277
8-4 Net present value relative to variations in sales prices and volumes 278
8-5 Critical sales and production volumes for two investment alternatives 279
8-6 Distribution function of the net present value of investment project A 283
8-7 Distribution function of the net present values of investment projects A and B 284
8-8 Formal structure of a decision-tree 287
8-9 Decision-tree of example 8-3 289

8-10 Decision-tree for a decision about investment timing 292
8-11 Differentiated expectations about future developments 295
8-12 Share prices, option values and value of the duplication portfolio in the binomial model 299
8-13 Cash flows and share prices during the investment period......................302

9-1 Linear membership function for a sales restriction 319
9-2 Expected profit and risk measures of portfolios 321
9-3 Development of share returns 322
9-4 Distribution of security returns 323
9-5 Iso-variance-ellipses 325
9-6 Iso-variance-ellipses, expected returns and efficient portfolios 326
9-7 Efficient portfolios in the return-variance diagram 327
9-8 Stochastic tree 329
9-9 Stochastic tree for the example model 332

Part I

Introduction

Chapter 1: Capital Budgeting and Investment Decisions

1.1 Characteristics and Classification of Investment Projects

Investments can be considered from different points of view. According to the cash flow oriented perspective an investment project can be characterised by a stream of cash flows starting with an initial investment outlay – a cash outflow. The basic task for investment decision-making then will be to ascertain whether the future benefits from the investment will make the initial outlay worthwhile.

> *Key Concept:*
> An investment project is a series of cash inflows and outflows, typically starting with a cash outflow (the initial investment outlay) followed by cash inflows and/or cash outflows in later periods (years).

This approach on the one hand leads to relatively easy solutions through the use of calculations that allow the stream of cash flows to be converted into (one or more) measures of the investment project's profitability. On the other hand, it limits the analysis of benefits and returns to the effects of cash flows. At this point it is crucial to remember that investment projects often show important effects other than those easily measurable in cash flows (e.g. research and development activities). Non-monetary effects are considered and described later in Chapter 6.

Other ways of looking at investments exist. Connecting investments to the company's balance sheet (since investments transform capital into assets) emphasises the tying-up of capital. This capital budgeting perspective implies a systematic approach to evaluating an investment as a long-term (or capital) asset. The benefit of an investment project is then seen as the monetary value gained by the company through acquiring a long-term asset in the form of increased future profits and cash flows attributable to that long-term asset.

The cash flow oriented concept that is used throughout most of the chapters of this book has the key advantage that anything that can be measured in cash flow(s) can be transformed and combined into target measures for deciding about a project's profitability. In accordance with the definition used, an investment project requires a long-term perspective and a long-term capital commitment. The investment appraisal methods mainly differ in the way they transform cash flows from different years, the target measure(s) they use as the decision criterion, and the assumptions they make.

Following the same line of argument, a financing alternative can be regarded in a similar way, i.e. it is a project that starts with an inflow typically followed by outflows and/or inflows. This reflects the close connection between investment and financing alternatives and the methods used for appraising each of them.

Investment projects can take many forms. One way to classify them is according to the *type* of investment. Financial investments can be either speculative or non-speculative and include, for example, shareholder deposits, the purchase of investment certificates and real-estate funds. Investments in assets can be subdivided into those concerning physical assets (e.g. goods, machines, equipment) and those concerning 'intangible' assets (e.g. education, advertising, research and development).

The following figure (adapted from KERN, 1974, p. 14) shows a differentiation of physical investment projects, classifying them according to *possible causes for investments*:

1. Foundational investment
2. Current investment
    a) Replacement investment
    b) Major repair or general overhaul investment
3. Supplementary investment
    a) Expansion investment
    b) Change investment (e.g. rationalisation, diversification)
    c) Certainty investment

Fig. 1-1: Classification of investments

The distinction between foundational, current and supplementary investments refers to the different phases of products or companies. Foundational investments are linked with a start-up and they can be either investments in a new company, or in an existing company's new branch at a new location. Current investments are replacement, major repair or general overhaul investments: a simple replacement investment is characterised by the substitution of equipment without a change in its characteristics. Frequently, however, the substitute is an improved, non-identical asset. In this case the substitution might also be viewed as a rationalisation and/or expansion investment, making its classification potentially ambiguous.

Supplementary investments refer to investments in equipment in existing locations and they can be classified as expansion, change, or certainty investments. The first type (expansion) leads to a rise in either the capacity or the potential of a company. Change investments are characterised by the modification of certain features of the company for varying reasons. Within this category, rationalisation investments are primarily driven by a requirement to reduce costs (e.g. caused by changed volumes of sales of existing products), while diversification investments arise from the need to prepare for changing production programmes. The demarcation between expansion and change investments can be problematical, since an increase in capacity is often accompanied by a change in the company's characteristic features.

Finally, certainty investments are those that aim to reduce risk in a wider sense. Examples might include buying shares in suppliers of raw material or in research and development companies.

Another possible classification criterion is the *operational area* that drives the investment. For example, investments can be categorised as being for procurement, production, sales, administration, or research and development. This can be a helpful classification when investment projects are isolated within one operational area and have little or no impact on other areas. However, many investments that are instigated by one operational area affect other parts and other decisions of a company, especially in regard to the availability of internal financial funds.

To illustrate, consider investments in a production plant. The procurement of these long-term assets is primarily decided based upon assumptions about future production. However, an expansion investment carried out to manufacture a new product type (for example) is an interdependent investment project, requiring considerable co-ordination of decisions from areas like sales, production, financing, human resources and research and development. Since the investment links to the company's environment in many ways, it is not just a production-related decision. In such instances, companies should be regarded as open systems and investment decisions should pay attention to the diverse effects that an investment can have. Sometimes, classifying investment projects by operational area can be counter-productive in this regard.

The final, very important, classification criterion is the *level of uncertainty* an investment entails. A situation of perfect certainty in regard to the effects of investments rarely exists, since investments generally show long-term future effects. However, uncertainty can vary substantially and it is possible to differentiate between relatively certain or uncertain investment projects. For example, a financial investment in fixed-yield bonds can be regarded as entailing little uncertainty. In contrast, investments to manufacture brand-new products usually involve considerable uncertainty in regard to sales potential, market success, and production processes that are not yet well established. Another example is investments in research and development, for which future resource requirements and outcomes (in terms of usable results) are extremely uncertain. For such investments, the necessary forecasting of uncertain cash flows is both difficult and inexact.

Although it is common to categorise investment projects as outlined above (based on cause, operational area, or level of uncertainty), some *other project characteristics* may be relevant to how they should be appraised. The first of these relates to whether the outcomes of the investment are readily quantifiable. The investment appraisal methods described in Part Two assume that all effects of an investment can be measured in monetary terms (e.g. cash flows or costs and profits) and attributed to both certain periods and certain projects. But, qualitative differences can exist between competing projects and therefore need to be considered. Projects with substantial qualitative outcomes require different appraisal methods to those with exclusively quantitative/financial outcomes.

Also, time-related differences may exist. A project could involve either a limited or an unlimited time horizon (e.g. for a financial investment), which will affect how it should be appraised. Other differences can result from whether a project is a stand-alone investment or links into subsequent projects. Investment projects can have no subsequent projects, a limited number, or an unlimited number of subsequent projects. These different forms may affect the profitability of the initial project (they are described in Chapter 5, Section 5.3).

In summary, investments exist in multiple forms: single or multi-purpose; certain or uncertain; isolated or interdependent; with limited or unlimited time horizons; stand-alone or connected with subsequent projects. All must be considered using appropriate investment appraisal methods. These are applied within a decision-making and control approach that primarily focuses on projects or programmes, i.e. makes decisions about a single investment project or a set of interrelated projects. The decision process usually is called *capital budgeting* and relates to long-term capital investment programmes and projects that must be assessed by investment appraisal.

Key Concept:
Investment projects can be categorised in many different ways. As they have substantially different characteristics, investment projects may require different investment appraisal methods to appropriately assess their impact, value and profitability.

1.2 Investment Planning and Investment Decisions

The life cycle of an investment can be regarded as consisting of specific phases. The main phases of this life cycle are: planning, implementation and utilisation. Since the appraisal of investment projects is part of the planning phase, this book focuses on planning rather than issues related to project implementation and utilisation.

In the following discussion, investment planning will be considered from different perspectives, first as part of the management process and second, in more detail, as part of the specific capital investment decision-making process.

1.2.1 Investment Planning as Part of the Management Process

The planning phase involves preparing to make decisions about one or more investments, including identifying the types of investment projects necessary to achieve the company's objectives. These projects should be closely linked to the company's strategy. The search for alternative projects and the information acquisition that is required to define and assess them form an important part of the planning process, which is concluded by the selection of the investment project to be undertaken. During the implementation phase, detailed project planning is followed by the construction or acquisition of the asset. As soon as this is finalised, utilisation can start and the investment project can begin to earn returns for the company.

The capital budgeting process can be regarded as a specific kind of management process within a company. Figure 1-2 (GÖTZE, 2006, p. 16, with further references) shows phases of the management process, which typically entails planning and control activities.

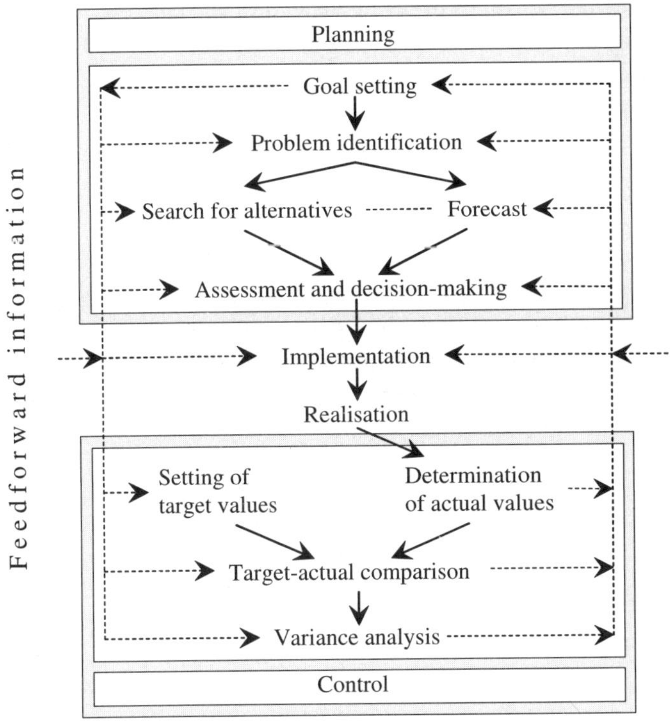

Fig. 1-2: Phases of the management process in companies

Planning requires many pieces of information and has multiple aims, including:

- Identifying risks and uncertainties
- Incorporating options and increasing flexibility

- Reducing complexity
- Identifying and exploiting synergistic effects
- Formulating targets
- Achieving early warning of problems
- Co-ordinating functional plans and sub-plans
- Enabling control processes
- Securing information
- Motivating employees and collaborators

Investment planning can be viewed as following the phases of the management process shown in Figure 1-2. *Goal setting* will both influence awareness of the problems (and thus the search strategies for solutions) and provide a framework for the assessment of possible solutions. Different forms of goals exist. *Formal goals* (for instance to increase shareholder value, profits, or employment stability) provide the high-level criteria for assessing the consequences of investments. *Substantive goals* are derived from these formal goals and relate to the steps required to fulfil the formal goals (such as adaptations of the product types and qualities to be produced). After the operationalisation of the goals, uncertainty and risk, and especially risk attitudes, must be considered.

Problem identification and analysis forms the next part of the investment planning process. The aim here is to assess the present situation, anticipate the forecasted future development and identify the deviation between the two, so that the benefits of a potential investment can be anticipated. The third phase, the *search for alternatives*, identifies possible investment alternatives that might be suitable options to address current problems and future needs.

Forecasting and assessment and decision-making form the final phases of the planning process. They require that information is gathered to forecast the future impact of alternative investment projects and that suitable analyses (usually mainly financial) are carried out to select the best investment options.

1.2.2 Investment Planning as Part of the Capital Investment Decision-Making Process

This book will present detailed calculative analyses that can be used to support capital investment decision-making, and there is no doubt that these sorts of rigorous financial analysis tools are important for supporting informed decisions. But, what else goes into capital investment decision-making in organisations? As noted in the introduction, there is more to planning capital investment projects than financial analysis alone.

A key theme of this chapter is the need for capital investment planning and analysis to be supported by an effective decision-making process that fits with, and enhances, organisational strategy. The capital investment choices that companies make are shaped by *current* strategy, but they also play a part in allocating substantial resources that will influence *future* strategy. This chapter will consider how investment analysis forms part of a broader, strategic decision-making activity. It describes how financial analyses fit into the overall decision-making process and what other activities are important in making well informed and effective capital investment decisions. In the next chapter, several emergent strategic analysis tools are described that have been proposed as useful supplements to existing capital investment analysis techniques. The discussion of these topics is motivated by the importance of taking a balanced approach to capital investment decision-making in practice, synthesising rigorous financial appraisal with good decision-making processes and sound strategic analysis.

The analysis tools presented in this book are used to evaluate the profitability of capital investment opportunities. However, before such analysis tools can be applied, several other decision-making steps are necessary. Similarly, further steps are required *after* the financial analysis is undertaken, to ensure that a capital investment project has a successful outcome. Taking account of all of the necessary steps, investment decision-making can be represented as an ordered process, as shown in Figure 1-3. The remainder of this section will describe each of the decision-making steps and show how financial appraisal methods fit into the overall process.

Developing the capital investment strategy

Capital investments should not be made on an ad hoc basis, but should link into the organisation's existing and planned investment programme. This investment programme should in turn be driven by the company's long-term strategy. Strategy will dictate the kinds of products, markets and technologies the organisation wants to invest in, and so proposals to invest in projects outside these guidelines are unlikely to gain support and commitment or to be approved for funding. Throughout this book it will be assumed that the strategic objective of capital investment decision-making is to invest in projects that will maximise the company's wealth (an exception is presented in Chapter 6). However, for some organisations, or at some stages of an organisation's life-cycle, other objectives are more appropriate or similarly important, such as the continued survival of the company, the maximisation of sales, or the provision of services at the lowest cost (for example, in public sector organisations). Whatever the organisation's strategy, it should be translated into guidelines and limitations as to what sorts of investment projects are likely to be acceptable from a strategic standpoint. These guidelines should be clearly communicated to organisational personnel when capital investment policies are developed and disseminated.

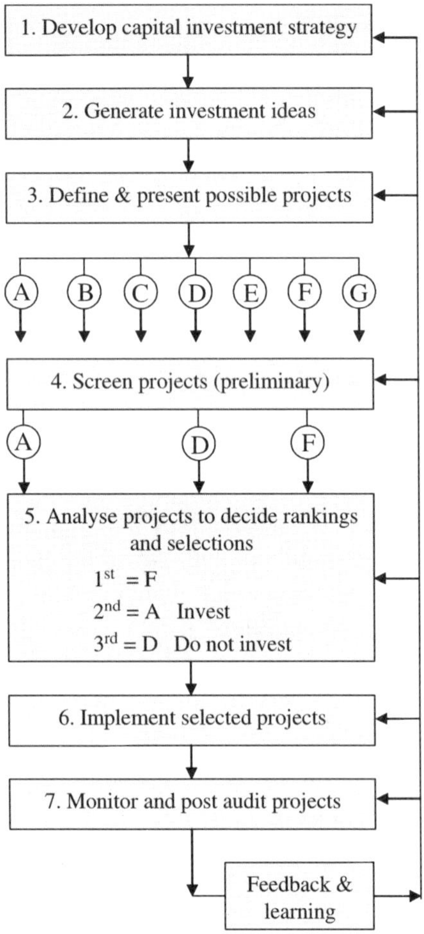

Fig. 1-3: The capital investment decision-making process

As part of integrating organisational strategy into the capital investment process, an investment budget should be planned for each year or preferably for several years to come (planning such a budget can be supported by the use of models for simultaneous decision-making, as described in Chapter 7). Project ideas should then be considered some time in advance of expected investment. For example, there may be a June deadline for proposing projects to commence in the year starting the following January. Projects that are eventually approved for investment are then included in the capital budget, which is a statement of spending intentions, and funds are earmarked to pay for budgeted projects. The advantages of this approach are that capital expenditure is planned according to agreed strategic aims, and decisions are based on direct comparisons between competing projects. Also, funding can be arranged in advance and there are fewer surprise expenditures to create cash flow problems for the organisation.

The disadvantage of this system, however, is that it is fairly inflexible and can reduce the organisation's ability to respond quickly to unplanned investment opportunities. If a project idea comes up that was not anticipated in the company's investment strategy or included in the capital budget, it may be delayed or even excluded. Indeed, it is often difficult to get funding for such last minute investments, since previously approved projects are usually given priority. To avoid this disadvantage, capital investment projects could be considered at any time of the year, without fixed deadlines for compiling a planned budget. However, this makes it difficult to compare projects that are competing for limited funds, since they are proposed at different times and decisions are made without knowledge of what opportunities might arise next. A balance between the first (planned) system and the second (ongoing) approach is usually best. Organisations should aim for a systematic approach that fits with strategic goals, while still retaining some flexibility and discretionary funds for unplanned investment opportunities that might arise during the year.

Generating investment ideas

Once the capital investment strategy is developed and budgetary processes are established, the rest of the process relies on the generation of good investment ideas (step 2 in Figure 1-3). Projects do not just exist simply to be discovered – opportunities for investment need to be recognised or created and then exploited. In fact, the success of a company's capital investment programme often depends more on its ability to *create* profitable investment opportunities than on its ability to appraise them.

Ideas for capital investment may come from people throughout the organisation, from senior managers to people working in technical or production positions. For instance, a plant manager might be able to identify ways in which expanded capacity or updated machinery could increase the efficiency of a production process. It is important to encourage everyone to communicate their ideas for investment and to seek advice on proposed projects from people in relevant areas of expertise.

A two-stage decision approach can be a good way of encouraging investment ideas. First, all organisational personnel are encouraged to put forward any preliminary, undeveloped ideas they have. These ideas are then reviewed in the first stage and those which do not seem viable are screened out using relatively simple decision criteria (see the next decision-making step, described below). The more promising ideas continue to stage two, in which thorough financial and strategic appraisals are carried out. It is important to recognise that even projects that do not come to fruition may generate ideas and information that benefit future investments; so unsuccessful projects are not just a waste of time and effort.

Defining and presenting potential investment projects

An investment idea cannot be evaluated until it has been properly defined and presented (step 3 in Figure 1-3). Consider an example where defective production output has been identified as a problem. Although an opportunity to invest in improving performance has been recognised, there is no real 'investment proposal' until possible solutions are identified, technical specifications collated, costs and time-scales ascertained, and likely benefits estimated.

At this definition stage of the decision-making process, the company must be clear about what information is required about a potential investment project and what format the proposal needs to take. The company's capital investment procedures manual should set out the requirements for project information and the format of the formal proposal. Preferred terminology must be specified and defined, and project appraisal methods and criteria should be made clear. Standardised proposal documentation should be used where possible to make project comparisons easier. However, since the nature and characteristics of projects can vary, project proposal forms need to allow for flexibility, for example in the life-span, costs and benefits of projects. Too much flexibility will reduce the comparability of proposals so a balance must be struck to suit the particular organisation and the types of projects it considers. The design of these forms should draw on experiences with a range of recent projects.

The project proposal documentation must contain all the information required to carry out a full financial analysis of the project. It should also demonstrate how the project links to the organisation's strategic plans and identify any qualitative benefits it might have. Since project proposals may be reviewed by high level managers or board members whose expertise lies in areas other than those associated with a particular project, it is important that project technical details are summarised and presented in a clear and comprehensible way. All facts and figures included in a project proposal should be supported by reference to sources of information or investigations carried out. Attached working papers should record any calculations and assumptions made when putting together the project proposal. These supporting papers should be well organised and clear because they may need to be consulted when the project is being analysed. The project proposal should identify the 'critical variables' that will determine the success or failure of the project. For example, the success of an expansion project may depend on the price of additional raw materials and the market demand for increased output. Once critical variables have been identified, the project proposal should indicate worst-case, best-case and most-likely scenarios for these variables. These scenarios will form the focus of sensitivity analysis to examine the riskiness of the project (for a detailed description of sensitivity analysis, see Chapter 8, Section 8.3). Finally, the formal project proposal should be signed by the people initiating the project, and should indicate who would be responsible for commissioning, installing and running the project.

At the project definition and presentation stage, more than one option should be considered where possible. In the case of a project to reduce production defects, for instance, options might include:

- Modifying the existing production plant.
- Replacing the plant with similar technology.
- Completely overhauling the production technology.

Each option may have quite different costs and benefits, even though it is directed at solving the same problem. It is important that the company's capital expenditure proposal documentation requires the project initiator to identify options that have been considered, and to justify why a particular choice is recommended.

Projects are often divided into categories as part of the definition stage. In Section 1.1 it has been outlined how projects might be classified according to their purpose (see Figure 1-1), their operational area (e.g. marketing, production, research and development etc.), or their level of uncertainty. Other categorisation options might focus on investment size, or the extent to which the investment is essential (e.g. for legal reasons, or to ensure business sustainability) or elective. In particular, the size of a capital project often dictates the organisational level at which it can be approved. Smaller projects may not have to be considered by a full capital investment committee. For example an organisation may allow a divisional manager to authorise expenditure up to €50,000 and a regional manager up to €100,000. However, larger projects usually require systematic review by a capital investment committee with final approval granted at a senior level, such as by the chief financial officer, chief executive officer, managing director or board of directors.

The classification of investment types also has implications for the subsequent financial analyses and decision criteria that will be applied to each project. First, the emphasis of financial appraisal will differ between project types. For example, equipment replacement projects may focus simply on incremental savings expected from a new asset. Expansion and strategic projects will need to consider less certain information about markets, competition and capacity constraints. The analysis of legislatively required projects focuses on finding the least-cost alternative for achieving the desired (or required) outcomes. Second, the uniform interest rate used (i.e. the required rate of return) for project acceptance can be varied for different categories of projects (this may be interpreted as a risk-adjusted analysis, an approach that is described in Section 8.2). The main reason for this is the different risk profiles of investments. Replacement projects concern activities the organisation is familiar with, so they involve relatively little risk. Expansion projects are of higher risk, because the inputs, outputs and scale of the project might be hard to predict. Strategic projects may be even riskier, because they move away from familiar activities towards new areas where the organisation has less knowledge of costs and benefits. In many cases, it is demanded that the greater the risk the higher should be a project's expected return to compensate for that risk, so the preliminary categorisation of a project during the definition stage can have a big impact on how it is appraised.

Once the definition and proposal-presentation phase of the decision-making process is complete, the company should have a good sense of what investment options exist, their scope and impact, and what likely costs and benefits they involve. However, they won't all be good investment prospects. So, the next stage is important to ensure that only promising projects, which fit with the company's strategy, proceed further to full financial appraisal.

Screening investment projects

The preliminary screening of capital investment proposals (step 4 in Figure 1-3) weeds out projects which are clearly not viable and which do not warrant further investigation. It is useful, particularly in large organisations, to have a capital investment committee that screens all but the smallest capital projects. Members of this committee should represent a range of expertise in key areas (such as production, marketing, engineering, strategic planning and finance) and be headed by a senior financial manager, or perhaps the organisation's chief executive officer or managing director.

The screening stage is critical to a successful capital investment process, since it is here that a first decision is made about which projects will be given serious consideration. Although screening criteria can be simple, they should be applied systematically to ensure that mistakes are minimised and promising investment opportunities are developed and exploited.

At its most simple level, screening can be based on a qualitative evaluation of a proposal. For example, a project idea might be eliminated at the screening stage if it is physically impractical, beyond the skills and experience of organisational personnel, or not in keeping with overall strategy. Qualitative screening relies on common sense and the experience of the capital investment committee. Simple financial analyses, such as the static payback period method (see Chapter 2) can be carried out in addition to qualitative screening, as a first test of the project's economic viability. Projects that take a long time to recoup their initial cost may be considered detrimental to the short to medium term liquidity of the organisation, so they may be screened out. Of course, it is dangerous to compare projects on the basis of their payback period if some projects are short lived (operating for say 2-5 years) while others are inherently very long-term in nature (running for say 10-20 years). Long-life projects are highly unlikely to pay back quickly, even though their eventual benefits might be substantial. In the screening stage, it is quite easy to spot unusually long-term projects and to ensure that they are not inappropriately ruled out.

Taking into account both qualitative and financial measures, the following questions should be asked when screening projects:

- Does the organisation have a choice about whether to invest in the project, or is it essential (perhaps for legislative or safety reasons)?
- Does the project fit within the organisational strategy?
- Is the idea technically feasible?
- Are the required resources (money, time and expertise) available to implement the project?
- Has this type of project been successful before, either for this organisation or for other organisations?
- Is the project considered too risky or uncertain?
- Does the project meet simple financial screening criteria?

After a project proposal has met preliminary requirements of feasibility and economic desirability (as for projects A, D and F in Figure 1-3), it then moves on to a more rigorous assessment in the next stages of the capital investment process.

Formal analysis of projects

At this stage of the capital investment process (step 5 in Figure 1-3), the company would employ a sophisticated financial and risk analysis using the methods outlined in this book to evaluate the economic viability of capital investment projects. Although accountants usually undertake this financial analysis, they should work in conjunction with the capital investment committee for all but the smallest projects, to draw on a wide range of expertise in areas such as production, marketing, engineering, strategic planning, and finance.

Before the financial analysis can be carried out, the capital investment committee must be satisfied that the formal project proposal contains sufficient information to complete a rigorous economic appraisal. Sometimes further information will be sought at this stage, or capital investment proposals may be sent back to the initiator for re-formulation. The committee should assess how realistic projected proposal cash flows are, and check that important variables are picked up in a project's sensitivity analysis. Of course, some types of proposals (for example those which are legislatively required) have less stringent information requirements at this stage, because the financial analysis results are less likely to determine the ultimate decision.

The various tools for financial and risk analysis are, of course, thoroughly reviewed in this book so are not discussed here. However, this analysis stage calls for a consideration of *both* financial and non-financial (or strategic) aspects of a project, so that a balanced evaluation of its overall costs and benefits can be made and it can be ranked against other competing projects. For some projects, for example low-risk replacements of existing assets, only financial results may be relevant. For projects where both financial and non-financial elements are important, there is no easy rule for weighing up these various factors. The final decision must be left to the judgment of the capital investment committee, since there are few hard-and-fast rules for how to incorporate qualitative aspects of a project into a capital investment appraisal (however, see Section 1.2.3 for some suggested approaches). Of course, intuition can be helpful at this stage of the decision-making process, particularly when it comes from experienced members of the organisation. People should be asked to justify and explain their intuitions, however, and intuition should complement the results of the financial analysis, not replace them.

To summarise, the analysis stage of the decision-making process does not begin and end with financial analysis. The capital investment committee must also:

- Review the organisation's capital investment strategy and how projects fit with it.
- Identify any constraints on the funds available for investment in the current period.
- Rank projects in order of desirability.
- Choose a portfolio of the best projects that can be afforded.
- For projects that have not been selected, check:
  a) Will there be unacceptable negative effects from rejecting these projects?
  b) Can any be delayed rather than rejected?
  c) Can any be modified to make them more acceptable?
- Make a final selection of projects to be funded.

Once the final project choices are decided upon, the planning phase of the capital investment activity is complete. However, further decisions and actions remain to ensure that capital projects are effective and that the organisation gets the most it can from its decision-making efforts.

Implementing capital investment projects

Even the best capital investment decisions may be ineffective if project implementation (step 6 in Figure 1-3) is poorly managed and executed.

It is the task of a designated project manager to oversee the physical construction or installation of a capital asset and to ensure that the project is adequately monitored (this is discussed next). The project manager should be someone technically skilled in the area, but who can consult with finance and accounting staff. Alternatively, some organisations may use implementation teams, where people with expertise in a variety of relevant areas contribute to the project's development.

Examples of specific tasks to be performed during implementation include: reviewing engineering specifications; finalising the contract price for equipment or construction requirements; ensuring that suppliers can meet the needs of the project; overseeing the development, commissioning and/or installation of the project; and arranging for any necessary re-training of employees. Project implementation also requires setting-up effective information systems that can provide feedback on progress, results and critical variables identified in the project proposal. It is useful at this stage to design any subsequent post audit of a project, taking into account the key variables the review will focus on, the responsibility of personnel for providing project information, and the timing of the audit. If post-audit requirements are considered from the start, it is much easier to identify and collect relevant information on the performance of a capital project. The post audit phase, which facilitates feedback and learning, is outlined next.

Project monitoring and post audit

Project monitoring and post audit provide information for the 'feedback loop' in the capital investment decision-making process. In some cases, this feedback can help to identify projects that are deviating from expectations so that problems can be rectified and poor financial outcomes avoided. In other cases, however, the feedback may come too late to help the current project, but it can still help the company to learn and improve future investment decisions and/or implementations.

This review process comprises two main stages. The first, *project monitoring*, is more likely to identify a need for intervention in a current project since it is conducted while the project is in its early stages of implementation. Project monitoring should focus on a combination of physical measures (e.g. early indications of production volumes from a new manufacturing installation), and financial measures (e.g. how much has been spent). Monitoring systems must be able to quickly identify deviations from 'benchmark' performance variables or timing criteria, and should utilise regular expenditure reports to monitor costs against the original, approved investment plan.

The second stage, *project post audit*, occurs once a project is well established and operating to its expected capability, so that the actual outcomes of the project can be assessed. For example, an investment to install a new production line might be reviewed after it has been in operation for an entire production cycle. That way, implementation costs and on-going performance can be observed and compared with initial estimates submitted in the project proposal. Because it occurs after a project is up and running, post audit has limited potential to correct problems in current projects. However, it does have four important benefits:

- To check that spending and specifications conform to the plan as approved.
- To increase the likelihood that capital expenditure proposals are realistic (since project initiators will know that the actual outcomes will be compared to their proposal).
- To identify factors that can lead to the success or failure of projects.
- To learn from past experiences and improve the capital investment process.

There are many possible sources of post-audit data, including: project files (for example: contractors' or engineers' reports, implementation log-books, warranty and service agreements, requests for specification or funding changes); organisational files (for example: accounting records, cost codes which trace expenditures to projects; legal/planning documentation); interviews with people involved with implementing and running the project; and customer feedback (for example about improvements achieved in quality or service).

While the overall aim of collecting this information is to facilitate feedback and learning, project post audit can also refer to particular stages of the capital investment decision-making process. For example, a *decision audit* reviews the effectiveness of the steps leading up to the decision to invest, i.e. project identification, screening, putting together the formal project proposal, the financial analysis, and the ranking and selection process. It checks that laid-down procedures were followed and notes any irregularities and their consequences. This type of audit can be very useful in improving the organisation's decision-making processes.

If, however, a company wishes to review the steps that occur *after* a decision is made to invest, it may choose to conduct an *implementation audit*. An implementation audit seeks to establish whether differences between planned and actual project outcomes are due to inaccurate planning or poor commissioning and implementation. The information generated can be a useful basis for assessing the performance of both the investment decision-makers and the project implementation team.

If a more general, strategic overview of a project's outcome is desired, a *final audit* may be appropriate. This considers how well the project supports the organisational strategy and identifies lessons for the future. It usually occurs a long time after the project is implemented so that the strategic impact of the project can be assessed. The success of the final audit depends on having a clear statement of organisational strategy and capital investment objectives, so that actual project outcomes can be compared with long-term plans. The sorts of questions that will be asked during a final audit include:

- Does the project fit within the organisational strategy (i) as it existed at the time of the investment decision and/or (ii) as it exists now?
- Have strategic benefits (e.g. increased market share, improved price competitiveness, expansion into overseas markets) been obtained?
- How do qualitative outcomes (e.g. product quality, employee working conditions, reduced environmental impact) compare to what was expected?
- How have changes in the operating environment affected the project?
- Has top management commitment to the project been appropriate?
- Has responsibility for mistakes been allocated and actioned?

Many companies choose to employ a combination of decision, implementation and final project post audits, since each provides feedback about different aspects of the decision-making process and outcomes. However, since post audits are time consuming and costly it is usually best to make a limited selection of projects to be post-audited, perhaps focusing on those that have experienced problems, required the greatest expenditure, or are perceived as particularly risky or strategically important. It is also helpful to post audit projects that are 'typical' for the company, since the lessons learnt can be applied to a good number of future projects.

In general, any post audit exercise should compare a project's actual financial results to the figures produced in the financial analysis stage of the capital investment process (e.g., the net present value that was calculated). It should focus on those aspects of an investment that were identified as critical to the success of the project, rather than necessarily being a comprehensive review of all aspects of the investment. For example, did the project really increase production output by 5%, reduce labour costs by 10% or increase market share by 15%? If not, then why not? Was it because the project was not implemented properly, because changes in operating conditions were not adequately anticipated, or because the original project proposal was poorly thought out or over-optimistic? If any of these problems are identified, the organisation can learn from the post-audit and improve future decision-making and implementation.

Summary: the capital investment decision-making process

This section has outlined the various stages of the capital investment decision-making process. The financial analysis models reviewed in this book are crucial to the rigorous examination of projects in step 5 of Figure 1-3 (analysis, ranking and selection of projects) and the less complex financial analysis methods (such as payback period calculations) are often employed at an earlier stage (step 4), when projects are screened so that only potentially viable projects are subjected to full appraisal.

The key message of this discussion, however, is that sound financial appraisal is not the only important part of investment decision-making. The success a company has in directing its capital expenditure towards projects that create wealth and promote organisational goals depends on the entire decision-making process. This means that the generation, definition and screening of project ideas have to be done well *before* thorough financial analyses are completed. Also, project implementation has to be well managed so that the potential benefits of an investment are realised. Finally, the company needs to review its capital investment processes and outcomes so that it learns for the future and continues to improve its investment activities. All stages of this decision-making process must be well planned and executed, so that good investment ideas are identified, appropriately analysed and effectively implemented. Rigorous financial analysis will not help projects that are bad ideas to start with, nor does it mean that projects are successfully implemented to achieve their maximum contribution to the company.

The capital investment decision-making process presented here is tightly coupled with the company's strategic planning. Strategy will shape the choice of investment projects and, in turn, the choice of projects will dictate the company's future strategic direction. The decision-making process, from idea generation to project post audit, must reflect the strategic goals of the company if capital investment projects are to support the achievement of those goals. With this in mind, now some emergent analysis tools that can be used to supplement rigorous financial analysis with an evaluation of the strategic dimensions of capital investment projects will be reviewed.

1.2.3 Strategic Analysis Tools Supporting the Capital Investment Decision-Making Process

While important in themselves, even the most rigorous financial analysis tools cannot capture all of the strategic dimensions of capital investment projects, since many of them are not amenable to quantification. Consequently, researchers have looked for other analysis tools that *do* help decision-makers to incorporate these important aspects.

Broadly, two avenues have emerged for developing alternative strategic investment appraisal techniques. The first involves modifying established approaches to incorporate neglected 'strategic' project benefits. *Fuzzy set theory* and the *analytic hierarchy process* fit into this category (an approach using these methods will be explained later, various methods supporting multi-criteria decision-making are presented in Chapter 6). The second avenue involves drawing on analytical frameworks that are significant departures from conventional financial and risk analyses. These latter approaches are usually drawn from outside the traditional accounting or finance domains, having emerged in project management, strategy and technology fields, for example. Three such approaches that have been linked with strategic investment decision-making will be described now.

The balanced scorecard

KAPLAN and NORTON (2001) devised the popular 'balanced scorecard' as a framework for linking financial measures of performance with non-financial measures (focused on customers, internal business processes, and innovation and learning), to give managers an integrated framework for managing and evaluating their businesses. They advocated the balanced scorecard as a strategic management and decision-making tool, which suggests that it may be a useful tool for capital investment decision-making, too (for a detailed description see KAPLAN and NORTON, 2001).

The balanced scorecard provides a framework within which financial analysis tools (such as net present value (NPV), see Section 3.2) can be used alongside non-financial considerations of customer/user outcomes, internal business impacts and innovation and learning outcomes. Using this approach, established financial analysis techniques can be combined with other metrics that evaluate the project's strategic fit. This multi-dimensional appraisal usually requires significantly more input from top management than traditional capital investment analysis, thus compelling top management to take a broad, strategic view of investment projects rather than leaving their assessment to financial experts. This increased involvement of senior managers is, in itself, a useful side effect of using this strategic analysis tool.

To use a balanced scorecard approach in investment appraisal, it is necessary to weigh up various (quantitative and qualitative) aspects of a project and arrive at some final project 'score' (techniques for multi-criteria making that may be useful to calculate this score are described in Chapter 6). This is not an easy process and may require long periods of negotiation and deliberation about what the key aims and outcomes of a project might be. However, the process of negotiating through these issues has some benefits. It forces managers to consider how the capital budget aligns to strategic goals, and it requires consensus building that focuses on the entire organisation rather than departmental concerns.

As a framework for aligning financial and strategic project considerations, the balanced scorecard appears to have some potential, therefore. The challenge in applying it relates to the usual practical considerations of implementing balanced scorecards – how to select the key indicators and operationalise the 'balancing' that must be achieved between them.

Strategic cost management analysis

Noting the need to evaluate projects' strategic issues as well as their cash flows, Shank and Govindarajan (1992) described strategic cost management (SCM) as an appropriate framework for giving strategic issues much more explicit attention in the investment decision-making process. Shank and Govindarajan's SCM framework comprises three related elements: value chain analysis, cost driver analysis and competitive advantage analysis. The first element, value chain analysis, is as a useful tool for identifying strategically important, value-creating activities and developing appropriate competitive strategies. The 'value chain' is "the linked set of value-creating activities all the way from basic raw materials through to component suppliers, to the ultimate end-use product delivered into the final consumers' hands" (Shank and Govindarajan, 1992, p. 40). Its analysis focuses on finding opportunities, within the company's segment of the value chain, to enhance customer value or lower costs. Value chain analysis can produce quite different investment decisions to those obtained using traditional financial analysis techniques, particularly where impacts on upstream and downstream value chain linkages are an important aspect of the decision.

Strategic cost management blends value chain analysis with cost driver and competitive advantage analyses. The first of these requires that cost drivers be carefully analysed so that their impact on the company's cost structure and competitive position are understood. In regard to capital investment decisions, *structural* cost drivers (i.e. those that relate to the company's explicit strategic choices) will flow from an investment decision, so their impact on future cash flows must be appropriately identified. Competitive advantage analysis completes the SCM picture with an evaluation of whether a project's achievable benefits are consistent with the company's competitive positioning strategy. Using an SCM approach to project appraisal requires that the project's ability to contribute to the chosen strategy (such as enhancing differentiation, or lowering costs) is explicitly considered. It offers a useful supplement to financial appraisal of investments, therefore.

Technology roadmapping

Since new technology projects comprise a substantial portion of strategic capital investments, developments in technology planning and appraisal offer insights for strategic project analysis. One such recent development is 'technology roadmapping', a planning process whereby a team of experts develops a framework for organising and presenting the information needed to make technology investment decisions. As part of the roadmapping process, this team attempts to project the needs of tomorrow's markets, and produces charts and graphs that identify the links between technology and business needs. This process can contribute to the definition of technology strategy by assisting managers to identify, select and develop technology alternatives to satisfy future service, product or operational needs.

The concept of technology roadmapping has gained widespread recognition, particularly in U. S. companies. According to its proponents, technology roadmapping: (1) helps an industry to predict the market's future technology and product needs, (2) defines the 'road' that industry must take to compete successfully in tomorrow's markets, (3) guides technology research and development decisions, (4) increases collaboration, shared knowledge and new partnerships, (5) reduces the risk of costly investment in technology, and (6) helps the industry seize future marketing opportunities.

Since a key aim of technology roadmapping is to look within and beyond the company to ensure that the right capabilities are in place to achieve strategic objectives, it has clear potential application to investment decision-making. The use of this approach for strategic investment analysis can help to balance long-term, strategic issues alongside near-term financial performance and to ensure that projects fit together well to enhance the company's value. However, the idea of using technology roadmapping to support capital investment decision-making is very new, so there is a lot to learn about how it works in practice.

Fuzzy set theory and the analytic hierarchy process

The three approaches outlined so far all avoid modifying the numerical calculations that support strategic project appraisal. ABDEL-KADER and DUGDALE's (2001) concept is very different. It is a mathematical approach that combines elements of the *analytic hierarchy process* (AHP) framework (which was developed SAATY, 1980 and is described in detail in Section 6.3) with the mathematical concept of *fuzzy set theory* to propose a model for evaluating advanced manufacturing technology investments.

The AHP decision model has been proposed as a means of structuring and systematising the evaluation of non-quantifiable project attributes. This approach requires that decision-makers formulate a decision problem as a hierarchical structure, breaking down the overall objective (of the investment decision) into its key criteria and sub-criteria. They must then assign subjective weights to the various criteria. Finally, then calculate an overall rating for each project alternative by adding up the weighted scores for each of the project's attributes. This approach allows decision-makers to focus on those project attributes most important to achieving the organisation's strategic goals. It cannot eliminate subjectivity from decision-making (it is inherent in the identification and weighting of project attributes), but it does promote the identification of both financial and non-financial project outcomes and provide a structured framework for evaluating and communicating their impact.

Fuzzy set theory allows ambiguous variables to be represented by a range of inexact, 'fuzzy' numbers (for a description see Section 9.1). Combining it with the AHP approach, ABDEL-KADER and DUGDALE propose a model for integrating the financial and non-financial elements of strategic project appraisal. A project's expected performance is evaluated in terms of three measures: financial return, intangible (strategic) benefits, and risk. While rigorous financial analyses (such as with the NPV) are still recommended as appropriate technique for determining financial returns, the model uses a *fuzzy* NPV to take into account that cash flow estimates are uncertain. Strategic and risk factors, which cannot be translated into cash flows, are given a similar treatment. This permits the assessment of non-financial and risk factors without the pressure or expectation of being precise. However, while the approach provides a mechanism for modelling and comparing the financial, strategic and risk attributes of investment projects, it does not provide a single measure of project desirability. Rather, the final accept-or-reject decision depends on decision-makers' preferences. So, despite the mathematical complexity of the method, subjective judgment remains critical to the decision-making process.

Summary: strategic analysis tools

The interpretation of investment planning as part of a (strategic) decision-making process, leads to the insight, that the strategic, non-financial aspects of capital investments need to be evaluated alongside financial factors. This book presents a range of rigorous financial analysis tools that can be used to evaluate a project's financial dimensions. This chapter has also pointed to some emergent strategic analysis tools that have the potential to complement financial analyses. The four appraisal approaches outlined above are all thought to have the potential to support investment decision-making by bringing together financial and strategic aspects of project appraisal. Some have been around in the accounting literature for a while now (the balanced scorecard and strategic cost management), whereas others are more recent, and relatively unproven, arrivals (technology roadmapping and fuzzy set theory combined with analytical hierarchy process).

While they are generally less well developed than the financial analysis tools, and are a lot more subjective in their application, these strategic analysis tools can help ensure that appraisals of capital projects are balanced and incorporate factors that are difficult to quantify in calculative models. The advantage of using strategic analysis tools like these is that they provide a framework for guiding decision-makers' considerations of strategic and non-financial aspects of capital investment projects, meaning that these issues are less likely to be overlooked. However, due to their inherently subjective nature, there is no clear 'rule book' for how these approaches should be applied. This makes them less appealing to decision-makers who prefer clear decision-making rules, such as those provided by most financial analysis tools. However, there is no avoiding the fact that managerial judgement and good strategic thinking are critical to the capital investment decision-making process. The tools outlined here help to support these skills, but they cannot replace them.

1.3 Investment Appraisal Methods as Tools for Investment Planning

Investment appraisal methods, as outlined in this book, are relevant to all the decisions that form part of the investment planning process. Understanding the different investment appraisal methods, their assumptions, limitations and possible usages will lead to an increased understanding of investment decision-making and an informed choice of methods. This should greatly enhance decision-making in regard to both single investment projects and investment programmes.

The key questions to be answered using investment appraisal methods can differ depending on problems identified during the analysis and search for alternatives. They are the following:

Key Decisions:

- Should an investment be undertaken or rejected?
  (⇨ *Absolute profitability* of an investment project)

- In the case of mutually exclusive investment projects, which one should be preferred?
  (⇨ *Relative profitability* of an investment project)
- For how long should an investment project be utilised?
  (⇨ *Optimum economic life* of an investment project)
- When should the investment project be started?
  (⇨ *Optimum investment point in time*)
- Which of the investment projects should be preferred and carried out when a limited financial budget restricts the number that can be undertaken at the same time?
  (⇨ *Optimum investment programme*)
- Which investment and financial projects should be undertaken, in what numbers and amounts and at what time?
  (⇨ *Optimum investment and financial programme*)
- Which investment projects and product types should be pursued and manufactured, in what number and at what time?
  (⇨ *Optimum investment and production programme*)

It should be pointed out here that the first four questions relate to single investment decisions. Suggested solutions for these, using various investment appraisal methods, are given in Chapters 2 to 6 and 8 including investment decisions made utilising multi-criteria models (presented in Chapter 6). The final three questions relate to programme decisions, when several decisions have to be made simultaneously. Models for this situation are presented in Chapters 7 and 9.

The various characteristics of decision models are illustrated in Figure 1-4, which highlights the distinction between the different methods described in this book.

<table>
<tr><th>Criterion</th><th colspan="9">Characteristics</th></tr>
<tr><td rowspan="2">(Un)Certainty</td><td colspan="4" rowspan="2">Certainty</td><td colspan="5">Uncertainty</td></tr>
<tr><td colspan="2">Unknown probabilities</td><td colspan="2">Estimated probabilities</td><td>Fuzziness</td></tr>
<tr><td rowspan="2">Alternatives</td><td colspan="4">Single project decision</td><td colspan="5" rowspan="2">Programme decision</td></tr>
<tr><td>Absolute profit-ability</td><td>Relative profit-ability</td><td>Econo-mic life</td><td>Date of invest-ment</td></tr>
<tr><td>Targets</td><td colspan="4">One target</td><td colspan="5">Several targets</td></tr>
<tr><td rowspan="3">Time</td><td colspan="4" rowspan="3">Static</td><td colspan="5">Dynamic</td></tr>
<tr><td rowspan="2">Single-tier</td><td colspan="4">Multi-tier</td></tr>
<tr><td colspan="2">Inflexible</td><td colspan="2">Flexible</td></tr>
</table>

Fig. 1-4: Characteristics of decision models

This book is structured in five major Parts: the introductory Chapter (Part 1), the basic methods of investment appraisal (Part 2) consisting of the static methods and (dynamic) discounted cash flow methods that can be found in most other text books; advanced methods and applications of investment appraisal (Part 3); multi-criteria methods and models for simultaneous decision-making (Part 4); and methods and models that consider uncertainty (Part 5). The structure of the book and its chapters is shown in Figure 1-5:

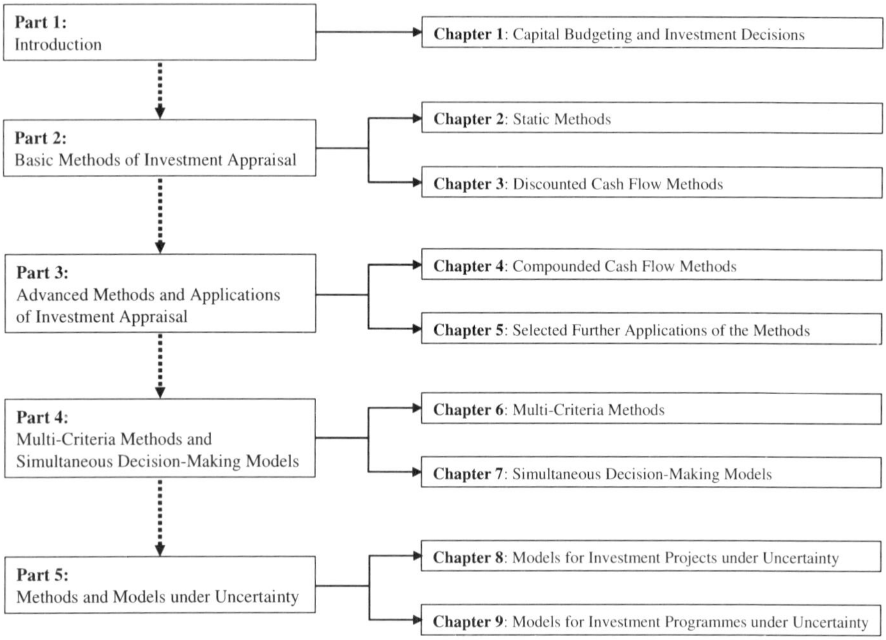

Fig. 1-5: Structure of the book

Further Reading Part I

Abdel-Kader, M. G., and D. Dugdale. 2001. Evaluating Investments in Advanced Manufacturing Technology: A Fuzzy Set Theory Approach. *British Accounting Review* 33 (4):455-489.

Bacon, P. W. 1977. The Evaluation of Mutually Exclusive Investments. *Financial Management* 6 (2):55-58.

Baldwin, R. H. 1959. How to Assess Investment Proposals. *Harvard Business Review* 37 (3):98-105.

Boulding, K. E. 1936. Time and Investment. *Economica* 3 (12):196-214.

Brealey, R. A., S. C. Myers, and F. Allen. 2007. *Principles of Corporate Finance*. 9 ed. Boston et al.: McGraw-Hill/Irwin.

Copeland, T. E., J. F. Weston, and K. Shastri. 2005. *Financial Theory and Corporate Policy*. 4 ed. Boston: Addison Wesley.

Götze, U. 2006. *Investitionsrechnung*. 5 ed. Berlin et al.: Springer.

Hirshleifer, J. 1958. On the Theory of Optimal Investment Decision. *The Journal of Political Economy* 66 (4):329-352.

Kaplan, R. S., and D. P. Norton. 2001. Transforming the Balanced Scorecard from Performance Measurement to Strategic Management: Part I. *Accounting Horizons* 15 (1):87-104.

Kern, W. 1974. *Investitionsrechnung*. Stuttgart: Poeschel.

Lutz, F. A., and V. Lutz. 1951. *The Theory of Investment of the Firm*. Princeton N.J.: Princeton University Press.

Ross, S. A., R. W. Westerfield, J. F. Jaffe, and D. J. Bradford. 2007. *Corporate Finance: Core Principles & Applications*. 6 ed. Boston, Mass. et al.: McGraw-Hill/Irwin.

Saaty, T. L. 1980. *The Analytic Hierarchy Process: Planning, Priority Setting, Resource Allocation*. New York et al.: McGraw-Hill.

Shank, J. K., and V. Govindarajan. 1992. Strategic Cost Analysis of Technological Investments. *SLOAN Management Review* 34 (1):39-51.

Part II

Basic Methods of Investment Appraisal

Chapter 2: Static Methods

This chapter considers simple 'static' analysis methods that assess the profitability of an investment for a time span of one (average) period. These methods focus on a single financial measure, so other target measures are ignored.

The term 'profitability' is, unless otherwise specified, used throughout this book to indicate the achievement of positive (or higher) economic returns from an investment project. However, it should not be confused with the concept of 'accounting profit', which includes non-cash items and accounting adjustments and is not always consistent with economic, wealth-maximising decision objectives. The profitability considered here can be thought of in two ways – in *absolute* terms or in *relative* terms.

> *Key Concept:*
> *Absolute profitability*: making an investment is better than rejecting it.
> *Relative profitability:* investing in project A is better than investing in project B (A being the more profitable investment: A and B are mutually exclusive).

In using financial analysis to assess an investment's absolute or relative profitability, specific assumptions are made:

- The model's data and linkages are known with certainty.
- All relevant effects can be isolated, allocated to a given investment project, and forecasted in the form of revenues and costs or cash inflows and outflows.
- No relationship exists between the alternative investment projects being analysed, apart from their mutual exclusivity.
- Other decisions, such as financing or production decisions, are made before the investment decision.
- The economic life of the investment projects is specified.

The last assumption means that time-related decisions, such as those related to the project's economic life or replacement time will not be covered at this point; they will be part of Chapter 5.

Furthermore, in assessing the profitability of alternative investment projects it is assumed that the alternatives are comparable in regard to their project type, the amount of capital tie-up and their economic lives. Strictly speaking, this requires identical amounts of invested capital and identical economic lives for all investment alternatives under consideration. If this is not the case, comparability can be achieved by additional premises, or by including additional activities to balance differences in the capital tie-up and/or economic lives. Such an additional assumption may be that all future investments yield at a specific interest rate which is used to calculate interest costs so that they do not have to be explicitly considered in the calculations.

The analysis models discussed in Part Two can be distinguished by their treatment of how time affects the value of future returns achieved from an investment project (often referred to as the 'time value of money'). Chapter 2 describes (simple) static models that analyse one average period – that is, they ignore the passage of time. In Chapter 3, 'dynamic' discounted cash flow models will be described. These models do take time into account. More advanced models will then be presented in Part Three of the book.

Static analysis models explicitly consider only one period (e.g. a year), which is assumed to be representative of all such periods (years). The data which characterise the average period are derived from data for the whole planning period (i.e. the expected life of the investment). The static models described in this book differ in regard to their target measures, but all target measures represent profit measures or are derived from them (i.e. cost, profit, average rate of return or payback time).

Accordingly the following methods are differentiated:

- The cost comparison method
- The profit comparison method
- The average rate of return method
- The static payback method

Each of the methods is explained using the following steps: (1) a description of the procedure, (2) key concepts concerning the absolute and the relative profitability measure, (3) an illustrative example and (4) an assessment of the method, with special emphasis on its underlying assumptions.

2.1 Cost Comparison Method

Description of the method

For the cost comparison method (CCM) the target measure is, as the name suggests, the cost(s) of an investment project. It is assumed when using the CCM that the revenues of mutually exclusive investment alternatives (and the option to forego the investment, if this is a permissible alternative) are identical and that only the costs differ. Costs analysed include: personnel expenditures (wages, salaries, social expenditure etc.), cost of raw materials, depreciation, interest, taxes and fees, and costs of outside services (such as repair or maintenance). The average costs for the planning period are determined for each investment alternative. Note that, for variable costs, the future production volume is a crucial determinant. Adding up all cost components gives a total cost for each alternative investment.

Assessing *absolute profitability* on the basis of total costs is not meaningful if the revenues generated by an investment differ from those that would be generated *without* the investment (i.e. the assumption of identical revenues is violated). This is usually the case for foundational or expansion investments. In these cases, absolute profitability can be judged only on the basis of profits (i.e. not using the CCM). However, for replacement or rationalisation investments, a comparison of total costs *with* the investment and total costs *without* the investment can be conclusive.

Relative profitability can be determined using the CCM in all situations where the projects under comparison have identical revenues. When considering relative profitability, it doesn't matter what the costs would have been *without* the project, since simply costs between the various project options are compared.

> *Key Concept:*
> *Absolute profitability* is achieved if the total cost of making an investment is lower than the total cost of rejecting it.
> *Relative profitability* is achieved if making an investment results in a total cost that is lower than that of the alternative investment project(s) under consideration.

The CCM is illustrated in the following example.

Example 2-1

To manufacture a new product, a metal-processing company needs a special component. This can be produced in the factory or bought in. To start production of the component, an investment is required for which the (mutually exclusive) projects A and B (representing different production processes) are available. The option to buy in from another company represents alternative C. The investment projects are characterised by the data given in Tab. 2-1. Please note that in this book interest rates always refer to a period of one year.

Data	**Project A**	**Project B**
Initial investment outlay (€)	240,000	600,000
Economic life (years)	6	6
Liquidation value (€)	0	60,000
Capacity (units per year)	8,000	10,000
Salaries (€ per year)	50,000	50,000
Other fixed costs (€ per year)	40,000	160,000
Wages (€ per year)	220,000	80,000
Costs of materials (€ per year)	400,000	450,000
Other variable costs (€ per year)	30,000	30,000
Rate of interest (% per year)	8	8

Tab. 2-1: Data for the investment projects A and B (CCM)

The buying in price of the component (alternative C) is €125 per unit.

Some of the specified cost components are variable and depend linearly on the production volume. The amounts stated for these components refer to the costs incurred at maximum production capacity.

The task now is to use the CCM to determine the cost of the three projects for a yearly production volume of 8,000 units. To find the solution, a distinction between fixed and variable costs is required. It is assumed here that the costs of materials and wages represent variable costs. In regard to wages, this can be justified by the assumption that employees can be shifted to other production departments, or that other appropriate uses of the personnel capacity are possible.

First, the average annual variable and fixed costs of the investment projects are identified. Investment project A's variable costs are taken from the sum of the given costs of materials, wages and other variable costs. The initial data are valid for a production volume of 8,000 units per year, which is identical to the production capacity of A. The variable costs of A (C_{vA}) therefore amount to:

$$C_{vA} = €650{,}000 \text{ per year}$$

The given data for investment project B refer to a capacity of 10,000 units per year and therefore a conversion to the production volume (x) of 8,000 has to be made. Variable costs of B (C_{vB}) are calculated as follows:

$$C_{vB}\ (x = 10{,}000 \text{ units}) = €560{,}000 \text{ per year,}$$

$$C_{vB}\ (x = 8{,}000 \text{ units}) = \frac{€560{,}000/\text{year} \cdot 8{,}000 \text{ units}}{10{,}000 \text{ units}} = €448{,}000 \text{ per year.}$$

The fixed costs consist of salaries, depreciation, interest and other fixed costs. Depreciation and interest have to be calculated from the given data. The average annual depreciation can be calculated by dividing the difference between the initial investment outlay and the liquidation value by the years of the economic life. The initial investment outlay comprises the purchase price paid and additional related costs like carriage costs etc. The liquidation value is the amount receivable when reselling the investment project, less any additional costs such as demolition costs etc. (there are none in this example).

The average depreciation therefore is:

$$\frac{\text{Initial investment outlay} - \text{Liquidation value}}{\text{Economic life (in years)}} \tag{2.1}$$

$$\text{Investment project A:} \quad \frac{€240{,}000}{6 \text{ years}} = €40{,}000 \text{ per year}$$

$$\text{Investment project B: } \frac{€600{,}000 - €60{,}000}{6 \text{ years}} = €90{,}000 \text{ per year}$$

The approach taken here corresponds to the straight-line depreciation method. Changing to a regressive (or 'diminishing value') depreciation method would not affect the amount of average depreciation, as the total amount written off would be the same. However, the chosen depreciation method does influence the average amount of capital tie-up and thus affects interest costs.

Interest costs must be included in the CCM if the competing projects differ in their initial investment outlays and therefore in the average amount of capital tie-up. Interest is calculated to achieve comparability concerning this capital tie-up. It is assumed as a rule that capital can be procured or reinvested at a given rate of interest. Interest cost is calculated by multiplying the average capital tie-up by the rate of interest. To determine the average capital tie-up, different approaches can be applied. A simple procedure assumes a steady decrease between the initial investment outlay at the beginning and the liquidation value at the end. Based on this assumption the capital tie-up during the life of project A is depicted in the following figure.

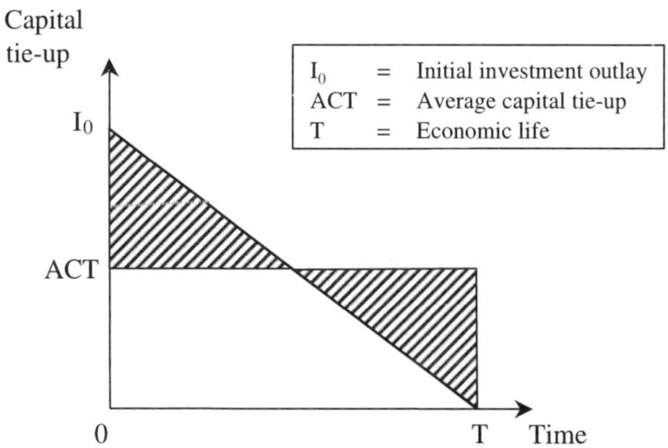

Fig. 2-1: Capital tie-up for investment project A (with zero liquidation value)

Assuming continuous capital reduction, the average capital tie-up can be determined computationally as the average of (i) the capital invested at beginning and (ii) the liquidation value at the end of the planning period (i.e. project life):

$$\text{Average capital tie-up} = \frac{\text{Initial investment outlay} + \text{Liquidation value}}{2} \tag{2.2}$$

Figure 2-1 shows that average capital tie-up is half of initial investment outlay if no liquidation value exists. This can be shown graphically (both of the marked triangles have the same sizes) or computationally (the average between the initial investment outlay and the liquidation value of zero). The average capital tie-up for project A therefore is:

$$\frac{€240{,}000}{2} = €120{,}000 .$$

The annual average interest (assuming an annual interest rate of 8%) for this project amounts to:

$$€120{,}000 \cdot 0.08 = €9{,}600$$

Project B shows a slightly different pattern of capital tie-up due to the positive liquidation value (see Figure 2-2).

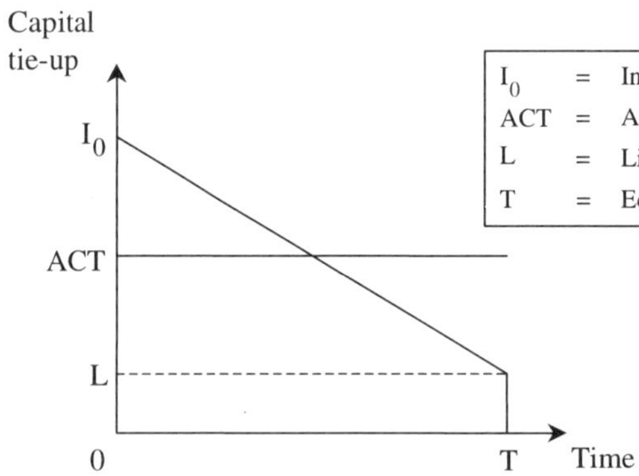

Fig. 2-2: Capital tie-up for investment project B (with positive liquidation value)

Thus, the average capital tie-up exceeds half of the initial investment outlay if a liquidation value exists. The average capital tie-up for project B in accordance with the general formula is:

$$\frac{€600{,}000 + €60{,}000}{2} = €330{,}000$$

The annual average interest (assuming an annual interest rate of 8%) for this project amounts to:

$$€330{,}000 \cdot 0.08 = €26{,}400$$

Now that interest costs have been calculated, the total average fixed costs can be determined as:

$$\text{Salaries} + \text{Other fixed costs} + \text{Depreciation} + \text{Interest costs} \qquad (2.3)$$

Investment project A:

€50,000/year + €40,000/year + €40,000/year + €9,600/year = €139,600/year

Investment project B:

€50,000/year + €160,000/year + €90,000/year + €26,400/year = €326,400/year

The total average costs of all three projects, given a production volume of 8,000 units per year, amount to:

Project A: €650,000/year + €139,600/year = €789,600/year

Project B: €448,000/year + €326,400/year = €774,400/year

Project C (assuming that only the component purchase price is relevant):

8,000 units/year · €125/unit = €1,000,000/year

The comparison of the average total costs shows that the investment project B is the cost minimising (and thus most profitable) alternative and therefore should be preferred. However, such a decision should be examined in light of the model's assumptions and the significance of any deviations from those assumptions.

Assessment of the method

The cost comparison method requires relatively simple calculations. Making predictions from the data can be difficult and time consuming and, despite the assumption of certainty, many elements of the data will be unreliably estimated. This is a general problem of investment appraisal methods and applies to all of the approaches described in this book.

The suitability of the calculated results for supporting decision-making depends on both the quality of the data and the validity of the model's assumptions. Therefore, the model's assumptions need to be evaluated. For example, the limitations of analysing only one target measure (and ignoring other factors) must be assessed in terms of their likely importance to the decision-making process.

The static perspective of the CCM (and other models described in this chapter) is also a weakness, since static models look at one 'average' period only. Differences in the timing of costs cannot be assessed, therefore. Such differences can result from changes in prices and/or consumption over the time for each cost category. They will usually arise in regard to interest costs. As an illustration, consider the interest costs in the example shown above (comparing projects A, B and C). Capital tie-up for projects A and B is relatively high at the beginning of the planning period and lower at the end (see Figure 2-1 and 2-2). This will result in higher interest at the beginning and lower interest towards the end of the investment. When using average data this is not considered.

Furthermore, the assumptions relating to the capital tie-up warrant more detailed discussion. Two concerns arise: the assumption of a continuous and steady decline of the capital tie-up, and the assumption that the total decrease of the capital tie-up equals the difference between initial investment outlay and liquidation value. The actual decrease in the capital tie-up, which can be interpreted as amortisation or pay back, will normally depend on the revenues (here assumed to be identical for all alternatives and, therefore, neglected) as well as on the resulting costs and the average profit (P). If these measures are equal to cash flows, apart from depreciation (D), and if no additional cash flow that is not affecting the operating result is gained, then the sum of depreciation and profit represents the total amount amortised or paid back (PB).

$$P + D = PB$$

In the case of positive (negative) average profits, this amount paid back will be higher (lower) than the difference between initial investment outlay and liquidation value. Besides, the total amounts amortised will usually differ between project alternatives, which is inconsistent with the assumption that the revenues are identical in all alternatives. Finally, interest charges depend on capital tie-up for each alternative and can affect the amounts available to reduce the capital tie-up.

A uniform interest rate, at which money can be borrowed and reinvestments made at any time (i.e. a perfect capital market), is also assumed. This is related to the assumption that differences in capital tie-up can be equalised between projects by (fictitious) additional investments that yield interest at the same given rate or by financing objects with this interest rate. This assumption is often invalid in practice, as is the assumption that all the investment projects under consideration have identical economic lives. Both of these ‘idealistic’ assumptions, and the determination of an appropriate rate of interest, will be discussed in Chapter 3.

Making a comparison of projects by simply analysing their total costs neglects the issue of capacity utilisation as well as the composition of the costs. Idle capacity and differences in the composition of total costs (i.e. between fixed and variable costs) can be extremely important for a company. Neglecting their analysis can have serious effects, therefore.

It should also be reiterated that the assumption of (data) certainty is usually unrealistic. For example, production volumes, which are crucial to decision-making, are often uncertain. If deviations occur between forecasted production volume and the actual units of production, relative profitability can be seriously affected. The dependence of profitability results on production volumes can be shown with the use of sensitivity analysis (described in Section 8.3).

Finally, it should be emphasised that the CCM model ignores any consideration of project revenues. Consequently, the assessment of absolute profitability is not possible for all investment projects, which is a significant limitation of this analysis method, as it requires that the products’ qualities and quantities produced with the different investment projects must be equivalent. A method that *does* incorporate project revenue data is discussed next.

2.2 Profit Comparison Method

Description of the method

As the name suggests, the profit comparison method (PCM) differs from the cost comparison method because it considers both the cost and revenues of investment projects. The target measure is the average profit, which is determined as the difference between revenues and costs. Apart from this difference, all of the other assumptions made in the CCM continue to apply for PCM.

> *Key Concept:*
> *Absolute profitability* is achieved if an investment project leads to a profit greater than zero.
> *Relative profitability* is achieved if an investment project leads to a higher profit than the alternative investment project(s).

Example 2-2

The PCM is illustrated in the following example. A company has the choice between the following two investment projects A and B:

Data	**Project A**	**Project B**
Initial investment outlay (€)	180,000	200,000
Freight charges (€)	15,000	25,000
Set-up charges (€)	2,000	2,000
Economic life (years)	5	5
Liquidation value at the end of the economic life (€)	12,000	17,000
Other fixed costs (€ per year)	4,000	20,000
Production and sales volume (units per year)	9,000	12,000
Sales price (€ per unit)	10	10
Variable costs (€ per unit)	2	1.90
Rate of interest (% per year)	6	6

Tab. 2-2: Data for the investment projects A and B (PCM)

To assess the absolute and relative profitability of the two investment projects, the projects' average revenues and costs must be determined. The annual revenues of projects A (R_A) and B (R_B) amount to:

$$R_A = 9{,}000 \text{ units/year} \cdot €10/\text{unit} = €90{,}000 \text{ per year and}$$

$$R_B = 12{,}000 \text{ units/year} \cdot €10/\text{unit} = €120{,}000 \text{ per year.}$$

The average cost can be determined in the same way as for the CCM approach described in Section 2.1. The amounts for each cost category, as well as the average total costs of projects A (C_A) and B (C_B), are shown in the following table:

Cost category (each in € per year)	**Project A**	**Project B**
Depreciation	37,000	42,000
Interest	6,270	7,320
Other fixed costs	4,000	20,000
Variable costs	18,000	22,800
Total costs	65,270	92,120

Tab. 2-3: Cost categories for the investment projects A and B (PCM)

The average profits for alternatives A (P_A) and B (P_B) amount to:

$$P_A = R_A - C_A = €90{,}000/\text{year} - €65{,}270/\text{year} = €24{,}730 \text{ per year}$$

$$P_B = R_B - C_B = €120{,}000/\text{year} - €92{,}120/\text{year} = €27{,}880 \text{ per year}$$

Both investment projects achieve absolute profitability, since they earn a positive profit. Project B achieves relative profitability because of its higher average profit.

Assessment of the method

The PCM acknowledges the fact that different investment opportunities (projects) lead to different revenues. Thus, the method has a wider range of use than the CCM. However, its application may be restricted by the fact that it is impossible to allocate revenues to some investment projects; in these cases the CCM has to be used. Apart from this difference, both methods have broadly the same strengths and weaknesses. Therefore the corresponding earlier assessment of the CCM applies equally to the PCM.

The next section introduces an analysis method that differs from the CCM and PCM in regard to the assumptions it makes about differences in capital tie-ups between competing investment projects.

2.3 Average Rate of Return Method

Description of the method

The average rate of return (ARR) method differs from the PCM in regard to its target measure. The ARR method combines a profit measure with a capital measure to focus on the return (expressed as a rate of interest) earned on the capital invested. Both the profit measure and the capital measure can be defined differently. Average capital tie-up can be used as the capital measure, while the profit measure can be determined by adding average profit and average interest. This leads to the following formula:

$$\text{Average rate of return} = \frac{\text{Average profit} + \text{Average interests}}{\text{Average capital tie-up}} \quad (2.4)$$

The average interest is derived by applying a given interest rate to the average tie-up capital. When using the PCM (Section 2.2), this interest is subtracted from revenues as a component of cost. For the ARR method this step is reversed by adding the interest amount back to the profit calculated using the PCM. The sum of average profit and average interest represents a surplus, which is compared to the average capital tie-up to determine the ARR method profitability measure.

The ARR method enables an assessment to be made of both absolute and relative profitability.

> *Key Concept:*
> *Absolute profitability* is achieved if an investment project leads to an average rate of return higher than a given percentage.
> *Relative profitability* is achieved if an investment project leads to a higher average rate of return than the alternative investment project(s).

The determination of a target average rate of return is at the decision-maker's discretion and depends on existing investment and financing opportunities. If it can be assumed that internal funds should be used and an alternative investment opportunity exists, which could earn a given rate of interest, then this rate is suitable as a target for investment options. If this rate equals that used by the PCM, both methods will produce the same result in regard to absolute profitability. Different results are possible in regard to relative profitability. The determination and interpretation of the average rate of return will be illustrated by the following example.

Example 2-3

In this example, Example 2-2 is considered again. The absolute and relative profitabilities are determined for the alternative investment projects. Assume that the relevant interest rate is 6% per year. The ARR method requires the determination of average profit, interest and capital tie-up for each project.

Relevant measures	**Project A**	**Project B**
Profit (€ per year)	24,730	27,880
Interest (€ per year)	6,270	7,320
Average capital tie-up (€)	104,500	122,000

Tab. 2-4: Relevant measures for the investment projects A and B (ARR method)

The average rates of return for projects A (ARR_A) and B (ARR_B) can be determined according to the formula given above, as follows:

$$ARR_A = \frac{€24{,}730/\text{year} + €6{,}270/\text{year}}{€104{,}500} = 0.2967/\text{year} \;\; (\text{or } 29.67\,\%) \quad \text{and}$$

$$ARR_B = \frac{€27{,}880/\text{year} + €7{,}320/\text{year}}{€122{,}000} = 0.2885/\text{year} \;\; (\text{or } 28.85\,\%).$$

It is obvious that both projects achieve *absolute* profitability, since the rate of return they generate exceeds the relevant interest rate of 6%. Investment project A achieves *relative* profitability due to its higher rate of return. This example illustrates that investment recommendations can be inconsistent between the PCM and the ARR method analyses if the considered alternatives require different capital tie-ups. An absolutely profitable investment project with lower capital tie-ups usually appears more attractive when using the ARR method than it does using the PCM.

Assessment of the method

In most respects, the ARR method resembles the CCM and the PCM. Therefore, the previous assessments of these models apply also to the ARR method. The PCM in particular has the same range of application and thus is competing. However, the following aspects should be noted. As for the PCM, the revenues of the investment alternatives are explicitly considered in the ARR method, but a different target measure is utilised.

Therefore, different investment assumptions are made about the balance of differences in capital tie-up. Using the PCM, it is assumed – as described above – that lower levels of capital tie-up are compensated by other investment(s) that yield the given uniform rate of interest used in the calculation (or a financing project with this interest rate). With the ARR method, however, it is implicitly assumed that smaller capital tie-up is balanced by a further (hypothetical) investment that earns the same rate of return as the project under consideration with the smaller capital tie-up. The reason for this is as follows: a comparison of average rates of return can only be meaningful, if the capital bases to which the rates refer are equal. This is not the case when differences exist in capital tie-up, so an adjustment is necessary which is achieved by assuming that the investment with the smaller capital tie-up is supplemented by a fictitious investment. In the case of the projects considered in the example above, A has to be supplemented by an investment yielding 29.67% with a capital tie-up of €17.500 (= €122.000 – €104.500).

If the project with the highest capital tie-up also yields the highest rate of return, then the compensation assumption made for the ARR method is not problematic because the hypothetical investment project has no influence on the profitability. But, if this is *not* the case (i.e. the highest rate of profitability is earned by an alternative project with a lower capital tie-up), then this can affect the profitabilities and it becomes important whether the above assumption is justified. That is, it has to be questioned whether the capital tie-up differences can be balanced by another investment or financial project that yields a return close to that of the project with the lower capital tie-up. The answer to this question will determine whether it is better to use the ARR method or the PCM. It should be noted here that the rate of interest used should reflect alternative investment and financing opportunities. If, in the example 1.3 above, the differences in capital tie-up are balanced by projects yielding 29.67%, a question arises as to why the given rate of interest is assumed to be only 6%. The changing orders of the relative profitability (between the PCM and the ARR method) can also be explained by the big differences in assumed interest rates.

If several investment opportunities exist with comparable rates of return, which are similar to that of the investment project with the lower capital tie-up and if the projects are competing for limited resources, the use of the ARR method may be appropriate. However, this can be considered as a special case. In reality, the profitability of the investment project under consideration will rarely correspond with the interest rate of investment or financing projects that are used to balance differences in capital tie-up. Besides this, an inconsistency of assumptions arises if several projects are included at the same time whose profitabilities drop with increasing capital tie-ups as in this case different assumptions are made during the selection process.

These problems are avoided by using the PCM. Additionally, the determination of the rate of interest used by the PCM should reflect and approximate the interest rate of the relevant investments and financing objects that balance the differences in capital tie-up. Thus, the assumptions underlying the PCM are closer to reality, making it a more suitable method. Further, if the interest rate of the balancing investment or financing objects is as high as is assumed in the average rate of return method, (e.g. alternative investments exist that yield a rate of about 30%, as in the example above), then the rate of interest should be adjusted towards this rate, and the result of the profit comparison method then becomes identical to that of the average rate of return method.

2.4 Static Payback Period Method

Description of the method

The target measure used for the static payback period (SPP) method is the time it takes to recover the capital invested in the project. It can be calculated based on average figures or on total figures. Average figures are used here.

> *Key Concept:*
> The payback period of an investment project is the period after which the capital invested is regained from the average cash flow surpluses generated by the project.

The SPP method offers a measure of the risk connected with an investment. Judging the absolute and the relative profitability of investment projects based only on the SPP method is not a suitable analysis, because any costs and revenues occurring after the payback period will be completely ignored. Thus the SPP method is only useful as a supplementary appraisal method. Notwithstanding this, the general decision rules offered by the SPP method can be expressed as follows:

> *Key Concept:*
> *Absolute profitability* is achieved if an investment project's payback period is shorter than a target length of time (usually expressed in years).
> *Relative profitability* is achieved if an investment project has a shorter payback period than the alternative investment project(s).

The SPP can be determined by dividing the capital tie-up by the average cash flow surpluses:

$$\text{Payback period} = \frac{\text{Capital tie-up}}{\text{Average cash flow surpluses}} \qquad (2.5)$$

The capital tie-up corresponds with the initial investment outlay. If the project has an expected liquidation value that can be estimated with some certainty, it may be useful to subtract it from the initial investment outlay, since the SPP is often viewed as a measure of project risk. Another option is to distribute it according to the average cash flow surpluses over the years of the project's economic life. Both options will be neglected here.

A project's average net cash flows are the key measures when using the SPP method. Average cash flow is not the same as average profit. While profit is defined as the difference between revenues and costs, cash flow represents the net balance of cash inflows and outflows. A number of differences exist between revenues and cash inflows and between costs and cash outflows. For investment appraisal, depreciation is the most relevant of these differences, since it is considered as a cost (thus influencing profit) but is not a cash outflow. Average net cash flow can be derived by adding the depreciation cost back into the average profit figure. Note that, since the SPP method relates a project's average net cash flow to the capital tie-up, using the average profit (including depreciation) instead of the average net cash flow would result in double counting.

The way in which interest costs are dealt with also warrants discussion. Interest costs are included in the calculation of profit, just as depreciation costs are. But, the inclusion of interest in a project's cash flows depends on whether it represents a relevant cash outflow (i.e. the project is financed by debt) or not (i.e. the project is financed using internal funds). The first case is assumed here. So, interest represents a cost (in the calculation of profit) as well as a cash outflow and, unlike for depreciation, there is no adjustment required to convert profit to net cash flow.

To sum up, a project's average net cash flow can be expressed as follows:

$$\text{Average net cash flow} = \text{Average profit} + \text{Depreciation} \qquad (2.6)$$

Example 2-4

The determination of the SPP method is illustrated with the help of an example. The data is taken from Example 2-2. Assume the company has decided that its investment projects must pay back their initial investment outlay within four years. The relevant information is:

Relevant measures	**Project A**	**Project B**
Profit (€ per year)	24,730	27,880
Depreciation (€ per year)	37,000	42,000
Capital tie-up (€)	197,000	227,000

Tab. 2-5: Relevant measures for the investment projects A and B (SPP method)

The static payback periods of the two projects A (PP_A) and B (PP_B) are calculated as follows:

$$PP_A = \frac{€197{,}000}{€24{,}730/\text{year} + €37{,}000/\text{year}} = 3.19 \text{ years}$$

$$PP_B = \frac{€227{,}000}{€27{,}880/\text{year} + €42{,}000/\text{year}} = 3.25 \text{ years}$$

These two projects, as shown, have similar payback periods. While project A is the relatively more profitable project, both are absolutely profitable because their payback periods are less than the required four years.

Assessment of the method

The comments made in regard to the previous three methods also apply to the SPP method, including the possible inconsistency between the assumptions concerning the capital tie-up when determining interest costs (see Figure 2.1) and the average cash flow surpluses which are available for amortisation according to the SPP method. It must be emphasised that the SPP should not be used as an exclusive decision criterion because it fails to incorporate any profits or cash flows occurring after the payback period. However, it is a useful supplementary investment appraisal tool since it provides some indication of the risk connected with an investment project. In this context the payback period can be interpreted as a critical factor in considering a project's economic life and, therefore, as a result of a sensitivity analysis.

All the methods described in this chapter omit any consideration of the time value of money, as they use average measures rather than tracking cash flows over time. The methods described in the following chapter will allow more meaningful analyses by discounting cash flows to one point in time (making them comparable) and by analysing different cash flows from different periods. This will enrich the investment appraisal process since the analysis of average indicators limits the usefulness of the results.

Assessment Material Chapter 2

Exercise 2-1 (Cost Comparison Method)

A car manufacturer wants to use the cost comparison method to assess whether he should continue to buy in a special component or manufacture it in-house instead. Two companies are offering different types of equipment to produce the part, giving the following data:

Data	Machine A	Machine B
Initial investment outlay (€)	120,000	80,000
Economic life (years)	10	10
Liquidation value (€)	10,000	0
Method of depreciation	straight-line	straight-line
Capacity (units per year)	12,000	10,000
Wages (€ per year)	24,000	28,000
Salaries (€ per year)	8,000	6,000
Materials (€ per year)	23,000	23,000
Other fixed costs (€ per year)	19,000	14,000
Other variable costs (€ per year)	8,000	9,000
Rate of interest (% per year)	5	5

Tab. 2-6: Data for the two machines A and B

The variable costs are in proportion to the volume produced; the above data relate to the capacity being fully utilised. The unit buying in price for the parts is €10.

a) Which of the alternatives (machine A, machine B or buying in (alternative C)) would you recommend if the number of these special components required each year was 6,000 units?

b) Which machine would you select if the required volume was 10,000 units per year?

c) Which assumptions have you used in question a) in respect of the amount of capital tied up? What other assumptions has the cost comparison been based on?

d) Describe the changes in average depreciation and interest that occur if, instead of straight-line depreciation, the declining balance method of depreciation for machine B is used, whereby

   d1) The rate of depreciation is 30% followed by a switch to the straight-line method to reach the liquidation value of €0.

   d2) Depreciation is carried out until there is a liquidation value of €10,000.

   It is not necessary to calculate the results; just discuss the general impact on the project appraisal.

Exercise 2-2 (Cost Comparison Method)

The cost comparison method is to be applied in assessing two alternative investment projects, A and B, as well as alternative C (buying in from outside). The following data are available:

Data	**Alternative A**	**Alternative B**
Initial investment outlay (€)	13,000	12,000
Liquidation value (€)	4,000	2,000
Economic life (years)	6	6
Capacity (units per year)	10,000	8,000
Rate of interest (% per year)	10	10
Variable costs (€ per year) (x = Production volume)	$-\frac{8}{100{,}000}x^2+1.7x$	$0.8x$
Other fixed costs (€ per year)	50	600

Tab. 2-7: Data for the investment projects A and B

The items can be bought in at a unit price of €1.50 for volumes of up to 10,000 units.

a) Ascertain the cost functions C_A, C_B and C_C for the various alternatives.

b) Which alternative is preferred when the production volume is
   b1) 4,000 units?
   b2) 8,000 units?
   b3) 10,000 units?

   What costs arise with this alternative?

Exercise 2-3 (Profit Comparison, Average Rate of Return and Payback Method)

A company is planning to undertake an investment project. The following data have been calculated for two alternatives, A and B:

Data	Alternative A	Alternative B
Economic life (years)	8	8
Sales volume (units per year)	20,000	24,000
Sales price (€ per unit)	8	8
Initial investment outlay (€)	200,000	240,000
Construction costs (€)	18,000	28,000
Freight costs (€)	2,000	2,000
Liquidation value at the end of the period (€)	16,000	16,000
Fixed operating costs (€ per year)	6,000	22,000
Variable unit costs (€ per unit)	4.60	4.40
Rate of interest (% per year)	6	6

Tab. 2-8: Data for the alternatives A and B

Ascertain the preferred project using

a) The profit comparison method.
b) The average rate of return method.
c) The static payback method.

Chapter 3: Discounted Cash Flow Methods

3.1 Introduction

The discounted cash flow methods described in this chapter are classified as dynamic investment appraisal methods, which, unlike the static methods described in Chapter 2, explicitly consider more than one time period and acknowledge the time value of money. Investment projects can be described as streams of (expected) cash inflows and outflows over the whole course of their economic life, i.e. over different periods. An assumption made here is that all relevant effects of the alternative investment projects are depicted by these cash inflows and outflows, and that no other effects need to be considered. Therefore, the target criterion used to evaluate investments takes only (discounted) cash flows into account. Additionally, it is assumed that all cash flows can be forecasted and allocated to defined periods of identical lengths (usually years) – more precisely to the beginning or the end of these periods as the representative points in time.

Common characteristics of the methods described in this and the following chapter include most of the assumptions referred to in Chapter 2. The explicit recognition of the time value of money, as the essential distinction between the discounted cash flow methods and the static methods, is discussed next.

The time value of money

Comparing cash flows from different periods can be achieved only by incorporating the time value of money. The values of the cash flows depend on the time at which they take place. Therefore transformations need to be carried out either by discounting or compounding cash flows to compare them at specific points in time. Using discounting, all future cash flows are converted to their equivalent value as at the *beginning* of the investment project. Using compounding, the cash flows are converted to their equivalent value as at the *end* of the investment project. The comparison can be made by multiplying the cash flows by:

- The discounting factor: $(1 + i)^{-t}$
- The compounding factor: $(1 + i)^{t}$.

Where t represents the number of time periods for which the cash flows are discounted or compounded. The interest or 'discount rate' (i) plays a major role in dynamic investment appraisal methods and will be further examined later on.

A simple example illustrates the logic behind the computation. With discounting, the value of a cash flow is determined for a certain point in time, regularly assumed to be the 'point in time 0' (which is the same as 'the beginning of year 1'). The value at point in time 0, the so called present value, is then calculated as the net cash flow divided by $(1 + i)^t$. If an interest rate (i) of 10% (remaining unchanged throughout the observed years) is assumed, a net cash flow of €10,000 that occurs at the end of the third year (t = 3) has a present value (PV) of:

$$PV = \frac{\text{Net cash flow}}{(1+i)^t} \tag{3.1}$$

$$PV = \frac{€10{,}000}{1.1^3} = €7{,}513.15$$

Remember that €10,000 represents a future cash inflow from an investment project. It has been shown that €7,513.15 'today' has the same value as €10,000 in three years' time. Thus, cash flows at two different times have been made comparable.

The same logic can be applied to compounding cash flows. A cash flow of €10,000 received now (point in time 0) can be regarded as identical in value to the future value (FV) of €12,597.12 received in 3 years, if an interest rate of 8% is assumed, since:

$$FV = \text{Net cash flow} \cdot (1+i)^t \tag{3.2}$$

$$FV = €10{,}000 \cdot 1.08^3 = €12{,}597.12$$

If the interest rate changes from year to year, however, separate discounting or compounding factors are determined for every period (up to the last period T). In the case of the compounding factor this can be described generally as:

$$FV = \text{Net cash flow} \cdot ((1+i_1) \cdot (1+i_2) \cdot \ldots \cdot (1+i_T)) \,. \tag{3.3}$$

Recalculating the above example, but now assuming that the relevant annual interest rates are $i_1 = 10\%$, $i_2 = 12\%$ and $i_3 = 15\%$, the future value becomes:

$$FV = €10{,}000 \cdot ((1+0.1) \cdot (1+0.12) \cdot (1+0.15)) = €14{,}168.00$$

Sometimes, the monetary value of an investment results from a stream of identical cash flows over several years (i.e. an annuity). In order to calculate the present value (as at time 0) of a stream of identical cash flows (annuity) the *capital recovery factor* (or annuity factor) can be used:

$$PV = \text{Annuity} \cdot \frac{(1+i)^t - 1}{(1+i)^t \cdot i} \tag{3.4}$$

An annuity of €10,000, occurring for three years and with an interest rate (discount rate) of 10%, has a present value of:

$$PV = €10{,}000 \cdot \frac{(1+0.1)^3 - 1}{(1+0.1)^3 \cdot 0.1} = €24{,}868.52$$

In a comparable way, a single cash flow received in time period 0 can be transformed into an annuity. This can be calculated by the use of the *annuity factor*, which is the inverse value of the above capital recovery factor:

$$\text{Annuity} = \text{PV} \cdot \frac{(1+i)^t \cdot i}{(1+i)^t - 1} \tag{3.5}$$

For example, €10,000 received at time 0 (with i = 10% and t = 3 years) is equivalent to an annuity of:

$$\text{Annuity} = €10{,}000 \cdot \frac{(1+0.1)^3 \cdot 0.1}{(1+0.1)^3 - 1} = €4{,}021.15$$

This means that receiving €4,021.15 at the end of each of three years has the same value as receiving €10,000 today, if the interest rate is 10%.

Summarising, it can be said that discounting and compounding calculations capture and reflect time preferences – that is, they are an expression of the preference an investor shows for receiving income, or consuming resources, at particular times.

The key concept relevant to investment appraisal is that an investment project is characterised by a series of cash inflows and outflows over several time periods, typically starting with a cash outflow (the initial investment outlay) at time 0, followed by inflows and/or outflows in later years. These multi-period cash flows will now be assessed using different investment appraisal methods. The methods described in this chapter are characterised by a uniform discount rate and (usually) by relating all future cash flows to the beginning of the project by discounting them to $t = 0$. Other investment appraisal methods, described in Chapter 4, will use differing debt and credit interest rates, and will compound values to the end of the investment project's life.

Figure 3-1 shows the investment appraisal methods described in this chapter.

Dynamic investment appraisal methods

Uniform discount rate	Differing debt and credit interest rates
- Net present value method (Section 3.2)	(Described in Chapter 4)
- Annuity method (Section 3.3)	
- Internal rate of return method (Section 3.4)	
- Dynamic payback period method (Section 3.5)	

Fig. 3-1: Dynamic investment appraisal methods

3.2 Net Present Value Method

Description of the method

The net present value method focuses on selecting projects that maximise the 'net present value' (NPV) generated for the company:

> *Key Concept:*
> Net present value is the net monetary gain (or loss) from a project, computed by discounting all present and future cash inflows and outflows related to the project.

Using the NPV method, all future cash flows related to an investment project are discounted back to time 0 (i.e. $t = 0$), taken to represent the start of the investment project. The NPV represents a specific kind of PV. While it is possible to discount and compound all the cash flows to a later point in time, for example to the end of the investment project, it is more common to use $t = 0$ as this is the time at which the decision to invest (or not to invest) has to be made. It will be explained later that other methods relate cash flows to other points in time, e.g. to the end of the investment project.

The most rigid assumptions of the NPV method relate to the existence of a perfect (unrestricted) capital market. The single, or uniform, interest rate for this market represents the rate at which it is possible to borrow or invest without limits. Therefore this rate is used for discounting or compounding cash flows to any point in time.

Using the NPV method, the profitability of investment projects is assessed as follows:

> *Key Concept:*
> *Absolute profitability* is achieved if an investment project's NPV is greater than zero.
> *Relative profitability:* An investment project is preferred if it has a higher NPV than the alternative investment project(s).

For the following examples it is assumed that the uniform discount rate (i) remains unchanged over the life of the investment. In that case, a project's NPV at $t = 0$ can be determined using the following equation:

$$NPV = \sum_{t=0}^{T} (CIF_t - COF_t) \cdot q^{-t} \quad (3.6)$$

Where:

t	=	Time index
T	=	The last year when cash flows take place

CIF_t = Cash inflows in t

COF_t = Cash outflows in t

q^{-t} = Discounting factor in t $\left(q^{-t} = \frac{1}{q^t} = \frac{1}{(1+i)^t} \right)$

The difference between cash inflows and cash outflows (CIF_t - COF_t) is the net cash flow (NCF_t). As shown in the following figure, all net cash flows after t = 0 are discounted back to this point in time.

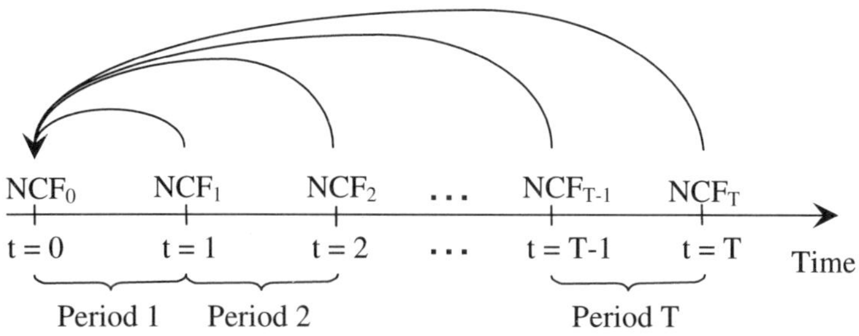

Fig. 3-2: Discounting net cash flows for the net present value method

The equation indicated above must be detailed if components of the net cash flows are to be considered in a differentiated way. A project's cash flows can be subdivided into: initial investment outlay, liquidation value(s), cash inflows (e.g. from sales) and cash outflows (e.g. from expenses). In addition, the following assumptions may be made when using the NPV method:

- Taxes and transfer payments can be ignored.
- Only one type of product is manufactured with the investment project.
- Production volume equals sales volume (i.e. no inventory produced).
- The cash flows are assigned to the following points in time:
  - Initial investment outlay: beginning of the first period (t = 0).
  - Cash inflows and outflows: end of each relevant period (t).
  - Liquidation value: end of the project's economic life (t = T).

The following formula for the NPV then can be derived:

$$NPV = -I_0 + \sum_{t=1}^{T} \left((p_t - cof_{vt}) \cdot x_t - COF_{ft} \right) \cdot q^{-t} + L \cdot q^{-T} \qquad (3.7)$$

Where:

t = Time index

T = The last year when cash flows take place (end of the project)

I_0 = Initial investment outlay

p_t = Sales price in period t

cof_{vt} = Production/sales dependent (variable) cash outflows per unit in period t
x_t = Production/sales volume in period t
COF_{ft} = Production/sales independent (fixed) cash outflows in period t
q = (1 + i)
L = Liquidation value

In concluding this discussion, it should be noted that the calculation of the NPV can be simplified when cash flows remain constant throughout the economic life of a project. In this case, the NPV of the cash flows at t = 0 can be determined by multiplying the cash flow by the annuity factor (described at the beginning of this chapter). The NPV is then the sum of the net present values of initial investment outlay, net cash flows and liquidation value.

An interesting feature of the NPV method is the potential use of differential cash flow analysis. This approach helps to simplify comparisons between competing projects, since the identical aspects of the projects can be omitted and less project data is required. For example, if two competing project options are both expected to generate the same revenue streams (but with different costs), the revenue streams can be omitted from the analysis since they are the same for both projects and therefore, don't need to be compared, provided absolute profitabilities exist. Only the costs need to be compared, because they differ between the projects.

When comparing two alternative projects, the critical point is the differences between their cash flows – i.e. the differential cash flows, which can also be interpreted as the cash flows of a fictitious 'differential investment'. By calculating the NPV of these differential cash flows (i.e. NPV_{diff}), the difference between the NPVs of the two projects under consideration is determined as a measure of relative profitability is determined.

I.e. for two investment projects A and B it can be shown that:

$$\begin{aligned} NPV_{diff} &= \sum_{t=0}^{T} \left((CIF_{tA} - COF_{tA}) - (CIF_{tB} - COF_{tB}) \right) \cdot q^{-t} \\ &= \sum_{t=0}^{T} (CIF_{tA} - COF_{tA}) \cdot q^{-t} - \sum_{t=0}^{T} (CIF_{tB} - COF_{tB}) \cdot q^{-t} \\ &= NPV_A - NPV_B \end{aligned} \tag{3.8}$$

If the net present value of NPV_{diff} is positive, then investment project A has a higher NPV than investment project B and is, therefore, *relatively* more profitable. This approach can be used to compare more than two competing projects, as long as care is taken to exclude only those cash flows from the analysis that are identical across all the project options. This can get complicated, so it is sometimes easier just to calculate the NPV for each project in its entirety and choose the project with the highest NPV. Note that *absolute* profitability cannot be assessed by calculating NPV_{diff}. To evaluate absolute profitability, the NPV calculation must include all the cash flows from a project. However, it may be useful to calculate NPV_{diff} to find the best project option, before calculating the NPV of this project (i.e. including all of its cash flows) to determine its absolute profitability.

A major assumption of the NPV method is that any net cash inflow that is not needed to cover a cash outflow will be reinvested at the relevant discount rate (i). This crucial assumption is further explained using an illustrative example.

Example 3-1

A company is considering an investment to expand their business. The necessary data for the two available investment options are listed in the following table:

Data	**Investment project A**	**Investment project B**
Initial investment outlay (€)	100,000	60,000
Economic life (years)	5	4
Liquidation value (€)	5,000	0
Net cash flows (€)		
t = 1	28,000	22,000
t = 2	30,000	26,000
t = 3	35,000	28,000
t = 4	32,000	28,000
t = 5	30,000	-
Relevant discount rate (%)	8	8

Tab. 3-1: Data for investment projects A and B (NPV method)

It is required to determine the absolute and relative profitability of the two projects by using the NPV method.

For investment project A the net present value (NPV_A) can be calculated as follows:

$$NPV_A = -€100{,}000 + €28{,}000 \cdot 1.08^{-1} + €30{,}000 \cdot 1.08^{-2} + €35{,}000 \cdot 1.08^{-3} + €32{,}000 \cdot 1.08^{-4} + €30{,}000 \cdot 1.08^{-5} + €5{,}000 \cdot 1.08^{-5}$$

$$NPV_A = €26{,}771.59$$

This result is interpreted as follows. Since NPV_A is positive it can be deduced that investment project A is profitable in *absolute* terms. The NPV of €26,771.59 is the net monetary gain achieved if investment project A is undertaken. This assumes a discount rate of 8% for the interest (payments). This result would be achieved regardless of the source of finance: from internal funds, debt financing or any combination of these.

The investor could choose to use this monetary gain (NPV_A) right now (t = 0) by taking out a loan of €26,771.59 for consumption purposes. Such a ‘consumption loan', together with interest charges, could be paid back from the cash flow surpluses of the investment project. The project's cash flow surpluses would also cover the loan repayments (including interest) on the capital employed for the investment (€100,000 for project A).

This is illustrated by a financial budget and redemption plan that contains the cash flows and net monetary values associated with the above investment, assuming that:

- A 100% debt financing is used, i.e. €26,771.59 to be consumed at the beginning of the planning period plus €100,000 for the initial investment outlay.
- At the end of every period, interest is paid at the discount rate (8%) on the debt remaining.
- Net cash surpluses are used for immediate loan repayments.

Point in time **t**	**Net project cash flow (€) (excluding initial investment outlay)** N_t	**Interest paid (€) (cash outflow)** $I_t\ (= i \cdot V_{t-1})$	**Net cash surplus (€) (used to repay the loan)** $\Delta V_t\ (= N_t + I_t)$	**Net monetary value (€) (amount of loan outstanding)** $V_t\ (= V_{t-1} + \Delta V_t)$
0	0	0	0	–126,771.59
1	28,000	–10,141.73	17,858.27	–108,913.32
2	30,000	–8,713.07	21,286.93	–87,626.39
3	35,000	–7,010.11	27,989.89	–59,636.50
4	32,000	–4,770.92	27,229.08	–32,407.42
5	35,000	–2,592.59	32,407.41	–0.01

Tab. 3-2: Financial budget and redemption plan with 100% debt financing

The financial budget and redemption plan shows that the initial loan of €126,771.59 is fully regained by the cash flow surpluses from investment project A.

The level of the NPV and, therefore, of the net monetary gain is the same regardless of the combination of internal funds and debt financing employed. This is a major outcome of the 'perfect capital market' assumption. To demonstrate this concept further, the financial budget plan is now given for a case where is financed by internal funds at 100%, in contrast to the 100% debt financing depicted above. In this case, the cash flow surpluses from the investment project are used for financial investments that – in accordance with the reinvestment assumption – are made in the capital market, and yield the relevant discount rate (8%).

Point in time	Net cash flow (€) (without initial investment outlay)	Interest received (€) (cash inflow)	Net cash surplus (€) (increase in internal funds)	Net monetary value (€) (total internal funds)
t	NCF_t	I_t (= $i \cdot V_{t-1}$)	ΔV_t (= $NCF_t + I_t$)	V_t (= $V_{t-1} + \Delta V_t$)
0	0	0	0	0
1	28,000.00	0	28,000.00	28,000.00
2	30,000.00	2,240.00	32,240.00	60,240.00
3	35,000.00	4,819.20	39,819.20	100,059.20
4	32,000.00	8,004.74	40,004.74	140,063.94
5	35,000.00	11,205.12	46,205.12	186,269.06

Tab. 3-3: Financial budget plan with 100% financing by internal funds

As the financial budget plan shows, the investor has internal funds of €186,269.06 at the end of the investment project's life. This amount cannot be compared directly to the outlay of €100,000, however, since the amounts occur at different points in time. Yet it can be shown that the end value, discounted back to $t = 0$ at the interest rate of 8%, equals the sum of NPV and initial investment outlay:

$$€186{,}269.06 \cdot 1.08^{-5} = €126{,}771.59$$

The difference between this amount and the capital employed (€100,000) corresponds to NPV_A (€26,771.59). Provided reinvestment at the discount rate is assumed, it can be seen that the internal funds-financed investment project yields the same net monetary gain of €26,771.59 as the debt-financed investment. This can also be shown by calculating the end value that an investor would hold if he or she invested capital of €100,000 over the economic life of the investment at an interest rate of 8%. The end value (EV) in this case is:

$$EV = €100{,}000 \cdot 1.08^{5} = €146{,}932.81$$

The difference between the end value of investment project A (€189,269.06) and the financial investment of €100,000 at the 8% discount rate (€146,932.81) is €39,336.25. If this amount is discounted back to $t = 0$ the difference becomes €26,771.59 which equals the project's NPV:

$$€39{,}336.25 \cdot 1.08^{-5} = €26{,}771.59$$

These examples illustrate the fact that an absolute profitability assessment made using the net present value model implies the operation of a uniform discount rate in a perfect capital market. This, is the alternative investment when an actual investment project is rejected.

Another interpretation of NPV is based on the possibility of investing in the capital market as an alternative to the investment project. The price of project A consists of the initial investment outlay. The alternative price is the financial investment amount required at the beginning of the planning period (t = 0) in order to generate the same expected cash flow surpluses ($CIF_t - COF_t$) in the future. This financial investment amount is the sum of separate investment amounts each arising from the cash flow surplus at time t discounted by the uniform discount factor:

$$(CIF_t - COF_t) \cdot (1+i)^{-t} \tag{3.9}$$

Altogether the sum of all separate financial investments and with it the price of the future payment surpluses amounts to:

$$\sum_{t=0}^{T} (CIF_t - COF_t) \cdot (1+i)^{-t} \tag{3.10}$$

Then the net present value represents the difference between this price and the initial investment outlay of the investment project under consideration:

$$NPV = \sum_{t=0}^{T} (CIF_t - COF_t) \cdot (1+i)^{-t} - I_0 \tag{3.11}$$

Or in the example:

$$NPV = €126{,}771.59 - €100.000 = €26{,}771.59$$

Because the difference is positive, the investment project under consideration is superior to a financial investment in the capital market. Thus, it is absolutely profitable.

For the assessment of relative profitability the net present value of the alternative project B (NPV_B) must also be calculated. It amounts to:

$$NPV_B = €25{,}469.32$$

As NPV_B is positive, investment project B is absolutely profitable. However, because NPV_A (€26,771.59) is greater, investment project A appears to be relatively more profitable. Where both projects are mutually exclusive, investment project A will be preferred, provided net present value is the decision criterion.

As described above, the relative profitability of two investment projects can also be determined by calculating the NPV of the differential cash flows or a fictitious differential investment ($NPV_{diff} = NPV_A - NPV_B$). This amounts in the example to:

$$\begin{aligned} NPV_{diff} &= -€40{,}000 + €6{,}000 \cdot 1.08^{-1} + €4{,}000 \cdot 1.08^{-2} + €7{,}000 \cdot 1.08^{-3} \\ &\quad + €4{,}000 \cdot 1.08^{-4} + €35{,}000 \cdot 1.08^{-5} \end{aligned}$$

$$NPV_{diff} = €1,302.27$$

This implies that project A's net monetary gain exceeds the net monetary gain from investment project B by €1,302.27. Project A therefore is relatively profitable.

However, it should be noted that the capital tie-up of investment project B is considerably lower (initial outlay is €60,000 compared to €100,000 for project A). Moreover, the economic life of project B is shorter by one year and, therefore, subsequent investments may be realised at an earlier time.

This raises the important question: to what extent are the net cash flow profiles used to calculate investment projects' NPVs suitable for the assessment of relative profitability if differences exist in regard to:

- The capital tie-up at the beginning (i.e. different initial investment outlays)?
- The capital tie-up during the course of the investment (i.e. from different net cash flows over the life of the project)?
- The projects' economic lives?

Needless to say, if none of these differences exist the investment projects under consideration can be regarded as equivalent, since the analysis is limited to the comparison of cash flow profiles regardless of the nature of the actual project (e.g. a machine). If differences in capital-tie up and/or economic life are not explicitly included in the analysis, however, they need to be balanced by additional investments (or by financing alternatives).

Differences in projects' capital tie-up are easy to consider if perfect capital market conditions are assumed. This implies that the differences between projects' initial outlays can be balanced by assuming that a financial investment is made at the relevant uniform discount rate (or by the corresponding assumption that a financing alternative with this interest rate is achieved). The following example illustrates the use of such a financial investment (NPV_F) (a fictitious investment project) to balance the initial capital tie-up difference between projects A and B for one period:

$$NPV_F = -€40,000 + (€40,000 \cdot 1.08) \cdot 1.08^{-1} = €0$$

The NPV of this balancing financial investment is zero. Accordingly, the differences in capital tie-up do not need to be analysed explicitly for competing investments. They can be ignored if perfect capital market conditions are assumed. A similar argument can be applied to differences in economic life. Subsequent investments that may be undertaken at different points in time because of different economic lives, have no influence on the profitability of alternatives if it is assumed that all future investments yield the relevant uniform discount rate and therefore have an NPV of zero. Under the assumed perfect capital market conditions it is not necessary to consider supplementary investments explicitly. The NPVs of projects under comparison determined on the basis of the cash flow profiles are sufficient for the assessment of relative profitability. In spite of differences in capital tie-up and/or economic life, competing investments can be treated as comparable alternative projects.

But what if it is unrealistic to assume current and future (re-)investment at the uniform discount rate? A modified application of the NPV method can be used if specific information exists for other current and future investment projects that may be used to balance differences in capital-tie up and/or economic life, whose interest rates deviate from the expected uniform discount rate. This might be the case if, for example, subsequent projects are pursued at the end of the initial project's economic life. They constitute so-called chains of investments might consist of identical or non-identical projects, and refer to limited or unlimited time horizons. In such situations, the NPVs of the investment chains may be used to assess relative profitability. This is described in Chapter 5. It is important to note that the profitability of investment projects also depends on subsequent projects: in calculating an isolated net present value this fact is overlooked. Unless the investment project under consideration is the final project for the company – i.e. truly is an isolated project – the decision conditions assumed may be not realistic. Companies usually envisage an unlimited or, at least, a long term planning horizon, which limits the simplistic use of NPVs in investment decision-making.

Assessment of the method

The NPV method is one of the most widely known and used methods in both theory and company practice. To assess its usefulness (as for all the alternative methods) its computational ease, data collection requirements and, most important of all, model assumptions must be considered.

The computational effort is low, as simple arithmetical calculations are sufficient. The data collection, however, may cause problems because, as a rule, several forecasts are necessary. The NPV model requires forecasts of the initial investment outlay, all future cash flows, the project's economic life, the liquidation value at the end of the economic life and the relevant discount rate. Nevertheless, this challenge applies to all investment appraisal models.

The NPV model makes more realistic assumptions compared to the static models described in Chapter 2 because all years of the investment project's economic life are explicitly included. Thus, as the required computational effort is only slightly greater, the methods described in this chapter are more appropriate for real-world company practice. Yet the net present value model does make some assumptions, the potential effects of which should be evaluated against the real situation. The model's assumptions include the following:

a) A single target measure (the NPV) is considered adequate.
b) The economic life is pre-determined and appropriate.

c) Other associated decisions (such as financing and production decisions) are made before the investment decision in order to be able to forecast cash flows for separate investment projects.
d) The data is certain.
e) The cash flows can be allocated to specified time periods and points in time.
f) All current and future investments not explicitly considered (financial investments due to cash inflow surpluses and investments to balance up the different capital tie-up and/or economic life of investments) will yield at the relevant uniform discount rate.
g) A perfect capital market exists.

The profitability of investment projects often depends on several performance targets. In such cases a single target measure (assumption a) may be insufficient for decision-making and other methods should be used, e.g. multi-criteria methods (described in Chapter 6).

The economic life must be known before applying the NPV method (assumption b). In order to gain this information, models may be used to determine the optimum economic life as described in Section 5.3. These models may be based on the NPV model.

Decisions about other investment projects, as well as actions of other company divisions and/or functional areas (e.g. production, sales and financing), can influence the cash flows associated with the project under consideration and, therefore, the profitability of this project. In the model described above, it is assumed the NPV is calculated after these decisions are taken (assumption c). In reality, the two are interdependent since these other decisions rely on information about the investment project currently under consideration. Such interdependencies mean that investment decisions cannot normally be allocated unambiguously to a single investment project, as assumed here. Models for simultaneous decision-making that can lead to overall optimum solutions are described in Chapter 7.

It is highly unlikely that all necessary present and future data will be known with 100% certainty (assumption d). Therefore, an additional analysis of the effects of uncertainty on the forecasted data should be made simultaneously with the determination of NPVs – at least for more important investment projects. Methods and models that take account of uncertainty are described in Chapter 8.

The models described in this chapter assume that all cash flows can be allocated to a specified point in time – usually the beginning or end of a year (assumption e). In reality cash flows will occur more often and several will take place over a year. This may be accommodated in the NPV model easily by increasing the number of periods monitored and adjusting the interest rate from yearly to for example monthly or daily. This will improve the accuracy of forecasts but increases computational efforts. As an alternative, a continuous yield and constant cash flows can be assumed.

The implications of assumed yields at the relevant discount rate (assumption f) have been discussed for the above example. Generally speaking, this assumption is unrealistic. The significance of deviations from the assumed yield, and the availability of information required to include supplementary investment projects, should be discussed during the decision-making process. The assumption that future investments will yield interest at the relevant discount rate implies that more profitable subsequent investment projects will not be made (unless their consequences are already captured within the cash flow profile of the investment project under consideration, as discussed in Section 5.3).

Additionally, the impact that one current investment project may have on the feasibility and profitability of future investment projects can be disregarded provided assumption (f) holds true. In this case, the NPV of future investments is zero, and ignoring these investments has neither negative nor positive financial consequences. However, in reality, uncertainty exists about future investment possibilities. Among other things, technological advancements may result in future projects earning positive NPVs. Under such circumstances, the question arises as to whether a current investment project with a positive NPV should be undertaken now or renounced in favour of future investment projects. This can be answered by the explicit inclusion of future investment projects in the investment decision-making process as described in Section 5.3.

Also problematic is the assumption of a perfect capital market (assumption g) under which loans can be taken and financial investments made at any time and in any amount, all yielding the relevant uniform discount rate. Only in a perfect capital market can investment and finance decisions be made independently without endangering their optimality. Additionally, only in a perfect capital market can an investor at any point in time transfer funds generated by an investment project to different points in time using a financial investment, yielding the uniform discount rate, without affecting the original value of the investment project. This leads to the fact that the temporal distribution of income can be chosen at will and, thus, investment, withdrawal or consumption decisions are independent. Such a perfect capital market simply does not exist in reality. Among other things, interest rates differ between those receivable for financial investments and those payable for loans. Moreover, it is impossible to determine one uniform discount rate that simultaneously fulfils all these different purposes. This consideration becomes important where the level of the assumed uniform discount rate is a key determinant of the NPV. The identification of a suitable discount rate is discussed in a separate section (3.6) below. But first, other approaches to investment appraisal are discussed, starting with the annuity method.

3.3 Annuity Method

Description of the method

The annuity method (AM) uses the same discounted cash flow model as the NPV method. The only change is a different target measure, the annuity:

> *Key Concept:*
> An annuity is a series of cash flows of equal amounts in each period of the total planning period.

The annuity can be regarded as an amount that an investor can withdraw in every period when undertaking the investment project. The annuity of an investment project is equivalent to the NPV of that project, i.e. it is possible to equate both measures mathematically.

A limitation of this approach is that the annuity method is not (completely) suitable for the assessment of relative profitability. This will be further outlined below. Setting this issue aside for now, however, the following profitability criteria can be applied:

> *Key Concept:*
> *Absolute profitability* is achieved if an investment project's annuity is greater than zero.
> *Relative profitability:* An investment project is preferred if it has a higher annuity than the alternative investment project(s).

When calculating an annuity, the cash flows are normally allocated to the end of each period (deferred cash flows) and this is assumed in the following notes. Initially, the time span used is the economic life of the project.

The annuity (ANN) of an investment project can be determined by multiplying the net present value (NPV) by the capital recovery factor (see Section 3.1). This is dependent on the uniform discount rate (i) and the economic life (T). The annuity is calculated as follows:

$$\mathrm{ANN} = \mathrm{NPV} \cdot \frac{(1+i)^T \cdot i}{(1+i)^T - 1} \tag{3.12}$$

As can be deduced from the formula, the annuity method leads to the same assessment of absolute profitability as the NPV method. Since any meaningful i and T are higher than zero, the capital recovery factor is higher than zero as well. Thus, a positive (negative) annuity is achieved as the result of a positive (negative) NPV. Similar reasoning applies to relative profitability assessments where the projects under comparison have identical economic life spans, as the recovery factors are identical. If this is not the case, and the assumptions of the NPV model are applied to subsequent projects used for balancing economic life differences, then the annuity method should be applied in modified form, e.g. using identical time spans. Then the assessment of profitability is again identical to that obtained by the NPV method. However, the annuity method can also be applied if a different assumption is made in regard to subsequent projects. This is illustrated in the following example.

Example 3-2

Here Example 3-1 is reconsidered using the annuity method. Investment project A's annuity can be calculated as:

$$\text{ANN}_\text{A} = €26{,}771.59 \cdot \frac{1.08^5 \cdot 0.08}{1.08^5 - 1} = €6{,}705.15$$

For project B a different capital recovery factor arises on account of its different economic life. The annuity amounts to:

$$\text{ANN}_\text{B} = €25.469{,}32 \cdot \frac{1.08^4 \cdot 0.08}{1.08^4 - 1} = €7{,}689.72$$

Both projects have a positive annuity and, thus, are profitable in absolute terms. For the assessment of relative profitability it should be noted that the annuities refer to different time spans – due to different economic lives – and therefore encompass different numbers of cash flows. The annuity of project B is higher, but it runs for a shorter time span. If the assumptions of the NPV method are maintained (in particular, that future investments yield at the uniform discount rate) then the annuity method should be replaced by the NPV method or, alternatively, the annuity method should be applied in a modified form, relating only to project annuities for the same number of periods. If the annuity of project B is recalculated for 5 years it becomes:

$$\text{ANN}_\text{B} = €25.469{,}32 \cdot \frac{1.08^5 \cdot 0.08}{1.08^5 - 1} = €6{,}378.96$$

Now, as might be expected, project A regains relative profitability. The obvious question of why the annuity method is used despite the results for absolute and relative profitability being identical, is taken up later.

If assumptions are modified so that a repetition of the investment project will follow, then a problem can arise with the NPV method. In particular, where a project will have unlimited, identical repetitions the annuity method should be used since, owing to the unlimited time horizon, no NPV can be determined. Using the annuity method, the NPV of an unlimited chain of identical projects can be calculated as follows:

$$\text{Net present value} = \frac{\text{Annuity}}{\text{Interest rate}} \tag{3.13}$$

In the example it amounts to:

$$NPV_A^{\infty} = \frac{€6{,}705.12}{0.08} = €83{,}814.00$$

$$NPV_B^{\infty} = \frac{€7{,}689.72}{0.08} = €96{,}121.50$$

In this situation, investment project B is relatively profitable on account of the higher NPV of the continuously repeated project: an effect due to the shorter economic life.

This argument and the calculation of limited and unlimited chains of investment projects are explored in more detail in Section 5.3.

Assessment of the method

The assessment of the annuity method is similar to that of the NPV method, since identical model assumptions and data requirements exist. The calculation of the annuity is only slightly more difficult than that of the NPV.

However, use of the annuity method is unnecessary in many situations. In the analysis of absolute profitability, the NPV method leads to identical results. When the economic lives of the projects under consideration are identical, or when the calculations are modified in the ways described, the assessments of relative profitability are identical as well. Also, annuities, in contrast to NPVs, can be calculated only approximately if the uniform discount rates change during the course of the project's life. Only two arguments remain after these reservations: annuities are needed to calculate the NPV of an unlimited identical investment chain; and the target measure for the annuity method can be interpreted more easily (esp. by the inexperienced user). As an annuity is a measure related to a period, it represents a specific form of 'average profit' and, thus, can be interpreted more easily than a NPV result.

3.4 Internal Rate of Return Method

Description of the method

The internal rate of return (IRR) method, considered next, is largely analogous to the NPV method. Only two assumptions are modified – concerning the reinvestment of free cash flow surpluses and the balancing of capital tie-up and economic life differences. Also, a different target measure is considered: the internal rate of return.

> *Key Concept:*
> The internal rate of return is the rate that leads to a NPV of zero when applied as the uniform discount rate.

The internal rate of return represents the interest earned on the capital employed at specific points in time by the investment project under consideration. The following profitability criteria are applied in the IRR method, although it should be recognised at this point that the method is not applicable to all decision contexts:

> *Key Concept:*
> *Absolute profitability* is achieved if an investment project's internal rate of return is higher than the uniform discount rate.
> *Relative profitability:* An investment project is preferred if it has a higher internal rate of return than the alternative investment project(s).

Accordingly, in assessing absolute profitability a comparison is made between the project's rate of interest and the cost of capital or the interest earned by an alternative financial investment, as represented by the uniform discount rate i. An investment project should be undertaken when its rate of interest is higher than the cost of capital and/or the interest that could be earned on alternative financial investments.

The meaningfulness of internal rates of return (and profitability assessments based on them) compared with that of the NPV or annuity methods depends on the cash flow profiles and, thus, on the type of investment. The following discussion concentrates on *isolated investment projects*. Such projects are characterised by the fact that the cash flow surpluses of the whole planning period only cover interest charges (at the internal rate of return) and repayment of the capital employed. That is, no reinvestment is made using the project's cash flow surpluses during the project's economic life. The investment is said to be 'isolated', and the internal rate of return is then independent of the interest rates that possible reinvestments might earn.

An isolated investment project has a project-specific cash flow balance that is negative for every period of its economic life if it is determined on the basis of the internal rate of return. This condition is fulfilled if:

- The sum of all net cash flows in the economic life is higher than or equal to zero:

$$\sum_{t=0}^{T} NCF_t \geq 0 \tag{3.14}$$

And:

- For all periods $t = 0,...,t^*$, with t^* signifying the period in which the last cash outflow surplus appears, the cumulative net cash flows are smaller than or equal to zero:

$$\sum_{\tau=0}^{t} NCF_\tau \leq 0 \quad \text{for} \quad t = 0,...,t^* \tag{3.15}$$

These conditions are in any case fulfilled with a 'normal' investment, i.e. an investment with a cash flow profile, where, only once, does a change in algebraic sign take place (one or more initial investment outlays in the beginning followed by cash inflows only in the subsequent periods). Thus, the normal investment is a special case of an isolated investment.

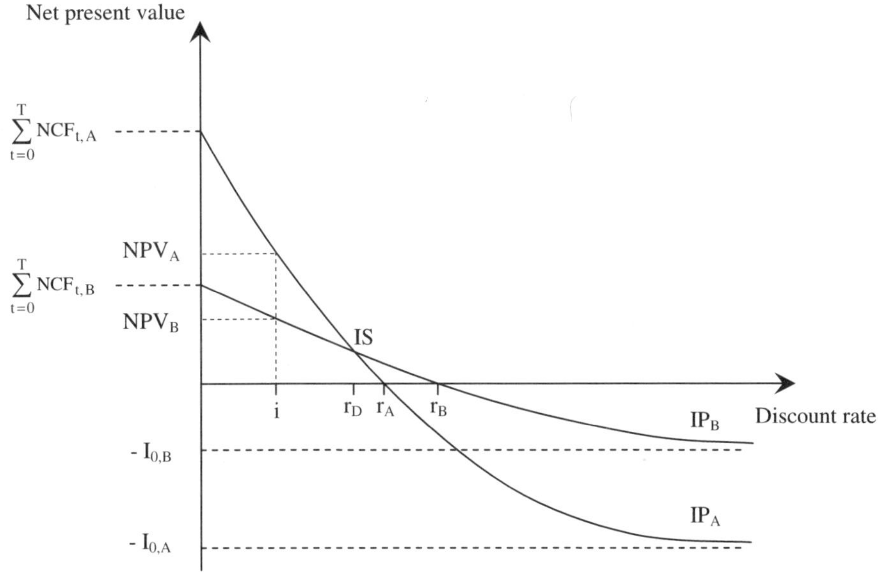

Fig. 3-3: The NPV of isolated investment projects as a function of the uniform discount rate

Figure 3-3 depicts the NPV of two isolated investment projects A (IP_A) and B (IP_B) as a function of the uniform discount rate. With this type of investment (isolated investments), the results of the NPV and IRR methods are the same in regard to absolute profitability because the NPV is always positive when the IRR is greater than the uniform discount rate. The profitability comparison of mutually exclusive projects, however, can lead to contradictory results from the NPV and IRR methods, as also shown in Figure 3-3. In this case, the NPV method assesses project A as superior, since $NPV_A > NPV_B$ (at the uniform discount rate i), whereas the IRR method favours project B, since $r_B > r_A$. The question of how to choose between mutually exclusive investments in such cases is taken up below.

From Figure 3-3 it can be deduced that, for an isolated investment project, only *one* positive internal rate of return exists, provided the sum of the cash inflows is greater than the sum of the outflows. For non-isolated (i.e. 'linked') investment projects, several internal rates of return may exist. The maximum number of these interest rates corresponds to the number of algebraic sign changes in accordance with DESCARTES' convention. It is also possible that no economically relevant internal rate of return exists.

Moreover, in the case of a linked investment project, a reinvestment assumption must be made. In contrast to the NPV model, the IRR method implicitly assumes that cash flows surpluses generated from a project (after covering interest charges and the repayment of the capital employed) can be used to make a financial investment that earns the internal rate of return. In general, this assumption is unrealistic and, thus, becomes a major disadvantage of the method. The application of the IRR method is therefore not meaningful for non-isolated investments – at least not without considering a specific supplementary investment or modifying the reinvestment assumption.

The internal rate of return (r) was defined above as the interest rate at which the NPV becomes zero. Therefore:

$$NPV = \sum_{t=0}^{T} (CIF_t - COF_t) \cdot (1+r)^{-t} = 0 \qquad (3.16)$$

Only in special cases can the IRR be isolated from the above formula and determined accurately. This is possible with an acceptable effort when the time span encloses only one or two periods or, in the case of a longer time span, if only two cash flows take place or all the future cash flows are identical.

For projects spanning three or more periods, where none of the other special cases apply, approximation procedures should be applied to the determination of the IRR. Such approaches include the NEWTON's procedure and a method developed by BOULDING (1936). Spreadsheet software usually also has programme functions that can be used to determine the IRR for multi-period projects.

In the following discussion an interpolation or extrapolation procedure is described for approximating the IRR of isolated investment projects.

For this procedure the net present value (NPV_1) is determined for a discount rate (i_1). If this is positive (negative), then a higher (lower) discount rate (i_2) is selected and the net present value is re-calculated (NPV_2). Then the two discount rates and their associated NPVs can be used to approximate the project's IRR. A linear interpolation (where a positive and a negative NPV have been determined) or an extrapolation (if both NPVs show the same algebraic sign) is executed. A formula supporting both the described interpolation and extrapolation can be derived with the help of the following figure.

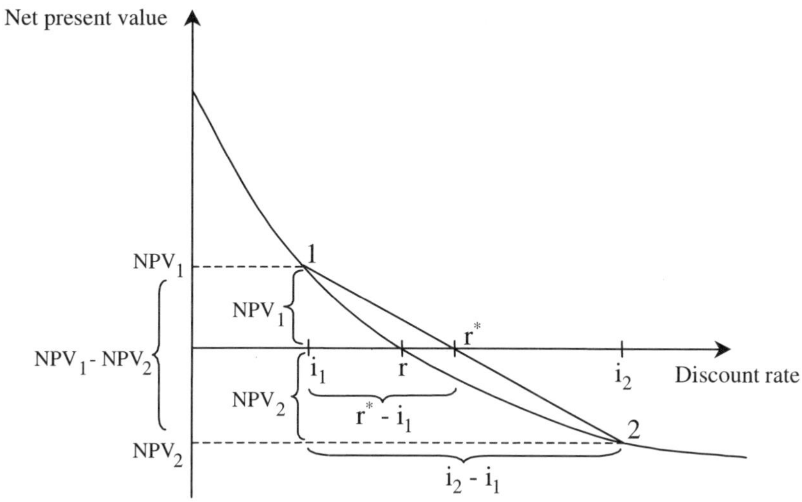

Fig. 3-4: Interpolation to determine the internal rate of return

In Figure 3-4 the IRR is represented by the point at which the NPV function and the abscissa intersect. This point can be approximated by drawing a straight line between the two determined NPV points (1 and 2 in Figure 3-4) and finding its intersection with the abscissa (r^*). The interpolation formula is derived based on the theorem on intersecting lines.

$$\frac{r^*-i_1}{i_2-i_1}=\frac{NPV_1}{NPV_1-NPV_2} \tag{3.17}$$

$$\Leftrightarrow \quad r^*-i_1=\frac{NPV_1}{NPV_1-NPV_2}\cdot(i_2-i_1)$$

$$\Leftrightarrow \quad r^* = i_1+\frac{NPV_1}{NPV_1-NPV_2}\cdot(i_2-i_1) \tag{3.18}$$

$$\Rightarrow \quad r \approx i_1+\frac{NPV_1}{NPV_1-NPV_2}\cdot(i_2-i_1) \tag{3.19}$$

The exactness of the approximation depends on how big the differences are between the discount or interest rates i_1 and i_2, and between their associated net present values NPV_1 and NPV_2. This determines the deviation of the approximating straight line from the course of the true NPV function. For a 'good' approximation it might be necessary to use several discount rates and to calculate their associated NPVs in order to identify two discount rates suitable for the interpolation. Two discount rates are suitable when their difference is relatively small, and the range of their associated NPVs around zero is also small. It may be helpful to apply an approximated IRR solution as a uniform discount rate and then use it for further interpolations. Thus, with an appropriate number of iterations, a reasonably accurate result can be reached for the IRR.

Example 3-3

For this example, the data from Example 3-1 is used again and the interpolation procedure is applied first to alternative A.

The NPV of project A with a uniform discount rate $i_1 = 8\%$ is already known ($NPV_{A1} = €26{,}771.59$). For a second chosen uniform discount rate $i_2 = 18\%$ the NPV_{A2} can be re-calculated as -€1,619.51.

Because the difference between i_1 and i_2 is relatively large and, thus, the exactness of the approximation would be poor, the NPV is re-calculated for another interest rate $i_1{}^* = 17\%$ to give an $NPV_{A1}{}^* = €740.69$. Now, the differences between the two discount rates and between the resulting NPVs are quite small.

Using the interest rates $i_1{}^*$ (17% or 0.17) and i_2 (18% or 0.18) together with their associated NPVs, the following interpolation result is obtained:

$$r_A \approx 0.17 + \frac{€740.69}{€740.69 - (-€1{,}619.51)} \cdot (0.18 - 0.17)$$

$$r_A \approx 0.1731 \quad \text{or} \quad 17.31\,\%$$

The IRR for project A is approximately 17.31%. Because this lies above the uniform discount rate of 8%, the project is profitable in absolute terms.

The fact that the IRR represents the interest on an investment project across different periods, based on the capital tie-up (remaining loan) in each period, can be illustrated by means of a finance and redemption plan. Such a plan is presented in the following table, which assumes the use of full debt financing at an interest rate of 17.31%.

Point in time **t**	**Net cash flow (€) (without initial investment outlay)** NCF_t	**Interest paid (€) (cash outflow)** $I_t (= i \cdot V_{t-1})$	**Change in capital tie-up (€) (redemption)** $\Delta V_t (= NCF_t + I_t)$	**Capital tie-up (€) (remaining loan)** $V_t (= V_{t-1} + \Delta V_t)$
0	0	0.00	0.00	–100,000.00
1	28,000	–17,310.00	10,690.00	–89,310.00
2	30,000	–15,459.56	14,540.44	–74,769.56
3	35,000	–12,942.61	22,057.39	–52,712.17
4	32,000	–9,124.48	22,875.52	–29,836.65
5	35,000	–5,164.72	29,835.28	–1.37

Tab. 3-4: Financial budget and redemption plan (IRR method)

At each period's end, the cash flow surpluses are used first to pay the interest on the capital tie-up at the beginning of the period. The remaining amount is available for the immediate redemption of capital. The net cash flows from the investment project enable the exact recovery of the capital and the payment of interest on capital employed at the internal rate of return (small rounding errors can be ignored). Correspondingly, the IRR equals the interests earned on the capital employed; this rate can also be interpreted as an upper limit for the cost of capital for the investment project. Since the amount of capital employed depends on the IRR, both must be determined simultaneously.

The results for project B are approximated in the same way. For discount rates of 25% and 26% the approximation of the internal rate of return is: 25.04%. Thus investment project B is also assessed as absolutely profitable.

However, in contrast to the NPV method, project B now appears to be relatively profitable owing to its higher IRR. This is because the IRR method uses the rate of interest earned on the capital that is tied-up as the target measure. Project B starts with a considerably lower initial investment outlay and, thus, its relative profitability increases. Absolutely profitable projects with lower capital tie-up often win in an IRR comparison of relative profitability, in contrast to the same comparison made using the NPV method.

Where competing projects differ in their capital tie-up or their economic life, the IRR method is of dubious suitability for assessing relative profitability. As with the NPV model, an implicit assumption is made in balancing such differences. It is assumed that a financial investment is made (or, alternatively, a corresponding financing alternative is realised), which yields an interest rate equal to the IRR of the investment project with the shorter economic life, or the smaller amount of capital tie-up. Among other things, this implies that financial investments yielding the IRR can be made without limit. This assumption is often unrealistic, because the IRR reflects the cash flows of the investment under consideration and *not* the opportunities in the capital market. Moreover, if in a comparison of two investment projects the capital tie-up is higher initially for one project and later, during the course of the economic life, for the other project, then it has to be assumed that the interest rate used to balance the capital tie-up changes with the IRRs. Finally, in any comparison of three or more different projects made by comparing two at a time, the inconsistency will be obvious as, in that situation, different rates will be used in the same decision process. In summary, the IRR method is not suitable for the assessment of (relative) profitability amongst two or more projects, since the assumption made for balancing capital tie-up and economic life differences at this very rate is unrealistic.

However, the IRR method *can* be used for the assessment of relative profitability when the IRRs are not taken from the investment projects themselves, but from differential investments (described in Section 3.2). An assumption in this case is that the differential investment is an isolated investment project.

The IRR of this differential investment corresponds to the discount rate that, used as a uniform discount rate, equalises the NPVs of the two projects under consideration (intersection IS of the NPV functions of projects A and B in Figure 3-4). This rate r_D is always higher than the uniform discount rate (i) if the project with the higher initial investment outlay has the higher NPV (project A in Figure 3-4). Accordingly, the IRR leads to assessments of relative profitability identical to the NPV method if the following rule is applied to the comparison of two investment projects A and B with A having the higher initial investment outlay:

Key Concept:
An investment project A is relatively profitable compared to a project B if the IRR of the differential investment is higher than the uniform discount rate.

If the differential investment does not have a positive IRR, investment project B is relatively profitable for all positive uniform discount rates.

Assessment of the method

For the assessment of the IRR method the reader is referred to the corresponding statements about the NPV method. Both methods require the same data. The calculation of an approximated IRR is slightly more difficult than the NPV calculation but, as shown above, these approximations lead to satisfactory results.

The underlying assumptions are largely the same for both models. The only exceptions are the assumptions regarding the financial investments of free cash flow surpluses (i.e. the reinvestment assumption) and those pertaining to how capital tie-up and economic life differences are balanced when comparing projects. The IRR model assumes that free surplus cash flows yielded by an investment project can be reinvested to earn exactly the IRR rate, which is – in general – unlikely.

Therefore, the IRR method should not be used to assess the absolute profitability of linked (non-isolated) investment projects unless (i) explicit consideration is given to supplementary investments, or (ii) the reinvestment assumption is modified. As an additional problem, it is possible that several economically meaningful IRRs exist for non-isolated projects. This makes it difficult to interpret the results of the IRR analysis.

Similarly, assessments of relative profitability should not be made by comparing project IRRs, because of the unrealistic balancing assumption noted above. Instead, differential investments should be analysed. If they are isolated investment projects, their IRRs may be compared to the uniform discount rate to achieve a meaningful profitability comparison. If a differential investment is a linked (non-isolated) investment project, then using the IRR method does not make sense.

The applicability of the IRR method is not limited to the assessment of investment projects. The method is also suitable for calculating the effective interest rate of financial projects like loans. The IRR of the cash flow profile of a financial project indicates its effective rate of interest. In this case, the application of the IRR method for the comparison of projects is less problematic. The projects under consideration are typically similar in amount, in the structure of their interest and redemption payments, and in their general terms; balancing differences is seldom required. Thus, assessments of relative profitability will regularly not deviate from those of the net present value method.

As with the annuity method, the IRR method shows some advantages over the NPV method when it comes to interpreting the results. A project's IRR can be seen as representing the interest earned on the capital employed – an intuitive approach that makes the IRR method popular in company practice.

Additionally, another relationship between the NPV and IRR methods can be pointed out. The IRR is the uniform discount rate at which a project's NPV equals zero. If the NPV method is used and the 'certainty of data' assumption is discarded, the IRR can be interpreted as a critical rate of return which must not be surpassed by the real cost of capital if the investment project is to remain favourable.

3.5 Dynamic Payback Period Method

Description of the method

The dynamic payback period method (DPP) combines the basic approach of the static payback period method (see Section 2.4) with the discounting cash flow used in the NPV model. The key measure is:

> *Key Concept:*
> The dynamic payback period is the period after which the capital invested has been recovered by the *discounted* net cash inflows from the project.

The static payback period method has already been discussed in Section 2.4, and the statements made there can largely be transferred to the dynamic payback period (DPP) method. As is true also for the static version, the DPP calculation should not be the sole criterion used to assess investment projects, but it can act as a supplement to other approaches. For the DPP approach:

> *Key Concept:*
> *Absolute profitability* is achieved, if the payback period of an investment project is shorter than a designated time limit.
> *Relative profitability:* An investment project is preferred if it has a shorter payback time than the alternative investment project(s).

The DPP method does not necessarily lead to the same results for absolute or relative profitability as the NPV method. Whether results differ for absolute profitability depends on the designated time limit as well as on the cash flows for the last period(s). Identical results are obtained if the designated time limit is assumed to be the project's economic life. Differences in comparing relative profitability, however, can result from cash flows that occur *after* the payback period has been achieved, as the DPP method does not systematically account for these subsequent cash flows.

The determination of the DPP involves calculating the NPV of the project as at the end of every period of its economic life. As long as this value remains negative, the payback period is not yet reached. When this value reaches zero (or becomes positive for the first time), the payback period is achieved (or exceeded). If the first non-negative value exceeds zero, then payback is achieved somewhere within that last period to be considered. The part of that period (year) which must pass before payback is achieved can be approximated by interpolation.

Example 3-4

The determination of the DPP is illustrated for the investment example discussed in the previous sections. The following table illustrates the calculations:

Point in time t	**Net cash flows (€)** NCF_t	**Present values of discounted net cash flows (€)** $NCF_t \cdot q^{-t}$	**Cumulative net present values (€)** $NCF_t \cdot q^{-t}$
0	–100,000	–100,000.00	–100,000.00
1	28,000	25,925.93	–74,074.07
2	30,000	25,720.17	–48,353.90
3	35,000	27,784.13	–20,569.77
4	32,000	23,520.96	+2,951.19

Tab. 3-5: Determination of the DPP

The table lists the net cash flows for each period, the present value of the discounted net cash flows and the cumulative NPVs. The DPP is exceeded in this example after four periods, because the cumulative NPV becomes positive. So, the DPP is achieved at a point in time somewhere between 3 and 4 years after the start of the project. To approximate the actual DPP, the following linear interpolation formula may be used. Here t^* indicates the period of the last cumulated negative net present value:

$$DPP \approx t^* + \frac{NPV_{t^*}}{NPV_{t^*} - NPV_{t^*+1}} \tag{3.20}$$

When using this interpolation it is assumed that cash flows occur in a linear fashion, i.e. evenly throughout each year. In the example above, a proportion (but not all) of year 4's discounted cash flow of €23,520.96 is required before payback is achieved. The amount required is €20,569.77 (i.e. the amount outstanding at the end of year 3). It may be assumed that this proportion of the year 4 cash flow corresponds to an equivalent proportion of time elapsed during year 4. Using this assumption, the DPP of the investment project A (DPP_A) is approximated as:

$$DPP_A = 3\,\text{years} + \frac{€20{,}569.77}{€23{,}520.96} = 3.87\,\text{years}$$

For project B (see Example 3-1) the DPP may be determined in the same way. It amounts to approximately 2.78 years. In contrast to the results of the NPV calculation, project B appears to be relatively profitable. Absolute profitability depends on the designated time limit. If 4 years is used, for example, then both projects are absolutely profitable. If the time limit was set at 3 years instead, then only project B would be judged absolutely profitable using the DPP criterion.

Assessment of the method

The DPP method has characteristics that are common to both the NPV and the SPP methods. The underlying assumptions (concerning the discounting of project cash flows) are the same as for the NPV model and so the same issues and problems of data collection apply (see the discussion of the NPV method).

Compared to the SPP method, the dynamic model has the advantage of using discounted cash flows. But, it still shares some of the limitations of the static model. A crucial problem is the omission of all cash flows occurring in periods after the DPP is achieved, which may be substantial for some long-running projects. Because of this limitation the DPP, like the SPP model, mainly serves as a measure of the risk connected with an investment project (in terms of the time needed to recover the investment outlay), but it is unsuitable as an exclusive decision criterion. However, it should be pointed out that the payback period represents a critical value of the economic life in the NPV model (this will be discussed further in Section 8.3).

3.6 Data Collection

As described above, the initial investment outlay, the future cash inflows and outflows, the economic life, the liquidation value and the discount rate all go into determining net present values for investment appraisal. Issues related to the collection of these data are discussed here. Also, an approach to the special problem of dealing with inflation is analysed. Although the following hints in this section refer to NPV examples, they also apply to other methods described in this book.

It is important to remember that NPV calculations involve a comparison between undertaking and rejecting an investment project. Therefore, a project's cash flow profile should indicate changes in the cash inflows and outflows that are a direct result of undertaking the project, i.e. the difference between the additional cash flows *created* and *eliminated* by the project. The intended subsequent activities and their consequences should be included as relevant data as well, e.g. the net cash flows of a known subsequent investment project. Finally, the cash flow effects may be influenced by various company decisions such as scheduling, project, cost or cash management decisions. Where known, these impacts should also be incorporated into the project appraisal.

Initial investment outlay

The initial investment outlay for an investment project is a cash outflow resulting from the acquisition of the project, and/or the company-wide activities necessary for its provision and establishment (i.e. any set-up costs). The purchase price should reflect any discounts received, but must also include any costs associated with procurement, for example freight and customs/import duties. Cash flows resulting from the in-company production of an investment project can be derived from the cost accounting system, as a calculation of production costs. However, any discrepancy between recorded costs and cash outflows should be scrutinised, as it might require adjustments to the data.

It is often difficult to work out the cash flows caused by additional in-company activities associated with the acquisition or production of an investment project, particularly where there are 'indirect cash flows' caused by the joint use of indivisible assets (staff, capital assets etc.) by several projects. This is comparable to the problem of indirect costs and revenues in cost accounting systems.

Investment projects can result in changes to current assets (e.g. increased inventories) or the initiation of projects needed to improve company-wide infrastructure, which themselves represent an investment by the company. Outflows caused by such 'subsequent investment projects' should also be included and considered as part of the investment analysis. The same applies to governmental or other institutional financial investment incentives, and to the cash inflows and/or outflows resulting from the directly associated release of other assets (particularly liquidation revenues from replaced projects, or outflows following their sale and disposal).

Current net cash flows

Current cash inflows and outflows, or current net cash flows, are the central components of the cash flow profile and must be explicitly forecasted for all periods of the project's economic life. Current cash inflows often result primarily from the sales of products produced as an outcome of the investment project. These cash inflows are calculated as the additional production volume multiplied by the unit sales price. Forecasting this data can be difficult. The forecasts need to be supported by detailed sales planning and control activities, differentiated by product types/markets served etc., and based on estimates of the additional production capacity that will be achieved as a result of undertaking the investment project.

Additionally, in contrast with the previously discussed assumption (c) (see Section 3.2), the cash inflows resulting from a particular investment project might not be determinable because they cannot be attributed to a single project (for example when several investment projects jointly increase the amount of saleable production by increasing the capacity of a production process). Such investment projects should be assessed using simultaneous investment and production decision models, as described in Section 7.3. The net cash flow effects resulting from investments in areas not directly related to the products and customers (e.g. investments in improving infrastructure or enhancing operational readiness), are even more difficult to estimate, making the identification of relevant net cash inflows very challenging for projects of this type.

The current cash outflows of a company can be either increased or reduced by investment projects. For example, a rationalisation investment can reduce current costs (cash outflows) and thus increase net cash flows. Such changes can impact on any production factors and in all company areas. Therefore, precise forecasts of relevant cash outflows may require a detailed analysis of effects across all of the company's areas and divisions and for all production factors. As with initial investment outlays and cash inflows, a frequent problem is the difficulty in isolating additional cash outflows caused by an investment project. Cost accounting data can provide some of the information needed, but usually not all of it. For planning consistency, estimated cash outflows should build on the same assumptions used for cash inflows, i.e. on factors like sales and production volumes, price levels, etc. If relevant, tax-related effects can also be included in the analysis of relevant cash inflows and outflows, as described in Section 5.1.

It is worth mentioning that, although cash inflows and outflows might appear to be equivalent to revenues and costs, the use of this (and other) data from the company's accounting system is not always appropriate for investment appraisal purposes. As mentioned above concerning the initial investment outlay, discrepancies between recorded costs and cash outflows (e.g. resulting from depreciation) should be identified and corresponding adjustments made to convert accounting data into cash flow information. The amount of adjustment work needed will depend on how divergent the accounting and cash flow measures are, and how aggregated the accounting data is. Theoretically, it can also be shown that investment appraisal decisions based on cash flow analysis are, under certain assumptions, identical to those based on traditional accounting measures (e.g. the LÜCKE and PREINREICH theorem (LÜCKE, 1955, LÜCKE 1991, PREINREICH, 1937). In practice, however, accounting data usually needs careful adjustments if it is to be used as a basis for capital investment decision-making.

Liquidation or residual value

Another part of an investment project's cash flows is the liquidation or residual value at the end of the project's economic life or planning period. Forecasts of liquidation value must include any cash inflows from the sale of the project or its components, together with any cash outflows resulting from its dismantling, sale or disposal. Therefore the liquidation value can be negative when there is an excess cash outflow. Forecasting liquidation cash flows is particularly difficult because they occur well into the future. The cash flows will depend on future prices that potential buyers will be willing to pay for the investment project and their planned utilisation of it. For some marketable projects, however, data or market prices exist that support the said forecast.

A simplified variation of the model can be constructed by setting the planning period shorter than the economic life of the investment project and summarising the remaining project cash flows as a residual value. That is, the cash flows expected *after* the designated planning period are discounted back to the end of the planning period and aggregated into a single 'residual value'. This approach simplifies the forecasting activity. For example, a constant cash flow surplus can be assumed for the period beyond the planning horizon. However, this approach is by no means uncomplicated since the data (cash flows generated after the planning period, the number of periods for which they will occur, and the relevant interest rate) are difficult to estimate beyond the designated planning period. Thus, both approaches are characterised by a high degree of uncertainty in regard to the liquidation or residual value. Moreover, defining the planning period also presents a decision problem for the model construction.

Relevant uniform rate of discount

The choice of a relevant discount rate is an important consideration for every net present value calculation. Choosing this discount rate presents challenges in itself. The discount rate must fulfil two functions: on the one hand it should permit comparability between alternative investments, and on the other hand it should reflect both current and future investment opportunities.

To compare alternatives, the cost of financing an investment (i.e. the 'cost of capital') needs to be considered. This cost is not included within the project's cash flows – instead, it must be reflected in the discount rate used in the NPV calculation. One way to determine the relevant discount rate is to derive it directly from financing costs. Where internal funds are used to finance a project, the relevant 'cost of capital' is the rate of return that could have been earned on the next best alternative investment. For example, if it has to be decided whether to invest in project A, and the best alternative use for the funds is to invest them in project B, then the (internal) rate of return that project B would earn should be used as the cost of capital for analysing project A.

With debt financing, the rate of interest is readily known (from the interest paid on the borrowed capital). Or, if a project is to be funded from a mix of internal funds and debt financing, a 'weighted average cost of capital' can be calculated by taking a proportion of the financing cost for each source (debt and internal funds).

However, deriving the relevant discount rate from financing costs brings certain problems:

- The forms of capital by which separate investment projects are financed are often not known (the company may have a combined 'pool' of debt and internal funds, from which several projects might be funded).
- It is hard to determine alternative return(s) that could be earned on internal funding.
- Interest payments for future investment opportunities will not always correspond with current financing costs.

An alternative approach is to consider opportunity costs. Here, it is assumed that a project's financing cost (or discount rate) is the rate of return that have been *given up* by not investing this money in an alternative project. However, it is often not known which investment project is crowded out by the investment under consideration and, thus, which represents the relevant alternative. Simultaneous planning models can help here (see Sections 7.1 and 7.2 later in the book). From their optimum solution, a uniform discount rate can be derived, based on the interest of the best 'crowded out' investment project: the so-called 'endogenous uniform discount rate'. However, this can be known only *after* the relative profitability of alternative investment projects has been assessed.

The second function of the uniform discount rate lies in balancing capital tie-up and economic life differences. Here, again the interest rate of the 'best crowded out' investment opportunity can be applied to fictitious current or future projects that 'balance out' differences in projects that are being compared.

Time-span dependent discount rates

Until this point, it has been assumed that the uniform discount rate is independent of the time-span between the occurrence of a cash flow (time t) and the beginning of the planning period ($t = 0$), i.e. a 'flat' interest curve exists. However, in reality, interest from bonds depends on their length: typically rates rise with increasing lengths of the bond. So, if the capital market is to be viewed as an alternative investment possibility, it is useful to fix uniform discount rates relative to time spans. To do this, interest rates from zero bonds that start in the planning period can be used. A zero bond is a loan that leads to only one cash inflow (CIF_t) at the end of its life span (a period lasting from $t = 0$ to point in time t). The rate of interest is derived from the difference between this cash inflow and the cash outflow (I_0) at the beginning of the period. For a period of length t, the rate of interest i_{ZBt} can be described by:

$$i_{ZBt} = \sqrt[t]{\frac{CIF_t}{I_0}} - 1 \qquad (3.21)$$

The NPV of an investment can then be determined by discounting (to the beginning of the planning period) the cash flows of any given point in time by the interest rate payable for a current loan up to that point in time:

$$NPV = \sum_{t=0}^{T}(CIF_t - COF_t) \cdot (1 + i_{ZBt})^{-t} \qquad (3.22)$$

Where zero bonds are traded only intermittently, i.e. interest rates are not available for all relevant periods, rates for other bonds or warrants can be used. Additionally, interest rates on zero bonds might in some cases correlate with the interest rates ($i_{T\tau}$) for all annual financial investments that jointly cover the same time span, according to the following relationship:

$$(1 + i_{ZBt})^t = \prod_{\tau=1}^{t}(1 + i_{T\tau})^{-1} \qquad (3.23)$$

Using this approach, the result is identical to the one for the NPV calculation described above, if the annual interest rates are applied to the discount rates for each period up to t:

$$NPV = \sum_{t=0}^{T}(CIF_t - COF_t) \cdot \prod_{\tau=1}^{t}(1 + i_{T\tau})^{-1} \qquad (3.24)$$

Whether time-span-specific interest rates are applied or not, a ‘correct’ uniform discount rate which fulfils the described functions (comparability as well as representing current and future investment opportunities) can be achieved only under the simplistic assumption of a perfect capital market. Therefore, practical applications of the NPV method must aim to find a uniform discount rate that leads to an approximate fulfilment of both functions.

Besides these considerations, the problem of determining a uniform discount rate can be reduced by finding an upper and a lower limit for the rate of interest and using both for NPV calculations. A minimum rate, for instance, could be the interest rate on risk-free securities, while an upper limit could be the maximum interest obtainable for the best alternative investment or the most expensive loan. It is then reasonable to assume that investment projects will show absolute profitability if they achieve a positive NPV using the upper limit discount rate. Conversely, if a negative NPV is obtained using the minimum discount rate, the project will normally be unprofitable.

In reality, interest rates are different for borrowing and investing. Methods have been developed to allow for these differential rates, thus accommodating an imperfect capital market. They are described in the next chapter. For instance, the 'compound value method' assumes different credit and debt interest rates. Moreover, the 'visualisation of financial implications method' (VoFI method) enables the utilisation of a large number of different credit and debt interest rates.

Further considerations are necessary if taxes, inflation, or risk need to be included in the derivation of a realistic uniform discount rate. The inclusion of taxes and risk is discussed in Chapters 5 and 8, and the case of inflation is taken up below.

Inflation

Because of the typical long-term effects of investment projects, a question arises as to whether inflation (and the purchasing power losses it causes) should be included in the investment appraisal method, and in what form. Increases in price levels usually affect the various components of cash flows associated with an investment project, as well as the discount rate(s) to be used. In regard to cash flows either nominal values or real values may be used. In general, the forecast of nominal values is less problematic. When using nominal values for cash flows, either a nominal interest rate i (nominal NPV method) or a real uniform discount rate i^r tied to the currency depreciation rate g (real NPV method) can be used as a uniform discount rate. Both approaches lead to the same discounting factors and, thus, to the same NPV result, provided interest rates and inflation rates remain constant throughout the planning period and the so-called FISHER condition applies (FISHER, 1930):

$$1 + i = (1 + i^r) \cdot (1 + g) \tag{3.25}$$

In this case, real interest rates are independent of inflation.

Finally, it should be noted that the ways in which a project's NPV is affected by incorporating inflationary effects, are governed by the specific inflationary outcomes for the cash flows as well as on the uniform discount rate. If both are affected in the same way, the NPV remains the same whether or not inflation is included in the calculation. However, if the project's net cash flows inflate more (or less) strongly than the uniform discount rate, the NPV will increase (decrease).

Assessment Material Chapter 3

Exercise 3-1 (Net Present Value Method and Annuity Method)

The initial investment outlay of an investment project is €100,000. Use the following data:
Economic life: 5 years
Liquidation value: €10,000

t	1	2	3	4	5
CIF_t (€)	45,000	55,000	50,000	45,000	40,000
COF_t (€)	15,000	15,000	20,000	25,000	30,000

Tab. 3-6: Cash inflows and outflows of the investment project

Where:

CIF_t = Current cash inflows in t
COF_t = Current cash outflows in t

The uniform discount rate is 5%. Is it a good idea to acquire this item? Ascertain:

a) The net present value.
b) Using a financing and redemption plan, the value that would arise if the item were to be wholly financed by internal funds.
c) The annuity.

Exercise 3-2 (Net Present Value Method and Internal Rate of Return Method)

A company has to decide between three investment projects. The characteristics of these are as follows:

Data	Project A	Project B	Project C
Initial investment outlay (€)	300,000	500,000	350,000
Net cash flows (€)			
t = 1	100,000	250,000	90,000
t = 2	100,000	200,000	90,000
t = 3	90,000	180,000	95,000
t = 4	80,000	80,000	95,000
t = 5	0	–50,000	100,000
Liquidation value (€)	20,000	–50,000	0

Tab. 3-7: Characteristics of the three investment projects A, B, and C

The economic life of all three projects is 5 years.

The uniform discount rate is 10%.

a) Calculate the net present values of the investment projects and assess the relative profitability of each.
b) Calculate the projects' internal rates of return.

Exercise 3-3 (Dynamic Investment Appraisal Methods)

To maintain production of an important product, a metal processing company is forced to replace a piece of equipment. As there is a good order book, an expansion of production could also follow from this investment. There are two investment projects to choose from with the following data (€):

		Project I		
Budget year	**1**	**2**	**3**	**4**
Cash inflows	60,000	64,000	76,000	76,000
Personnel expenses	18,000	18,000	18,000	18,000
Material expenses	12,000	16,000	18,000	18,000
Maintenance expenses	2,000	2,000	4,000	8,000
Other cash outflows	3,000	3,000	3,000	4,000
Initial investment outlay:			100,000	
Liquidation value at the end of four periods:			10,000	

		Project II		
Budget year	**1**	**2**	**3**	**4**
Cash inflows	124,000	113,000	87,000	75,000
Personnel expenses	22,000	22,000	22,000	22,000
Material expenses	20,000	18,000	18,000	18,000
Maintenance expenses	0	0	14,000	12,000
Other cash outflows	5,000	3,000	3,000	3,000
Initial investment outlay:			180,000	
Liquidation value at the end of four periods:			12,000	

Tab. 3-8: Data for the investment projects I and II

The uniform discount rate is 6%.

a) Assess the relative profitability of the two projects using
   a1) The net present value method.
   a2) The annuity method.

a3) The internal rate of return method.

a4) The dynamic payback period method.

b) What is the reason for possible different results while using the net present value method and the internal rate of return method?

c) Assess the premises and applicability of each method; in particular refer to the consideration of different initial investment outlays und economic lives. Which possibilities exist to balance these differences?

Further exercises will be included in the assessment material for Chapters 4 and 5 in the context of advanced investment appraisal methods and applications.

Further Reading Part II

Alesii, G. 2006. Payback Period and Internal Rate of Return in Real Options Analysis. *Engineering Economist* 51 (3):237-257.

Ang, J. S., J. H. Chua, and R. Sellers. 1979. Generating Cash Flow Estimates: An Actual Study Using the Delphi Technique. *Financial Management* 8 (1):64-67.

Baldwin, C. Y., and R. S. Ruback. 1986. Inflation, Uncertainty, and Investment. *Journal of Finance* 41 (3):657-669.

Baron, D. P. 1979. Investment Policy, Optimality, and the Mean-Variance Model. *Journal of Finance* 34 (1):207-232.

Baumol, W. J., and R. E. Quandt. 1965. Investment and Discount Rates Under Capital Rationing - a Programming Approach. *Economic Journal* 75 (298):317-329.

Berkovitch, E., and R. Israel. 2004. Why the NPV Criterion does not Maximize NPV. *Review of Financial Studies* 17 (1):239-255.

Block, S. 2005. Are There Differences in Capital Budgeting Procedures Between Industries? An Empirical Study. *Engineering Economist* 50 (1):55-67.

Blohm, H., K. Lüder, and C. Schaefer. 2006. *Investition: Schwachstellenanalyse des Investitionsbereichs und Investitionsrechnung*. 9 ed. München: Vahlen.

Boulding, K. E. 1936. Time and Investment. *Economica* 3 (12):196-214.

Boyle, G., and G. Guthrie. 2006. Payback without apology. *Accounting & Finance* 46 (1):1-10.

Breuer, W. 2007. *Investition I. Entscheidungen bei Sicherheit.* 3 ed. Wiesbaden: Gabler.

Brown, R. J. 2006. Sins of the IRR. *Journal of Real Estate Portfolio Management* 12 (2):195-199.

Burton, R. M., and W. W. Damon. 1974. On the Existence of a Cost of Capital Under Pure Capital Rationing. *Journal of Finance* 29 (4):1165-1173.

Cooper, W. D., R. G. Morgan, A. Redman, and M. Smith. 2001. Capital Budgeting Models: Theory vs. Practice. *Business Forum* 26 (1/2):15-19.

Doenges, R. C. 1972. The 'Reinvestment Problem' in a Practical Perspective. *Financial Management* 1 (1):85-91.

Dorfman, R. 1981. The Meaning of the Internal Rate of Return. *Journal of Finance* 36 (5):1011-1021.

Elton, E. J. 1970. Capital Rationing And External Discount Rates. *Journal of Finance* 25 (3):573-584.

Elton, E. J., and M. J. Gruber. 1971. Valuation and the Cost of Capital for Regulated Industries. *Journal of Finance* 26 (3):661-670.

Fama, E. F. 1970. Efficient Capital Markets: A Review of Theory and Empirical Work. *Journal of Finance* 25 (2):383-417.

Fama, E. F., and K. R. French. 1999. The corporate cost of capital and the return on corporate investment. *Journal of Finance* 54 (6):1939-1967.

———. 2002. The Equity Premium. *Journal of Finance* 57 (2):637-659.

Fama, E. F., and M. R. Gibbons. 1982. Inflation, Real Returns and Capital Investment. *Journal of Monetary Economics* 9 (3):297-323.

Fama, E. F., and A. B. Laffer. 1971. Information on Capital Markets. *Journal of Business* 44 (3):289-298.

Fisher, I. 1930. *Theory of Interest*. New York: Macmillan.

Franke, G., and H. Hax. 2008: *Finanzwirtschaft des Unternehmens und Kapitalmarkt,* 6 ed. Berlin: Springer.

Götze, U. 2006. *Investitionsrechnung*. 5 ed. Berlin et al.: Springer.

Hirshleifer, J. 1958. On the Theory of Optimal Investment Decision. *Journal of Political Economy* 66 (4):329-352.

———. 1961. Risk, the Discount Rate, and Investment Decisions. *American Economic Review* 51 (2):112-120.

Ingraham Jr, H. G. 1979. An Analysis of Two Cost Comparison Methods - Interest Adjusted Cost vs. Linton Yield. *CLU Journal* 33 (4):34-43.

Keane, S. M. 1979. The Internal Rate of Return and the Reinvestment Fallacy. *Abacus* 15 (1):48-55.

Keef, S. P., and M. L. Roush. 2001. Discounted cash flow methods and the fallacious reinvestment assumption: a review of recent texts. *Accounting Education* 10 (1):105-116.

Kelleher, J. C., and J. J. MacCormack. 2005. Internal rate of return: A cautionary tale. *McKinsey Quarterly*:70-75.

Kruschwitz, L. 2007. *Investitionsrechnung*, 11 ed. München, Wien: Oldenbourg.

Kruschwitz, L., and A. Loeffler. 2006. *Discounted Cash Flow: A Theory of the Valuation of Firms*. Chichester et al.: Wiley.

Lewellen, W. G., H. P. Lanser, and J. J. McConnell. 1972. Payback Substitutes for Discounted Cash Flow. *Financial Management* 8 (2):195-206.

Little, J. D. C. 2004. Models and Managers: The Concept of a Decision Calculus. *Management Science* 50 (12):1841-1853.

Longbottom, D. A., and L. Wiper. 1977. Capital Appraisal and the Case for Average Rate of Return. *Journal of Business Finance and Accounting*, 4 (4): 419-426.

———. 1979. Capital Appraisal and the Case for Average Rate of Return: A Reply. *Journal of Business Finance & Accounting* 6 (2):243-244.

Lücke, W. 1955. Investitionsrechnungen auf der Grundlage von Ausgaben oder Kosten? *Zeitschrift für handelswissenschaftliche Forschung, NF* 7:310-324.

Lücke, W. 1991. *Investitionslexikon*. 2 ed. München: Vahlen.

Meyer, R. L. 1979. A Note on Capital Budgeting Techniques and the Reinvestment Rate. *Journal of Finance* 34 (5):1251-1254.

Miller, M. H., and F. Modigliani. 1966. Some Estimates of the Cost of Capital to the Electric Utility Industry, 1954-57. *American Economic Review* 56 (3):333-392.

———. 1967. Some Estimates of the Cost of Capital to the Electric Utility Industry: 1954-57: Reply. *American Economic Review* 57 (5):1288-1300.

Modigliani, F., and M. H. Miller. 1958. The Cost of Capital, Corporation Finance and the Theory of Investment. *American Economic Review* 48 (3):261-297.

———. 1959. The Cost of Capital, Corporation Finance, and the Theory of Investment: Reply. *American Economic Review* 49 (4):655-669.

Modigliani, F., and R. Sutch. 1966. Innovations in Interest Rate Policy. *American Economic Review* 56 (2):178-197.

Modigliani, F., and H. M. Weingartner. 1958. Forecasting Uses of Anticipatory Data on Investment and Sales. *Quarterly Journal of Economics* 72 (1):23-54.

Nicol, D. J. 1981. A Note on Capital Budgeting Techniques and the Reinvestment Rate: Comment. *Journal of Finance* 36 (1):193-195.

Perridon, L., and M. Steiner, M. 2007. *Finanzwirtschaft der Unternehmung*. 14 ed. München: Vahlen.

Pogue, M. 2004. Investment appraisal: A new Approach. *Managerial Auditing Journal* 19 (4):565-569.

Pratt, J. W., and J. S. Hammond III. 1979. Evaluating and Comparing Projects: Simple Detection of False Alarms. *Journal of Finance* 34 (5):1231-1241.

Preinreich, G. A. D. 1937. Valuation and Amortization. *The Accounting Review* 12 (3):209-226.

Remer, D. S., and A. P. Nieto. 1995a. A Compendium and Comparison of 25 Project Evaluation Techniques.: Part 1: Net Present Value and Rate of Return Methods. *International Journal of Production Economics* 42 (1):79-96.

———. 1995b. A Compendium and Comparison of 25 Project Evaluation Techniques. Part 2: Ratio, Payback, and Accounting Methods. *International Journal of Production Economics* 42 (2):101-129.

Weingartner, H. M. 1969. Some New Views on the Payback Period and Capital Budgeting. *Management Science* 15 (2):594-607.

Part III

Advanced Methods and Applications of Investment Appraisal

Chapter 4: Compounded Cash Flow Methods

This chapter describes methods that do not assume a perfect capital market – i.e. the following methods use differing debt and credit interest rates instead of a uniform discount rate. An overview over all dynamic investment appraisal methods described in this and the previous chapter is shown in the following figure:

Dynamic investment appraisal methods

Uniform discount rate

- Net present value method (Section 3.2)
- Annuity method (Section 3.3)
- Internal rate of return method (Section 3.4)
- Dynamic payback period method (Section 3.5)

Differing debt and credit interest rates

- Compound value method (Section 4.1)
- Critical debt interest rate method (Section 4.2)
- Visualisation of financial implications (VoFI) method (Section 4.3)

Fig. 4-1: Dynamic investment appraisal methods

The discussion of compounded cash flow methods will start with the compound value method.

4.1 Compound Value Method

Description of the method

The compound value (CV) method is a dynamic investment appraisal method that uses the compound value as its target measure – i.e. all cash flows are compounded to the end of the investment project.

Key Concept:
The compound value is the overall net monetary gain or loss resulting from the investment project and is related to the end of its economic life.

The method is characterised by three assumptions about the capital market. First, it is assumed that different interest rates exist: a debt interest rate for borrowings and a credit interest rate for financial investments. Second, it is assumed that unlimited amounts can be borrowed or invested at these rates. Third, interest rates are assumed to be independent of the amount borrowed or invested.

Apart from these assumptions and the use of compound values as target measures, the CV model parallels the net present value (NPV) model. The profitability of projects according to the CV method can be assessed as follows:

> *Key Concept:*
> *Absolute profitability:* is achieved if an investment project's compound value is greater than zero.
> *Relative profitability:* is achieved if an investment project has a higher compound value than the alternative investment project(s).

Absolute and relative profitability assessments obtained using the CV method might differ from those obtained using the NPV method due to the different capital market assumptions. In contrast to the NPV method, the comparison of alternative projects using the CV method does not employ a fictitious differential investment. A fictitious investment would not always lead to usable results with the CV method, as its end value might not match the difference between the end values of the investment projects under comparison.

Since two interest rates are involved in the CV method, an assumption has to be made about the amount and timing of existing loan repayments using project net cash inflows. In general this assumption can be specified separately for every period. Here, for reasons of simplification only two special cases are examined – *mandatory* and *prohibited* account balancing – where cash inflows from a project *must* be used, or *cannot* be used, to redeem project-related debts.

Prohibited account balancing prevents cash inflows from being applied to debt redemption during the economic life of the investment project and prohibits the use of existing cash for financing net cash outflows. Separate accounts are established for the net cash inflows and net cash outflows. The inflows earn the credit interest rate (c) (in the account CV_T^+) and the outflows incur the debt interest rate (d) (in the account CV_T^-). Accordingly, the compound values at the end of the planning period (or the project's economic life) are:

$$CV_{T^+} = \sum_{t=0}^{T} NCF_{t^+} \cdot (1+c)^{T-t} \tag{4.1a}$$

$$CV_{T^-} = \sum_{t=0}^{T} NCF_{t^-} \cdot (1+d)^{T-t} \tag{4.1b}$$

The compound value (CV_T^+) is the sum of the compounded cash inflows (NCF_t^+) at the end of the planning period, using the credit interest rate. The (negative) compound value (CV_T^-) is the sum of the negative net cash flows (NCF_t^-) compounded using the debt interest rate. The difference between these two accounts, i.e. the overall compound value (CV_T) of the investment project, can be calculated by summing the compound values of the two accounts:

$$CV_T = CV_{T^+} + CV_{T^-} \tag{4.2}$$

In contrast *mandatory account balancing* implies that any net cash inflows have to be applied to the redemption of existing debt. Existing cash is immediately used (if required) to finance any net cash outflows. Thus, it is sufficient to have only one account (CV) to which all cash inflows and outflows (NCF_t) are assigned. Interest on this account accrues at the end of the period (t) and is calculated using the debt interest rate (d) if the project-specific financial assets at beginning of the period (CV_{t-1}) are negative, or using the credit interest rate (c) if CV_{t-1} is positive. Financial resources at time t (CV_t) are given by the following formula:

$$CV_t = NCF_t + \begin{cases} CV_{t-1} \cdot (1+c), & \text{for } CV_{t-1} \geq 0 \\ CV_{t-1} \cdot (1+d), & \text{for } CV_{t-1} < 0 \end{cases} \tag{4.3}$$

The compound value (CV_T) therefore is:

$$CV_T = NCF_T + \begin{cases} CV_{T-1} \cdot (1+c), & \text{for } CV_{T-1} \geq 0 \\ CV_{T-1} \cdot (1+d), & \text{for } CV_{T-1} < 0 \end{cases} \tag{4.4}$$

The following example illustrates the amortisation assumptions outlined above.

Example 4-1

The standard example introduced in Chapter 3, Example 3-1, is used again, but is slightly modified in regard to the interest rates. Now, a debt interest rate (d) of 10% and a credit interest rate (c) of 6% are assumed.

First, the compound value is calculated for investment project A using the *prohibited account balancing* assumption. The accounts CV^+ and CV^- are then combined at the end of the project's life into the CV, the sum of the two accounts:

$$\begin{aligned} CV_{5A^+} &= €28{,}000 \cdot 1.06^4 + €30{,}000 \cdot 1.06^3 + €35{,}000 \cdot 1.06^2 + €32{,}000 \cdot 1.06 \\ &\quad + €30{,}000 + €5{,}000 \\ CV_{5A^+} &= €179{,}325.83 \end{aligned}$$

$$CV_{5A^-} = -€100{,}000 \cdot 1.10^5 = -€161{,}051.00$$

$$CV_{5A} = CV_{5A^+} + CV_{5A^-} = €18{,}274.83$$

The compound value for investment project B can be calculated in the same way and amounts to:

$$CV_B = €25{,}249.95$$

Since both projects yield positive compound values, both are absolutely profitable. With regard to relative profitability it must be noted that the compound values are not directly comparable, because they refer to different points in time. Comparability can be achieved by compounding CV_B (determined as at t = 4) by one year (to t = 5) using the credit interest rate, and thereby assuming that the prohibited account balancing assumption is abandoned at the end of the project's economic life. The new compound value is then €26,764.95 (i.e. €25,249.95 · 1.06). Thus project B is relatively profitable because it has a higher compound value.

In contrast, the *mandatory account balancing* assumption requires only one account to which both net cash inflows and outflows (NCF_t) are assigned. The calculation of the compound value using the formula indicated above is shown in the following spreadsheet for project A:

Point in time **t**	**Net project cash flow (€)** NCF_t	**Interest (€)** $I_t = \begin{cases} c \cdot CV_{t-1}, \text{ for } CV_{t-1} \geq 0 \\ d \cdot CV_{t-1}, \text{ for } CV_{t-1} < 0 \end{cases}$	**Net cash change (€)** $\Delta CV_t \ (= NCF_t + I_t)$	**Net monetary value (€)** $CV_t \ (= CV_{t-1} + \Delta CV_t)$
0	–100,000	0.00	–100,000.00	–100,000.00
1	28,000	–10,000.00	18,000.00	–82,000.00
2	30,000	–8,200.00	21,800.00	–60,200.00
3	35,000	–6,020.00	28,980.00	–31,220.00
4	32,000	–3,122.00	28,878.00	–2,342.00
5	35,000	–234.20	34,765.80	32,423.80

Tab. 4-1: Calculation of the compound value for project A using the mandatory account balancing assumption

The compound value of project A is now €32,423.80 and the project remains absolutely profitable. Project B's compound value can be determined in the same way and amounts to €31,561.60 (related to t = 4) or €33,455.30 (related to t = 5). Again, project B maintains relative profitability.

In comparing profitabilities, capital tie-up and economic life differences must be considered. Compound value comparisons work well also in cases where capital tie-up differs between projects. Since financial investments in the capital market will normally yield at a credit interest rate that is lower than the debt interest rate, the compound values of such investments will be negative, these investments cannot be advantageous and they will not affect the profitability. So, it is sufficient to compare the compound values that arise from the cash flow profiles of the investment projects.

As in the example given above, differences in economic lives may be balanced by reinvesting the compound value of the shorter-term investment project (B) until the end of the economic life of the other project (A), using the credit interest rate. Thus, it is assumed that future investments will yield interest at this credit interest rate. This assumption is sometimes questionable, for example when information exists about yields of specific subsequent projects. In this case, investment chains should be compared.

In the example above, the assessment of profitabilities was unaffected by account balancing assumptions. However, differences can appear concerning absolute and relative profitability results due to account balancing assumptions. For instance, if the example shown above is modified and a debt interest rate of 13% is assumed, the absolute profitability of A depends on the account balancing assumption: the object is absolutely profitable under the mandatory account balancing assumption but not under the prohibited account balancing assumption. The choice of an appropriate assumption is discussed below.

Assessment of the method

The CV method evaluation is largely the same as that presented for the NPV method. The required data are identical except that the CV method requires both debt and credit interest rates. The calculation of the target measure, the compound value, is no more difficult.

But, some differences do exist between CV and NPV. The CV method avoids the assumption of a perfect capital market and with it the use of a uniform discount rate. In assuming unlimited borrowing capacity and unlimited financial investment opportunities, but at different interest rates, the CV model assumptions are more realistic than those of the NPV method. However, if debt and credit interest rates deviate only slightly from each other, the results of both the CV and NPV calculations will be often the same in practice.

Additionally, assumptions are made about the use of net cash inflows for debt redemption (and interest payments) and about the use of existing funds to finance net cash outflows. Two options for account balancing assumptions were presented above: prohibited and mandatory. Since debt interest rates usually exceed credit interest rates, companies often prefer to repay debt rather than invest surplus cash, in which case mandatory account balancing assumptions are most appropriate. However, the assumption concerning the 'account balancing' is problematic, since finance and investment policy is determined for a whole company rather than for separate projects.

Finally, the use of only two interest rates is another limitation of the CV method. This can be overcome by a method described in Section 4.3 – the visualisation of financial implications (VoFI) method – which allows a greater number of debt and credit interest rates to be used. An approach that is strongly related to the CV method, the critical debt interest rate method, is considered next.

4.2 Critical Debt Interest Rate Method

Description of the method

The critical debt interest rate (CDIR) method, like the compound value method, assumes separate debt and credit interest rates. The critical debt interest rate serves as the target measure for this method.

> *Key Concept:*
> The critical debt interest rate is the rate that (with a given credit interest rate) results in a compound value of zero.

This approach indicates the interest earned on capital tied-up over each period of the investment project, given a specified credit interest rate.

The CDIR method and the CV method have a relationship similar to that of the internal rate of return (IRR) method and the net present value (NPV) method.

Assuming the likely case that the debt interest rate exceeds the credit interest rate, the absolute profitability of investment projects can be defined as follows:

> *Key Concept:*
> An investment project is absolutely profitable if its critical debt interest rate exceeds the market's debt interest rate.

Absolute profitability results are the same for the CDIR method as they are for the CV method, in the case of isolated investment projects.

Relative profitability assessments produced using the CDIR method have the same limitations that were outlined for the internal rate of return (IRR) method (see Section 3.4). Critical debt interest rate comparisons usually fail to yield meaningful results, since capital tie-up and economic life differences are assumed to be balanced by the critical debt interest rate. The use of the CDIR method with a fictitious differential investment is problematic, because the resulting compound value does not always equate to the difference between the compound values of the projects under consideration. Therefore, the CDIR method can be used to assess relative profitability only in some cases. Since all of these cases can also be assessed using the CV method, the CDIR method is not recommended for assessing relative profitability.

An approximation of the critical debt interest rate (d_c) can be made as described for the IRR (see Section 3.4). First, the compound value CV_1 is calculated for a debt interest rate d_1. If CV_1 is positive (negative), a higher (lower) debt interest rate d_2 is selected and used to calculate a lower (higher) compound value CV_2. Using these two results, an interpolation or extrapolation can be executed using a formula similar to the one used to calculate with the IRR method:

$$d_c \approx d_1 + \frac{CV_1}{CV_1 - CV_2} \cdot (d_2 - d_1) \tag{4.5}$$

As for the IRR method, the accuracy of the approximation depends on the difference between the debt interest rates and how far from zero the resulting compound values lay.

With an isolated investment project, and assuming mandatory account balancing, the critical debt interest rate equals the internal rate of return (IRR). Under the prohibited account balancing assumption and when only one cash outflow exists, the critical debt interest rate can be calculated easily and without interpolation, as shown at the example below.

The CDIR method generally may use different account balancing assumptions. In the following example both mandatory and prohibited account balancing are considered, so the approach parallels that taken for CV analysis in Section 4.1. The determination of critical debt interest rates assuming mandatory account balancing is based on the approach suggested by TEICHROEW, ROBICHEK and MONTALBANO (1965).

Example 4-2
This example draws on data used for Example 4-1.

Prohibited account balancing

Investment project A is reconsidered. As mentioned, the critical debt interest ratc can be calculated using the interpolation procedure presented in Section 3.3. However, a simpler determination of the critical debt interest rates can be made, provided that prohibited account balancing is assumed and only one negative cash flow (i.e. one cash outflow) exists. The compound value of the cash inflows is 'given' and independent of the debt interest rate. To obtain the critical debt interest rate, the compound value of the cash outflows must be identical (though negative) in order to achieve a net compound value of zero. Thus, in the example:

$$CV_{5A^+} = €179{,}325.83 = -CV_{5A^-}(d_{cA})$$

$$CV_{5A^-} = -€100{,}000 \cdot (1 + d_{cA})^5 = -€179{,}325.83$$

$$d_{cA} = 0.1239 \text{ or } 12.39\ \%$$

For investment project B, a critical debt interest rate of 17.17% can be calculated in the same way. Because the debt interest rate is 10%, and therefore lower than the critical debt interest rates, both projects are absolutely profitable.

Mandatory account balancing

For investment project A a compound value CV_{A1} of €32,423.80 has already been calculated using a debt interest rate of $d_1 = 10\%$. An approximate solution can be determined using the interpolation formula indicated above. When the debt interest rates are $d_1^* = 17\%$ and $d_2 = 18\%$ and their associated compound values are $CV_{A1}^* = €1{,}623.93$ and $CV_{A2} = -\,€3{,}705.04$, the formula is:

$$d_{cA} \approx 0.17 + \frac{€1{,}623.93}{€1{,}623.93 - (-€3{,}705.04)} \cdot (0.18 - 0.17)$$

$$d_{cA} \approx 0.1730 \quad \text{or} \quad 17.30\%$$

In the same way, a critical debt interest rate of 25.04% can be calculated for investment project B using the debt interest rates of 25% and 26% and their respective compound values.

Both projects are absolutely profitable because their critical debt interest rates exceed the debt interest rate of 10%. The critical debt interest rates are equal (apart from rounding errors) to the project's internal rates of return (IRRs). However, whether account balancing is prohibited or mandatory, the identical assessments of absolute and relative profitability in this example cannot be generalised to all circumstances.

Assessment of the method

The assessment of the CDIR method can be derived from the assessments of the IRR and CV methods. The data required is the same as for the CV method and the computational effort is only slightly higher. The model's assumptions correspond largely to those of the CV method, except that capital tie-up and economic life differences are balanced in a manner equivalent to that used for the IRR method. Because the assumptions of the CV method reflect the reality more closely, this method is preferable to the CDIR method.

4.3 Visualisation of Financial Implications (VoFI) Method

Description of the method

The visualisation of financial implications (VoFI) method is based on the ideas of HEISTER (1962) that were later developed by GROB (1993). Its defining feature is a comprehensive financial plan that considers all cash flows connected with an investment project.

Key Concept:
The VoFI comprehensive financial plan considers the economic consequences of an investment project, specifically in regard to:

- The amounts and proportions of internal funds and debt capital used.
- The amounts and timing of debt redemption from cash inflows.
- The alternate yield on the long-term financial investment of the initial internal funds (the opportunity interest rate that generates the so-called opportunity income value) – not necessarily identical to the yield on short-term financial investments during the project's economic life.
- The existence of different forms of loans, with differing payback and interest conditions.

The VoFI method explicitly analyses both the cash flow profile of an investment project itself (the so-called *original* cash flows) and the cash flows from the project's financing and financial investments (the *derivative* cash flows). Assumptions (e.g. about payback structures, financial investment opportunities and balancing differences in capital tie-ups and economic lives) that are only implicit in other models (such as NPV and IRR) are made explicit in the VoFI method. Moreover, different assumptions can be applied to different financial arrangements when there are different forms of loan or financial investment.

Target measures for the VoFI method can be compound values, initial values, intermediate values, withdrawals, or specific rates of return. Compound values are considered here, primarily because of their clarity. They represent the value of the accounts (including the loans) at the end of the economic life of an investment project, and are discernable directly from comprehensive financial plans.

Key Concept:
An investment project is *absolutely profitable* if its compound value exceeds the opportunity income value at the end of its economic life.
An investment project is *relatively profitable* if its compound value exceeds the compound values of alternative projects.

Standardised tables can be used to work out comprehensive financial plans. Figure 4-2 shows the structure of such a table.

	t=0	t=1	t=2	t=3	t=4	...
Series of net cash flows						
Internal funds						
– Withdrawal of capital						
+ Contribution of capital						
Instalment loan						
+ Borrowing						
– Redemption						
– Debt interest						
Loan with final redemption						
+ Borrowing						
– Redemption						
– Debt interest						
Annuity loan						
+ Borrowing						
– Redemption						
– Debt interest						
Current account loan						
+ Borrowing						
– Redemption						
– Debt interest						
Financial investment						
– Reinvestment						
+ Disinvestment						
+ Credit interest						
Financial balance						
Balances						
Loans:						
Instalment loan						
Loan with final redemption						
Annuity loan						
Current account loan						
Financial investment						
Net balance						

Fig. 4-2: The VoFI table

The first part of this table contains the cash flows, consisting of: the cash flow profile of the investment project; the project-assigned internal funds and their changes; the borrowing, repayments and interest payments for four typical forms of loans; and the payments resulting from the execution, release and interest transactions of financial investments taken. The comprehensive financial plan always has to be balanced, i.e. the balance of all cash flows is zero in every point in time. In the second part of the table relevant loans and financial investments, together with their resulting net balances, are recorded. At the end of the economic life, the net balance obtained corresponds to the compound value of the investment project.

The comprehensive financial plan and compound value calculation for an investment project require the following steps:

Step 1: at $t = 0$ the initial outlay of the investment project and allocated internal funds are recorded. In addition, the loan amount to be raised is calculated and the status of loans and financial investments is recorded.

Step 2: for $t = 1$ and every subsequent period the net cash flows of the investment project are recorded. Interest payments, any borrowing or redemption of loans, and any making or discontinuation of financial investments is calculated in order to update the status of loans and financial investments.

To assess absolute profitability, a compound value is calculated using a comprehensive financial plan. Then, the project-assigned internal funds are compounded with an opportunity interest rate into an opportunity income value, which is compared to the expected compound value of the project. To assess relative profitability, the inclusion of supplementary investments may be required under specific circumstances. This issue will be addressed in the example below.

Before that, the use of alternative target measures should be explained. For example, a rate of return for the internal funds invested (r_{IF}) can be derived from the expected compound value (CV_T) at the end of the economic life (T) (assumed to be non-negative) using formula 3.6 below. This formula assumes that internal funds (IF) at the beginning of the planning period yields at a constant annual (interest) rate:

$$r_{IF} = \sqrt[T]{\frac{CV_T}{IF}} - 1 \tag{4.6}$$

An investment project is considered absolutely profitable if its rate of return exceeds the opportunity interest rate. The project with the highest rate of return is relatively profitable. Assuming identical allocated internal funds and economic lives, results for both absolute and relative profitabilities are identical to those achieved by using the compound value as the target measure.

Another possible target measure is the periodic withdrawal which can be realised assuming a given compound value. The withdrawal amounts need not be constant throughout the different years, as it is also possible to consider a series of timed withdrawals as a target measure. The maximum withdrawal, or series of withdrawals, that a project can sustain can be determined iteratively (as in the IRR interpolation procedure) or with the help of spreadsheet software such as Lotus 1-2-3 or Microsoft Excel. In an imperfect capital market – as it is often assumed in VoFI models – differing assessments of profitability can arise from analyses of withdrawal maximisation and compound value maximisation.

Example 4-3

Example 4-2 can be usefully extended by assuming that €20,000 is available in cash (representing the allocated internal funds) at the beginning of the planning period. Its alternate use is a financial investment opportunity yielding 7% interest. The interest rate available for the short-term investment of surpluses is 6%. To finance the investment project – A or B – a loan with final redemption and an instalment loan, each about 25% of the initial investment outlay are available at 9% interest for a term of four years. Any remaining financing can be raised as a current account loan (at 11% interest). All payments are made at the period end, and the interest charges are based on the capital employed at the beginning of each period.

Using this data, and assuming that surpluses are used for the immediate redemption of the current account loan, the comprehensive financial plan for investment project A is as follows:

	t=0	t=1	t=2	t=3	t=4	t=5
Series of net cash flows	-100,000	28,000	30,000	35,000	32,000	35,000
Internal funds						
– Withdrawal of capital						
+ Contribution of capital	20,000					
Instalment loan						
+ Borrowing	25,000					0
– Redemption		-6,250	-6,250	-6,250	-6,250	0
– Debt interest		-2,250	-1,687.50	-1,125	-562.50	0
Loan with final redemption						
+ Borrowing	25,000					
– Redemption					-25,000	0
– Debt interest		-2,250	-2,250	-2,250	-2,250	0
Annuity loan						
+ Borrowing						
– Redemption						
– Debt interest						
Current account loan						
+ Borrowing	30,000					
– Redemption		-13,950	-16,050	0	0	0
– Debt interest		-3,300	-1,765.50	0	0	0
Financial investment						
– Reinvestment			-1,997	-25,494.82		-36,624.73
+ Disinvestment					412.99	0
+ Credit interest				119.82	1,649.51	1,624.73
Financial balance	0	0	0	0	0	0
Balances						
Loans:						
Instalment loan	25,000	18,750	12,500	6,250	0	0
Loan with final redemption	25,000	25,000	25,000	25,000	0	0
Annuity loan						
Current account loan	30,000	16,050	0	0	0	0
Financial investment			1,997	27,491.82	27,078.83	63,703.56
Net balance	-80,000	-59,800	-35,503	-3,758.18	27,078.83	63,703.56

Fig. 4-3: VoFI plan for investment project A

The compound value of project A amounts to €63,703.56. Because this exceeds the opportunity income value (by €20,000 $\cdot$ 1.07^5 = €28,051.03), the project is absolutely profitable.

The VoFI financial plan for investment project B is shown in Figure 4-4:

	t=0	t=1	t=2	t=3	t=4
Series of net cash flows	-60,000	22,000	26,000	28,000	28,000
Internal funds					
– Withdrawal of capital					
+ Contribution of capital	20,000				
Instalment loan					
+ Borrowing	15,000				
– Redemption		-3,750	-3,750	-3,750	-3,750
– Debt interest		-1,350	-1,012.50	-675	-337.50
Loan with final redemption					
+ Borrowing	15,000				
– Redemption					-15,000
– Debt interest		-1,350	-1,350	-1,350	-1,350
Annuity loan					
+ Borrowing					
– Redemption					
– Debt interest					
Current account loan					
+ Borrowing	10,000				
– Redemption		-10,000		0	0
– Debt interest		-1,100		0	0
Financial investment					
– Reinvestment		-4,450	-20,154.50	-23,701.27	-10,460.85
+ Disinvestment					
+ Credit interest			267	1,476.27	2,898.35
Financial balance	0	0	0	0	0
Balances					
Loans:					
Instalment loan	15,000	11,250	7,500	3,750	0
Loan with final redemption	15,000	15,000	15,000	15,000	0
Annuity loan					
Current account loan	10,000	0	0	0	0
Financial investment		4,450	24,604.50	48,305.77	58,766.62
Net balance	-40,000	-21,800	2,104.50	29,555.77	58,766.62

Fig. 4-4: VoFI plan for investment project B

Investment project B is also absolutely profitable, because its compound value (€58,766.62) exceeds the opportunity income value (which is €20,000 $\cdot$ 1.07^4 = €26,215.92).

Assessing relative profitability requires determining the extent to which the projects are comparable, given their differences in investment outlay and economic life, and, if necessary, working out how comparability can be achieved. The VoFI method explicitly considers the manner in which the initial investment outlay is financed. Therefore, different initial investment outlays impair project comparability only if one (or more) of the mutually exclusive projects has an initial outlay less than the allocated internal funds. In that case (not shown in the example), an assumption about a supplementary investment is needed to balance the difference in the allocated equity. For example, it can be assumed that the excess amount is invested to yield the opportunity interest rate.

Economic life differences must be balanced in every case; otherwise compound values referring to different points in time will not be comparable. The capital available at the end of the shorter investment project has to be compounded by an appropriate interest rate to balance the life differences. In the example given, the compound value of project B has to be compounded by a further year before it can be compared with the compound value of project A. Assuming an interest rate of 7%, the compound value of B is €62,880.28 at t = 5 (€58,766.62 · 1.07). Because the compound value of the project A (€63,703.56) is higher, A is relatively profitable.

The rates of return derived from the VOFI are:

$$r_{IFA} = \sqrt[5]{\frac{€63{,}703.56}{€20{,}000}} - 1 = 0.2607 \quad \text{or } 26.07\,\%$$

$$r_{IFB} = \sqrt[5]{\frac{€62{,}880.28}{€20{,}000}} - 1 = 0.2575 \quad \text{or } 25.75\,\%$$

Both projects are absolutely profitable, because their rates of return exceed the opportunity interest rates. Project A emerges as relatively profitable due to its higher VoFI capital profitability.

Assessment of the method

The VoFI method is a relatively simple method for assessing alternative investment projects. Data required are: the cash flow profiles of the investment projects; the amounts of available internal (financial) funds; debt capital components and their relevant financial conditions (redemption types, interest rates etc.); the opportunity income interest rate; and the credit interest rate for short-term investments. Some of this data are determined independently of which investment appraisal method is chosen and, therefore, have to be available in each case. Other data would have to be obtained especially for the VoFI method, in which case it should be asked whether the additional effort is justifiable. Since financing and investment policies are usually tailored to the whole company rather than to individual projects, the allocation of internal funds and specific loans to individual projects can be difficult. However, this problem does not occur with, for example, *strategically important* investments (e.g. foundational investments for new plant or business locations, and foreign investments) or with certain projects such as real-estate purchases, which require their own financial plans.

The assumptions of the VoFI method are largely the same as those of the NPV method: only one target measure is pursued (although various target measures may be employed); a given economic life is assumed; other decisions concerning production, sales etc. are assumed to be already made and therefore cash flows are attributable to specific projects and points in time; and the data is assumed to be certain. It should additionally be pointed out that the VoFI method can also be used to determine the optimum economic lives and the replacement times and that uncertainty can be included in VoFI models as well. For instance, a payback period can be determined (it ends when the existing net balance equals the compounded opportunity income value). In the examples given, it was assumed that all payments take place at the end of a period (year). This assumption can be changed by adjusting the VoFI analysis to a monthly (or other) timeframe (although this might be problematic when calculating the tables manually without spreadsheet software).

Decisions in other company areas are considered solely in relation to financial decisions, because at the beginning of the second and following periods decisions may be needed about the extent of debt use (or repayment) that results from net cash outflows (or inflows). Moreover, in an extension to the examples presented here, the optimum financing of individual investment projects can be determined. This may be useful because in an imperfect capital market the optimum investment and financing decisions are not independent (i.e. the FISHER separation theorem does not apply). The way in which investment projects are financed is, therefore, relevant to the assessment of those projects. In the case of decisions about a single investment project, the aim is to identify the optimum set of financing alternatives and use this as a basis for the project appraisal. Therefore, a compound value can be calculated for every combination of investment and financing using the comprehensive financial plan. The combination with the maximum compound value represents the optimum. Alternatively, optimisation models, which include financing possibilities as variables, can be used to determine the optimum financing for each project. In the same way, it can be determined whether any financial surpluses should be used to pay back loans. However, the VoFI method cannot assist with optimising the allocation of funds between *different* investment projects. The VoFI approach does not consider all interdependencies between different investment projects and financial investments, so optimum investment and financing programmes cannot be determined (for models allowing this see Chapter 7).

In contrast with the NPV method, the VoFI method does not assume that cash flows are reinvested and differences in capital tie-up and/or economic life are balanced at a uniform discount rate – assumption (f) of the NPV method. The short-term investment of cash flow surpluses is assumed to earn an adequate credit interest rate, at least for the standard case (which can be modified). Capital tie-up differences are limited to the internal funds available at the beginning of the planning period, and can be balanced individually. The same applies to economic life differences although it can be difficult to determine the relevant interest rate. In summary, the VoFI method also requires simplifying assumptions about financing and investment opportunities in order to avoid the planning scenario becoming too complicated.

An advantage of the VoFI method over other investment appraisal methods is that assumptions about the reinvestment of surpluses and the balancing of differences in capital tie-up are transparent within the standardised tables. Also, the comprehensive financial plans can be modified in regard to assumptions (f) and (g) (see Section 3.2) in order to illustrate the premises of the other dynamic investment appraisal methods such as NPV. Overall, VoFI analysis results are well suited to presentation and control, so they are likely to be highly acceptable to decision-makers.

A major difference between the VoFI and NPV methods concerns assumptions about the capital market. While the NPV method assumes a perfect capital market (assumption g), the VoFI method can include not only differences between credit and debt interest rates (like the compound value method), but also the capacity for self-financing and a huge variety of loan and financial investment conditions (especially different interest rates for short and long term investment opportunities). This is a second reason for preferring the VoFI method.

In an imperfect capital market, investment and consumption decisions are not separable, but under the VoFI method consumption can be considered in a simplified form by maximisation of the withdrawals attainable. Moreover, where capital markets are imperfect, certainty – assumed throughout Chapters 2 to 4 – cannot exist. In reality, investing companies do face an imperfect capital market and uncertainty, so to assume otherwise is a simplification. However, the arguments presented here reflect the view of the authors that these simplifying assumptions can be appropriate in some situations. In other cases, the models presented here are a first step towards dealing with uncertainty *and* imperfect capital markets within the investment appraisal process.

Assessment Material Chapter 4

Exercise 4-1 (Compound Value Method, Critical Debt Interest Rate Method and VoFI Method)

Two investment projects are available, with the following relevant cash flows:

Data	Project I	Project II
Initial investment outlay (€)	580,000	760,000
Economic life	7	5
Net cash flows (€)		
t = 1	–60,000	240,000
t = 2	0	320,000
t = 3	140,000	180,000
t = 4	150,000	120,000
t = 5	270,000	160,000
t = 6	290,000	–
t = 7	180,000	–

Tab. 4-2: Cash flows of the investment projects I and II

a) Use the compound value method to decide which project to accept. Assume a credit interest rate of c = 5% and a debt interest rate of d = 8%. Calculate the compound values of the two projects, assuming:
   (i) Mandatory account balancing.
   (ii) Prohibited account balancing.
b) Calculate the critical debt interest rate, assuming:
   (i) Mandatory account balancing.
   (ii) Prohibited account balancing.
c) Assess the underlying assumptions and meaningfulness of the compound value method.
d) Assess the absolute profitability of project II above, using the visualisation of financial implications (VoFI) method. In so doing, assume that the opportunity interest rate is 6% and the credit interest rate for short-term deposits is 5%. The project is to be 20% financed by internal funds. Thirty percent of the initial outlay is to be financed with an annuity loan (with annual interest and capital repayments, an interest rate of 8% and a 5 year term). A further 30% is financed by a loan repayable at the end of its term (with an initial payment at a 'below par' rate of 5%, with annual interest payments, a nominal interest rate of 7% and a 5 year term) and the remainder with a current account loan (10% interest rate).

e) In the case of project II, what is the maximum amount that can be withdrawn at the end of each period of its economic life, taking the assumptions in d) as valid?

Exercise 4-2 (Dynamic Investment Appraisal Methods)

A choice has to be made between two investment projects. The following budgets are forecasted:

Data	**Project I**	**Project II**
Initial investment outlay (€)	10,000	12,000
Economic life	3	4
Net cash flows (€)		
t = 1	5,000	3,000
t = 2	5,000	4,000
t = 3	3,000	4,000
t = 4	–	6,000

Tab. 4-3: Data for the investment projects I and II

The uniform discount rate is 10%.

a) Assess the alternatives using the net present value method. What is the net present value of the fictitious differential investment?

b) Calculate the internal rates of return for each investment project and draw the net present value curves.
Assess the relative profitability using the internal rate of return method.

c) Calculate the projects' discounted payback period.

d) Now assume a debt interest rate of d = 0.12 and a credit rate of c = 0.08 for the next four years. Calculate the compound values of the projects, assuming:
(i) Mandatory account balancing.
(ii) Prohibited account balancing.

e) Calculate the critical debt interest rates, for each project, assuming:
(i) Mandatory account balancing.
(ii) Prohibited account balancing.

f) Assess the absolute and relative profitability of the two investment projects using the visualisation of financial implications (VoFI) method. In each case, €5,000 of internal funds should be used for financing. The opportunity interest rate is 9% and the credit interest rate for short-term deposits is 7%. Project I is financed with an instalment loan of €4,000 (interest of 11%; annual interest payments calculated on the remaining balance; term matches the project's economic life) and with a current account loan (annual interest payments at 13%). In the case of project II there is an additional loan for €2,000, repayable at the end of its four year term (annual interest at 10%).

Chapter 5: Selected Further Applications of Investment Appraisal Methods

This chapter examines some further applications of the investment appraisal methods already discussed: the inclusion of taxes in investment appraisals; the assessment of foreign investments; and the use of selected investment appraisal methods for determining optimum economic lives, replacement times and investment timing – all decisions under the assumption of certainty.

5.1 Income Taxes and Investment Decisions

Taxes should be included in the analysis of investment projects since they may affect project profitability. Their consideration in the assessment of investment projects is illustrated here using both the net present value (NPV) and visualisation of financial implications (VoFI) methods. The influence of taxes on the profitability of investment projects is affected by several factors, including: the form of the tax laws; the legal form of the company (in particular whether it has limited or unlimited liability); and the perspective from which the appraisal is made (particularly whether from the perspective of the company or the shareholders). Some simplifying assumptions usually have to be made in regard to these factors. For example, the following discussion assumes that only the perspective of the company is considered.

5.1.1 Taxes and the Net Present Value Method

Description of the method

In modifying the NPV method to include tax considerations, a simplified model variant is chosen that considers only profit-dependent taxes. The relevant profit measure can be derived from the original cash flow profile modified by (i) depreciation and (ii) the difference between the liquidation value and the remaining book value of assets sold at the end of a project's economic life.

In addition to the premises of the NPV model, the following assumptions are made:

- The company pays profit-dependent tax at the same time as the profit is reported: at the end of each period.
- Tax payments are proportional to the profit made.
- The company makes a profit in each period, independent of the project under consideration. Therefore, immediate loss compensation is possible in each period for which the proposed investment results in a loss, so a loss carry-forward is neither necessary nor possible.

- The original cash flow profile of an investment project (before the inclusion of tax payments) remains unaffected by taxes (e.g. there are no price increases as a result of taxation).
- Interest paid to creditors reduces profit and therefore reduces taxes; interest received from debtors raises profit and taxes.
- All cash inflows or outflows resulting from a project – with the exception of the initial investment outlay(s) and possibly the liquidation value – are counted in that same period as yields or expenses for the purposes of calculating profit. The initial investment outlay is initially capitalised in the balance sheet. Its subsequent depreciation annually reduces the profit, and the sale (liquidation) of the project generates a cash flow, that simultaneously may influence the profit.

The NPV calculation requires two additional steps to account for taxes:

- The original cash flow profile must be modified by payments directly resulting from taxation.
- The uniform discount rate must be adjusted to recognise the effects of tax paid on the yields of alternative (financial) investments, as well as tax deducted from the interest paid on debt capital (to determine the 'after-tax cost of debt').

First, *changes to the original cash flow profile* are discussed. Net cash flows before taxes (NCF_t) must be corrected for taxes paid in the point in time t (T_t). These may be calculated, assuming the premises specified above are valid, by multiplying the rate of taxation (rt) by the profit change accruing to the investment project in the period t (ΔP_t). After-tax net cash flows, represented by NCF_t^* (t = 0,1,...,T), are then:

$$NCF_t^* = NCF_t - T_t \qquad \text{or} \qquad (5.1)$$

$$NCF_t^* = NCF_t - rt \cdot \Delta P_t \qquad (5.2)$$

The changes to net cash flows resulting from tax payments depend on whether the investment project results in an increased profit ($\Delta P_t > 0$) or a loss ($\Delta P_t < 0$). In the first case $rt \cdot \Delta P_t$ is positive; in the second case it is negative.

Next, the profit change resulting from an investment project is analysed, based on the assumptions specified above. Therefore, net cash flow before taxes (NCF_t) is divided between a profit-affecting portion (NCF_t^{pa}) and a portion that does not affect profit (NCF_t^{np}). The latter comprises only the initial investment outlay and (possibly) the liquidation value, because all other cash inflows and outflows are assumed to be yields and expenses that impact profit calculations. The profit change (ΔP_t) may be calculated from the profit-affecting portion before taxes (NCF_t^{pa}), including any income/loss (i.e. gain or loss on sale) from the liquidation of the project, less any depreciation (D_t). This can be expressed as follows:

$$\Delta P_t = NCF_t^{pa} - D_t \qquad \text{for } t = 0,1,...,T \qquad (5.3)$$

Net cash flows after taxes therefore amount to:

$$NCF_t^* = NCF_t - rt \cdot (NCF_t^{pa} - D_t) \qquad \text{for } t = 0,1,...,T \qquad (5.4)$$

The inclusion of taxes affects both the cash flow profile of an investment project *and the uniform discount rate* that is used. As discussed earlier, the uniform discount rate takes into account the yields of alternative investment opportunities as well as the costs of debt capital. If taxes are assumed to be relevant, the interest yield on alternative investments changes in the following way:

$$i^* = i - rt \cdot i$$

Where i is the pre-tax return, and i* is the after-tax yield of the alternative investment opportunity. For example, if an alternative project yields a 10% pre-tax return and the company's tax rate is 30%, the relevant after-tax yield is 7% (i.e. 10% – 10% · 30%).

Similarly, the costs of debt capital must be adjusted for taxes. If these amount to i before the consideration of taxes, then a tax saving arises to the amount of $rt \cdot i$ and the adjusted interest equals $i^* = i - rt \cdot i$.

Therefore, in relation to both alternative investment opportunity yields and the cost of debt capital, the appropriate uniform discount rate (i^*) to be applied in a tax-adjusted NPV model is:

$$i^* = i - rt \cdot i \qquad (5.5)$$

Taking this into account, the modified net present value (NPV^*) can be calculated as follows:

$$NPV^* = \sum_{t=0}^{T} NCF_t^* \cdot (1 + i^*)^{-t} \qquad \text{or} \qquad (5.6)$$

$$NPV^* = \sum_{t=0}^{T} \left(NCF_t - rt \cdot (NCF_t^{pa} - D_t) \right) \cdot (1 + i - rt \cdot i)^{-t} \qquad (5.7)$$

In the tax-adjusted NPV^* model, the same decision rules apply as for the basic model that does not consider taxes. As a rule, the consideration of taxes changes the value of the NPV calculated. This may lead to different absolute and/or relative profitability results. For example, an investment project may be absolutely profitable with inclusion of taxes ($NPV^* > 0$) while, without the inclusion of taxes, it is absolutely not profitable ($NPV < 0$): a case referred to as a tax paradox. Such changes in profitability can be explained by two effects. On the one hand, a negative effect on NPV typically arises because the net cash flows are lower due to tax payments. On the other hand, the smaller tax-adjusted discount rate (i^*) acts to increase the NPV. The structure of the underlying cash flow profile, together with the changes in depreciation rates over time, decides which of these effects dominates.

Example 5-1

In the calculations below, Example 3-1 is reconsidered including tax considerations.

Data	Investment project A	Investment project B
Initial investment outlay (€)	100,000	60,000
Economic life (years)	5	4
Liquidation value (€)	5,000	0
Net cash flows (€)		
t = 1	28,000	22,000
t = 2	30,000	26,000
t = 3	35,000	28,000
t = 4	32,000	28,000
t = 5	30,000	-
Uniform discount rate (%)	8	8

Tab. 5-1: Data for the two investment projects A and B

Assume that the rate of taxation t is 40% and the entire initial outlay value is depreciated over each project's life using linear (straight-line) depreciation. For project A, then the depreciation is €20,000 per annum, and the profit resulting from the liquidation, which is part of the profit-affecting portion of the net cash flows before taxes (NCF_t^{pa}), is €5,000. This is because the depreciated book value of the project is zero by the end of year 5. Since the liquidation value is €5,000, a gain of €5,000 is reported and taxed. Thus, the profit-affecting and the profit-neutral portions of the pre-tax net cash flows (NCF_{tA}^{p} and NCF_{tA}^{np}), the annual depreciation D_{tA}, the profit resulting from the project liquidation, the profit change ΔP_{tA}, the tax payments T_{tA} and the modified cash flows NCF_{tA}^{*} may be determined as follows (in €'000):

Point in time t	0	1	2	3	4	5
NCF_{tA}	–100	28	30	35	32	35
D_{tA}	–	20	20	20	20	20
NCF_{tA}^{pa}	–	28	30	35	32	35
NCF_{tA}^{np}	–100	–	–	–	–	–
ΔP_{tA}	0	8	10	15	12	15
$T_{tA} = rt \cdot \Delta P_{tA}$	0	3.2	4	6	4.8	6
$NCF_{tA}^{*} = NCF_{tA} - T_{tA}$	–100	24.8	26	29	27.2	29

Tab. 5-2: Modified cash flows and other measures for each period (€'000)

The modified uniform discount rate in this example is 4.8% ($i^* = i - rt \cdot i$; 0.048 = 0.08 - 0.4 · 0.08). Then the modified net present value NPV_A* amounts to:

$$NPV_A^* = -100{,}000 + 24{,}800 \cdot 1.048^{-1} + 26{,}000 \cdot 1.048^{-2} + 29{,}000 \cdot 1.048^{-3}$$
$$+ 27{,}200 \cdot 1.048^{-4} + 29{,}000 \cdot 1.048^{-5}$$

$$NPV_A^* = €18{,}020.69$$

In the same way, the modified net present value NPV_B^* of the alternative project B can be calculated at €16,696.98.

Thus, both alternatives are absolutely profitable, and project A is relatively profitable. The assessments of profitability in this case remain identical to those achieved without considering taxes.

Assessment of the method

The model described here is based on the general NPV model and, therefore, its assessment is broadly as outlined in Section 3.2.

What is new, however, is the treatment of taxes in the model. It should be noted that only profit-dependent taxes are considered. Although this might be sufficient in most cases, a conclusive and thorough investment appraisal could also need to include other kinds of taxes and their resultant effects (which can be incorporated by adjustments of the cash flows).

More problematic is the assumption that only one type of profit-dependent tax is levied, and that it is a proportional tax (i.e. a linear function of profit). In reality, differential taxation of profit occurs using several kinds of taxes (e.g. in Germany: income tax, church tax, corporation and trading profit tax) whose inter-connecting effects can be complicated to recognise. Moreover, the rate of taxation is not always constant, given the high incidence of tax-free allowances and/or progressive taxation schemes. The linear tax rate assumption might often be unrealistic, therefore.

Where a single profit assessment basis and only one rate of taxation (a proportional tax) are not justifiable assumptions, extended models involving further analysis should be employed.

5.1.2 Taxes and the Visualisation of Financial Implications (VoFI) Method

Description of the method

The VoFI method explicitly records changes in tax payments that result from an investment project in an exhaustive financial plan. The VoFI table presented in Section 4.3 is extended by two columns for additional or reduced tax-dependent cash outflows, i.e. by tax payments and tax refunds. The determination of these changes is made in a separate calculation linked to the VoFI tables. Adjusted interest rates for loans or for short-term investments are not required. Instead, taxes are included when determining the compound value. Additionally, either a simple, after-tax opportunity interest rate may be used to determine the compound value of the internal funds, or tax payments may be included in a VoFI plan for the alternative opportunity investment.

The VoFI method, with its separate calculations, allows an investment appraisal to incorporate a specific tax system's known characteristics, such as the relevant kinds of tax, the tax bases, and the tax rates. However, no such specific tax system is included here, since no one system could adequately represent the wide variability in international tax systems.

The slight modifications of the VoFI needed to include taxes and their associated calculations are shown in the following example. For clarity, the tax-related assumptions of Section 5.1.1 are used, implying a highly simplified 'world of taxes' with one kind of tax only.

Example 5-2

Example 4-3 is extended here to consider tax effects. The determination of compound values for investment projects A and B requires separate calculations for their relevant tax cash payments, which then can be incorporated into the VoFI table. After this, the financial surplus or deficit can be determined, and a financial arrangement for its use or coverage can be considered. The following figures show the exhaustive financial plan and the separate calculations for investment project A. Again, as in Example 5-1, a tax rate of 40% is assumed.

	t=0	t=1	t=2	t=3	t=4	t=5
Series of net cash flows (€)	-100,000	28,000	30,000	35,000	32,000	35,000
Internal funds (€)						
– Withdrawal of capital						
+ Contribution of capital	20,000					
Instalment loan (€)						
+ Borrowing	25,000					0
– Redemption		-6,250	-6,250	-6,250	-6,250	0
– Debt interest		-2,250	-1,687.50	-1,125	-562.50	0
Loan with final redemption (€)						
+ Borrowing	25,000					
– Redemption					-25,000	0
– Debt interest		-2,250	-2,250	-2,250	-2,250	0
Annuity loan (€)						
+ Borrowing						
– Redemption						
– Debt interest						
Current account loan (€)						
+ Borrowing	30,000					
– Redemption		-13,870	-16,130	0	0	0
– Debt interest		-3,300	-1,774.30	0	0	0
Financial investment (€)						
– Reinvestment			-192.92	-20,731.95		-29,573.86
+ Disinvestment					4,984.21	
+ Credit interest			0	11.58	1,255.49	956.44
Taxes (€)						
– Tax payments		-80	-1,715.28	-4,654.63	-4,177.20	-6,382.58
+ Tax refunds						
Financial balance (€)	0	0	0	0	0	0
Balances (€)						
Loans:						
Instalment loan	25,000	18,750	12,500	6,250	0	0
Loan with final redemption	25,000	25,000	25,000	25,000	0	0
Annuity loan						
Current account loan	30,000	16,130	0	0	0	0
Financial investment		0	192.92	20,924.87	15,940.66	45,514.52
Net balance (€)	-80,000	-59,850	-37,307.08	-10,325.13	15,940.66	45,514.52

Fig. 5-1: VoFI plan for investment project A considering taxes

The following table shows the separate calculations necessary to determine the tax payments resulting from project A.

	t=1	t=2	t=3	t=4	t=5
Net cash flow	28,000.00	30,000.00	35,000.00	32,000.00	30,000.00
- Depreciation	-20,000.00	-20,000.00	-20,000.00	-20,000.00	-20,000.00
+ Gain of liquidation					5,000.00
- Interest expenses	-7,800.00	-5,711.80	-3,375.00	-2,812.50	0.00
+ Interest income	0.00	0.00	11.58	1,255.49	956.44
= Change of profit	200.00	4,288.20	11,636.58	10,442.99	15,956.44
Change of tax payment (tax rate 40%)	80.00	1,715.28	4,654.63	4,177.20	6,382.58

Fig. 5-2: Separate calculations to determine the tax effects of investment project A

Taking taxes into account, the compound value of investment project A is €45,514.12 (as shown in Figure 5-1). The opportunity income value is calculated using an after-tax interest rate (c_t), which is derived from the assumed taxation rate of 40%:

$$c_t = 0.07 - 0.4 \cdot 0.07$$

$$c_t = 0.042 \quad \text{or} \quad 4.2\%$$

Using this figure, the compound value of the alternative income opportunity amounts to €24,567.93 (= $20.000 \cdot 1.042^5$). Project A remains absolutely profitable, therefore. For investment project B, a compound value of €42,676.33 is obtained when taxes are included (as at point in time $t = 4$). Because this is higher than the compound value of the alternative income opportunity (€23,577.67), this project is also absolutely profitable. In order to assess relative profitability, the compound value for project B as at $t = 5$ may be used. Assuming the after-tax interest rate determined above to be relevant, this compound value is:

$$€42{,}676.33 \cdot 1.042 = €44{,}468.74$$

Therefore investment project A remains relatively profitable.

Assessment of the method

In assessing this appraisal method including tax effects, our previous evaluation of the underlying VoFI method remains valid. The compound value calculations, and the successive inclusion of cash flows and tax payments, give the VoFI method an advantage over the NPV method in considering tax payments resulting from an investment. The VoFI method may better reflect the variety of tax regulations that exist in reality and is more transparent. Although the example presented assumes a highly simplified set of circumstances (see the assessment in Section 5.1.1), the method can be applied quite readily to other situations as well.

The following section on the assessment of foreign investments discusses the VoFI methodology's inclusion of differing perspectives which might also be applied to the consideration of taxes from the perspective of the company and the shareholders.

5.2 The Assessment of Foreign Direct Investments

5.2.1 Special Characteristics of Foreign Direct Investments

A foreign direct investment (FDI) includes the establishment, expansion or acquisition of sales outlets, storage or production plants abroad, and the direct influencing of the decisions made by a foreign company unit. The investing 'home' company sustains cash outflows in its domestic currency (i.e. the 'home currency') to finance assets in the 'investment country', so that future cash flow surpluses may be achieved in the currency of that country (i.e. the 'investment currency'). In view of the relatively high investment amounts and the complexity of these decisions, a model-supported assessment of foreign direct investments seems particularly advisable. Additionally, foreign direct investments have special characteristics that make it useful to present a separate discussion of models and methods for their appraisal.

(i) For foreign direct investments, at least two company units are involved: the unit that views the investment as an FDI (the 'mother company'); and the existing or newly-formed unit abroad (the 'daughter company'). For these two company units, the cash flows resulting from the FDI may differ in their amounts and timing for several reasons (such as exchange rate differences, subsidies, tax payments and transfer payments). Therefore, the profitability of an FDI from the daughter company's point of view (project-related view) may be different to the profitability from the mother company's perspective (investor-related view). In the following discussion, the perspective of the mother company is adopted, since this unit usually supplies most of the necessary investment funds, its targets are dominating and this approach therefore allows incorporating most of the decision-relevant factors.

As a basis for the investment appraisal, project cash flows that accrue to the mother and/or daughter company must be identified. Then, factors influencing these cash flows have to be analysed in order to forecast their amounts and timing. The necessary analysis and forecasting activities can be summarised in sequential steps:

1. Identify the cash flow changes at the daughter company in the investment currency (initial investment outlay, cash flows, liquidation value, payments resulting from the financing of the investment project and financial investments connected with it, cash flows from and to the mother company, and tax payments).
2. Identify the cash flow exchanges between daughter and mother company from the point of view of the mother company and in the home currency (cash flows for financing, interest and amortisation, for mutual supplies of semi- or fully-finished products, for claims on patents or licences, for management services and from the transfer of surpluses from the investment including the liquidation value or residual value, etc.).
3. Identify other cash flow changes within the mother company, in the home currency (resulting particularly from the financing of the investment project, associated financial investments, risk management, changes to production and sales processes as well as tax payments in the home country).

(ii) The effects of an FDI are often influenced by differing tax systems in the home and investment countries. These tax systems may be crucial for the absolute and relative profitability assessments of direct investments, so it is advisable to include taxes in models for their appraisal.

Double taxation plays a special role and the nature and extent of taxation in the investment country must be taken into account in the home country. The existence and particularities of double taxation agreements are crucial to this issue.

(iii) Inflation rates are another important influence on the profitability of an FDI project. If, for example, the daughter company supplies goods to the mother company when inflation rates are higher in the investment country and the exchange rates remain constant, the consequences will be negative. Existing savings may be destroyed and cost advantages lost. In many cases, however, differential inflation rates will be offset by changes in the exchange rates.

(iv) The cash flows associated with an FDI will accrue in different currencies. Therefore, from the investor's perspective, monitoring the relationship between the investment currency and the home currency is important, since the daughter company's cash flows will lose or gain value in terms of the home currency if exchange rates alter.

Exchange rate changes are often driven by differing price trends in two countries. For example, comparatively high price increases often lead to a devaluation of the currency. The extent to which such adjustments take place and how exchange rates develop in general, depend on market conditions and on exchange rate systems. Different exchange rate determinations exist in the form of fixed, semi-flexible and flexible/floating rates of exchange.

For a floating exchange rate system, the purchasing power parity theory has been formulated to explain the link between inflation rates and exchange rates. This is based on the hypothesis that currencies are exchanged at a price that maintains purchasing power parity so that both currencies can be used to acquire the same goods. Therefore, relative purchasing power, resulting from the price levels in both countries, is crucial to the exchange rates between currencies. Additionally, it can be shown that changes to the exchange rate and relative price levels often correspond in the two countries, so that inflation differences are being compensated by exchange rate changes. However, the validity of this link depends on a perfect market for international products with market transparency, homogeneous products and standardized consumption patterns. It also excludes consideration of trade restrictions and transportation costs. As these conditions do not apply in reality, the purchasing power parity theory has only long-term effects, if any. In reality, the effects of inflation and exchange rate changes on investment success will not always be balanced as this theory suggests.

Therefore, given a forecasted exchange rate, a judgement must be made as to whether purchasing power parity can be assumed. If no available information points to future deviations from purchasing power parity, the assumption will be justifiable. However, in every case, exchange rate forecasts should include likely changes to the inflation rates of both countries.

(v) Foreign direct investments potentially allow access to several national capital markets and, thus, to an international capital market formed with different currencies and different inflation and interest rates. In a perfect international capital market the so-called International FISHER Condition applies (FISHER, 1930). This states that the interest rate in one country's capital market equals the interest rate in another adjusted by the change in exchange rate (Δer). The change in exchange rate can be expressed as:

$$\Delta er = \frac{er_{t+1} - er_t}{er_t} \qquad (5.8)$$

If the exchange rate changes and interest rates are constant over time, then the following is valid:

$$1 + i_h = (1 + i_f) \cdot (1 + \Delta er) = (1 + i_f) \cdot \frac{er_{t+1}}{er_t}, \qquad \text{for} \quad t = 1,...,T\text{-}1 \qquad (5.9)$$

Additionally, in a perfect international capital market – as in perfect capital markets in general – investment and financing decisions may be made independently of each other (as in the FISHER Separation Theorem).

However, limitations on the exchange of capital and property rights, restricted or fixed exchange rate systems, delays of arbitration processes and subsidies paid on national markets mean that an imperfect international capital market is more likely. The International FISHER Condition may not apply, therefore.

FDI financing should also be addressed in relation to the capital market, as the involvement of two company units presents various possibilities for financing. Financing can be undertaken by the daughter and/or the mother company. Each will have different financing opportunities available in different capital markets. Often it is advantageous to have at least some financing by the daughter company and/or in the investment country's currency, since this helps to protect from exchange rate fluctuations or the effects of any limitations on international capital exchanges, and may lead to comparatively low interest rates in the home currency.

In constructing a model for the appraisal of an FDI, it has to be decided whether to make the simplifying assumption of a perfect international capital market. In any case, likely developments in inflation and exchange rates should be considered when forecasting interest rates. Even though the International FISHER Condition might not be completely valid, it may be worth using it as an assumption or an orientation when making the necessary forecasts.

(vi) An FDI often involves greater uncertainty than a home investment. Economic, political-legal, socio-cultural and national infrastructural risks may be higher in the investment country than in the home country. In addition, dangers arise from changes in relative prices and exchange rates, and additional forecasting difficulties increase the uncertainty of information. Potential negative effects of risk may be reduced by suitable risk management measures that typically influence cash flows.

The characteristic features of foreign investments can be considered using different models for investment appraisal. In the following discussion, the NPV and VoFI models are employed.

5.2.2 Net Present Value Model and the Assessment of Foreign Direct Investments

Description of the method

This section will outline how NPV calculations can be used to assess foreign investments. Some special characteristics of such investments are taken into account, primarily concerning the consideration of different currencies and the inclusion of an international capital market (which may be perfect or imperfect). Any cash flow differentials between mother and daughter companies that exceed the currency differences are totally (with a perfect capital market) or largely (with an imperfect capital market) omitted. They can usually be recorded as a correction to the cash flows of the mother company; later an example of this is shown where financing is realised in an imperfect capital market. Taxes (as discussed before), inflation and uncertainty (taken up later – see Chapter 8) are not considered in the following model analyses.

In a perfect international capital market, the International FISHER Condition stipulates that interest rates in different national capital markets are equivalent after accounting for exchange rate changes. So, if the uniform discount rate is based on capital market interest rates for investments or loans, it is independent of the investment country. With a constant uniform discount rate in the home country (i_h), the NPV from the point of view of the mother company and in the home currency (NPV_{mh}) may be determined from the net cash flows in the foreign currency (NCF_{ft}) and the relevant exchange rate (er_t) to convert to the home currency:

$$NPV_{mh} = \sum_{t=0}^{T} NCF_{ft} \cdot er_t \cdot (1+i_h)^{-t} \tag{5.10}$$

Assuming a constant exchange rate change (Δer) and using the following relationship:

$$er_t = er_0 \cdot (1+\Delta er)^t \tag{5.11}$$

The NPV from the mother company's perspective can also be determined as:

$$NPV_{mh} = er_0 \cdot \sum_{t=0}^{T} NCF_{ft} \cdot (1+\Delta er)^t \cdot (1+i_h)^{-t} \tag{5.12}$$

On account of the International FISHER Condition, the relationship between the uniform discount rate in the home country and the interest rate in the investment country (i_f) is assumed to be constant and can be expressed as follows:

$$1+i_h=(1+i_f)\cdot(1+\Delta er) \tag{5.13}$$

Therefore, the net present value from the perspective of the mother company and in the home currency is:

$$\begin{aligned} NPV_{mh} &= er_0\cdot\sum_{t=0}^{T} NCF_{ft}\cdot(1+\Delta er)^{t}\cdot(1+i_f)^{-t}\cdot(1+\Delta er)^{-t} \\ &= er_0\cdot\sum_{t=0}^{T} NCF_{ft}\cdot(1+i_f)^{-t} = er_0\cdot NPV_{df} \end{aligned} \tag{5.14}$$

Accordingly, the net present value to the mother company in the home currency (NPV_{mh}) is proportional to that of the daughter company in the investment currency (NPV_{df}). The NPV to the mother company can therefore be determined using the relevant uniform discount rates in either the home or the foreign currency. The exchange rate and the relationship between the inflation rates in the two countries do not affect profitability. Therefore, as long as the International FISHER Condition applies, no confounding factors will follow from currency differences or the choice of national capital market.

The above consideration assumes – as a simplification – that the exchange rate changes are constant over time. However, the argument can be also transferred to the cases of period-specific exchange rate changes and varying home and foreign uniform discount rates.

Uniform discount rates can be derived from home capital market interest rates for financial investments, or from the costs of capital (using an average cost of capital of the relevant company-specific or project-specific capital components).

The procedure described for the NPV model is based on the assumption of a perfect international capital market, but can be also applied in modified form for an imperfect market. In the following, it is assumed that the mother company finances the FDI partly in the (perfect) home capital market and partly using a foreign loan raised in the capital market of the investment country. Because of the imperfection of the international capital market, the cash inflows (CIF_{flt}) and outflows (COF_{flt}) resulting from the foreign loan must be considered in addition to the initial investment outlay (I_{0ft}), the net cash flows (NCF_{ft}) and the liquidation value (L_f) when calculating the NPV from the perspective of the mother company. Because these cash flows are measured in the investment currency, they must be converted using the appropriate exchange rate into the home currency. Then, the NPV is calculated as follows:

$$NPV_{mh} = \sum_{t=0}^{T} (NCF_{ft} - I_{0ft} + CIF_{flt} - COF_{flt}) \cdot er_t \cdot (1+i_h)^{-t} + L_f \cdot er_T \cdot (1+i_h)^{-T} \tag{5.15}$$

In the case of constant exchange rate change (Δer) it amounts to:

$$NPV_{mh} = er_0 \cdot \left(\begin{array}{l} \sum_{t=0}^{T} (NCF_{ft} - I_{0ft} + CIF_{flt} - COF_{flt}) \cdot (1+\Delta er)^t \cdot (1+i_h)^{-t} \\ + L_f \cdot (1+\Delta er)^T \cdot (1+i_h)^{-T} \end{array} \right) \tag{5.16}$$

Now, the NPV – and possibly also the profitability of the investment – is dependent on the financing decision. The financing alternative that maximises NPV can be determined by comparing the home interest rate ($1 + i_h$) with the exchange rate-adjusted interest rate of the investment country ($1 + i_f$) · ($1 + \Delta er$). If the home interest rate is lower (higher), financing should be obtained from the home capital market (capital market of the investment country).

It should be pointed out that the approach above assumes the uniform discount rate of the mother company's home country will be used to discount cash flows and, therefore, that investment and financing projects (with the exception of explicitly recorded financing investments) are only made in the home country. If investment and financing opportunities exist on other capital markets, the interest rates of the optimum investment and financing projects may differ and the determination of the uniform discount rate becomes more problematic.

Additionally, the so-called 'adjusted net present value' approach may be used to calculate NPVs in imperfect capital markets. Using this approach, NPVs are determined as the sum of the basic NPV and other NPV components due to subsidised debt financing or tax effects. In the adjusted present value approach, various risk profiles are considered to determine the uniform discount rate used to calculate the basic NPV and other NPV components. That approach is presented later, along with the inclusion of uncertainty in investment methods, in Chapter 8 (Section 8.2).

Example 5-3

In the following example, it is assumed that investment project A – considered in the previous examples – is a foreign investment. The cash flows resulting from the project, as again shown below, are measured in the investment currency. At the beginning of the planning period an exchange rate er_0 of 0.5 is in place, defined as the ratio of the currency units of the investment country (CU_f) to those of the home country (CU_h). A constant decrease in this exchange rate (Δer) of 2% is assumed. The resulting cash flow values, in the home currency, are shown below. All cash flows, including the liquidation value, should be transferred entirely to the mother company. The uniform discount rate i_f in the investment country remains, as in the initial example, at 8%.

Point in time t	0	1	2	3	4	5
Currency units of the investment country (CU_f)	-100,000	28,000	30,000	35,000	32,000	35,000
Currency units of the home country (CU_h)	-50,000	13,720	14,406	16,470.86	14,757.89	15,818.61

Tab. 5-3: Currency units of the home and the investment country

In the first variant of the example, a perfect international capital market is assumed. In accordance with the International FISHER Condition the following relationship between capital market interest rates in the home country $(1 + i_h)$ and the investment country $(1 + i_f)$ applies (Formula 5.13):

$$1+i_h = (1+i_f)\cdot(1+\Delta er)$$

From this, the uniform discount rate in the home country can be derived at:

$$1 + i_h = (1 + 0.08) \cdot (1 - 0.02) \Rightarrow i_h = 5.84\%$$

The relevant NPV (from the perspective of the mother company, i.e. NPV_{mh}) can be determined from NPV_{df} (the NPV from the perspective of the daughter company, which is €26,771.59) multiplied by the exchange rate at the beginning of the planning period (Formula 5.14):

$$NPV_{mh} = er_0 \cdot NPV_{df} \Rightarrow 0.5 \cdot €26{,}771.59 = €13{,}385.80$$

Or by discounting the home currency cash flows using the home country's uniform discount rate (Formula 5.10):

$$NPV_{mh} = \sum_{t=0}^{T} NCF_{ft} \cdot er_t \cdot (1+i_h)^{-t}$$

$$NPV_{mh} = -€50.000 + €13.720 \cdot 1{,}058.4^{-1} + €14.406 \cdot 1{,}058.4^{-2}$$
$$+ €16{,}470.86 \cdot 1{,}058.4^{-3} + €14{,}757.89 \cdot 1{,}058.4^{-4}$$
$$+ €15{,}818.61 \cdot 1{,}058.4^{-5}$$

$$NPV_{mh} = €13{,}385.80$$

Under the assumptions made, the results of these alternative calculations are equal (apart from rounding errors) and the investment is found to be absolutely profitable.

The second example relates to an imperfect international capital market and, thus, the International FISHER Condition does not apply. Data remain unchanged, except for an interest rate of 7% in the home country: in the investment country financial investment opportunities continue to yield at 8%. A loan with annual interest payments and final amortisation can be used: in this case the NPV (from the perspective of the mother company) is dependent on the investment's financing. The NPV can be determined using the general formula (5.16):

$$NPV_{mh} = er_0 \cdot \begin{pmatrix} \sum_{t=0}^{T} (NCF_{ft} - I_{0ft} + CIF_{flt} - COF_{flt}) \cdot (1+\Delta er)^t \cdot (1+i_h)^{-t} \\ + L_f \cdot (1+\Delta er)^T \cdot (1+i_h)^{-T} \end{pmatrix}$$

The proportions of financing raised in the home and foreign country will affect the NPV, as follows.

With 100% home country financing:

$$NPV_{mh} = 0.5 \cdot \begin{pmatrix} -€100{,}000 + €28{,}000 \cdot 0.98 \cdot 1.07^{-1} + €30{,}000 \cdot 0.98^2 \cdot 1.07^{-2} \\ + €35{,}000 \cdot 0.98^3 \cdot 1.07^{-3} + €32{,}000 \cdot 0.98^4 \cdot 1.07^{-4} \\ + €35{,}000 \cdot 0.98^5 \cdot 1.07^{-5} \end{pmatrix}$$

$$NPV_{mh} = €11{,}387.49$$

With 50% financing in each of the home and foreign countries:

$$NPV_{mh} = 0.5 \cdot \begin{pmatrix} (-€100{,}000 + €50{,}000) + (€28{,}000 - €4{,}000) \cdot 0.98 \cdot 1.07^{-1} \\ + (€30{,}000 - €4{,}000) \cdot 0.98^2 \cdot 1.07^{-2} + (€35{,}000 - €4{,}000) \\ \cdot 0.98^3 \cdot 1.07^{-3} + (€32{,}000 - €4{,}000) \cdot 0.98^4 \cdot 1.07^{-4} \\ + (€35{,}000 - €54{,}000) \cdot 0.98^5 \cdot 1.07^{-5} \end{pmatrix}$$

$$NPV_{mh} = €12{,}533.05$$

And finally, with 100% foreign country financing:

$$NPV_{mh} = 0.5 \cdot \begin{pmatrix} (-€100{,}000 + €100{,}000) + (€28{,}000 - €8{,}000) \cdot 0.98 \cdot 1.07^{-1} \\ + (€30{,}000 - €8{,}000) \cdot 0.98^2 \cdot 1.07^{-2} + (€35{,}000 - €8{,}000) \\ \cdot 0.98^3 \cdot 1.07^{-3} + (€32{,}000 - €8{,}000) \cdot 0.98^4 \cdot 1.07^{-4} \\ + (€35{,}000 - €108{,}000) \cdot 0.98^5 \cdot 1.07^{-5} \end{pmatrix}$$

$$NPV_{mh} = €13{,}678.60$$

The investment has a positive NPV under all financing alternatives and is, therefore, absolutely profitable. The NPV increases with increased foreign financing. This is due to the fact that the home interest rate $(1 + i_h)$ is higher than the exchange rate-adjusted interest rate of the investment country $(1 + i_f) \cdot (1 + \Delta er)$:

$$1+i_h = 1.07 > (1+i_f)\cdot(1+\Delta er) = 1.08\cdot 0.98 = 1.0584 .$$

Therefore, in this example, the foreign investment should be financed entirely in the investment country.

Assessment of the method

In this section, two models, which differ in their assumptions about the capital market, have been presented for the assessment of foreign direct investments using the NPV method. The assumption of a perfect international capital market in which the International FISHER Condition is valid might not apply in reality and, therefore, the corresponding model may be suitable only in some cases. Nevertheless, the accuracy of the results depends on the situation in the relevant capital markets, as well as on how the investment is financed.

The usual assumptions of the NPV model apply should be taken into account when assessing both model variants. It should be noted that, even in the case of an imperfect international capital market, perfect national capital markets are assumed. It is also assumed that the cash flow surpluses from a project can be (re)invested at the uniform discount rate, and that financial investments and financing measures included to balance capital tie-up and economic life differences also yield this same rate. This assumption might be unrealistic, particularly since two company units and several segmented capital markets are involved. Finally, the NPV method, in contrast to the VoFI method considered next, has the disadvantage of less transparency, particularly regarding details of the relationships between mother and daughter companies, or cash flow differences and other effects resulting from these relationships.

5.2.3 The Visualisation of Financial Implications (VoFI) Method and the Assessment of Foreign Investments

Description of the method

This section demonstrates how foreign investments can be assessed in detail using the visualisation of financial implications (VoFI) method. For this purpose, the standard version of the VoFI method must be modified slightly.

A comprehensive financial plan must now be constructed in the respective national currencies of both the daughter and mother companies for all cash flows that result from the project. The appropriate tables must be adapted and expanded for the typical cash flows of foreign investments. Cash flows from the mother company may be included in the VoFI table of the daughter company and vice versa. The same applies to any other cash inflows and outflows resulting from the investment project, including payments used to finance it and tax payments or refunds in the investment country. The following figure shows an example of a daughter company financial plan.

Daughter company		t=0	t=1	t=2	t=3	t=4	t=5
Series of net cash flows							
Cash flows for deliveries of semi-finished and finished products to/from the mother company	+ Cash inflows – Cash outflows						
Cash flows for patents, licences etc. to/from the mother company	+ Cash inflows – Cash outflows						
Cash flows for other services to/from the mother company	+ Cash inflows – Cash outflows						
Cash flows due to debt financing to/from the mother company	+ Borrowing – Redemption – Debt interest						
Cash flows to the mother company due to equity changes as well as the transfer of surpluses and the liquidation or residual value	+ Contribution of capital – Withdrawal of capital – Transfer payments						
Further loans of the daughter company	+ Borrowing – Redemption – Debt interest						
Taxes	– Tax payments + Tax refunds						
Financial investment	– Reinvestment + Disinvestment + Credit interest						
Financial balance		**0**	**0**	**0**	**0**	**0**	**0**
Balances **Loan from mother company** **Further loan** **Financial investment**							
Net balance							
Untransferred surplus **Total amount of untransferred surpluses**							

Fig. 5-3: VoFI table of a daughter company

The balance of the financial investment indicates any surpluses that are not transferred to the mother company. In the second part of the exhaustive financial plan, the liabilities associated with the investment are also recorded, including the loan from the mother company. The comprehensive financial plan determines the transferable surpluses, including any relevant taxes. On this basis, the transfer payments to the mother company can be determined. Any remaining difference can be balanced by an investment project or by borrowing.

The comprehensive financial plan of the mother company includes, in the first part of the table, cash flows to and from the daughter company after deduction of associated taxes and fees. Because the latter, like all other cash flows, must be recorded in the home currency, a conversion from the investment currency will be required. Also included in the comprehensive financial plan are cash flows that: relate to the supply of the necessary finance for the mother company; are due to changes in production and sales processes of the mother company; result from investments of any surpluses; or result from any changes to tax payable. The second part of the table records balances, including loan claims against the daughter company. In addition, information may be included in the third part about non-transferred after-tax cash flow surpluses and their accumulated amounts. The exhaustive financial plan for the mother company looks similar to that of the daughter company (see Figure 5-4).

The VoFI method illustrates changes in tax payments in a transparent and realistic way. Tax payments (and allowances) for the daughter and mother companies may be included as described in Section 5.1.2, after considering the fiscal laws relevant to foreign activities.

When determining the compound value of an investment, inflation may be taken into account using a combination of nominal cash flow values and nominal interest rates (including inflation effects). This allows differences in price trends for various product types in the relevant countries to be considered. For consistency, expected inflation rates should also be included when forecasting the opportunity income yields (i.e. expected real interest rates are multiplied by the inflation rate). A comparison of the compound values will indicate whether a project is more profitable than the opportunity income, given the expected exchange rates; or which of several mutually exclusive projects are relatively profitable when inflationary effects are included.

Exchange rates are required, as with the NPV model, to convert cash flows in the investment currency into the home currency. When appraising foreign investments using the VoFI method, either perfect or imperfect international capital markets may be assumed. Imperfect international markets may be accounted for by explicitly including known financing and investment opportunities, possibly in different countries, in the exhaustive financial plan. To forecast future interest rates in the relevant countries, likely movements in their inflation and exchange rates should be considered, as mentioned above. The assessment of alternative financing, redemption and other financial decisions using the VoFI method that are at disposal was discussed in Section 4.3.

An *example* of the assessment of foreign investments using the VoFI method is not included here due to lack of space, but several similar VoFI examples are presented elsewhere in this textbook.

Mother company		t=0	t=1	t=2	t=3	t=4	t=5
Series of net cash flows							
Cash flows for deliveries of semi-finished and finished products to/from the daughter company	+ Cash inflows – Cash outflows						
Cash flows for patents, licences etc. to/from the daughter company	+ Cash inflows – Cash outflows						
Cash flows for other services to/from the daughter company	+ Cash inflows – Cash outflows						
Cash flows due to loans to/from the daughter company	– Granting of loans + Redemption + Debt interest						
Cash flows due to equity changes of the daughter company as well as the transfer of surpluses and the liquidation or residual value	– Contribution of capital + Withdrawal of capital + Transfer payments						
Cash flows due to changes in the range of economical performances	+ Cash inflows – Cash outflows						
Equity of the mother company	– Withdrawal of capital + Contribution of capital						
Debt of the mother company	+ Borrowing – Redemption – Debt interest						
Taxes	– Tax payments + Tax refunds						
Financial investment	– Reinvestment + Disinvestment + Credit interest						
Financial balance		0	0	0	0	0	0
Balances **Loan from daughter company** **Further loan** **Financial investment**							
Net balance							
Untransferred surplus **Total amount of untransferred surpluses**							

Fig. 5-4: VoFI table of a mother company

Assessment of the method

The visualisation of financial implications (VoFI) method was evaluated in Section 4.3 as well as in the special case of tax inclusion (Section 5.1.2). Building on these discussions, the VoFI method is now evaluated in terms of its ability to appraise foreign investments.

The VoFI method is well suited to considering both national and international imperfect capital markets and offers a realistic view of foreign direct investments' profitability across the spectrum of country-specific financing and investment opportunities. However, the assessment of alternative financing and investment possibilities via the VoFI method assumes that these possibilities can be explicitly assigned to separate investment projects. This may not always be the case. But, in view of its importance, project-specific financing for foreign direct investments should be based on such information, especially regarding the conditions underlying loans, opportunity income yields and interest rates available on short-term investments.

The high transparency of the VoFI method is another one of its advantages. Currency changes for mother and daughter companies can be illustrated clearly, as well as cash flow streams between both and the tax effects of investments. As a result of this high transparency, alternative scenarios can be evaluated quite easily, and the calculation and interpretation of the financial plan results might suggest options for financing, repayment, financial investment, transfer of surpluses, or the appropriate pricing of part- or fully-finished products supplied between daughter and mother company.

5.3 Models for Economic Life and Replacement Time Decisions

5.3.1 Overview

The 'lifetime' of an investment project – i.e. the period for which it operates – is crucial to its financial results and its profitability. A project's lifetime may be limited for different reasons. For example, legal determinations or contractual agreements might impose an upper limit on the economic life (e.g. in the form of a license period), or technical reasons might limit how long the investment project can fulfil its function (the project's 'technical life'). Technical life expiry might be due to the nature and use of the project itself, or it might be caused by an independent factor, such as the passage of time. In some cases, technical life can be extended by maintenance and repairs.

Often, technical life should not be completely exhausted in order to maximise financial success. Product market changes may make it uneconomic to continue with a project because it becomes dysfunctional, obsolete or in need of economic overhaul. Or, technical developments may present alternative investment opportunities that can better fulfil the assigned functions – perhaps at lower costs or higher qualities.

Economic factors also influence the optimum 'economic life' – i.e. the period of project utilisation that best fulfils company aims. Economic life is, by necessity, always shorter than or equal to the project's technical life.

In this chapter models are discussed that can be used to determine the optimum economic life of an investment project. It is assumed from here that:

- The economic life of an investment project can be determined in isolation from other investment decisions.
- Maintenance policy is given.
- Tax payments are not relevant.
- The data are certain.
- The cash flows underpinning the assessment of economic life alternatives can be assigned to the beginning or the end of separate periods of equal lengths (usually years).

Decisions about the economic life of investment projects will be considered in two situations. First, before the inception of the project, as an *ex ante decision* or an *economic life decision* in the strict sense – one that is necessary to assess a project's absolute and relative profitability. Second, after a project's inception, decisions about extending an existing project – this is an *ex-post decision* or a so-called *replacement time decision*. Such a decision becomes necessary if the data have varied from those used for the initial, ex-ante decision. Then, the optimum economic life previously determined should be re-examined during the course of the investment project and revised if this will improve financial success.

Economic life and replacement time decisions are made in different situations, yet the decision-support models are in many ways the same. For both types of decision, the number and type of subsequent project(s) are crucial. Subsequent projects are projects whose inception depends on the cessation of the considered investment and, if started at the end of the economic life of the preceding investment, may be said to constitute a chain (or stream) of investments. In regard to the *number* of subsequent projects, models for calculating economic lives can accommodate a limited or unlimited number of subsequent projects, or none. These alternatives largely determine the length of the planning period. The *types* of subsequent projects can be divided into those identical to the one under consideration – i.e. having an identical cash flow profile – and those not identical.

Models for economic life and replacement time determination may differ (as did the models discussed in Chapters 2 to 4) in their target measures, their inclusion of one or several periods, and their assumptions about the capital market. In the following discussion, the NPV model is used because of its particular relevance in theory and company practice. Consequently, the assumptions of the NPV model apply. In addition, optimum economic life and replacement time analyses require the following assumptions:

- The declining performance of an investment project is indicated by cash flows dropping over time, possibly after passing a maximum in earlier years.
- A project has a determinable liquidation value at the end of each period, with this value decreasing from year to year.

The following analysis covers most of the possible combinations of numbers and types of subsequent projects, as categorised in the figure below. It begins with a single economic life decision in the narrow sense, when there is no subsequent project. It then considers increased numbers of subsequent identical projects, from one to an unlimited chain (or stream) of investments, and finishes with replacement time decisions.

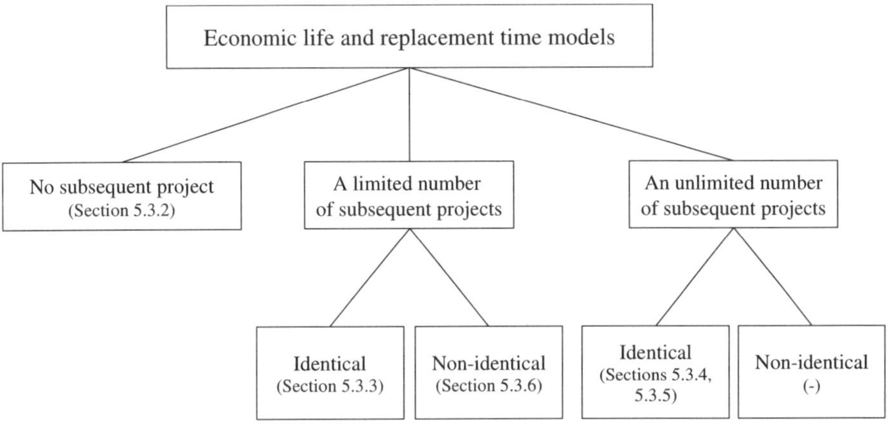

Fig. 5-5: Number and types of subsequent projects in economic life and replacement time models

5.3.2 Optimum Economic Life without Subsequent Projects

Description of model and procedure

This section outlines ways to determine optimum economic life, i.e. decisions about how long an investment project should be pursued, in the case of a single investment with no subsequent project. This situation may occur, for instance, where the products generated by an investment project cannot, or should not, be sold after the end of the economic life.

> *Key Concept:*
> Using the NPV model, the *optimum economic life* of a single investment is achieved at that point in time when the maximum NPV is reached.

The maximum NPV can be determined in the following two ways:

(1) By determining the NPV for every economic life alternative n, using the formula:

$$NPV_n = -I_0 + \sum_{t=1}^{n} NCF_t \cdot q^{-t} + L_n \cdot q^{-n} \tag{5.17}$$

With:

NPV_n	=	NPV with an economic life of n periods
I_0	=	Initial investment outlay
NCF_t	=	Net cash flow in the period t (at time t)
L_n	=	Liquidation value at the end of period n
q^{-t}	=	Discount factor for point in time t

Using this approach, the value for n that produces the maximum NPV indicates the optimum economic life of the project.

(2) By determining the marginal profits. This requires the calculation of two components that result from continuing the project for an additional period t:

(i) An additional cash flow (NCF_t) that is gained in period t.

(ii) A delay and reduction in the investment's liquidation value, i.e. instead of liquidating the investment in period $t-1$ and receiving L_{t-1}, a lower liquidation value (L_t) is achieved one period later.

By compounding the liquidation value in period $t-1$ (receivable at time $t-1$) to the end of the period t (time t), the marginal profit of the period t (P_{mt}) is determined as follows:

$$P_{mt} = NCF_t + L_t - q \cdot L_{t-1} \tag{5.18}$$

From the marginal profit, the change in NPV achieved by continuing the project for another period can be determined. This marginal NPV is the marginal profit discounted to the beginning of the planning period.

The marginal profit may be used as an unambiguous criterion for determining the optimum economic life, if the NPV function has only one local maximum which is then also the over-all or global maximum. In that case, each period can be examined to determine whether the marginal profit remains positive, i.e. whether the additional cash flow exceeds the decreased liquidation value plus interest foregone on the liquidation value achievable in the preceding period. If marginal profit remains positive, the economic life of the investment should be extended by another period. If marginal profit becomes negative (i.e. $P_{mt} < 0$) for the first time, the project should be discontinued. Therefore, the decision criterion based on marginal profits is:

Key Concept:

The economic life ends at the close of period $t-1$ if the following period t is the first, whose marginal profit is negative.

The validity of assuming that the NPV function achieves only one maximum may be verified by determining marginal profits for all following periods t + 1, t + 2, ... until the end of the technical life of the investment project. If at least one of these periods is associated with a positive marginal profit, several local NPV maxima exist. Then, the optimum economic life can be identified by comparing the respective NPVs.

The marginal profit approach may also be used to clarify the effects of data changes on decisions about optimum economic life. From the above formula, it can be seen that a decreased interest rate, reduced liquidation value, or rise in cash flows all favour an extension of the investment's economic life.

Example 5-4

A company wants determine the optimum economic life of a single investment. The initial investment outlay amounts to €600,000 and the uniform discount rate is 10%. The following cash flows and liquidation values (in €'000) have been identified for the relevant periods (t) of the project's technical life (8 periods):

Periods t	1	2	3	4	5	6	7	8
Cash flows	190	160	150	140	130	90	80	60
Liquidation values	480	380	300	270	250	220	170	120

Tab. 5-4: Cash flows and liquidation values of the investment project for different periods and technical lives

First, thc NPV determination approach is used. The following table displays undiscounted and discounted values for the initial investment outlay, the cash flows ($-I_0$ resp. NCF_t and $-I_0$ resp. $NCF_t \cdot q^{-t}$) and the liquidation values (L_n and $L_n \cdot q^{-n}$) for each period. The net present value (NPV_n) is calculated for every economic life alternative as the sum of the initial investment outlay and the discounted cash flows:

$$-I_0 + \sum_{t=1}^{n} NCF_t \cdot q^{-t}$$

And the present value of the initial investment outlay:

$$L_n \cdot q^{-n}$$

n or t	$-I_0$ or NCF_t (€)	L_n (€)	$-I_0$ or $NCF_t \cdot q^{-t}$ (€)	$-I_0 + \sum_{t=1}^{n} NCF_t \cdot q^{-t}$ (€)	$L_n \cdot q^{-n}$ (€)	NPV_n (€)
0	–600,000	600,000	-600,000.00	–600,000.00	600,000.00	0
1	190,000	480,000	172,727.27	–427,272.73	436,363.64	9,090.91
2	160,000	380,000	132,231.40	–295,041.32	314,049.59	19,008.26
3	150,000	300,000	112,697.22	–182,344.10	225,394.44	43,050.34
4	140,000	270,000	95,621.88	–86,722.23	184,413.63	97,691.41
5	130,000	250,000	80,719.77	–6,002.46	155,230.33	149,227.88
6	90,000	220,000	50,802.65	44,800.21	124,184.26	168,984.47
7	80,000	170,000	41,052.65	85,852.86	87,236.88	**173,089.74**
8	60,000	120,000	27,990.44	113,843.30	55,980.89	169,824.19

Tab. 5-5: Determination of the net present value

In this example, the economic life has its optimum at seven periods, and a maximum NPV of €173,089.74 can be achieved.

Next, the marginal profit analysis is illustrated. In the first six periods the marginal profits are positive. They are (in €):

$$P_{m1} = 10{,}000 \qquad P_{m2} = 12{,}000$$

$$P_{m3} = 32{,}000 \qquad P_{m4} = 80{,}000$$

$$P_{m5} = 83{,}000 \qquad P_{m6} = 35{,}000$$

The calculation of the marginal profit of the seventh period (G_7) is presented in detail. This is as follows:

$$P_{m7} = NCF_7 + L_7 - q \cdot L_6 = €80{,}000 + €170{,}000 - 1.1 \cdot €220{,}000 = €8{,}000$$

For the eighth period the marginal profit amounts to €–7,000. Because this is the first period with a negative marginal profit, the optimum economic life ends at the close of the seventh period.

The marginal profit calculated above for the seventh period refers to the point in time t = 7. Discounted to the beginning of the planning period, it is the change in NPV resulting from the inclusion of a seventh period, as shown here:

$$€8{,}000 \cdot 1.1^{-7} = €4{,}105.27 \; = €173{,}089.74 \; - €168{,}984.47$$

$$P_{m7} \cdot q^{-7} \qquad\qquad = \qquad NPV_7 \; - \; NVP_6$$

Model assessment

The earlier assessment of the underlying NPV model can largely be transferred to the model presented here, including the observation that marked differences in economic life are assumed be balanced by investment projects yielding an interest rate equal to the uniform discount rate.

The assumptions about data certainty are applicable here also. Uncertainty may be accommodated using the criteria and procedures discussed in Chapter 8. Sensitivity analyses, risk analyses, the decision-tree method, or options pricing models may all be applied.

Assuming a given maintenance policy, or considering the economic life of each investment project in isolation, might be problematic in many situations. Also, it should be noted that the suitability and precision of the described model depend largely on whether it is realistic to assume there will be no subsequent investment project(s). As companies usually intend to operate long term, this assumption would be justifiable only in exceptional cases. Therefore, model variants that include subsequent investments are now examined.

5.3.3 Optimum Economic Life with a Limited Number of Identical Subsequent Projects

Description of model and procedure

This section considers the determination of optimum economic life when a limited number of identical subsequent investment projects are available. These projects should be undertaken sequentially, so that a limited chain of identical projects is considered. The identical feature of the investment projects – as mentioned above – is their cash flow profile; other characteristics can differ.

First, it is assumed that the investment chain consists of a basic project and a single subsequent investment project, i.e. a *two-project chain* is planned. For both the basic and second investment projects, the optimum economic life is achieved at the maximum NPV of the investment chain.

Because the second investment project is the final one, its optimum economic life can be determined as previously described. In calculating the economic life of the basic investment, however, another (usually economic life-shortening) component must be considered, which results from the temporal linkage of the two projects. The longer the duration of the basic investment, the later the uptake of the second project. Therefore the maximum net present value calculated for the second investment project (NPV_{2max}) is available at a later point in time. The following figure illustrates this:

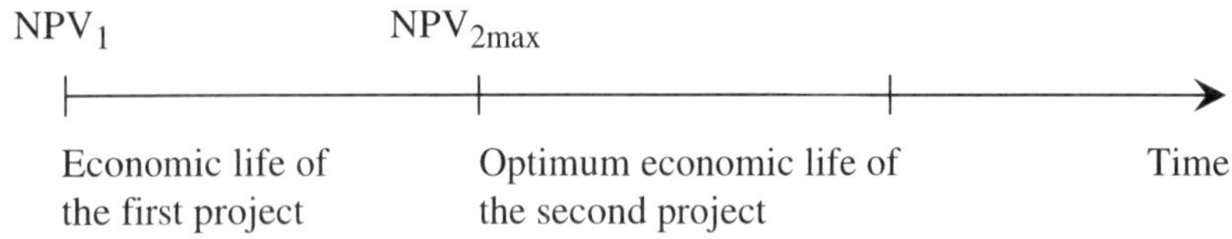

Fig. 5-6: Temporal linkage between projects in a two-project investment chain

The NPV approach can be applied to appraising a chain of two investment projects by calculating, for all the basic investment project economic life alternatives (n_1), the NPV of the investment chain (NPV_C). That chain comprises (i) the discounted NPV of the second investment project (used for its optimum economic life) and (ii) the NPV of the basic investment (NPV_1), with both related to the beginning of the planning period:

$$NPV_C = NPV_1(n_1) + NPV_{2\,max} \cdot q^{-n_1} \tag{5.19}$$

Using this relationship, the maximum NPV of the investment chain and, thus, the optimum economic life of the basic investment, can be calculated.

In the alternative approach, using marginal profit analysis, the interest on the NPV of the second investment project must be included in the analysis. To justify extending the economic life by one period, the marginal profit must exceed the interest earned on the maximum NPV of the second investment project for that period ($i \cdot NPV_{2max}$). The criterion for an optimal economic life where only one maximum NPV of the investment chain exists is as follows:

> *Key Concept:*
> If period t is the first period for which the basic investment's marginal profit is lower than the interest on the maximum NPV of the second investment project for that period, then the optimum economic life of the basic investment ends at the close of period t – 1.

Accordingly, t – 1 is the optimum period if:

$$P_{mt} < i \cdot NPV_{2max} \tag{5.20}$$

Is true for the first time. The optimum economic life may then be determined using marginal profit analysis, as shown in the previous section.

A similar approach can be used to find the optimum economic life of a *multi-project chain* of investments, e.g. a chain in which a basic investment is followed by two or more identical subsequent projects. For a chain of three identical projects, for instance, the optimum economic life and the associated maximum NPV should be calculated *first* for the final project and *second* for the intermediate project in the chain. Then, the optimum economic life of the basic investment can be determined using either the NPV or a marginal profit analysis. The marginal profit should be higher than the interest on the maximum NPV from the chain of subsequent projects ($NPV_{(2+3)max}$), if extending the initial project by one period is to be profitable.

If a period t is the first one for which

$$P_{mt} < i \cdot NPV_{(2+3)max} \qquad (5.21)$$

Then the optimum economic life of the basic investment is t - 1. For a chain consisting of three identical projects this condition tends to be fulfilled earlier than for a chain of only two projects, because higher levels of interest on the maximum NPV from both the second and third projects ($NPV_{(2+3)max}$) must be considered.

The following statement generally applies with regard to the economic life of separate projects in a limited chain of identical projects:

> *Key Concept:*
> In a limited investment chain of identical projects, the optimum economic life of the separate projects tends to decrease as the number of subsequent projects increases.

This phenomenon is known as the *chain effect*. Accordingly, the optimum economic life of a basic investment tends to be shorter than that of an investment without subsequent projects.

However, despite the chain effect, the projects in such a limited investment chain may have identical optimum economic lives if a discrete number of periods of considerable length are assumed. In contrast, where a project chain is dealt with by using a so-called continuous calculus assuming infinitesimally small periods, differing optimum economic lives arise for every project, and the economic life of any project is always longer than that of its predecessor(s) and shorter than that of its successor(s).

Example 5-5

The previous example is now considered for a single identical replacement project (i.e. a chain of two projects). Since the replacement project is the final one, its optimum economic life is as determined in the previous section (seven periods, with the associated maximum NPV of €173,089.74). This result is now used to determine the optimum economic life of the basic investment.

First, the NPV of the chain of two identical investments (NPV_C) is calculated as a function of the economic life of the first project (n_1). It consists of the NPV of the first project as a function of its economic life (NPV_{n1}), added to the maximum NPV of the second project discounted back to the start of the first project's economic life ($NPV_{2max} \cdot q^{-n_1}$). The following table shows the results for the example (the NPV of the chain is not calculated for an 8-year usage of the first project, because this cannot be optimal due to the chain effect):

n_1	NPV_{n_1} (€)	$NPV_{2max} \cdot q^{-n_1}$ (€)	NPV_C (€)
0	0	173,089.74	173,089.74
1	9,090.91	157,354.31	166,445.22
2	19,008.26	143,049.37	162,057.63
3	43,050.34	130,044.88	173,095.22
4	97,691.41	118,222.62	215,914.03
5	149,227.88	107,475.11	256,702.99
6	168,984.47	97,704.65	**266,689.12**
7	173,089.74	88,822.41	261,912.15

Tab. 5-6: Determination of the optimum economic life of the basic investment

In this case, the optimum economic life of the basic (first) investment is now six periods, and the associated maximum NPV of the chain of two identical investments is €266,689.12.

The same result can be determined using the second approach, the marginal profit analysis. For the third up to sixth period of the economic life, the marginal profits are higher than the interest on the NPV of the second investment project ($i \cdot NPV_{2max}$ = €17,308.97).

The marginal profit analysis for the first and the seventh period are shown below:

P_{m1}	$<$	$i \cdot NPV_{2max}$	P_{m7}	$<$	$i \cdot NPV_{2max}$
€10,000	$<$	€17,308.97	€8,000	$<$	€17,308.97

Therefore the optimum might be either to forgo the basic investment project (corresponding to an optimum economic life of 0 periods) or to utilise the investment project for about six periods (since, as shown above, an expansion of the basic investment's economic life beyond the sixth period is not profitable). Regarding the high positive differences between each of the marginal profits of the periods 3 to 6 and the interest on the NPV of the second investment project it can easily be concluded that six periods is the optimum economic life of the basic investment.

Model assessment

For an assessment of this model, refer to the previous section. Again, assumptions made about subsequent projects are problematic. On the one hand repetition of identical investments may be unrealistic; on the other hand it remains unclear how the relevant number of subsequent projects can be determined for every specific situation.

5.3.4 Optimum Economic Life with an Unlimited Number of Identical Subsequent Projects

Description of model and procedure

For all investment projects in an unlimited chain of identical projects, economic life reaches an optimum when the NPV of the unlimited chain is at its maximum. In contrast to the previous examples, it is now assumed that a basic investment is followed by an infinite number of identical, sequential investment projects. Therefore, the interest that is part of the calculated marginal profit is identical for each successive project in the investment chain. From this, it follows that all the projects in an unlimited chain of identical investments have identical optimum lives. This concept is expressed in the following:

> *Key Concept:*
> For all investment projects in an unlimited chain of identical projects, economic life reaches a common optimum when the NPV of the unlimited chain is at its maximum.

Again, the optimum economic life may be determined using both NPV and marginal profit analyses. In both cases annuities are calculated.

To determine the NPV of an unlimited cash flow profile, in general its annuities should be divided by the uniform discount rate. The NPV of the unlimited chain therefore reaches its maximum at the maximum of the annuities. Because all projects are identical, the annuities of the chain equal the annuities of all individual projects. This is illustrated by Figure 5-7, in which the selected levels of annuities are presented for the first projects of an investment chain as a function of the economic life.

Based on the above, it is sufficient to determine the economic life that leads to the maximum annuity of a single investment project, since that also maximises the NPV of the unlimited chain. To do this, annuities should be calculated for all economic life alternatives. The optimum economic life is indicated by the highest annuity achieved.

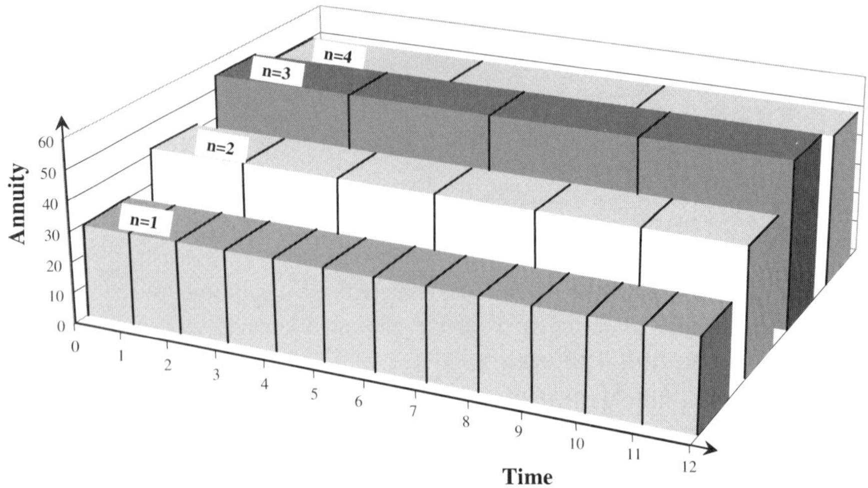

Fig. 5-7: Annuities for a chain of identical investment projects as a function of economic life

For a marginal profit analysis, marginal profit is compared with the interest on the NPV of subsequent projects as a function of their economic lives ($i \cdot NPV_{\infty t}$). These interest payments make up its annuity. In order for the extension of a project by one period (t) to be profitable, the marginal profit from this period should be higher than the corresponding annuity. Again assuming NPV as a function of economic life reaches only one maximum, the criterion for optimality is as follows:

> *Key Concept:*
> The end of the optimum economic life of a project in an unlimited chain of identical projects occurs at the close of period t – 1, if the following period t is the first one whose marginal profit is lower than its annuity.

Formally, the criterion is:

$$P_{mt} < ANN_t \tag{5.22}$$

Comparing marginal profit with the annuity for the preceding period (t – 1) will also show whether this criterion is fulfilled. Only if the marginal profit at t is higher than this annuity can this marginal profit exceed the annuity of the period t, which is comprised of the marginal profit and the annuity for the preceding period.

> *Key Concept:*
> The end of the optimum economic life of a project in an unlimited chain of identical projects occurs at the close of period t – 1 if the following period t is the first one whose marginal profit is lower than the annuity achieved up to the period t – 1.

Formally, the criterion is:

$$P_{mt} < ANN_{t-1} < P_{mt-1} \quad (5.23)$$

The following figure illustrates this optimum situation. The marginal profits exceed the annuities before its maximum; afterwards they show lower values. If there were a continuous calculus of infinitesimally small periods, the optimum economic life would occur at the intersection of the two continuous curves.

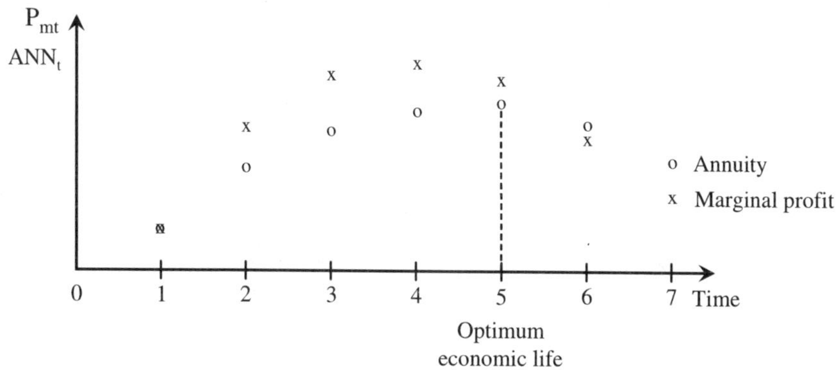

Fig. 5-8: Marginal profit criterion and the optimum economic life

Example 5-6

An illustrative example is now presented. The optimum economic life of projects in an unlimited identical chain may be determined, as shown above, by calculating annuities for different economic lives. The following table contains the net present values (NPV_n) and the capital recovery factors described in Section 3.1 (CRF_n) as a function of economic life: in each case their products are the annuities (ANN_n). The calculations here can be stopped at n = 6 with respect to the chain effect.

n	NPV_n (€)	CRF_n (€)	ANN_n (€)
1	9,090.91	1.1	10,000.00
2	19,008.26	0.5761905	10,952.38
3	43,050.34	0.4021148	17,311.18
4	97,691.41	0.3154708	30,818.79
5	149,227.88	0.2637975	**39,365.94**
6	168,984.47	0.2296074	38,800.08

Tab. 5-7: Net present values, capital recovery factors and annuities for different economic lives

The optimum economic life of all projects in this unlimited chain is five periods. The associated annuity is €39,365.94, and the maximum NPV of the unlimited chain is €393,659.40 (= €39,365.94/0.1). As described in Section 3.3 (see Formula 3.12) the NPV of an unlimited chain of annuities is the annuity divided by the uniform discount rate, in this example 10%.

The marginal profit analysis is also shown below for the sixth period:

P_{m6}	<	ANN_5
€35,000	<	€39,365.94

Thus, an expansion of the investment's economic life beyond the fifth period is not profitable.

Model assessment

This assessment will refer only to the new assumption concerning subsequent projects. Since a company normally expects to continue operations over a long period of time, assuming an unlimited planning period may be realistic. Additionally, in most cases no usable information exists on the potential length of the planning period or the types of subsequent projects. Therefore, the simplification of assuming an unlimited chain of identical projects may be regarded as justifiable.

Unlimited chains of non-identical subsequent projects are not presented here. The relevant models developed in the literature involve considerable simplification, e.g. including the assumption of a linear change in cash outflow while all other measures remain constant. It is doubtful whether such models are helpful for real investment decisions and preferable to those models presented here. Detailed and accurate analyses seem impossible where the planning period is unlimited, due to the data procurement problems described above.

One useful model variant deals with a limited chain of non-identical subsequent projects. This is taken up later in association with replacement time determination.

5.3.5 Optimum Replacement Time with an Unlimited Number of Identical Subsequent Projects

Description of model and procedure

In the previous sections, economic life decisions were discussed that are made before the inception of an investment project (ex-ante decisions). Now the focus will turn to replacement time decisions made after a project's inception (ex-post decisions) to determine for how long its use should be extended (see also Section 5.3.1). For the model variant considered first, it is assumed that the project is followed by an unlimited chain of identical projects, as in Section 5.3.4.

The replacement decision requires analyses of profitability in order to determine which investment project is the best replacement. From the profitability comparison, the investment project is selected that produces the maximum NPV for the unlimited chain. This choice assumes that an appropriate NPV, based on an optimal economic life, has been determined for each project. In the profitability comparison an investment project identical to the existing one may, of course, also be analysed. If a replacement is profitable for this investment type, then the replacement time can be derived from its optimum economic life, provided no data changes have occurred since the original economic life decision was made. In the following discussion, however, it is assumed that the replacement is a chain of identical investment projects of a different type.

During the replacement time decision process, the original forecasted data for current projects should be checked and, if necessary, adapted to changed expectations. For simplicity, the following examples assume that the data did not change.

If the investment project intended as the replacement is known, the optimum replacement time may be determined using the following rule:

Key Concept:
The replacement time reaches its optimum when the combined NPV of the cash flows from the existing investment project plus the unlimited chain of new investment projects, achieves its maximum.

As before, this optimum replacement time may be determined using either an NPV or marginal profit analysis. The total NPV of all possible replacement times is:

$$NPV_{C\tau} = \sum_{t=t^*}^{t^*+\tau} NCF_{et} \cdot q^{-t+t^*} + L_{et^*+\tau} \cdot q^{-\tau} + NPV_{r\infty} \cdot q^{-\tau} \tag{5.24}$$

With:

$NPV_{C\tau}$	=	Total net present value at the replacement time τ
t^*	=	Optimum economic life of the existing investment project
NCF_{et}	=	Net cash flow of the existing investment project in the period t
$L_{et^*+\tau}$	=	Liquidation value at the replacement time τ
$NPV_{r\infty}$	=	Net present value of the unlimited chain of new investment projects
q^{-t}	=	Discount factor for point in time t

Using this calculation and comparing the values obtained, the optimum replacement time can be identified. The marginal profit analysis is based on a comparison of the marginal profit for the existing investment project (P_{met}) with the maximum annuity of the replacement investment project (ANN_{rmax}) which can be interpreted as its 'average profit'. The current investment project should be pursued as long as its marginal profit exceeds the annuity of the new investment projects, since it is contributing more to the total NPV. Accordingly the replacement criterion is:

Key Concept:
The optimum replacement time is the end of the period t – 1 if the following period t is the first one in which the marginal profit of the existing investment project is lower than the maximum annuity of the new investment projects.

Formally, the criterion is:

$$P_{met-1} < ANN_{rmax} < P_{met} \quad (5.25)$$

It is assumed that, once this criterion is fulfilled, the existing project will not achieve further average profits that exceed the maximum annuity of the new investment projects. The following figure illustrates this assumed condition.

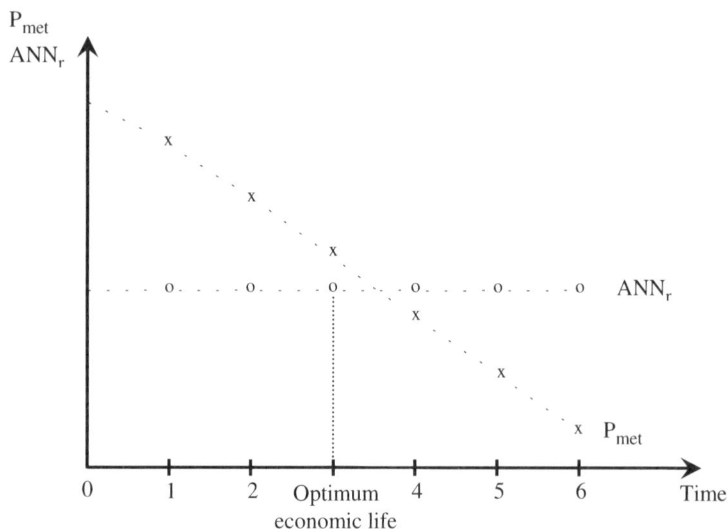

Fig. 5-9: Replacement criterion for an unlimited chain of identical projects

Example 5-7

Building on Example 5-6, it is now assumed that, as at 1st January 2007, an investment project of type A has been in operation four years and has a remaining technical life of three years.

Now, in addition to replacement by an identical investment project of the same type (A), there is the option to replace the existing project with one of a different type (B) that will fulfil the same functions. For both investment projects, the assumption of an unlimited identical chain is made. The cash flows from investment project B, and its liquidation value at the end of each year of its technical life (t_B), are shown below (in €'000):

t_B	0	1	2	3	4	5	6	7
Initial investment outlay/Cash flows	-700	200	190	190	180	150	120	90
Liquidation values	700	600	510	420	330	250	180	120

Tab. 5-8: Cash flows and liquidation values of the investment project of type B for different technical lives

The questions are whether the existing investment project should be replaced with an identical investment project (type A), or with an investment project of type B, and when the replacement should be made.

As a first step towards answering these questions, the optimum economic life for the type B project and the associated maximum annuity should be determined. In this example, the optimum economic life of all type B investment projects is four years. The associated maximum annuity is €40,989.01 and the maximum NPV is €409,890.11.

In a second step, the relative profitability of the different investment types is assessed. Because of their higher maximum annuity, investment projects of type B are preferable.

The third step is to determine the optimum replacement time. First, marginal profit analysis is used. For the fifth and following periods, the marginal profits for the existing investment project (A) are: P_{me5} = €83,000, P_{me6} = €35,000 and P_{me7} = €8,000.

The replacement criterion is met in the sixth period, because marginal profit falls below the maximum annuity from the type B investment project (i.e. €40,989.01). The existing investment project should be replaced after the fifth period (i.e. on 31st December 2007 or 1st January 2008).

The same result is obtained using total net present values (NPV_C) for the potential replacement times:

Immediate replacement:

$$NPV_C = €270{,}000 + €409{,}890.11 = €679{,}890.10$$

Replacement after one more period of utilisation:

$$NPV_C = (€130{,}000 + €250{,}000 + €409{,}890.11) \cdot 1.1^{-1} = €718{,}081.92$$

Replacement after two more periods of utilisation:

$$NPV_C = €130{,}000 \cdot 1.1^{-1} + (€90.000 + €220.000 + €409{,}890.11) \cdot 1.1^{-2}$$
$$= €713{,}132.32$$

Replacement after three more periods of utilisation:

$$\begin{aligned} NPV_C &= €130{,}000 \cdot 1.1^{-1} + €90{,}000 \cdot 1.1^{-2} + (€80{,}000 + €170{,}000 \\ &\quad + €409{,}890.11) \cdot 1.1^{-3} \\ &= €688{,}347.19 \end{aligned}$$

The approach to determining the optimal replacement time can also be applied to a limited chain of identical replacement projects, or to a replacement project without a successor. In these cases, the appropriate NPVs of the projects used as replacements (NPV determination), or the interest on these NPVs (marginal profit analysis), should be considered.

A *model assessment* is not necessary here, since it was presented in the previous section.

5.3.6 Optimum Replacement Time with a Limited Number of Non-Identical Subsequent Projects

Description of model and procedure

This section discusses the replacement of an existing investment project, over a limited planning period, by non-identical investment projects. It is assumed that now the potential replacement projects' start times, their initial outlays, cash flows and liquidation values are known. Furthermore, it is assumed that production operations are to be maintained until the end of the planning period.

Given these assumptions, the optimum replacement strategy can be found using the following rule:

> *Key Concept:*
> The replacement projects and times that generate the maximum total NPV – as the sum of the NPVs of both the existing project and the new investment project(s) – are optimal.

The determination of this optimum replacement strategy can be difficult, especially when a long planning period, with a high number of possible replacement times, is being considered. However, modern analyses and computer technology simplifies the task; for instance, the solution can be found using a 'branch and bound' procedure, the dynamic optimisation, or a complete enumeration of the available options. The latter procedure is applied in a slightly modified form in the following example.

Example 5-8

Again, Example 5-6 is considered here. It is now assumed that the existing type A investment project manufactures a product that can be sold only for another six years. Therefore, the planning period is limited to six years. The target is to maximise the NPV. Additionally, it is assumed that the type A investment project has been operating for four years. It is to be replaced with one or several type B investment projects, which are also suitable for the production of this product. The type B project has been shown to be the most profitable option, and this is also the expectation for the remaining six years. For the type B project it is assumed that the relevant data are as given at the previous example, regardless of the starting period. In determining the optimum replacement strategy, the choices now are as follows.

In the first set of alternatives, an immediate replacement of the existing investment project is made. This option may be subdivided into various numbers of type B investment projects that are pursued over the remaining six years. These sub-groups also represent different alternatives, because it is possible to combine projects of different economic lives. For example, if two type B projects are used over the next six years, the possibilities are: one lasting 5 years followed by a second lasting 1 year; one lasting 4 years followed by a second lasting 2 years; two lasting for 3 years each etc. However, the number of alternatives that need to be explicitly considered can be reduced by comparing opposite sequences of differing-length projects in a chain of two or more investment projects (e.g. 5 years and 1 year against 1 year and 5 years). Because of discounting effects, it is usually preferable to start with those projects having higher net present values (usually the ones with longer economic lives).

In the second, third and fourth sets of alternatives the replacement of the current investment project occurs after one, two and three years. These groups also consist of a 'row' of different sub-alternatives, as described above for the first group.

The optimum replacement strategy can be determined using a limited enumeration in the form of calculating NPVs for all alternatives that are not excluded from the analysis as being unprofitable.

The NPV of a type B investment project (NPV_{nB}) as a function of its economic life (n_B) – both are needed for the calculation – is specified below:

n_B	1	2	3	4	5	6
NPV_{nB}	27,272.73	60,330.58	97,145.00	129,929.65	152,903.74	167,015.59

Tab. 5-9: Net present values of a type B investment project for different economic lives

The *first* set of investment alternatives is analysed first. For all alternatives in this group, the NPV contribution for the existing investment project is identical. However, there are differences in the NPVs of the subsequent projects (NPV_{SP}). The NPVs of the potentially profitable alternatives are:

Use of one type B project for 6 years: NPV_{SP} = €167,015.59

Use of two type B projects:

- For 5 years first and then 1 year: NPV_{SP} = €152,903.74 + €27,272.73 $\cdot 1.1^{-5}$ = €169,837.96
- For 4 years and then 2 years: NPV_{SP} = €171,136.25
- For 3 years and then again for 3 years: NPV_{SP} = €170,131.48

Use of three type B projects:

- For 3 years, then 2 years and finally 1 year: NPV_{SP} = €159,406.48
- For 4 years and then twice for 1 year: NPV_{SP} = €165,491.51

The total net present value NPV_C of the best alternative in this first group – the immediate replacement of the existing type A project with two sequential type B projects of four and two years' duration – consists of the NPV of the subsequent projects (NPV_{SP}) plus the liquidation value of the existing investment project:

$$NPV_C = €171{,}136.25 + €270{,}000 = €441{,}136.25$$

For the *second* group, i.e. assuming that the current type A project is retained for one further year), the alternative subsequent project strategies have the following NPVs:

Use of one type B investment project for 5 years: NPV_{SP} = €152,903.74

Use of two type B investment projects:

- For 4 years and then 1 year: NPV_{SP} = €148,557.29
- For 3 years and then 2 years: NPV_{SP} = €142,472.26

The optimum alternative from the second group has a total net present value NPV_C (resulting from the maximum NPV of the subsequent projects, and the cash flow and liquidation values for the existing investment project) of:

$$NPV_C = (€152{,}903.74 + €130{,}000 + €250{,}000) \cdot 1.1^{-1} = €484{,}457.94$$

For the *third* group, the only apparent alternative is to pursue a type B investment project for four years. The total NPV for this alternative is:

$$\begin{aligned} NPV_C &= €130.000 \cdot 1.1^{-1} + (€129{,}929.65 + €90{,}000 + €220{,}000) \cdot 1.1^{-2} \\ &= €481{,}760.04 \end{aligned}$$

For the *fourth* group, the most profitable option again is the use of one type B project. The total NPV for this alternative is:

$$\begin{aligned} NPV_C &= €130{,}000 \cdot 1.1^{-1} + €90{,}000 \cdot 1.1^{-2} \\ &\quad + (€97{,}145 + €80{,}000 + €170{,}000) \cdot 1.1^{-3} \\ &= €453{,}377.16 \end{aligned}$$

Comparing the total NPV of the best alternative in each group, the maximum total NPV can be identified. The best option is to continue the existing investment project for one more year and then replace it with one type B project lasting five years. The total NPV of this alternative is €484,457.94.

Model assessment

The model presented here is relatively complex in terms of both calculations and the collection of data. It might be impossible to identify the fixed planning period, or to estimate the potential (non-identical) replacement projects' initial outlays, cash flows and liquidation values with sufficient precision. If all of this *were* possible, however, this model would be superior to those discussed previously in supporting decision-making, because it provides for more realistic scenarios.

The NPV model can also support other kinds of investment decision, such as the acquisition of used assets or the pursuit of multiple projects of different durations, although these might require slight modifications of the model. Similar calculations can be used to support replacement decisions that are underpinned by different basic models and assumptions (e.g. with static characteristics, a different target measure such as internal rate of return, or an imperfect capital market). However, the procedure described for the NPV method must then be adapted to the basic model being regarded.

5.4 Models to Determine Optimum Investment Timing

Characterisation of the problem

This section will illustrate models for determining optimum investment timing. A particular aspect of this was discussed in the previous section – replacement time. However, investment projects that are not part of replacement decisions may share similar decision issues, as they may have a range of possible start times that substantially influence a company's success.

Examples of such decision problems are: the acquisition of companies (units); financial investments; and investments in novel products or wider marketing of current products (e.g. R&D, extending production capacity). For instance, the decision as to whether to enter a market as a pioneer or a follower may be seen as such a specific investment decision. The remainder of this chapter describes models developed for single investments and assuming certainty. The key factors in such decisions are assumed to be economic consequences that can be measured, for instance, as cash flows. They depend on a number of influences, of which the more important are listed in the following:

- *Interdependencies between different investment projects* available at the same time (time-horizontal interdependencies) or at different times (time-vertical interdependencies).
- *Pioneering advantages* resulting from early investment (e.g. securing market position and distribution channels, improved access to key resources, early use of learning and experience curve effects, establishment of product standards or external barriers such as patents).
- *Pioneering disadvantages* in the form of additional costs or cash outflows (e.g. for gaining access to resources, establishing the infrastructure, gaining necessary consents and complying with legal regulations).
- *Technological progress* achieved over time, which might influence investment project outcomes.
- The *specificity of investment projects* – i.e. the degree to which an investment is tied to a specific use and, therefore, prospects for alternate usage, adaptability, or value loss if the wrong project is pursued.
- The *uncertainty of available information* and its resulting risks, and the *anticipation of improved future information*, which may be reasons to delay the investment.

Time-vertical interdependencies might take the form of effects on future investments caused by current investments. A current investment may render a future one unprofitable: for instance if both projects have identical purposes, or if the funds are insufficient for a second project after the first has been started. Similarly, future investment opportunities can influence the profitability of current investments. Such time-vertical interdependencies require models designed to identify the best start time for an investment project.

In order to be most useful, models to determine optimum investment timing should consider the following factors: pioneering advantages and disadvantages; technological progress; and specificity of investment projects. Where project (asset) specificity is high, a disinvestment opportunity might be included (model variation 2).

The models described here are based on the assumptions of certainty and completeness of the necessary data. Therefore, uncertainty and anticipated information improvement cannot be included in the analysis, and must be accommodated using decision tree models, options pricing models, or flexible planning models presented later in Chapters 8 and 9.

Description of model and procedure

The following model uses the NPV approach, including its underlying assumptions and the NPV target measure. As described in Chapter 3, an investment project is considered absolutely profitable if its NPV is greater than zero. One assumption made is that no time-vertical interdependencies exist – reflecting the underlying assumption that all future investments, including any reinvestments of cash surpluses, will yield at the uniform market discount rate. This assumption is necessary to determine correct results for absolute and relative profitability, but it eliminates investment time decisions from the analysis.

Complications arise if the assumption is invalid because an investment project may be started at different times to yield positive or negative NPV results. In this case, the crucial issue is whether or not the cash flow profile would be affected by the investment start date. If cash flows are unaffected and will lead to a positive NPV, the investment should be made as soon as possible. A similar logic applies for a mandatory investment (i.e. required by law) that has a negative NPV – it should be postponed as long as it is allowed by the legal restrictions.

If cash flows are affected by the investment date, these rules do not apply. If delayed investment reduces the NPV of a profitable project, the investment should be made as early as possible. If delay increases the NPV, an expanded NPV calculation is necessary. Current investment projects then should be assessed using the various models described below.

Model variation 1:

Optimum investment date for investment opportunities at t = 0 and t = 1, with no disinvestment opportunity at t = 1

A two-tier model is described here, as the investment project may be started at either t = 0 or t = 1. This simplified situation is used to establish the basic decision rules.

Thus, two investment projects are available: the current one at t = 0 (characterised by the index 0), and the future one at t = 1 (index 1). Initial investment outlays, cash flows, economic lives and liquidation values are known. Because of technological progress or changes in the market, the cash flow profile and the economic life of the future investment are not identical to those of the current one. The usual assumption of the NPV model applies, i.e. all future investments after t = 1 (including subsequent projects) are irrelevant, since they yield the uniform discount rate. When analysed independently, both investment projects are relatively (compared with alternative projects available at the same point in time) and absolutely profitable.

In this model variation, we assume that after investing at t = 0, disinvestment at t = 1 is not possible. This might be due to high specificity of the project, resulting in a low liquidation value or a high termination cost. The investment at t = 0 should be compared with the investment at t = 1. The first alternative is relatively profitable if its NPV exceeds the NPV of the investment project at t = 1 discounted to t = 0:

$$\underbrace{-I_0 + \sum_{t=1}^{T_0} NCF_{0t} \cdot q^{-t} + L_0 \cdot q^{-T_0}}_{\text{NPV of immediate investment}} \; > \; \underbrace{q^{-1} \cdot \left(-I_1 + \sum_{t=2}^{T_1+1} NCF_{1t} \cdot q^{-t+1} + L_1 \cdot q^{-T_1} \right)}_{\text{Discounted NPV of future investment}} \qquad (5.26)$$

With:

I_τ = Initial investment outlay for the investment project to be started at the time τ ($\tau = 0,1$)

t = Time index

T_τ = Economic life of the investment project to be started at the time τ

$NCF_{\tau t}$ = Net cash flow at t of the investment project started at the time τ (t refers to the beginning of the planning period, not of the economic life of the project. For example, NCF_{12} indicates the cash flow at $t = 2$ from an investment project started at $\tau = 1$)

q^{-t} = Discount factor at t

L_τ = Liquidation value of the investment project to be started at the time τ at the end of the project's economic life

According to this criterion, for the case under consideration a current investment (at $t = 0$) becomes relatively more profitable:

- The smaller the difference between the initial investment outlay and the discounted liquidation value of the present project:

$$(-I_0 + L_0 \cdot q^{-T_0})$$

- Then the higher the NPV of the difference between the initial investment outlay and the discounted liquidation value of the future investment:

$$q^{-1} \cdot (-I_1 + L_1 \cdot q^{-T_1})$$

And also:

- The smaller the difference between the sums of discounted cash flows of the future ($t = 1$) and present ($t = 0$) investments:

$$\left(q^{-1} \cdot \sum_{t=2}^{T_1+1} NCF_{1t} \cdot q^{-t+1} - \sum_{t=1}^{T_0} NCF_{0t} \cdot q^{-t} \right)$$

The difference between the NPVs of future and present investment projects is of particular relevance. Such differences may, for example, result from future technological progress, or possible pioneering advantages/disadvantages. Future technological progress can lead to a positive NPV difference and, therefore, reduces the relative profitability of an investment project starting at $t = 0$. Opportunities for gaining pioneering advantages may generate less positive (or even negative) differences and therefore favour an immediate investment.

The influence of the discount rate can be examined by transforming the above criterion as follows:

$$q^{-1} \cdot \left(\left(\sum_{t=1}^{T_0} NCF_{0t} \cdot q^{-t+1} + L_0 \cdot q^{-T_0+1} \right) - \left(-I_1 + \sum_{t=2}^{T_1+1} NCF_{1t} \cdot q^{-t+1} + L_1 \cdot q^{-T_1} \right) \right) > I_0 \quad (5.27)$$

The formula indicates that an immediate investment at t = 0 becomes more attractive as the discount factor q (resulting from the uniform interest rate) is lowered. This is because the factor by which the discount rate must be multiplied is usually positive, as it does not include the initial investment outlay of the current investment project (the only cash flow not discounted). However, with increasing interest (discount) rates, the NPVs of *both* current and future investment projects diminish. This implies that the influence of interest rates on serial investment decisions is not as great as might be suggested by the graph of NPV as a function of the uniform discount rate (Figure 3-3 in Section 3.4) for single and independent investment projects.

An important result of the analysis above is, that in decisions situations including future investment projects, the standard criterion for absolute profitability (NPV > 0) is no longer sufficient. The net present value (NPV_0) must now be not only positive, but also greater than the discounted future net present value (NPV_1):

$$NPV_0 > NPV_1 \cdot q^{-1} \quad (5.28)$$

If this condition is not met, an investment project should not be undertaken, even if it has a positive NPV. Using the positive NPV criterion to assess single investment projects can, therefore, lead to suboptimal decisions if future investment opportunities arise or current projects may be postponed. Different investment times must then be explicitly included in the investment appraisal.

The following variation of the model assumes a disinvestment opportunity due to low specificity of the current investment (thus allowing its alternate use).

Model variation 2:

Optimum investment date with investment opportunities at t = 0 and t = 1 and with a disinvestment opportunity at t = 1

In the previous example, it was assumed that an investment following one started at t = 0 was impossible, as there was no opportunity to divest the first (t = 0) investment. Now, this is changed such that the initial investment project may be sold with a liquidation value (L_{01}) if another investment project is started at t = 1. Simultaneous use of the two projects is not possible. Both projects are profitable when regarded in isolation. Therefore the options are:

At t = 0: Invest in project 0 or do not invest.
At t = 1: If investment project 0 was not taken up, invest in project 1.
At t = 1: If Investment project 0 was started at t = 0

(i) Invest in project 1 and divest project 0.
(ii) Continue project 0 and refrain project 1.

The opportunity to replace project 0 by project 1 must now be considered. This replacement should be pursued if the sum of the NPV of project 1 and the liquidation value of project 0 (at t = 1) exceeds the value of the remaining cash flows plus the liquidation value of project 0 discounted to the same point in time:

$$\underbrace{NPV_1 + L_{01}}_{\text{NPV of the cash flows including disinvestment}} > \underbrace{\sum_{t=2}^{T_0} NCF_{0t} \cdot q^{-t+1} + L_0 \cdot q^{-T_0+1}}_{\text{NPV of the cash flows without disinvestment, discounted to } t=1} \quad (5.29)$$

NPV of the cash flows including disinvestment — *NPV of the cash flows without disinvestment, discounted to t = 1*

If replacement is favoured, the cash flow profile of the current investment project must be supplemented by cash flows from the future project. The NPV of an investment at t = 0 considering the possibilities of disinvestment and a new project at t = 1 is:

$$-I_0 + q^{-1} \cdot \left(NCF_{01} + \max \begin{cases} NPV_1 + L_{01} \\ \sum_{t=2}^{T_0} NCF_{0t} \cdot q^{-t+1} + L_0 \cdot q^{-T_0+1} \end{cases} \right) \quad (5.30)$$

In order for an investment at t = 0 to be relatively profitable, its NPV must exceed the NPV (as discounted to t = 0) of the 'don't invest at t = 0, then invest at t = 1' alternative. This can be expressed as:

$$-I_0 + q^{-1} \cdot \left(NCF_{01} + \max \begin{cases} NPV_1 + L_{01} \\ \sum_{t=2}^{T_0} NCF_{0t} \cdot q^{-t+1} + L_0 \cdot q^{-T_0+1} \end{cases} \right) > q^{-1} \cdot NPV_1 \quad (5.31)$$

NPV of an immediate investment, with a disinvestment opportunity at t = 1 — *Discounted NPV of the future investment project*

If no replacement investment is made at t = 1, this criterion is identical to the one described for model variation 1 (5.27); on the left side of the equation, only the NPV of investment project 0 appears.

In model variation 2, the basic NPV criterion (NPV > 0) is again no longer sufficient. The NPV of an immediate investment is now higher if a disinvestment and simultaneous new investment is profitable. This tends to make a current investment (t = 0) appear more profitable and gives rise to a new criterion:

$$NPV_0 + q^{-1} \cdot \max \begin{cases} NPV_1 + L_{01} - \left(\sum_{t=2}^{T_0} NCF_{0t} \cdot q^{-t+1} + L_0 \cdot q^{-T_0+1} \right) \\ 0 \end{cases} > q^{-1} \cdot NPV_1 \quad (5.32)$$

And:

$$NPV_0 \quad > \quad q^{-1} \cdot NPV_1 \quad - \quad q^{-1} \cdot \max\begin{cases} NPV_1 + L_{01} - \left(\sum_{t=2}^{T_0} NCF_{0t} \cdot q^{-t+1} + L_0 \cdot q^{-T_0+1} \right) \\ 0 \end{cases} \qquad (5.33)$$

NPV of immediate investment — *Discounted NPV of future investment* — *Discounted value of cash inflows from divesting the initial investment*

The NPV of the present (t = 0) investment project must now exceed the discounted NPV of the future investment project, less any additional cash flow surpluses if they are positive and a disinvestment and simultaneous new investment follows. The possible additional cash flow surpluses are the key advantage of the combined disinvestment/new investment opportunity, resulting from enhanced flexibility.

The replacement decision and resultant future cash flow surpluses largely depend on the specificity of the investment project. This can be measured by identifying the value loss from divesting rather than continuing the project – i.e. the difference between the NPV of the cash flows from continued use (discounted to t = 1) and the liquidation value at divestment (at t = 1). With decreasing specificity and, therefore, decreasing value loss, a replacement becomes more desirable. And, as additional cash flow surpluses increase, the relative profitability of an immediate investment increases. Low specificity, therefore, supports an investment project at t = 0. In the case of a completely non-specific investment project, the liquidation value at t = 1 may be identical to the discounted sum of all future cash flows plus the liquidation value. Then, there is no distinction between further use and liquidation of the current investment. Therefore this investment does not affect the future investment and an investment at t = 1 is always profitable if it has a positive NPV. For the current investment, the general criterion of absolute profitability (NPV > 0) becomes valid again.

Example 5-9

Example 3-1 from Section 3.2 is re-examined here. Two investment projects A and B are under consideration, and A is both absolutely and relatively profitable.

As a modification of this example, it is now assumed that instead of considering only projects A or B, another project C is available which can be started only at t = 1. The cash flows from C deviate from those of A and, thus, an investment appraisal is necessary. As the basis for this, the net cash flows of the two projects (A and C) are shown in the following table, with the uniform discount rate remaining at 8%:

t_A or t_C	0	1	2	3	4	5
NCF_{tA} (€)	–100,000	28,000	30,000	35,000	32,000	35,000
NCF_{tC} (€)	–120,000	40,000	42,000	42,000	40,000	40,000

Tab. 5-10: Net cash flows for the investment projects A and C

In the first variation of this example, replacement at t = 1 is rejected, due to the high specificity of investment project A, which generates only a small liquidation value of €5,000 at t = 0 (included in NCF_{5A}). To determine the optimum investment time, the NPV of project A must be compared with the discounted NPV of project C:

$$€26,771.59 \; < \; 1.08^{-1} \cdot €43,010.74$$

Since the discounted NPV of project C (€39,824.76) exceeds the NPV of project A, project A should not be pursued at t = 0, but project C should be started at t = 1. That is, the (until now) absolutely profitable project A should not be undertaken.

In the second variation of the example, we assume that a promising disinvestment opportunity at t = 1 has arisen for project A, as other companies have become interested in it. At t = 1 a liquidation value of €85,000 can be obtained, reflecting the low specificity of the project (the difference between the cash flows from continued use and the liquidation value from divestment related to t = 1 is now only €108,913.31 - €85,000 = €23,913.31).

To determine the optimum investment time, the outcome of project initiation at t = 1 must first be assessed. This requires adding the NPV from C to the liquidation value of A (at t = 1) and comparing the total with the value of the remaining net cash flows from A (also related to t = 1):

$$€43,010.74 + €85,000 \; > \; €108,913.31$$

As the replacement is profitable, the cash flow profile of project A is modified before examining whether its NPV exceeds the realisable value of investment project C (at t = 1) discounted to t = 0:

$$\begin{aligned} -€100,000 + (€28,000 + €43,010.74 + €85,000) \cdot 1.08^{-1} &> 1.08^{-1} \cdot 43,010.74 \\ 44,454.39 &> 39,824.76 \end{aligned}$$

The replacement investment is now profitable, since project A's low specificity and resultant high liquidation value at t = 1 increases the overall NPV. The optimum investment strategy, therefore, is to start with project A at t = 0 and (provided data remain unchanged at t = 1) replace it with project C at t = 1.

Model assessment and modifications

The models discussed here present little additional problems of data collection and calculation over the basic NPV model, so the assessment already presented holds for these models. The additional assumptions can, however, affect the meaningfulness of the results. This might require some modifications to the models shown above which are discussed in the following.

Regarding time-vertical interdependencies, it was assumed either that no substitution projects were available, or that only projects starting at t = 0 or t = 1 were acceptable.

The inclusion of existing investment projects generates specific replacement problems that can be solved by integrating their cash flows into the model. For example, in a corresponding extension of Example 5-9 the liquidation values of an existing project at the possible replacement times t = 0 and t = 1, plus its cash flow surpluses in the first period, would also have to be included. Model variation 2 then largely corresponds to the replacement time model discussed in Section 5.3.6 (optimum replacement time with a limited number of non-identical subsequent projects).

When considering future investment projects, the number of investment timing options to be considered will depend on the planning system. In the case of periodic planning it may be sufficient to consider two possible investment times, i.e. an immediate investment at t = 0 and a delayed investment at t = 1. More investment times must be included if a project commencing at t = 2 or later could be more profitable than an investment at t = 0 or t = 1. This situation might arise as a result of technological progress beyond t = 1. Such a (multi-tier) problem can be solved using dynamic programming techniques. Additional insights may be gained via multi-tier model analyses, for example they may show that faster technological progress has a greater impact on the current investment.

For the investment alternatives analysed here, it is important to note the assumptions that they are absolutely and relatively profitable and cannot be used simultaneously. Absolute profitability can be assured in advance for a pre-determined optimum economic life by calculating the resulting NPV (which has to be positive). The relative profitability of suitable replacement projects cannot always be determined based on their isolated NPVs alone. Where several investment alternatives are available, a simultaneous optimisation of investment projects and times is needed.

Since the models described are specific NPV models, most of the assumptions of the general NPV model apply. For instance, certainty (i.e. accuracy and predictability) of the data is a major assumption, so uncertainty and anticipated information improvement are not considered in the analyses. They can be incorporated using decision tree models, options pricing models, or flexible planning models (described later in this book).

Further on, time-horizontal interdependencies can be only partially accommodated using NPV-based models. Mutual dependencies call for programming models, some of which are multi-tier. These are analysed in Chapter 7.

Some other assumptions can be addressed by making specific model modifications or by using different basic models. For example, another investment appraisal method can be used that accommodates imperfect capital markets, such as the VoFI method. An alternative modelling approach is to use a multi-criterion decision model, as discussed in the next chapter.

Assessment Material Chapter 5

Exercise 5-1 (Taxes in the Investment Appraisal)

The following investment decision problem should be solved considering tax issues.

a) Calculate the net present values of investment projects I and II, the data relating to Exercise 4-2 and a tax rate of 40%. Assume that depreciation is linear.

b) Assess the absolute profitability of project II using the visualisation of financial implications (VoFI) method and assuming a tax rate of 40%.

Exercise 5-2 (Economic Life)

A company in the metal processing industry is planning to acquire a new machine to produce special parts. Calculate its optimum economic life using the net present value method.
The following data have been forecasted for the machine:

Initial investment outlay: €500,000
Technical economic life: 8 years

Point in time	Net cash flows	Liquidation values
1	140,000	400,000
2	120,000	350,000
3	110,000	300,000
4	100,000	250,000
5	90,000	200,000
6	80,000	150,000
7	75,000	95,000
8	70,000	30,000

Tab. 5-11: Cash flows and liquidation values for the new machine

The uniform discount rate is 10%.

a) Calculate the machine's net present value assuming that the machine will be in operation until the end of its technically useful life.

b) Calculate the machine's optimum economic life and the related net present value assuming that the machine:
b1) Will not be replaced.
b2) Will be replaced with an identical project at the end of its economic life.

b3) Will be replaced twice with an identical project at the end of the economic life (i.e. an investment chain consisting of three machines in total).
b4) Will be replaced an infinite number of times with identical projects.

c) What is the reason for – possibly – differing terms of optimum economic life?

Exercise 5-3 (Economic Life)

The initial investment outlay for a machine is €54,000. In addition, the following data is available:
The sales price of products manufactured with this machine is €9 per unit. The cash outflows for each unit depend on the accumulated production volume, as follows:

Accumulated production volume (€)			Cash outflows per unit (€)
of		to	
1	-	6,000	4.00
6,001	-	9,000	4.50
9,001	-	12,000	5.00
12,001	-	13,000	5.70
13,001	-	14,000	5.80
14,001	-	15,000	5.90
15,001	-	17,000	6.00
17,001	-	19,500	6.50
19,501	-	23,000	7.00
23,001	-	24,000	7.40
24,001	-	27,000	8.00

Tab. 5-12: Cash outflows per unit according to the accumulated production volume

The maximum volume that can be produced is 27,000 units; there should be no further cash outflows.
The unit's liquidation value at the end of each year depends on its age as well as on the production volume. It falls by €1 per unit produced plus another €7,000 in the first year, €5,000 in the second, €3,000 in the third and €2,000 in each year thereafter.
The annual production volume amounts to 3,000 units; the uniform discount rate is 10%.

a) Calculate the machine's net present value assuming it will be used until the end of its economic life.

b) Calculate the machine's optimum economic life and related net present value if:
b1) The machine will not be replaced.

b2) The machine will be replaced once with an identical project.

b3) The machine will be replaced an infinite number of times with identical projects.

Exercise 5-4 (Economic Life and Replacement Time)

A company wants to determine the optimum economic life and replacement policy for its machines.

a) Machine A has the following cash flows and liquidation values in dependence on its economic life t_A (in €'000):

t_A	0	1	2	3	4	5	6	7
Cash flows	–500	160	140	130	120	120	100	70
Liquidation value	–	400	330	270	220	170	120	70

Tab. 5-13: Cash flows and liquidation values of machine A for different economic lives

The uniform discount rate is 10%.

a) Determine the machines' optimum economic life and the related net present value when:

a1) There is no replacement.

a2) There is one identical replacement.

a3) The machines are replaced twice by identical machines.

a4) The machines are replaced an infinite number of times by identical machines.

b) Now assume there is a machine of type A in operation that is (as at 1 January 2007) two years old. Assume further that there will be an unlimited stream of identical replacements, as in a4) above.
In addition to replacements with identical machines of type A, it is now possible to replace the machines with others of type B. It is expected that there will be an infinite stream of identical replacements for these machines. The net present values of machines of type B (t_B) as a function of economic life, have already been calculated as follows (in €'000):

t_B	0	1	2	3	4	5	6	7
Net present value	–	30	20	60	90	120	140	135

Tab. 5-14: Net present values of machines of type B for different economic lives

Should a machine of type A be replaced with an identical one or with a machine of type B?
If there is to be a replacement with a machine of type B, when should this occur?

c) Now assume, again, the situation described in a4) (unlimited stream of identical replacements) and that a two-year old used machine as in b) is available. Machines of type B are not available.
Investigate whether it would be advantageous to buy used machines of type A. This is possible for machines of type A of any age, at the liquidation value given in a) plus €10,000. Assume that in the following years the economic life, differential cash inflows and liquidation values are as given in a). A further assumption is that equivalent machines are also available in the future (infinite stream).
Only one- and two-year old machines are being considered for purchase. Using appropriate calculations, judge whether new, one-year-old or two-year-old machines should be put into operation in the future. In case that there is a change in the optimum economic life calculated compared with that found in a4), how high is the net present value now, and what is the optimum time to replace this machine?

Exercise 5-5 (Determining Economic Life)

A mining operation is investing, sequentially, in two investment projects: A (for the removal and recycling of waste) and B (for the extraction of hard coal). The cash flows contained in the following tables may be allocated to these investment projects. The uniform discount rate is 10%.

Investment project A					
t	0	1	2	3	4
Cash outflows (€'000)	7,000				
Cash inflows (€'000)		3,500	3,500	1,500	1,000
Liquidation value in t (€'000)		4,500	2,300	1,900	1,200

Investment project B				
t	0	1	2	3
Cash outflows (€'000)	4,500			
Cash inflows (€'000)		3,500	1,800	1,300
Liquidation value in t (€'000)		3,500	2,500	1,400

Tab. 5-15: Cash flows and liquidation values of the investment projects A and B

a) Determine the optimum economic lives and the total net present value of the investment projects A and B if the investment is made firstly on a type A investment project and then on a type B.

b) Determine the optimum economic lives of the investment projects if, starting with investment project A and alternating between A and B, repeated investments are made over an infinite period.

Exercise 5-6 (Determining Economic Life with the Net Present Value, Internal Rate of Return and Compound Value Method)

A company wants to determine the optimum economic life for a machine.
The machine A being reviewed has the following net cash flows and liquidation values as a function of economic life t_A (in €'000):

t_A	0	1	2	3	4	5	6
Cash flows	–580	180	150	150	140	140	85
Liquidation value		490	410	310	250	210	150

Tab. 5-16: Cash flows and liquidation values of the machine for different economic lives

a) To determine economic life using the net present value method:
   a1) Assume the investment project under review will not be replaced. What is the optimum economic life that maximises the net present value (uniform discount rate is 10%)? What is the maximum net present value?
   a2) Imagine that the investment project under review will be replaced by an identical one. What are the economic lives for the initial and subsequent investments that maximise the net present value (the rate of interest again is 10%)? What is the maximum net present value?
   a3) Using the sample data, explain the so-called 'chain effect'.

b) To determine economic life using the internal rate of return method:
   b1) Assume the investment project under review will not be replaced. What is the optimum economic life that maximises the internal rate of return?
   b2) Imagine that the investment project under review will be replaced with an identical one. What are the optimum economic lives for the initial and subsequent investment projects?

c) To determine economic life using the compound value method:
   Assume that the investment project under review will not be replaced. What is the optimum economic life that maximises the compound value (mandatory

accounts balancing; debt rate of interest 12%; credit rate of interest 8%)? What is the maximum compound value?

Exercise 5-7 (Profitability Assessment and Investment Timing Decisions)

a) There is a choice between two investment projects, A and B, having the following data at time t = 0:

Project	**A**	**B**
Initial investment outlay (€)	240,000	190,000
Liquidation value at the end of its useful life (€)	20,000	10,000
Useful life (years)	4	4
Net cash flows (€)		
t = 1	75,000	50,000
t = 2	75,000	55,000
t = 3	70,000	60,000
t = 4	70,000	65,000

Tab. 5-17: Data for the two investment projects A and B

Assume a uniform discount rate of 10%. Assess the absolute and relative profitability of the projects using the net present value method.

b) There is now an opportunity to invest in project B at time t = 1. A €15,000 reduction of the initial outlay compared to the realisation at t = 0 is expected. All other data given in part a) of this exercise remain unchanged.

b1) What is the optimum investment policy now? (Support the finding with appropriate calculations.)

b2) Which assumption in the basic net present value method is no longer valid?

b3) How can this expanded decision problem b) be solved using the VoFI method (brief description)?

Further Reading Part III

Baldwin, C. Y. 1982. Optimal Sequential Investment When Capital is Not Readily Reversible. *Journal of Finance* 37 (3):763-782.

Blohm, H., K. Lüder, and C. Schaefer. 2006. *Investition: Schwachstellenanalyse des Investitionsbereichs und Investitionsrechnung*. 9 ed. München: Vahlen.

Derbes Jr, M. J. 1987. Economic Life Concepts. *Appraisal Journal* 55 (2):216-224.

Fisher, I. 1930. *Theory of Interest*. New York: Macmillan.

Gaddis, P. O. 1966. Analyzing Overseas Investment. *Harvard Business Review* 44 (3):115-122.

Götze, U. 2006. *Investitionsrechnung*. 5 ed. Berlin et al.: Springer.

Grob, H. L. 1993. *Capital Budgeting with Financial Plans: An Introduction*. Wiesbaden: Gabler.

Heister, M. 1962. *Rentabilitätsanalyse von Investitionen*. Köln et al.: Westdeutscher Verlag.

Jääskeläinen, V. 1966. *Optimal Financing and Tax Policy of the Corporation*. Helsinki: Helsinki Research Institute for Business Economics.

Kruschwitz, L. 2007. *Investitionsrechnung*, 11 ed. München, Wien: Oldenbourg.

Lessard, D. R. 1985. Evaluating International Projects: an Adjusted Value Approach. *International Financial Management. Theory and Application*, edited by D. R. Lessard. New York et al.: Wiley, 570-584.

Maloney, K. J., and T. I. Selling. 1985. Simplifying Tax Simplification: An Analysis of Its Impact on the Profitability of Capital Investment. *Financial Management* 14 (2):33-42.

Miller, M. H. 1977. Debt and Taxes. *Journal of Finance* 32 (2):261-275.

Modigliani, F. 1982. Debt, Dividend Policy, Taxes, Inflation and Market Valuation. *Journal of Finance* 37 (2):255-274.

———. 1983. Debt, Dividend Policy, Taxes, Inflation, and Market Valuation: Erratum. *Journal of Finance* 38 (3):1041-1042.

Modigliani, F., and M. H. Miller. 1963. Corporate Income Taxes and the Cost of Capital: A Correction. *American Economic Review*: American Economic Association, 433-443.

Preinreich, G. A. D. 1940. The Economic Life of Industrial Equipment. *Econometrica* 8 (1):12-44.

Scarf, P. A., and M. H. Hashem. 1997. On the Application of an Economic Life Model with a Fixed Planning Horizon. *International Transactions in Operational Research* 4 (2):139-150.

Teichroew, D., A. A. Robichek and M. Montalbano. 1965. An Analysis of Criteria for Investment and Financing Decisions under Certainty. *Management Science* 12 (3):151-179

Terborgh, G. 1949. *Dynamic Equipment Policy*. New York et al.: McGraw-Hill.

Yu, Z., and I. Friend. 1986. The Effects of Different Taxes on Risky and Risk-Free Investment and on the Cost of Capital. *Journal of Finance* 41 (1):53-66.

See also: Further Reading Part II.

Part IV

Multi-Criteria Methods and Simultaneous Decision-Making

Chapter 6: Multi-Criteria Methods

6.1 Introduction

For many investment decisions, the decision-maker wishes to pursue several targets, rather than a single target as the earlier chapters have assumed. Such a decision-making problem is typical in strategic investment decision-making as, for example, when installing a new plant in a new location, using new technology and/or manufacturing a new product.

The following chapter describes and discusses models and procedures developed to satisfy several target measures simultaneously, i.e. for multi-criteria decision-making. Multi-criteria decision-making (MCDM) may be divided into two groups. Decisions about alternative investment projects require multi-attribute decision-making (MADM); and decisions about alternative programmes require multi-objective decision-making (MODM). The first of these is explored in this chapter.

Multi-criteria decision-making affects all phases of the planning process. Initially, an extensive analysis is required to ascertain targets, their significance and likely conflicts. Where several targets exist, as assumed here, the decision-maker's preferences play a decisive role and must be investigated in detail. The MADM procedures discussed in this chapter support these processes of goal setting and decision-planning.

For a clear understanding of MADM procedures, some basic knowledge of utility theory is required.

First, an appropriate scale is necessary to measure targets quantitatively, in order to assess options as, in this case, alternative investment projects. The various types of available scales differ in the degree of measurability they imply.

A *nominal scale* is used to assign outcomes of a target criterion to different classes without ambiguity. No measurable relationship exists between the nominal classes and, therefore, no arithmetic operations are possible. Bank account numbers would be an example of the use of a nominal scale.

An *ordinal scale* allows statements about relationships, like 'smaller than' or 'bigger than'. Although differences between points on this scale cannot be measured, comparisons can be made. One example of an ordinal scale is the sequential list of place-getters in a competition.

The measurement of differences between points on the scale, and mathematical operations like addition, subtraction and averaging, may all be performed using an *interval scale*. A baseline may be fixed arbitrarily but, since a natural neutral point does not exist for an interval scale, the calculation of quotients is not meaningful. Examples of the use of interval scales include times and dates.

A *relational scale* differs from an interval scale in that a natural baseline exists and quotients can be calculated. Examples of values measured with a relational scale are lengths and weights.

For an *absolute scale* the scale unit is defined and consists of real numbers only, the values measured being dimensionless. Examples are absolute frequencies or probabilities. This scale type shows the highest level of measurability.

Interval, relational and absolute scales are all referred to as *cardinal scales*.

Having described the various scales that can be used to measure targets, it is now relevant to consider, first, the preference relationships and, second, the orders of preference that might apply to the alternatives being assessed.

From the relevant elements (alternatives) of a set A in a decision problem, a set of all possible ordered pairs (a, b) may be derived. This set is expressed as:

$$A \times A = \{(a, b) \mid a \in A, b \in A\} \quad (6.1)$$

Preference (or priority) relationships R are determined for pairs of alternatives belonging to A. One single preference relationship R is a partial set of A x A, so the relationship is not necessarily valid for all pairs of alternatives. If R links a given pair (a, b), e.g. (a, b) is an element of R, this is symbolised as 'aRb'. Characteristic features of relationships between pairs might be:

- *Completeness*: For all pairs (a, b) from the elements of a set A at least one of the relationships aRb or bRa exists and, therefore, all elements can be compared with one another.
- *Transitiveness*: The relationships aRb and bRc, for all elements a, b, c $\in$ A, determine the relationship aRc. This, for example, is the case for the greater than relation ($a > b$ and $b > c$, therefore: $a > c$).
- *Reflexivity*: For all a $\in$ A, the relationship aRa is valid. The greater than or equality relation is reflexive, e.g. $a \geq a$.
- *Irreflexivity*: In a set A, for all a $\in$ A the relationship aRa is not valid. For example, the greater than relation (e.g. $a > a$) is not valid.
- *Symmetry*: In a set A, from the relationship aRb it follows that bRa. For example, the equality relationship is symmetrical (i.e. from $a = b$, $b = a$ may be derived).
- *Asymmetry*: From aRb it follows that bRa is not valid. This is the case in a greater than relation, because if $a > b$, then $b > a$ cannot be correct.
- *Anti-symmetry*: In a set A, for all a, b $\in$ A, the relationships aRb and bRa imply that $a = b$. For example, in a greater than or equality relationship, if $a \geq b$ and $b \geq a$ it follows that $a = b$.

To further characterise relationships in general, and especially the preference (or priority) relationships relevant here, the relationships mentioned above may be combined to obtain so-called *preference orders*. One kind of preference order is the *indifference order*, for which the characteristic features of transitiveness, reflexivity and symmetry are valid. According to this order, two alternatives are essentially equivalent, as symbolised by $\sim$ ($a \sim b$ indicates that a and b are regarded as equivalent). A *strict preference order* is characterised by completeness, transitiveness and asymmetry. This order is symbolised by $\succ$ ($a \succ b$ indicates a preference for a over b). For a *weak preference order,* completeness, transitiveness, reflexivity and anti-symmetry are characteristic. Here, the symbol $a \gtrsim b$ indicates that a is either better than or equivalent to b.

A *weak preference order* may be represented by a quantitative utility function (also called a preference or value function). The utility function transforms the preferential relationships '$\succ$' and '$\sim$' into the numerical relationships '>' and '=' concerning the utility (U) of alternatives. For all alternatives $a, b \in A$ it is valid that:

$$a \succ b \Leftrightarrow U(a) > U(b) \tag{6.2}$$

$$a \sim b \Leftrightarrow U(a) = U(b) \tag{6.3}$$

To conclude this introductory section, an overview of the methods applicable for MADM is given. These may be classified in various ways. For example, a distinction might be made between methods that assume a weak preference order (so that all alternatives can be ordered transitively and entirely and, thus, the optimum decision/action can be defined unambiguously), and the so-called decision technology-based procedures, like the fuzzy set approaches, which are not based on this assumption. Another classification suggested by HWANG and YOON (1981) is based on the types of information that are used. This is summarised in Figure 6-1.

A discussion of all the methods shown in Figure 6-1 would exceed the scope of this book. However, the most important multi-criteria decision-making methods are described and discussed using examples related to a location decision - a typical strategic investment decision with multiple target criteria.

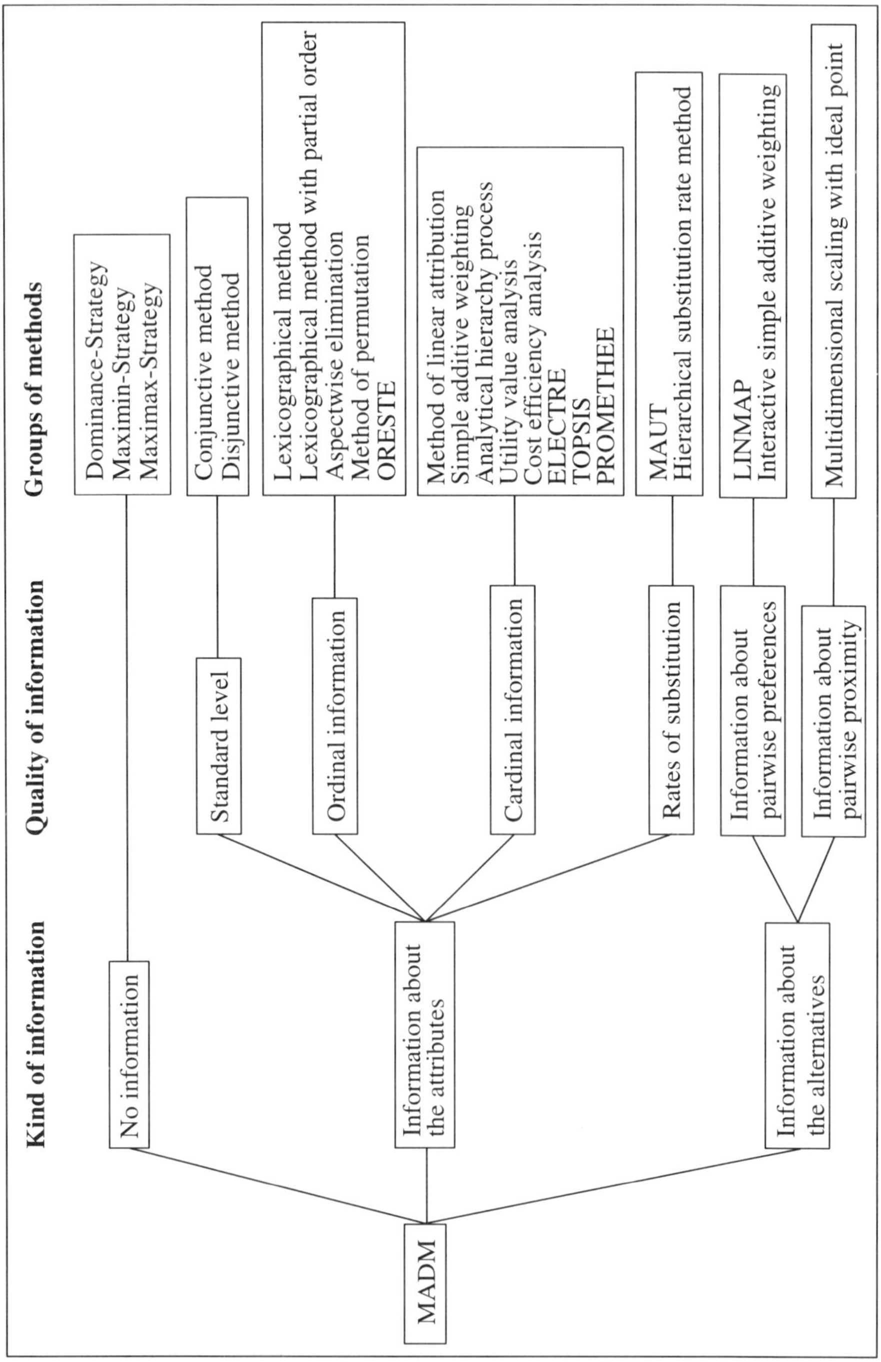

Fig. 6-1: MADM methods according to the type of information

6.2 Utility Value Analysis

Description of the method

This method seeks to analyse a number of complex alternatives, with the aim of ordering them according to the preferences of the decision-maker in a multi-dimensional target system. The ordering is carried out by calculating so-called *utility values* for the alternatives.

In utility value analysis, multiple target criteria are weighted according to their importance to the decision-maker. The ability of the different alternatives (here, the investment projects) to fulfil each target is measured and a corresponding partial utility value is given. The weighted partial utility values are summed to obtain a total value for every alternative – the utility value. For any one alternative, the aggregation of (weighted) partial utility values allows unfavourable results on one target measure to be compensated by better results on others. If certain criteria have minimum requirements, those must be fulfilled before carrying out a utility value analysis.

The utility value analysis consists of the following steps:

1. Determination of target criteria.
2. Weighting of each target criterion.
3. Calculation of partial utility values.
4. Calculation of (total) utility values.
5. Assessment of profitability.

In the first step of the utility value analysis, the *determination of target criteria*, a measurement scale (which may be nominal, ordinal or cardinal) is required for every criterion. The consideration of project attributes should not be duplicated by applying more than one criterion per attribute, and the extent to which an investment project fulfils one target criterion should be measured independently of the assessments made for other criteria. Monetary criteria are not normally included in a utility value analysis, since cash inflows and outflows, or yields and expenditures, are typically affected by many characteristics of investment projects that fall under some of the other criteria. Determining the target criteria requires a careful structuring and analysis of the target system. In complex decision problems, it is often worthwhile to split target measures into a multi-level hierarchy.

In the second step of the utility value analysis, a *weighting* w_c is determined for each criterion c in order to rank its importance to the decision-maker. The weightings should total 1 or 100 in order to simplify the interpretation of analysis results.

In the third step, the alternative projects are evaluated with respect to each criterion using, as appropriate, a nominal, ordinal or cardinal scale. Then, the results are transformed into partial utility values u_{ic} for each alternative i and for each criterion. The *partial utility values* are measured using a uniform cardinal scale, preferably with a range of 0 to 1, or 0 to 100.

In the fourth step, a (total) *utility value* U_{Ui}, is calculated as follows:

$$U_{Ui} = \sum_{c=1}^{C} u_{ic} \cdot w_c \tag{6.4}$$

Finally, an *assessment of profitability* is made using the following definitions:

> *Key Concept:*
> *Absolute profitability* is achieved if an investment project's utility value is higher than a given target value.
> *Relative profitability:* an investment project is preferred if its utility value is higher than that of any alternative project.

In some situations the utility value is not the only result of model analyses used for profitability assessment. As mentioned above, monetary target measures (e.g. net present value) should not be included in a utility value analysis, but considered separately. In such situations, goal conflicts are possible and a new multi-criteria problem can arise.

Example 6-1

In the following example, a utility value analysis is carried out in order to assess the relative profitability of three location alternatives: A_1, A_2 and A_3.

As a first step, the targets shown in Figure 6-2 have been determined. The main target, selection of the optimum location, is split into sub-targets as illustrated. The weightings, which are determined in the second step, also appear in Figure 6-2. The third step, the calculation of partial utility values is illustrated using the criterion 'size of land' in Figure 6-3. The alternatives under consideration have sizes of 60,000 m^2 (A_1), 42,500 m^2 (A_2) and 35,000 m^2 (A_3A_3).

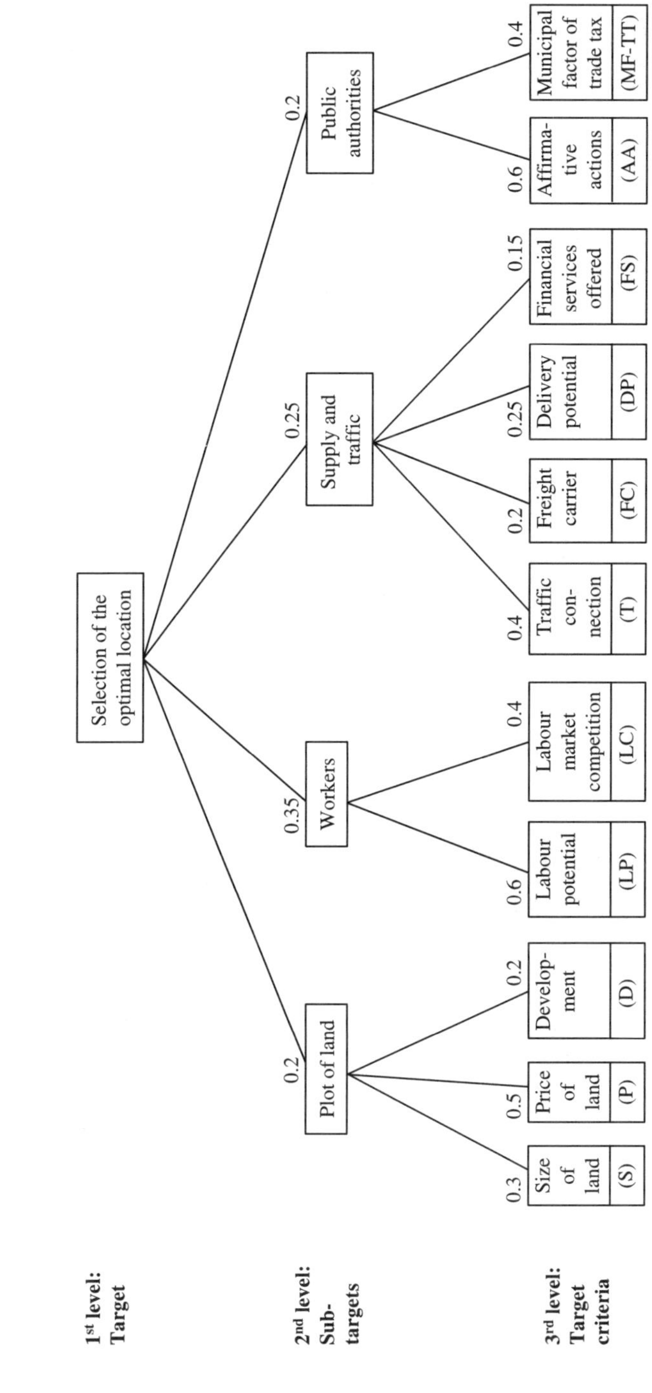

Fig. 6-2: Hierarchy of targets

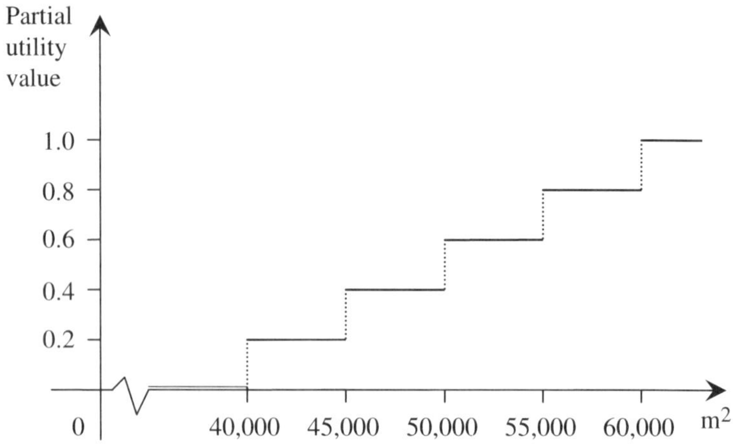

Fig. 6-3: Transformation function for the criterion 'size of land'

In accordance with this function, the partial utility values of the alternatives for this criterion are: 1 (A_1), 0.2 (A_2) and 0 (A_3). For the other criteria, partial utility values have been determined as follows:

Target criteria / Alternative	S	P	D	LP	LC	T	FC	DP	FS	AA	MF-TT
A_1	1	0.4	1	0.2	0.4	0.6	0.4	0.6	0.8	0.4	0.6
A_2	0.2	0.4	0.2	0.6	0.8	0.4	0	1	0.8	0.8	1
A_3	0	0.6	0.8	0.9	1	0.8	1	0.2	0.8	0.4	0.4

Tab. 6-1: Partial utility values of the alternatives A_1, A_2 and A_3

In the fourth step, the total utility values are calculated. The weighted partial utility values are determined by multiplying the partial utility values by the weightings of the associated criterion and sub-target. For alternative A_1 and the criterion 'size of land', for example, it is:

$$1 \cdot 0.3 \cdot 0.2 = 0.06$$

This value indicates the contribution of the criterion 'size of land' to the fulfilment of the highest-level target. By multiplying other partial values by their weightings, and adding the resulting weighted partial utility values, (total) utility values U_{Ui} for the three alternatives A_i can be determined:

$$U_{U1} = 0.48 \qquad U_{U2} = 0.61 \qquad U_{U3} = 0.67$$

It can be concluded, that Alternative A_3 is relatively profitable because it has the highest utility value.

Assessment of the method

Utility value analysis is a comparatively simple method for multi-criteria decision-making. It is easily comprehended and requires only minor computational effort. Also, its application encourages systematic structuring of the underlying problem.

The results of a utility value analysis can be easily interpreted, especially if standardised scales are used for the weightings and partial utility values, as proposed above. Then, a utility value of 1 or 100 is the maximum attainable and the utility value of an alternative can be interpreted as a proportion or percentage of this maximum value. Perhaps for these reasons, utility value analysis is a popular method in practice.

However, data collection can be problematic as target criteria, weightings and partial utility values must be determined and, for the latter two, cardinal measuring scales are required. The target criteria, target weightings and transformation into partial utility values must be based on personal, subjective judgements and estimates, often requiring extensive effort. It might also be questionable whether these criteria, weightings and transformations fully reflect the preferences of the decision-maker, whether target criteria are completely independent, and whether each project characteristic is examined under only one criterion. Effects caused by uncertainty and subjectivity of data, and deviations from assumptions, may by analysed by combining utility value analysis with appropriate procedures for investment methods under uncertainty (especially sensitivity analysis and risk analysis, as described in Chapter 8).

Some other reservations concern the weightings used. These represent overall statements about the relative importance of targets only, i.e. the relationship between two weightings must not be interpreted as a substitution rate for the outcomes of these two targets. Therefore, the utility function is not necessarily additive as this method implies. These aspects are reconsidered in Section 6.4, in the context of multi-attribute utility theory.

Another method for multi-criteria decision-making is now described: the analytic hierarchy process.

6.3 Analytic Hierarchy Process

Description of the method

The analytic hierarchy process (AHP) was developed by SAATY (1980) in the early 1970s to structure and analyse complex decisions. One important application of the method is the support of decision-making involving multiple objectives.

The AHP splits the decision process into partial problems in order to structure and simplify it. A hierarchy containing multiple target levels, such that the main target is broken down into sub-targets. At the lowest level(s) of the hierarchy, the alternatives (here, the investment projects) are included.

Using the AHP, both qualitative and quantitative criteria can be considered. In each case, the relative importance (weightings) of the different criteria, and the relative profitability of alternatives, is determined with respect to each element of the higher level by using pair comparisons. Then, a total value is calculated for sub-targets to determine their relative importance for the whole hierarchy, and, ultimately, to assess the overall profitability of the alternative investment projects.

The AHP is carried out using the following steps:

1. Formation of the hierarchy.
2. Determination of the priorities.
3. Calculation of local priority vectors (weighting factors).
4. Examination of the consistency of the priority assessments.
5. Determination of (global) priorities for the sub-targets and alternatives with respect to the whole hierarchy.

Under certain circumstances some of these steps must be repeated, particularly where priority estimations are inconsistent. Evaluation of the subjective priority assessments for consistency is another characteristic feature of the method.

The initial *formation of the hierarchy* requires segmentation and hierarchical structuring of the decision problem. In this step, an unambiguous demarcation must be drawn between different alternatives and sub-targets. Relevant relationships should exist between the elements of successive levels only. This implies that no (or only minor) relationships exist between the elements of a single level. In addition, the elements of a single level should be comparable and belong to the same category of importance. Finally, assessments should be independent of other assessments at the same and other levels. Usually, it is also assumed that all relevant alternatives and target measures will be considered. The measurability of target criteria has not to be considered in this step of the AHP.

The second step is the *determination of priorities* for all elements of the hierarchy. This involves estimating and quantifying the relative importance of every element in relation to each element of the hierarchy immediately above. This is done using pair comparisons with other elements at the same level. Thus, each element's relative importance for fulfilling target criteria is ranked at each level, as a contribution to the fulfilment of the overall target. For alternative investment projects, this relative importance represents a degree of profitability.

With regard to the pair comparisons, it is assumed that the decision-maker is able to determine values v_{ic} for all pairs i and c from the set A (target criteria or alternatives) on a relational scale. This will indicate, for an element at the next level up, the relative importance of i and c, and must be estimated for all elements of the higher level and for all levels. Reciprocity should apply for the estimated values. That is, the comparative value of i relative to c must equal the reciprocal of the comparison between c and i. Then, for an element at the next level up it applies:

$$v_{ic} = \frac{1}{v_{ci}} \quad \text{for all i, c} \in A \qquad (6.5)$$

Moreover, a comparative value v_{ic} should never be infinite. An infinite relative importance would mean the target criteria or alternatives regarded were not comparable, and a renewed target and problem analysis would be required.

For the pair comparisons, the nine-point scale suggested by SAATY (1980) and illustrated in Figure 6-4 may be used.

Scale value	Definition	Interpretation
1	Equal importance	Both compared elements have the same importance for the next higher element.
3	Slightly greater importance	Experience and estimation suggest a slightly greater importance of one element in comparison with the other element.
5	Considerably greater importance	Experience and estimation suggest a considerably greater importance of one element in comparison with the other element.
7	Very much greater importance	The very much greater importance of one element in comparison with the other element has been shown clearly in the past.
9	Absolutely dominating	The maximum difference of importance between two elements.
2,4,6,8	Intermediate values	

Fig. 6-4: SAATY's nine-point scale for pair comparisons

This scale has the advantage of converting verbal comparisons into numerical values, so that measurability on a relational scale is possible. A more detailed scale is not regarded as meaningful. Using this scale, comparisons can yield only values between one and nine, or their reciprocals (which apply where an element is of lesser importance than the other element).

The results of pair comparisons related to an element of the next level up may be shown in the form of a C x C matrix [denoted 'V'] with C elements being compared. The values along the main diagonal of this pair comparison matrix are always 1.

To obtain a pair comparison matrix for C elements being compared, $0.5 \cdot C \cdot (C-1)$ pair comparisons must be made, since the values across the main diagonal are 1 and reciprocity is assumed. Therefore, the determination of a comparative value v_{ic} is not required if the reciprocal value v_{ci} is known. The required number of pair comparisons increases steeply with an increasing number of elements at a single level; this should be considered when determining a hierarchy.

A perfect (i.e. consistent) execution of all pair comparisons has been made if, for every matrix element v_{ic}, and all elements j different to i and c, the following equation is valid:

$$v_{ic} = v_{ij} \cdot v_{jc} \tag{6.6}$$

If such a consistent execution of the pair comparisons can be assumed, some values can be derived from prior assessments, and the required number of pair comparisons may be reduced to $C - 1$.

In the third step, *local priority vectors (weighting factors)* are calculated for every pair comparison matrix. From the totality of the pair comparisons, the relative importance of the elements (alternatives, target criteria) is determined and summarised in the form of a priority vector. Accordingly, every component of this vector indicates the relative importance of its associated element to the relevant element at the next level up.

The calculation of the priority vectors [denoted 'W'] may be carried out by means of the *eigenvector* method, as explained below. Based on the pair comparison matrix V, and (temporarily) assuming that the estimations are perfect and the relative importance w_c of all the separate elements of c is known, the matrix elements v_{ic} can be calculated as follows:

$$v_{ic} = \frac{w_i}{w_c} \qquad \text{for all } i, c \in A. \tag{6.7}$$

Moreover, on account of the reciprocity condition:

$$v_{ic} = \frac{1}{v_{ci}} = \frac{1}{\frac{w_c}{w_i}} \qquad \text{for all } i, c \in A \tag{6.8}$$

Or:

$$v_{ic} \cdot \frac{w_c}{w_i} = 1 \qquad \text{for all } i, c \in A \tag{6.9}$$

Additionally:

$$\sum_{c=1}^{C} v_{ic} \cdot \frac{w_c}{w_i} = \sum_{c=1}^{C} \frac{w_i}{w_c} \cdot \frac{w_c}{w_i} = C \qquad \text{is valid for all } i \in A \qquad (6.10)$$

And also:

$$\sum_{c=1}^{C} v_{ic} \cdot w_c = C \cdot w_i \qquad \text{for all } i \in A \qquad (6.11)$$

Because this relationship applies to all lines i (i = 1,...,C) of the pair comparison matrix, the following system of C equations can be formulated:

$$\begin{pmatrix} v_{11} & v_{12} & \cdots & v_{1C} \\ v_{21} & v_{22} & \cdots & v_{2C} \\ \vdots & \vdots & & \vdots \\ v_{C1} & v_{C2} & \cdots & v_{CC} \end{pmatrix} \cdot \begin{pmatrix} w_1 \\ w_2 \\ \vdots \\ w_C \end{pmatrix} = C \cdot \begin{pmatrix} w_1 \\ w_2 \\ \vdots \\ w_C \end{pmatrix} \qquad (6.12a)$$

Or:

$$V \cdot W = C \cdot W \qquad (6.12b)$$

This system of equations represents a specific so-called *eigenvalue problem.* Such a mathematical problem is generally defined as follows: for a C x C matrix (B), real numbers L and corresponding vectors X must be found which fulfil the following system of equations:

$$B \cdot X = L \cdot X \qquad (6.13)$$

The numbers (L) are called *eigenvalues* of B, and the assigned vectors (X) are called *eigenvectors*. The sum of the eigenvalues in an eigenvalue problem equals the sum formed by the elements of the main diagonal. As for the pair comparison matrices considered here, these elements are each equal to 1 and so the sum of the eigenvalues is the same as the dimension (C) of the matrix. If all assessments are consistent, there is only one positive eigenvalue with the value C.

However, in a multi-criteria decision problem priority estimates are often inconsistent and the weighting vectors are not known. Therefore, in the following discussion the corresponding assumptions must be abandoned. If priority estimates are inconsistent, several eigenvalues and eigenvectors will result. Thus, the maximum eigenvalue L_{max} of the pair comparison matrix and the associated eigenvector must be determined. The latter should be standardised so that the sum of its components is 1, then it can be regarded as the weighting vector W. The calculation of such a weighting vector is meaningful, even with an inconsistent pair comparison matrix, as small inconsistencies will show only a slight effect on the weighting vector.

To determine the maximum eigenvalue and the weighting vector, the following eigenvalue problem must be solved:

$$V \cdot W = L \cdot W \quad \text{or} \quad (V - L \cdot U) \cdot W = 0 \qquad (6.14)$$

Here, U represents a C x C unit matrix. For the eigenvalues L in this problem, the determinant of the matrix (V - L · U) is zero, i.e.:

$$\det | V - L \cdot U | = 0 \qquad (6.15)$$

The maximum value L fulfilling this condition is the maximum eigenvalue L_{max}. By inserting this value in the equation system given above, the eigen- or weighting vector may be calculated. For this vector it applies:

$$(V - L_{max} \cdot U) \cdot W = 0 \qquad (6.16)$$

And:

$$\sum_{c=1}^{C} w_c = 1 \qquad (6.17)$$

The calculation of the maximum eigenvalue and weighting vector involves substantial computational effort. Therefore, approximations are suggested, e.g. the weighting vector can be approximated from the pair comparison matrix V by using the following arithmetical rule to generate matrix products gradually:

$$V \cdot U;\ V^2 \cdot U;\ V^3 \cdot U;\ \ldots;\ V^o \cdot U \qquad (6.18)$$

Where:

V = C x C (pair comparison matrix)
U = C x 1 (unity vector)

With a sufficiently high value o, the vector $V^o \cdot U$ is a good approximation for the eigenvector.

An *examination of the consistency of priority assessments* takes place in the fourth step of the AHP for all pair comparison matrices. This step is necessary because the consistency of all estimates cannot be taken for granted.

If all the assessments are totally consistent, the maximum eigenvalue is C. Where there are inconsistencies, however, a higher eigenvalue L_{max} arises. This value L_{max} might not be known exactly if, in the third step, the eigenvectors were calculated using an approximation. Then, L_{max} can only be approximated (e.g. using the well known NEWTON method to determine zero points). The difference between L_{max} and C increases with increasing inconsistency, so it provides an indication of the consistency of the estimates. An index of consistency (IOC) can be formulated using an additional calculation:

$$IOC = \frac{L_{max} - C}{(C-1)} \qquad (6.19)$$

In assessing consistency, the matrix dimension should also be taken into account, since it influences the extent of typical inconsistencies. To do this, a *value of consistency* (VOC) is calculated. The VOC indicates the relationship between the index of consistency (IOC) and an average value of indices of consistency (RI) derived from reciprocal matrices of the same size, which are produced randomly based on SAATY's nine-point scale:

$$VOC = \frac{IOC}{RI} \qquad (6.20)$$

Figure 6-5 shows the average values, calculated by SAATY, in dependance on the matrix dimension.

Matrix dimension	1	2	3	4	5	6	7	8
Average value (RI)	0.00	0.00	0.58	0.90	1.12	1.24	1.32	1.41

Matrix dimension	9	10	11	12	13	14	15
Average value (RI)	1.45	1.49	1.51	1.48	1.56	1.57	1.59

Fig. 6-5: Average values of indices of consistency

SAATY suggests 0.1 as a critical limit for the value of consistency. Accordingly, pair comparison matrices with a consistency value $VOC \leq 0.1$ are regarded as being sufficiently consistent, while matrices with $VOC > 0.1$ require an examination and revision of the pair comparisons.

Up to this point in the analysis, each estimated priority has been related to only one element at the next level up the hierarchy. In the fifth step of the AHP, the *determination of target and alternative priorities for the whole hierarchy*, the weighting vectors are aggregated with respect to all elements in the next level up and all other higher levels. This facilitates the assessment of both the global priority (or relative importance) of each target criterion and the ultimate profitability of alternatives.

As a result of the pair comparisons for the second level of the hierarchy, a weighting vector is generated. This indicates the importance of target criteria at this level relative to the overall target, thereby showing both the local and global priority of the targets. The weighting vector is a starting point for the calculation of global priorities for the elements of each subsequent level. It is multiplied by a weighting matrix, which incorporates the weighting vectors of the level subsequent to it. The product is also a weighting vector, whose components represent the global priorities of the elements of the subsequent level. The successive continuation of this step leads to the calculation of the global priority for the alternatives at the lowest level of the hierarchy.

This procedure for determining global priorities for alternatives may also be interpreted as the additive calculation of a utility measure U_{Ai} for each alternative A_i with the formula:

$$U_{Ai} = \sum_{c=1}^{C} w_c \cdot u_{ic} \tag{6.21}$$

The index c refers to the elements of the next level up, which here represents target criteria. The symbol w_c indicates the global priority of these target criteria, and u_{ic} is the relative importance (profitability) of the alternative i concerning the criterion c. Therefore, the global priority (as for the utility value analysis described in the previous subchapter) is calculated as a sum of weighted partial priorities.

The global priorities determined in this step represent weightings of the target criteria. Concerning the alternatives under consideration, they estimate the contribution made to the fulfilment of the overall target. In assessing the relative profitability of (investment) alternatives when the overall target is to be maximised, the following key concept applies:

> *Key Concept:*
> *Relative profitability:* an investment project is preferred if its global priority is higher than that of every other project under consideration.

The isolated assessment of absolute profitability by AHP is not possible, as the procedure is based on pair comparisons and, therefore, assessment of one alternative depends on the other alternatives selected. However, the alternative of *not* investing may be included in the procedure. In that case, an estimate of absolute profitability can be made by comparing the global priority of not investing with that of the remaining alternatives.

Example 6-2

The following example draws on Example 6-1.

The first step of the AHP is the formation of the hierarchy. In this example, the target system is drawn from the previous section. Figure 6-6 depicts this target system and contains, in addition to the previous example, the location alternatives A_1, A_2 and A_3 as elements of the lowest hierarchy level.

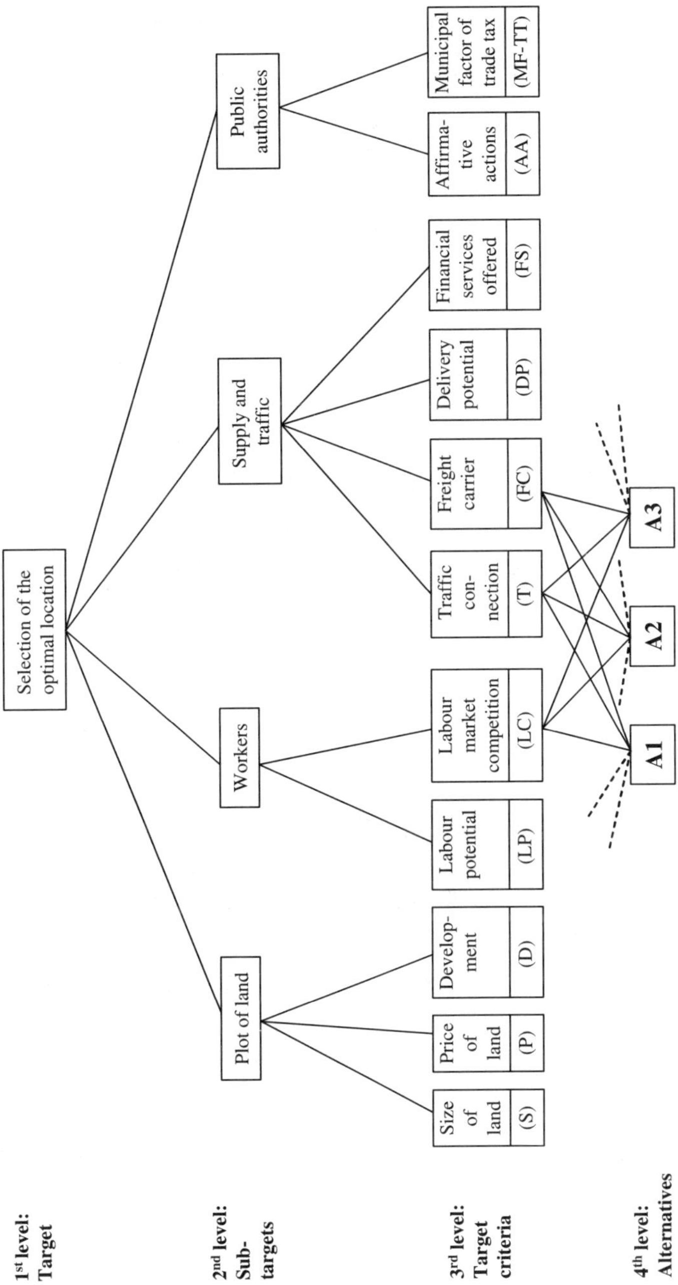

Fig. 6-6: Decision hierarchy

The second, third and fourth step of the AHP (the determination of priorities, the calculation of local priority vectors or weighting factors, and the examination of the priority assessments for consistency) are now presented together. First, the level of the alternatives is considered. For the criterion 'size of land', the following pair comparison assessments are obtained with regard to the profitability of the alternatives.

$$V = \begin{pmatrix} 1 & 4 & 5 \\ \frac{1}{4} & 1 & 3 \\ \frac{1}{5} & \frac{1}{3} & 1 \end{pmatrix}$$

To determine the exact weighting vector, the maximum eigenvalue L_{max} of the pair comparison matrix V must first be calculated. For all eigenvalues L of the matrix, the determinant of the matrix (V - L · U) represented below is zero.

$$(V - L \cdot U) = \begin{pmatrix} 1\text{-}L & 4 & 5 \\ \frac{1}{4} & 1\text{-}L & 3 \\ \frac{1}{5} & \frac{1}{3} & 1\text{-}L \end{pmatrix} \begin{matrix} 1\text{-}L & 4 \\ \frac{1}{4} & 1\text{-}L \\ \frac{1}{5} & \frac{1}{3} \end{matrix}$$

The determinant of a 3 x 3 matrix can be calculated using the SARRUS rule. For this, the first and second columns of the matrix are repeated after the third column. Then, the products of the elements of (i) the main diagonal of the original matrix and (ii) the components of the diagonals which lie parallel to it, are calculated and summed.

The determinant is this sum, less the products of the elements of the side diagonal and its parallel diagonals. In the example it is:

$$\det|V - L \cdot U| = (1-L)^3 + 4 \cdot 3 \cdot \frac{1}{5} + 5 \cdot \frac{1}{4} \cdot \frac{1}{3} - \frac{1}{5} \cdot (1-L) \cdot 5 - \frac{1}{3} \cdot 3 \cdot (1-L) - (1-L) \cdot \frac{1}{4} \cdot 4$$

$$\det|V - L \cdot U| = (1-L)^3 - 3 \cdot (1-L) + 2.8167$$

Based on the necessary condition

$$\det|V - L \cdot U| \stackrel{!}{=} 0$$

The maximum eigenvalue (L_{max}) can be determined using a suitable procedure such as the NEWTON procedure:

$$L_{max} = 3.0858$$

The associated eigen- or weighting vector can be determined using the equation system:

$$(V - L_{max} \cdot U) \cdot W = 0$$

Or:

$$(1\text{-}\ 3.0858) \cdot w_1 + 4 \cdot w_2 + 5 \cdot w_3 = 0$$

$$\frac{1}{4} \cdot w_1 + (1\text{-}\ 3.0858) \cdot w_2 + 3 \cdot w_3 = 0$$

$$\frac{1}{5} \cdot w_1 + \frac{1}{3} \cdot w_2 + (1\text{-}\ 3.0858) \cdot w_3 = 0$$

First, the relationship between the weighting factors is derived. Then, the (local) weighting factors are calculated using the condition $w_1 + w_2 + w_3 = 1$. Here, these factors are:

$$w_1 = 0.6738 \qquad w_2 = 0.2255 \qquad w_3 = 0.1007$$

They indicate the profitability (local priority) of the location alternatives A_1, A_2 and A_3 in regard to the criterion 'size of land'.

The index of consistency (IOC) arises from the maximum eigenvalue (L_{max}):

$$IOC = \frac{3.0858}{3-1} = 0.0429$$

The value of consistency (VOC) amounts to:

$$VOC = \frac{0.0429}{0.58} = 0.0740$$

Because the VOC is below 0.1, the assessment from this pair comparison matrix can be regarded as sufficiently consistent.

In the same manner, pair comparison matrices can also be formulated and evaluated to compare alternatives concerning the other target criteria. Figure 6-7 shows these matrices as well as the maximum eigenvalues, the weighting vectors, and the indices and values of consistency determined for each of the different target criteria.

Price of land

	A_1	A_2	A_3
A_1	1	3	1/4
A_2	1/3	1	1/6
A_3	4	6	1

Maximum eigenvalue: 3.0536
Weighting vector: (0.2176; 0.0914; 0.6910)
Value of consistency: 0.0462

Development

	A_1	A_2	A_3
A_1	1	7	3
A_2	1/7	1	1/4
A_3	1/3	4	1

Maximum eigenvalue: 3.0323
Weighting vector: (0.6586; 0.0786; 0.2628)
Value of consistency: 0.0278

Labour potential

	A_1	A_2	A_3
A_1	1	1/4	1/9
A_2	4	1	1/5
A_3	9	5	1

Maximum eigenvalue: 3.0713
Weighting vector: (0.0633; 0.1939; 0.7428)
Value of consistency: 0.0615

Labour market competition

	A_1	A_2	A_3
A_1	1	1/5	1/7
A_2	5	1	1/3
A_3	7	3	1

Maximum eigenvalue: 3.0649
Weighting vector: (0.0719; 0.2790; 0.6491)
Value of consistency: 0.0559

Traffic connection

	A_1	A_2	A_3
A_1	1	1/2	1/2
A_2	2	1	1
A_3	2	1	1

Maximum eigenvalue: 3
Weighting vector: (0.2000; 0.4000; 0.4000)
Value of consistency: 0

Forwarding agents

	A_1	A_2	A_3
A_1	1	8	4
A_2	1/8	1	1/3
A_3	1/4	3	1

Maximum eigenvalue: 3.0183
Weighting vector: (0.7167; 0.0782; 0.2051)
Value of consistency: 0.016

Delivery potential

	A_1	A_2	A_3
A_1	1	8	4
A_2	1/8	1	1/3
A_3	1/4	3	1

Maximum eigenvalue: 3.0093
Weighting vector: (0.7166; 0.0783; 0.2051)
Value of consistency: 0.008

Bank facility offer

	A_1	A_2	A_3
A_1	1	3	3
A_2	1/3	1	1
A_3	1/3	1	1

Maximum eigenvalue: 3
Weighting vector: (0.6000; 0.2000; 0.2000)
Value of consistency: 0

Affirmative actions

	A_1	A_2	A_3
A_1	1	1/7	1/2
A_2	7	1	6
A_3	2	1/6	1

Maximum eigenvalue: 3.0324
Weighting vector: (0.0905; 0.7583; 0.1512)
Value of consistency: 0.0279

Municipal trade tax rate

	A_1	A_2	A_3
A_1	1	6	4
A_2	1/6	1	1/3
A_3	1/4	3	1

Maximum eigenvalue: 3.0536
Weighting vector: (0.6910; 0.0914; 0.2176)
Value of consistency: 0.0462

Fig. 6-7: Pair comparison assessments for the alternatives and their evaluation

Analogous assessments and calculations are also made for the higher levels of the decision hierarchy. Figure 6-8 shows the results of the pair comparison assessments and their evaluations for the target criteria (with regard to the sub-targets) and the sub-targets (with regard to the overall target).

Plot of land

	S	P	D
S	1	1/3	4
P	3	1	9
D	1/4	1/9	1

Maximum eigenvalue: 3.0093
Weighting vector: (0.2499; 0.6813; 0.0688)
Value of consistency: 0.008

Workers

	LP	LC
LP	1	5
LC	1/5	1

Maximum eigenvalue: 2
Weighting vector: (0.8333; 0.1667)
Value of consistency: 0

Supply and traffic

	T	FC	DP	FS
T	1	7	5	9
FC	1/7	1	1/4	3
DP	1/5	4	1	5
FS	1/9	1/3	1/5	1

Maximum eigenvalue: 4.2314
Weighting vector: (0.6474; 0.0899; 0.2165; 0.0462)
Value of consistency: 0.0857

Public authorities

	AA	MF-TT
AA	1	3
MF-TT	1/3	1

Maximum eigenvalue: 2
Weighting vector: (0.7500; 0.2500)
Value of consistency: 0

Upper target: Optimal location

	PL	W	SP	PA
PL	1	1/8	1/3	2
W	8	1	4	6
SP	3	1/4	1	5
PA	1/2	1/6	1/5	1

Maximum eigenvalue: 4.1670
Weighting vector: (0.0871; 0.6238; 0.2281; 0.0610)
Value of consistency: 0.0619

Fig. 6-8: Pair comparison assessments for the target criteria and sub-targets, and their evaluation

As the consistency values of all pair comparison matrices of the hierarchy are smaller than 0.1, sufficient consistency may be assumed.

The fifth step of the AHP consists of determining target and alternative priorities for the whole hierarchy, which can be done in a way similar to the corresponding step of utility value analysis. The contribution that the alternative A_1 makes to fulfilling the overall target via the criterion 'size of land' can be calculated by multiplying the local priority of the alternative (0.6738) by the local priority of this criterion (0.2499) and that of the associated sub-target 'plot of land' (0.0871). This contribution amounts to 0.0147. By calculating results for all other criteria in the same way and adding them up, the global priority of the alternative under consideration is determined. Here, the global priorities of the three alternatives are:

$$U_{A1} = 0.172 \qquad U_{A2} = 0.244 \qquad U_{A3} = 0.584$$

Alternative A_3 shows the highest global priority and is, therefore, relatively the most profitable.

Assessment of the method

The assessment of the AHP method focuses on the effort it requires and its underlying assumptions.

The computational effort is high compared with utility value analysis. With a high number of elements at a single level, approximation procedures must be applied. Also, the data collection is relatively complicated because, for all pairs of elements at a given level, pair comparisons are needed with regard to every element at the next level up. For these pair comparisons it is assumed that a relational scale measurement is possible. Fundamentally, this sets high requirements for measurability, although the use of SAATY's nine-point scale allows the comparison of attributes of lower measurability. However, the nine-point scale has some problems of its own. Unlike a true relational scale, it has no natural neutral point. This can produce errors in the pair comparison judgements. Generally, it is doubtful whether a decision-maker is able to differentiate between statements like 'considerably greater' (scale value 5) and 'very much greater' (scale value 7), and additionally may consider their intermediate values. In addition, the nine-point scale can lead to inconsistencies. If, for example, the scale value 7 is assigned to an element C_1 compared to C_2, as well as to C_2 compared to C_3, the priority of C_1 compared to C_3 would have to be represented by the scale value 49. This, however, is not possible, because the scale value 9 is the upper limit.

A crucial point is the assumption that all relevant alternatives have been considered. Since it makes pair comparisons, the ranking determined using the AHP depends on the choice of alternatives. The consideration of additional alternatives can lead to changes in the ranking, so the ranking is not stable and the result of the AHP is valid only amongst the alternatives included in the comparison. For this set of alternatives, in spite of any inaccuracies caused by approximations, the preferences of the decision-maker are quite accurately represented. The examinations of consistency, which are an essential component of the procedure, support this claim.

The condition that judgements must be independent is restrictive, as it is with utility value analysis. In general, the AHP procedure resembles utility value analysis in its structuring of the decision problem, the utility function, and the interpretation of the criteria weightings. Thus, a combination of both procedures is possible.

Within the framework of the AHP it is also possible to include elements of uncertainty by creating a level in the hierarchy that reflects possible environmental conditions or scenarios. Uncertainties about the preferences expressed in the pair comparison judgements can be examined with the help of sensitivity analysis.

A central criticism of the AHP is that it is not based on an additive utility function. This criticism was also noted for the utility value analysis method described earlier. The weightings merely represent overall statements about the importance of the targets, and an additive utility function cannot be taken for granted.

A method more soundly based on utility theory is described in the following section.

6.4 Multi-Attribute Utility Theory

Description of the method

The multi-attribute utility theory (MAUT) was originally developed for the analysis of multi-criteria problems under uncertain conditions, but it can also be applied in more predictable conditions (of certainty), as assumed here. A characteristic feature of the method is that a multi-criteria problem is solved using cardinal utility functions (or 'preference functions') based on substitution rates between the attributes.

Using MAUT, cardinal utility functions are assigned to each attribute according to the preferences of the decision-maker (called *individual utility functions* in the following). The total utility (value) U_M then arises as a function of the individual utilities u_c assigned to the outcomes o_c (c = 1,...,C) of the target criteria:

$$U_M(o_1, o_2,...,o_C) = f(u_1(o_1), u_2(o_2),..., u_C(o_C)) \quad (6.22)$$

Because each separate criterion is analysed, specific value assessments can be made for them, and exchange relationships between them can be explicitly considered. It is assumed that the criteria are interchangeable, i.e. all changes to the fulfilment of a target criterion can be balanced by changes in other target criteria. This requires that the outcomes of the different alternatives lie close to each other, a prerequisite that can only be fully achieved with an unlimited number of alternatives. Furthermore, it is assumed that the substitution rate (i.e. the relationship between the utility changes that lead to a utility balance between two attributes) can be quantified.

The determination of total utilities requires criteria whose fulfilment is clearly independent of the fulfilment of the other criteria. Depending on the type of independence, different total utility functions may be used. For the multi-criteria decisions under conditions of certainty discussed here, an additive total utility function of the following form may be applied:

$$U_M = \sum_{c=1}^{C} w_c \cdot u_c \tag{6.23}$$

Where:

w_c = weighting factor for target criterion c

In addition to interchangeability of the attributes, this approach assumes that:

- For the alternatives, a weak order of priority can be formed.
- The decision-maker regards the attributes as mutually preference independent.

Mutual preferential independence can be said to occur if every subset of the set of all criteria has a preference assessment for its criteria outcomes that is independent of the outcomes of the remaining criteria in the target system.

In the following discussion, it is assumed that the conditions specified above are fulfilled, and only an additive utility function as shown above is analysed. MAUT resembles utility value analysis in this regard except that, in MAUT, the utility theory assumptions indicated above are taken into consideration. Moreover, both the individual utility functions u_c and the weighting factors w_c are determined using attribute comparisons in a consistent format.

A multi-criteria problem under certainty is solved with the MAUT using the following steps:

1. Choice of the attributes or criteria.
2. Examination of the independence of the criteria.
3. Determination of an individual utility function for each attribute.
4. Determination of a weighting factor for each criterion.
5. Calculation of the total utility for each alternative.

In the first step, *the choice of criteria*, the overall target is split hierarchically into sub-targets. The lowest target level contains the attributes that measure the achievement of objectives (targets) by the alternatives. These may be quantitative or qualitative. In the case of qualitative criteria, an appropriate measurement scale must be chosen, depending on the attributes (in contrast to AHP no generally applicable scale is suggested).

The *examination of independence* follows in the second step, as this independence is a prerequisite for the meaningful aggregation of the individual utilities assigned to single criteria to find an alternative's total utility. Using an additive utility function, mutual preferential independence is assumed; this must be proven for the present system of attributes and their outcomes.

In the third step, *individual utility functions u_c for the separate attributes c are formulated* to assign cardinal utility measures to the attributes. This requires knowledge of the relevant possible outcomes for the attributes. The individual utility functions are standardised so that their values u_c are restricted to the interval [0;1], for example by assigning the individual utility value of zero ($u_c(o_c^0) = 0$) to the worst outcome o_c^0 for criterion c and the utility value of one ($u_c(o_c^1) = 1$) to the best outcome o_c^1.

The individual utility functions may take different forms - they can be linear, concave or convex. Their course can be determined using a sequence of queries in accordance with the so-called mid-value splitting technique. Using this approach, an attribute C_1 with o_1^0 and o_1^1 is assigned a 'midvalue' $o_1^{0.5}$ that represents the outcome for which the increase in utility achieved by the change from o_1^0 to $o_1^{0.5}$ equals the utility increase resulting from the change from $o_1^{0.5}$ to o_1^1. Then, an individual utility of 0.5 is assigned to this outcome $o_1^{0.5}$, e.g. $u_1(o_1^{0.5}) = 0.5$. To determine $o_1^{0.5}$, a second attribute C_2 is used in successive querying so that, starting from a level of $o_2^{'}$, the change Δo_2 that balances the step from o_1^0 to $o_1^{0.5}$ with the step from $o_1^{0.5}$ to o_1^1 can be identified.

Accordingly, the following indifference judgments must apply:

$$(o_1^0, o_2^{'}) \sim (o_1^{0.5}, o_2^{'} - \Delta o_2) \qquad (6.24)$$

$$(o_1^{0.5}, o_2^{'}) \sim (o_1^1, o_2^{'} - \Delta o_2) \qquad (6.25)$$

This procedure is illustrated in Figure 6-9.

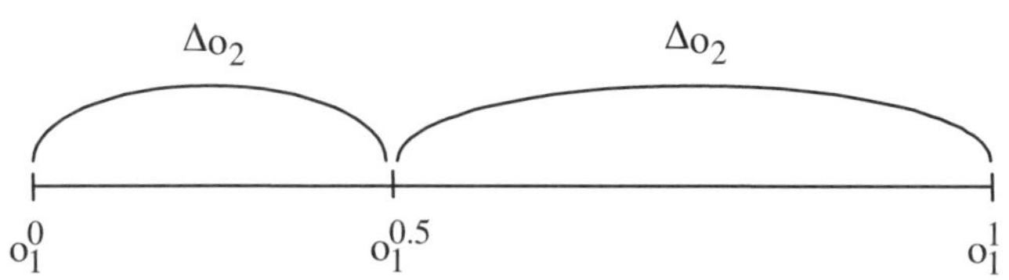

Fig. 6-9: Utility measurement by attribute comparison

Additional querying for the partial intervals $[o_1^0; o_1^{0.5}]$ and $[o_1^{0.5}; o_1^1]$ will determine the mid-values ($o_1^{0.25}$ and $o_1^{0.75}$). These values often allow a sufficient approximation of the individual utility function u_1, especially if their type is known (e.g. a linear function). However, additional values for the individual utility function u_1 may be calculated in the same way. An example showing the determination of an individual utility function is given in Figure 6-10.

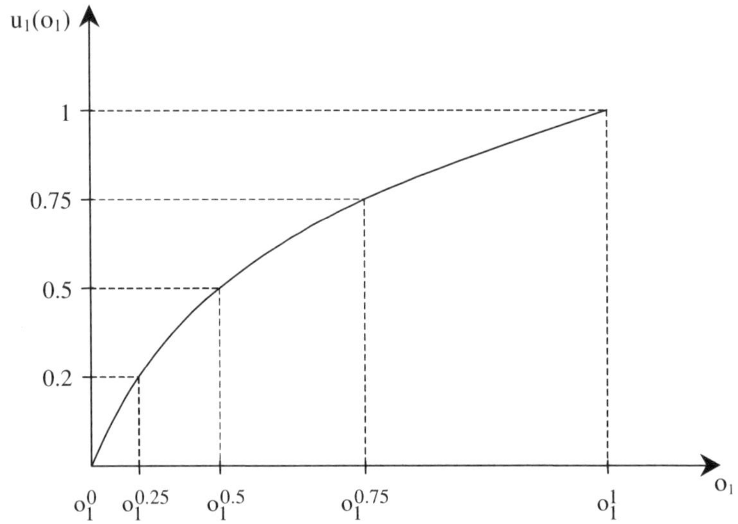

Fig. 6-10: Determination of an individual utility function

Individual utility functions ($u_2,...,u_C$) can be determined for the remaining criteria in the same way. In each case, a consistency examination should be carried out – e.g. the value $o_1^{0.5}$ may be verified by re-calculating it as the mid-value of the interval $[o_1^{0.25}; o_1^{0.75}]$, and repeated determination of an individual utility function can be performed using different other attributes.

If it is sufficient to know the individual utility values only for specific attributes of the relevant alternatives, it is not necessary to ascertain the full individual utility functions.

Determination of the weighting factors for the criteria, the fourth step, is achieved using the relationship between the weighting factors (also known as scale factors) of two attributes, which can be interpreted as substitution rates and derived from the indifference judgments made in the third step. To help explain this, the case of two target measures (C = 2) is considered first. Then the linear and additive total utility function is:

$$U_M = w_1 \cdot u_1 + w_2 \cdot u_2 \tag{6.26}$$

For a given utility level $\overline{U}_M$ the following equation applies:

$$\overline{U}_M = w_1 \cdot u_1 + w_2 \cdot u_2 \tag{6.27}$$

This relationship can be represented in a u_1/u_2 diagram in the form of a straight line representing the utility combinations u_1 and u_2 that lead to the same total utility $\overline{U}_M$. This may be interpreted as an indifference curve and, together with other indifference curves embodying different levels of the total utility, it is presented in Figure 6-11.

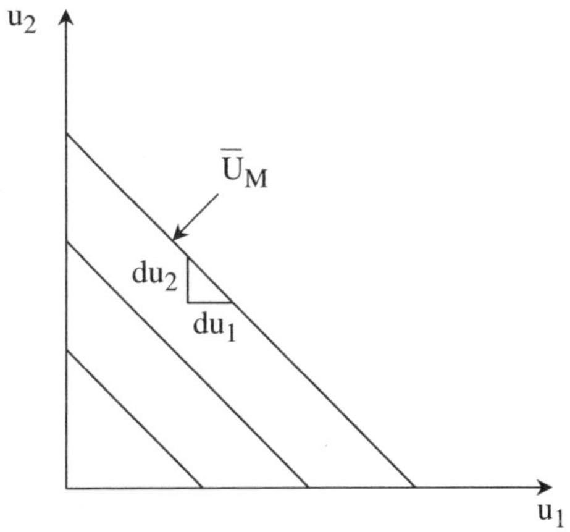

Fig. 6-11: Indifference curves

The slope of the straight lines $\frac{du_2}{du_1}$ equals the substitution rate between u_1 and u_2. It specifies how many units u_2 must be reduced by in order to gain the same utility with one more unit of u_1. The slope, or substitution rate, can be derived from the equation for the indifference curve as follows:

$$\frac{du_2}{du_1} = -\frac{w_1}{w_2} \tag{6.28}$$

The substitution rate equals the negative reciprocal quotient of the weighting factors of two attributes. Therefore, the relationship between two attributes is also characterised by:

$$|\Delta u_2| \cdot w_2 = |\Delta u_1| \cdot w_1 \tag{6.29}$$

The value changes Δu_1 and Δu_2 can be derived from the indifference estimates obtained in order to determine their mid-values:

$$(o_1^0, o_2') \sim (o_1^{0.5}, o_2' - \Delta o_2) \tag{6.30}$$

$$(o_1^{0.5}, o_2') \sim (o_1^1, o_2' - \Delta o_2) \qquad (6.31)$$

The difference Δu_1 between $u_1(o_1^0)$ and $u_1(o_1^{0.5})$ is known as $\Delta u_1 = 0.5$. The value difference Δu_2 between $u_2(o_2')$ and $u_2(o_2' - \Delta o_2)$ can be derived from the individual utility function $u_2(o_2)$. Then Δu_1 and Δu_2 can be inserted in the equation given above to determine the numeric relationship between the weighting factors w_1 and w_2:

$$w_1 = \frac{|\Delta u_2|}{|\Delta u_1|} \cdot w_2 \qquad (6.32)$$

Since the mutual preferences are independent, the procedure presented here can be used where there are several target measures. Relationships between w_1 and the remaining weighting factors (w_3, ...,w_C) can be determined in the same way. Then, using these relationships and the condition (6.17),

$$\sum_{c=1}^{C} w_c = 1$$

A system of equations can be formulated and used to determine the weighting factors w_c.

In the fifth step, *calculation of the total utilities of the alternatives*, individual utility functions are used to convert the attributes of the alternatives into individual utilities. Then, taking account of the weighting factors, they are summed to obtain a total utility (using Formula (6.23)). The maximum achievable total utility is 1. The following conditions for profitability then apply:

> *Key Concept:*
> *Absolute profitability* is achieved if an investment project's total utility is higher than a given target value.
> *Relative profitability:* an investment project is preferred if its total utility is higher than those of every other project under consideration.

Example 6-3

The example considered in the previous sections (a location decision) is used again here, assuming that the prerequisites for an additive utility function apply.

The choice of attributes, the first step, draws on the target criteria list given above. Using MAUT, the lowest level criteria serve as indicators for analysing the achievement of objectives. In this example, for reasons of complexity only four of the eleven lowest level criteria will be considered: one from each criteria group. Accordingly, it is assumed that only the attributes 'size of land (S)' (in m^2), 'labour potential (LP)', 'freight carrier (FC)' and 'municipal factor of trade tax (MF)' (in %) are relevant. The 'labour potential' is measured on the basis of the available workers, and the criterion 'freight carrier' on the number of carriers resident in the locality.

For the location alternatives A_1, A_2, A_3 the following data are available:

Alternative	S	LP	FC	MF
A_1	60,000	800	15	350
A_2	42,500	1,100	12	250
A_3	35,000	1,300	25	450

Tab. 6-2: Data for the location alternatives A_1, A_2 and A_3

In the second step, the criteria are examined for independence and in this instance it is assumed that they are mutually preference independent, thus an additive utility function may be applied.

Steps 3 and 4 (determinations of the individual utility functions u_c and the weighting factors w_c) can, because of the relationships described above, be presented together.

The minimum and maximum outcomes for the attributes can be read from the data given. Their individual utility values are fixed at 0 and 1: thus, the lowest outcome should score an individual utility of 1 if the aim is to minimise the attribute (e.g. tax) or 0 if the aim is to maximise the attribute (e.g. labour potential):

$$
\begin{aligned}
&u_1(35{,}000) = 0 \qquad && u_1(60{,}000) = 1\\
&u_2(800) = 0 && u_2(1{,}300) = 1\\
&u_3(12) = 0 && u_3(25) = 1\\
&u_4(450) = 0 && u_4(250) = 1
\end{aligned}
$$

Furthermore, it is assumed that the individual utility function has already been determined for attribute C_1 (size of land) with the help of the mid-value splitting technique and corresponding indifference estimates. Figure 6-12 shows this individual utility function: increasing the size of land from 35,000 m^2 initially results in a relatively high increase in the utility, but after reaching 42,500 m^2 the utility increases diminish.

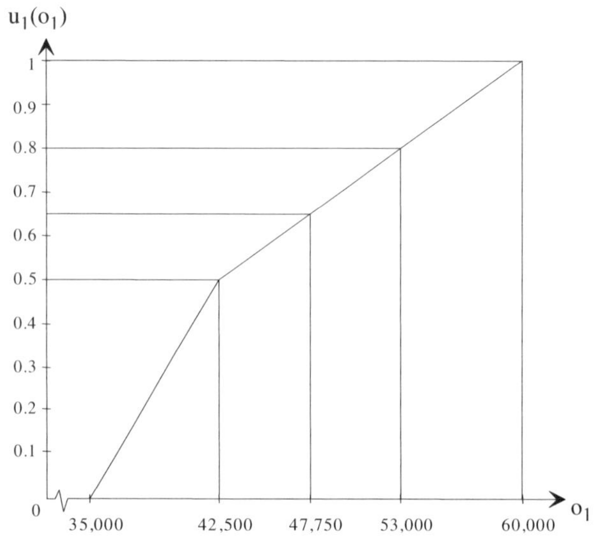

Fig. 6-12: Individual utility function for the attribute 'size of land'

Next, the individual utility function for the second attribute is determined using mid-values. First, the outcome $o_2^{0.5}$ is identified, which leads to an individual utility of 0.5. Using the first criterion and starting at $o_1^{'} = 42{,}500$, the change Δo_1 for the step from o_2^0 to the required $o_2^{0.5}$ and from this to o_2^1 is estimated. In the example this would be $\Delta o_1 = 7{,}500$, as the following indifference assessments demonstrate:

$$(o_1^{'}, o_2^0) \sim (o_1^{'} - \Delta o_1,\ o_2^{0.5}) \qquad \Rightarrow (42{,}500;\ 800) \sim (35{,}000;\ 1{,}100)$$

$$(o_1^{'}, o_2^{0.5}) \sim (o_1^{'} - \Delta o_1,\ o_2^1) \qquad \Rightarrow (42{,}500;\ 1{,}100) \sim (35{,}000;\ 1{,}300)$$

Therefore, $o_2^{0.5}$ is found at 1,100 and the utility value $u_2(1{,}100)$ is 0.5. As all individual utility values for all outcomes of the three alternatives are now known, a further analysis of the individual utility function u_2 is not required.

From the indifference estimates, the relationship between the weighting factors w_1 and w_2 may also be derived. For the first criterion, the difference between the individual utilities (resulting from the increase from 35,000 to 42,500) is $\Delta u_1 = 0.5$, as shown in Figure 6-12.

Since the variation of Δu_2 (the second criterion's individual utility that is compensated by this difference) is also 0.5, the following applies:

$$\begin{aligned} |\Delta u_2| \cdot w_2 &= |\Delta u_1| \cdot w_1 \\ 0.5 \cdot w_2 &= 0.5 \cdot w_1 \\ w_2 &= w_1 \end{aligned}$$

Therefore, the first and second criteria are weighted identically.

To determine the individual utility function u_3 and its weighting factor w_3 the first criterion is used again. The following indifference estimates may be considered for the outcomes for the first and third criteria:

(53,000; 12) ~ (42,500; 17)

(53,000; 17) ~ (42,500; 25)

This means:

$u_3(17) = 0.5$

The relationship between the weighting factors w_1 and w_3 can now be determined as:

$$\begin{aligned} |\Delta u_3| \cdot w_3 &= |\Delta u_1| \cdot w_1 \\ 0.5 \cdot w_3 &= 0.3 \cdot w_1 \\ w_3 &= 0.6 \cdot w_1 \end{aligned}$$

To determine the individual utility from $o_3 = 15$, which is necessary to assess the first alternative, other indifference assessments must be included:

(47,750; 12) ~ (42,500; 15)

(47,750; 15) ~ (42,500; 17)

Therefore, that individual utility is:

$u_3(15) = 0.25$

Determination of the individual utility function u_4 and the relationship between w_4 and w_1 will not be presented here. It is simply assumed that the relevant value $o_4 = 350$ results in an individual utility $u_4(350)$ of 0.5. The relationship between w_4 and w_1 is: $w_4 = 0{,}4 \cdot w_1$.

All relevant individual utility functions or values are now known. With the help of the standardisation condition:

$$w_1 + w_2 + w_3 + w_4 = 1$$

The weighting factors may be determined as well:

$$w_1 = \frac{1}{3} \qquad w_2 = \frac{1}{3} \qquad w_3 = \frac{1}{5} \qquad w_4 = \frac{2}{15}$$

In the fifth step, the total utility U_M of the alternatives is calculated. The following additive total utility function is used for this:

$$U_M = \frac{1}{3} \cdot u_1(o_1) + \frac{1}{3} \cdot u_2(o_2) + \frac{1}{5} \cdot u_3(o_3) + \frac{2}{15} \cdot u_4(o_4)$$

Finally, by inserting the relevant outcomes for the three alternatives, the following total utilities can be determined. Their comparison shows, that location alternative A_3 is relatively profitable:

Alternatives	A_1	A_2	A_3
Total utilities	9/20	7/15	8/15

Tab. 6-3: Total utilities of the alternatives A_1, A_2 and A_3

Assessment of the method

The MAUT approach is quite similar to utility value analysis and, where an additive total utility function is assumed, it also corresponds in this regard with the AHP. However, MAUT has stronger utility theory foundations and a framework in which individual utility functions and criterion weightings can be determined in a consistent way, taking into account the conditions that must be considered for particular total utility functions. For an additive total utility function these are, as mentioned, the existence of a weak order, interchangeability, and mutual preference independence. Interchangeability of criteria, as shown, suggests that the alternatives are similar. However, this condition can be fully achieved only in the unrealistic case of an unlimited number of alternatives. Furthermore, it is assumed that the relationship between the utility changes leading to a utility balance between two attributes can be quantified.

These are relatively strict conditions, which will not be fulfilled in all decision situations and tend to impose high demands on the decision-maker. Since, in reality, only a limited number of alternatives will be available, interchangeability is usually not possible and the decision-maker may be forced to include hypothetical alternatives in order to find substitution rates.

The requirement for mutual preferential independence (with an additive total utility function) restricts the range of applications for MAUT in comparison to utility value analysis and AHP, as these require less strict independence conditions. Moreover, it is difficult to examine the mutual independence of preferences and this requires considerable effort. In fact, the MAUT can also be applied on a utility theory basis assuming a weaker independence condition, but then other forms of total utility function must be used.

The data collection requirements for MAUT present another particularly serious problem. Individual utility functions and weighting factors must be determined with the help of indifference estimates, and the effort involved is a considerable disadvantage of the procedure.

The relationships between the weightings of the attributes may be interpreted as substitution rates between the scale units of the criteria. However, this assumes the use of an interval scale to measure the individual utility value for all attributes. For qualitative attributes in particular, it is difficult to find a suitable scale. Additionally, it may be difficult to decide which outcomes the individual utility values of 1 and 0 should be assigned to. Apart from the worst and the best outcomes from the set of alternatives (as in the example), other outcomes may also be used for this standardisation, e.g. the best or worst conceivable outcomes, or maximum or minimum outcomes.

A consistency examination of the estimations may also be carried out within MAUT, as shown. The effects of possibly incorrect assessments can be examined with the help of sensitivity analysis. As well, uncertain environmental conditions in the future can be explicitly considered with MAUT, as mentioned, since the procedure was originally developed for uncertain conditions.

Compared with AHP, one advantage of MAUT is that it always leads to a stable ranking of the alternatives.

The MAUT approach represents a utility theory-based method for multi-criteria decision-making. Its theoretical foundation is an advantage over utility value analysis and AHP, but strict conditions and high data collection requirements limit the realisation of that advantage. The method described in the next section, PROMETHEE, requires far less strict conditions.

6.5 PROMETHEE

Description of the method

PROMETHEE (preference ranking organisation method for enrichment evaluations) is one of the so-called *outranking methods* (also called prevalence methods), along with ELECTRE (elimination et choix traduisant la realité) and ORESTE (organisation, rangement et synthèse de données relationelles). These procedures differ from the classic methods of multi-criteria decision-making in their basic assumptions about the decision-maker. In contrast to the classic methods, the outranking procedures' starting point is that a decision-maker does not have access to the information needed to form at least a weak order and make an optimum choice. The classic procedure assumptions that (a) a complete compensation or balancing between the attributes is possible and (b) an unambiguous estimate of the indifference or preference between two alternatives can be made are often unrealistic in multi-criteria problems. The assumptions underpinning outranking procedures differ on these points. Using PROMETHEE, graded preference estimations are permitted when assessing two alternatives, as well as strict preference and indifference judgements. Critical values, which indicate the difference in a criterion outcome at which a preference emerges, can also be included. Incomparability of alternatives caused by an inability to compensate may be considered as well, so often neither strong nor weak orders can be formed and no full ranking can be determined. However, the determination of an optimum alternative is not the purpose of the outranking procedures. Rather, they aim to support problem solving and contribute to identifying suitable alternatives.

To describe differentiated preference situations, the outranking procedures use a graduated relationship, the so-called outranking relationship (or prevalence relationship). This indicates the likelihood π_{ij}, that the decision-maker estimates alternative i to be at least as good as alternative j. It must be formulated for every possible alternative pair. Pair comparisons between the alternatives are, as with the AHP, an essential feature of outranking procedures, so this approach is primarily suited to the assessment of relative profitability.

An evaluation of outranking relationships should help to solve any problem that is defined as the selection, arranging or ordering of alternatives. Since PROMETHEE has been primarily developed to determine rank orders, it aims to do so in the form of so-called *pre-orders,* for some or all alternatives. A pre-order is a specific order to which transitivity must not apply, and via which non-comparable factors can be incorporated.

Another fundamental characteristic of PROMETHEE is the use of *generalised criteria*. These consist of a typical series of so-called preference functions, which indicate the intensity of the preference for one alternative against another regarding a particular criterion. On the basis of the preferences determined using these functions, an outranking relationship and an outranking graph are produced.

This can be illustrated for a multi-criteria problem of the form:

$$\text{Max } \{f_1(A_i), f_2(A_i),..., f_c(A_i),..., f_C(A_i)\} \text{ with: } A_i \in A \tag{6.33}$$

$A = \{A_1,A_2,...,A_i,...,A_I\}$ represents the set of all alternatives and $f_c(A_i)$ represents A in real numbers in each case. Accordingly, $f_c(A_i)$ indicates the cardinally measured outcome of an alternative A_i with regard to the criterion c. This formulation of the multi-criteria problem assumes that all target measures are to be maximised. Therefore, criteria that are minimised must be transformed into a maximisation task (e.g. by multiplying by -1).

In PROMETHEE, a pair-wise comparison of all alternatives takes place for every criterion c. Thus, for an alternative $A_i \in A$, a preference against the alternative $A_j \in A$ can be determined by calculating the difference d_c between the outcomes $f_c(A_i)$ and $f_c(A_j)$ and converting this difference into a preference value using the preference function. For the preference function $p_c(A_i,A_j)$:

$$p_c(A_i,A_j) = p_c(f_c(A_i) - f_c(A_j)) = p_c(d_c(A_i,A_j)) \tag{6.34}$$

The preference value $p_c(A_i,A_j)$ indicates the level of dominance of alternative A_i over alternative A_j in regard to criterion c, and may have values between 0 and 1. For $d_c \leq 0$, i.e. indifference or negative preference of A_i over A_j, a value of 0 is assigned to $p_c(A_i,A_j)$. For a strict preference for A_i over A_j, $p_c(A_i,A_j)$ amounts to 1.

With PROMETHEE it is possible to consider preference estimations (preference intensities) lying anywhere between indifference and strict preference. These are represented by preference values between 0 and 1. The higher the preference value, the more intense the preference: the increased intensity being the result of increasing differences d. The flexible means of assigning preference values p_c to value differences using preference functions is another characteristic of PROMETHEE. Critical values can be included, as mentioned, for indifference and/or preference.

For most practical applications, six typical kinds of preference functions (the 'generalised criteria' mentioned above) are sufficient. Figure 6-13 shows these generalised criteria.

Usual criterion

$$p(d) = \begin{cases} 0, \text{ for } d \le 0 \\ 1, \text{ for } d > 0 \end{cases}$$

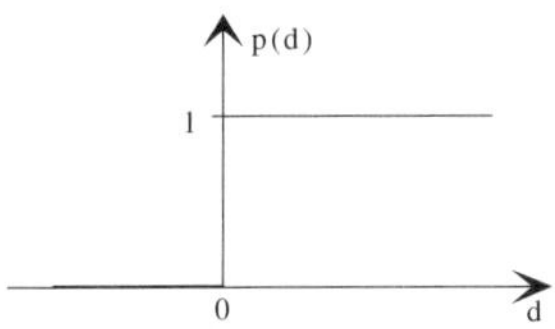

Quasi-criterion

$$p(d) = \begin{cases} 0, \text{ for } d \le q \\ 1, \text{ for } d > q \end{cases}$$

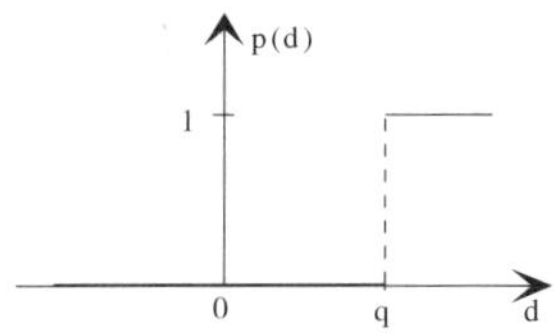

Criterion with linear preference

$$p(d) = \begin{cases} 0, \text{ for } d \le 0 \\ \frac{d}{s}, \text{ for } 0 < d \le s \\ 1, \text{ for } d > s \end{cases}$$

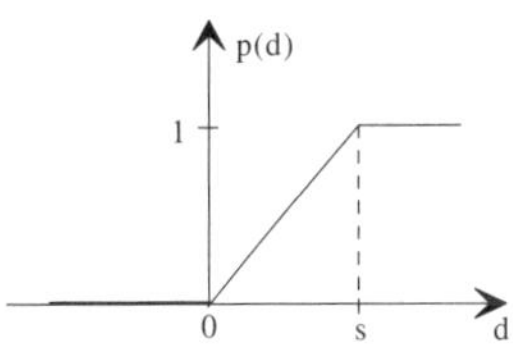

Step-criterion

$$p(d) = \begin{cases} 0, \text{ for } d \le q \\ 0.5, \text{ for } q < d \le s \\ 1, \text{ for } d > s \end{cases}$$

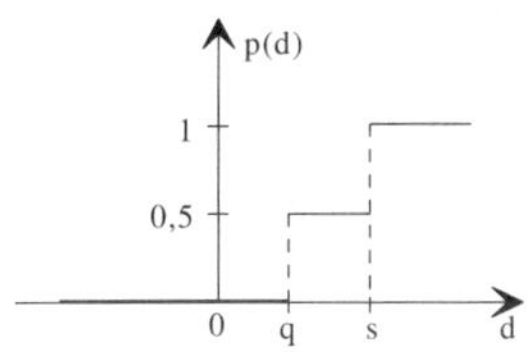

Criterion with linear preference and indifference area

$$p(d) = \begin{cases} 0, \text{ for } d \le q \\ \frac{d-q}{s-q}, \text{ for } q < d \le s \\ 1, \text{ for } d > s \end{cases}$$

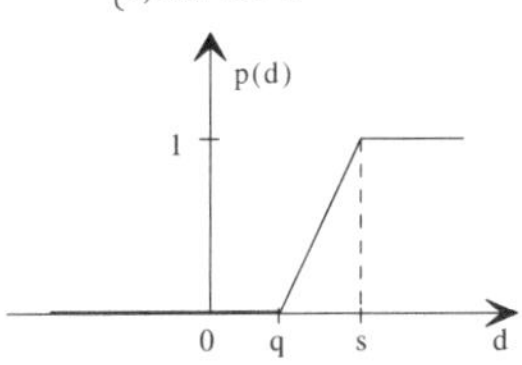

GAUSS-criterion

$$p(d) = \begin{cases} 0, \text{ for } d \le 0 \\ 1 - \exp\left(-\frac{d^2}{2\sigma^2}\right), \text{ for } d > 0 \end{cases}$$

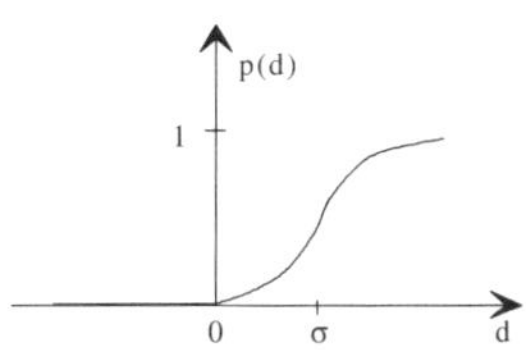

Fig. 6-13: Generalised criteria with PROMETHEE

The *usual criterion* represents the classic case in decision theory, with a strict division between indifference ($p(d) = 0$, if $d \leq 0$ or $f(A_i) \leq (A_j)$) and strict preference ($p(d) = 1$, if $d > 0$ or $f(A_i) > f(A_j)$). The intensity, or degree, of preference is not considered.

The *quasi-criterion* differs from the usual criterion in that it includes a critical value (q) for indifference. This critical value equals the highest value of d at which indifference still exists. Small differences are then irrelevant. Strict preference, with $p(d) = 1$, applies to all values of $d > q$.

For a *criterion with linear preference,* a critical value for preference (s) is included, which represents the smallest value of the difference for which a strict preference exists. In the range between 0 and this critical value, preferences rise linearly, i.e. there is a proportionate relationship between differences and preference intensities.

For a *step-criterion,* critical values are considered for both indifference (q) and preference (s). Differences of $d \leq q$ lead to indifference, differences above s indicate strict preference. In the range between q and s (including s), a weak preference with $p(d) = 0.5$ can be assumed. Alternatively, other preference values between 0 and 1, and more than two gradations, can be included as well.

A *criterion with a linear preference and an indifference area* also uses two critical values. This criterion represents a combination of the two previous criteria. It differs from the step-criterion in that a linear preference function is assumed to exist between the critical values.

Using the *GAUSS-criterion,* preference is strictly increasing with the difference d, beginning at $d = 0$. Even for high values of d, a strict preference ($p(d) = 1$) is not fully reached. With this criterion, a parameter σ, which determines the turning point of the preference function, must be identified. The GAUSSIAN distribution is included in the generalised criteria since the preference function based on it is quite stable, i.e. small changes in σ result in only slight changes in preference.

PROMETHEE is carried out using the following steps:

1. Determination of the target criteria and data collection.
2. Selection of generalised criteria and definition of preference functions.
3. Determination of an outranking relationship.
4. Evaluation of the outranking relationship.

The first step, *definition of the target criteria*, requires a detailed analysis of the target system, as in all multi-criteria methods. After defining the targets, the possible outcomes for the available alternatives must be assigned cardinal numbers with respect to each criterion.

The second step, *selection of generalised criteria and definition of preference functions* is performed for every criterion and includes, if necessary, the specification of the generalised criteria by determining the associated parameters (s, q, σ). This second step implies the assumption that the preference functions accurately reflect the preferences of the decision-maker in regard to the outcomes, or more precisely outcome differences, of each criterion.

To *determine an outranking relationship* (the third step), value differences must be calculated for all criteria and alternative pairs. Then, using the preference functions, the preference values are derived from the value differences. For every pair of alternatives (A_i,A_j) and every criterion *two* preference values are determined: a preference value indicating the preference for A_i against A_j; as well as one indicating the preference for A_j against A_i. One of the two values is always zero.

The relative importance of the criteria must also be fixed in this step. This is achieved using cardinally measured weighting factors w_c for all criteria c. As with other methods, the weighting factors must fulfil the Condition (6.17):

$$\sum_{c=1}^{C} w_c = 1$$

Then, for the preference of every alternative A_i against another A_j, an outranking relationship can be determined using the weighted means of all criteria-specific preference values $p_c(A_i,A_j)$.

$$\pi(A_i, A_j) = \sum_{c=1}^{C} w_c \cdot p_c(A_i, A_j) \tag{6.35}$$

The values of the outranking relationship can be interpreted as preference indications that reflect the level of preference for A_i against A_j. After including all criteria, they can be interpreted similarly to the values $p_c(A_i,A_j)$ for a criterion c, that is $\pi = 0$ indicates indifference and $\pi = 1$ indicates strict preference. Between 0 and 1, the degree of preference rises with increasing values of π. For each alternative pair A_i,A_j, two values of the outranking relationship are determined (as for a single criterion).

The outranking relationships identified may be summarised as a square matrix. The elements of the main diagonal of this matrix represent the values $\pi(A_i,A_i)$ at zero. Alternatively, the outranking relationship may be illustrated in the form of a graph. The nodes of the graph correspond to the alternatives, and the arrows correspond to the values of the outranking relationship between alternatives. Because, for two alternatives A_i and A_j, two outranking values are calculated, the graph contains two arrows between two nodes.

The fourth step of PROMETHEE is the *evaluation of the outranking relationship*. Based on the outranking graph, two flow measures can be determined for every node and every alternative. The outflow measure of a node (F^+) is the sum of the assessments of all arrows (values of the outranking relationship) starting at the node:

$$F_i^+ = \sum_{j=1}^{I} \pi(A_i, A_j), \qquad \text{for all i, i = 1,...,I} \qquad (6.36)$$

It indicates the level of preference for one alternative against all others. The greater it is, the more preferable that alternative.

The inflow measure of a node (F^-) is determined in the same way, as the sum of the estimates of all arrows flowing into the node:

$$F_i^- = \sum_{j=1}^{I} \pi(A_j, A_i), \qquad \text{for all i, i = 1,...,I} \qquad (6.37)$$

The inflow measure shows the extent to which an alternative is dominated by other alternatives. The higher it is, the greater the dominance by other alternatives.

Now, to set up a rank order of alternatives, each alternative is evaluated on the basis of the inflow and outflow measures. A suitable pre-order can be formulated to assess relative profitability. As a basis for this, an entire (pre)order is derived from both measures.

The pre-order resulting from the outflow measures, characterised by the symbols P^+ (preference) and I^+ (indifference), contains the following statements:

A_i is preferred to A_j ($A_i P^+ A_j$), if $F^+(A_i) > F^+(A_j)$

A_i is indifferent to A_j ($A_i I^+ A_j$), if $F^+(A_i) = F^+(A_j)$

Accordingly, a pre-order based on the inflow measures (with the symbols P^- and I^-) may be formed:

A_i is preferred to A_j ($A_i P^- A_j$), if $F^-(A_i) < F^-(A_j)$

A_i is indifferent to A_j ($A_i I^- A_j$), if $F^-(A_i) = F^-(A_j)$

After simultaneous inclusion of outflow and inflow measures, a pre-order of the following form can be produced to assess profitability (with the symbols P, I and U):

A_i is preferred to A_j ($A_i P A_j$),

if ($A_i P^+ A_j$ and $A_i P^- A_j$)

or ($A_i P^+ A_j$ and $A_i I^- A_j$)

or ($A_i I^+ A_j$ and $A_i P^- A_j$)

A_i is indifferent to A_j ($A_i I A_j$),

> if $A_i I^+ A_j$ and $A_i I^- A_j$
>
> A_i and A_j cannot be compared ($A_i U A_j$),
>
> if not $A_i P A_j$ *and* not $A_i I A_j$

If the relationship $A_i P A_j$ is valid, the alternative A_i is clearly preferable to A_j – i.e. 'A_i outranks A_j'. For $A_i I A_j$ the decision-maker is indifferent between these options, and for $A_i U A_j$ the alternatives are not comparable. A pre-order derived in this way is always a so-called *partial pre-order* when the alternatives (U) are not comparable. This is another difference between PROMETHEE and the methods discussed previously.

Example 6-4

Now the MAUT example is reconsidered. As in all outranking procedures, PROMETHEE is particularly suitable for decisions involving many alternatives. Therefore, the example is extended by a further two alternatives (A_4, A_5).

In the first step of PROMETHEE, the determination of target criteria and data collection, the following data are recorded for four target criteria (size of land (S), labour potential (LP), freight carrier (FC) and municipal factor of trade tax (MF)):

Target criteria / **Alternative**	**S**	**LP**	**FC**	**MF**
A_1	60,000	800	15	350
A_2	42,500	1,100	12	250
A_3	35,000	1,300	25	450
A_4	35,000	900	14	300
A_5	40,000	1,000	17	400

Tab. 6-4: Data for the five alternatives

The second step involves selecting generalised criteria and defining preference functions for the four target criteria. Figure 6-14 contains the relevant generalised criteria and preference functions. It is assumed that they reflect the preferences of the decision-maker.

Criterion	**Generalised criterion and preference function**
Size of land (Criterion 1)	Quasi-criterion with parameter q = 5,000 $p_1(d_1) = \begin{cases} 0, \text{ for } d_1 \le 5{,}000 \\ 1, \text{ for } d_1 > 5{,}000 \end{cases}$
Labour potential (Criterion 2)	Step-criterion with parameters q = 50 and s = 200 $p_2(d_2) = \begin{cases} 0, \text{ for } d_2 \le 50 \\ 0.5, \text{ for } 50 < d_2 \le 200 \\ 1, \text{ for } d_2 > 200 \end{cases}$
Freight carrier (Criterion 3)	Criterion with linear preference and indifference area; parameters q = 1 and s = 4 $p_3(d_3) = \begin{cases} 0, \text{ for } d_3 \le 1 \\ \frac{d_3 - 1}{3}, \text{ for } 1 < d_3 \le 4 \\ 1, \text{ for } d_3 > 4 \end{cases}$
Municipal factor of trade tax (Criterion 4)	Criterion with linear preference, parameter s = 100 $p_4(d_4) = \begin{cases} 0, \text{ for } d_4 \le 0 \\ \frac{d_4}{100}, \text{ for } 0 < d_4 \le 100 \\ 1, \text{ for } d_4 > 100 \end{cases}$

Fig. 6-14: Generalised criteria and preference functions in the example

In the third step, the outranking relationship is determined, with the weightings w_c being assigned first. In this example they are:

$$w_1 = 0.3 \qquad w_2 = 0.35 \qquad w_3 = 0.2 \qquad w_4 = 0.15.$$

Substituting into the Formula (6.35) for the value of the outranking relationship $\pi(A_1,A_2)$ for an alternative A_1 compared to alternative A_2:

$$\pi(A_1, A_2) = \sum_{c=1}^{C} w_c \cdot p_c(A_1, A_2)$$

The following is obtained:

$$\pi(A_1, A_2) = 0.3 \cdot p_1(A_1, A_2) + 0.35 \cdot p_2(A_1, A_2) + 0.2 \cdot p_3(A_1, A_2) \\ + 0.15 \cdot p_4(A_1, A_2).$$

By inserting the outcome differences between A_1 and A_2 in the preference functions and, subsequently, transforming the preference values, the following can be determined:

$$\pi(A_1, A_2) = 0.3 \cdot p_1(60{,}000 - 42{,}500) + 0.35 \cdot p_2(800 - 1{,}100) + 0.2 \cdot p_3(15 - 12) + 0.15 \cdot p_4(-350 - (-250))$$

$$\pi(A_1, A_2) = 0.3 \cdot p_1(17{,}500) + 0.35 \cdot p_2(-300) + 0.2 \cdot p_3(3) + 0.15 \cdot p_4(-100)$$

$$\pi(A_1, A_2) = 0.3 \cdot 1 + 0.35 \cdot 0 + 0.2 \cdot \frac{2}{3} + 0.15 \cdot 0$$

$$\pi(A_1, A_2) = 0.43$$

In the same way, the value $\pi(A_2,A_1)$ can be calculated:

$$\pi(A_2, A_1) = 0.3 \cdot p_1(-17{,}500) + 0.35 \cdot p_2(300) + 0.2 \cdot p_3(-3) + 0.15 \cdot p_4(100)$$

$$\pi(A_2, A_1) = 0.3 \cdot 0 + 0.35 \cdot 1 + 0.2 \cdot 0 + 0.15 \cdot 1$$

$$\pi(A_2, A_1) = 0.50$$

The other values of the outranking relationship can be determined in the same way. The matrix in Figure 6-15 shows the entire outranking relationship.

	A_1	A_2	A_3	A_4	A_5	F^+
A_1	0	0.43	0.45	0.30	0.38	**1.56**
A_2	0.50	0	0.45	0.55	0.33	**1.83**
A_3	0.55	0.38	0	0.55	0.55	**2.03**
A_4	0.25	0.07	0.15	0	0.15	**0.62**
A_5	0.24	0.20	0.08	0.31	0	**0.83**
F^-	**1.54**	**1.08**	**1.13**	**1.71**	**1.41**	

Fig. 6-15: The outranking relationship

The fourth step is the evaluation of the outranking relationship. Firstly, flow measures are determined. The outflow measure F^+ results from adding the values of the columns for each alternative; the inflow measure F^- results from summing up the values of the rows (see Figure 6-15). By simultaneously considering outflow and inflow measures, the partial pre-order shown in Figure 6-16 can be formulated.

	A_1	A_2	A_3	A_4	A_5
A_1	x	-	-	A_1PA_4	A_1UA_5
A_2	A_2PA_1	x	A_2UA_3	A_2PA_4	A_2PA_5
A_3	A_3PA_1	A_3UA_2	x	A_3PA_4	A_3PA_5
A_4	-	-	-	x	-
A_5	A_5UA_1	-	-	A_5PA_4	x

Fig. 6-16: The partial pre-order

In the matrix above it can be seen that the alternative A_1 is preferable to A_4 (A_1PA_4, there is: $F_1^+ > F_4^+$ and $F_1^- < F_4^-$); A_2 is preferable to A_1 (A_2PA_1, indicated by: $F_2^+ > F_1^+$ and $F_2^- < F_1^-$). The alternatives A_1 and A_5 are not comparable (A_1UA_5) because: $F_1^+ > F_5^+$ and $F_5^- < F_1^-$.

This result can also be presented in the form of a directional graph. In this graph, the nodes represent the alternatives. An arrow from A_i towards A_j indicates that alternative i is preferable to alternative j. Indifference is expressed by lines without arrows drawn between the nodes. No connection between two nodes signifies a lack of comparability, i.e. no preference can be stated for either alternative.

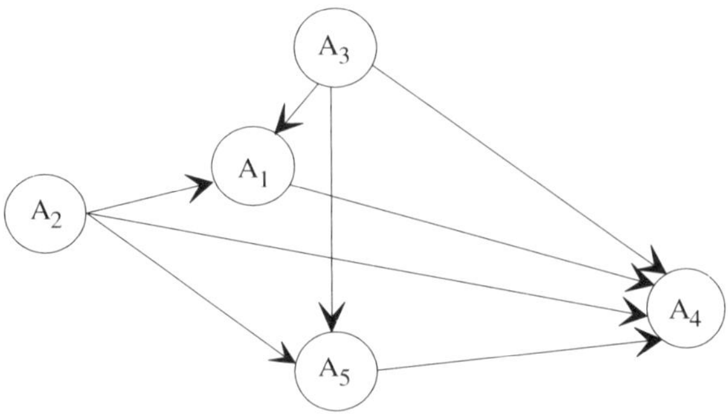

Fig. 6-17: Graphical presentation of the partial pre-order

From this analysis it is obvious that the alternatives A_4, A_1 and A_5 are not relatively profitable (A_4 is dominated by all the other alternatives; A_1 and A_5 are dominated by A_2 and A_3). Accordingly, either A_2 or A_3 should be selected; for these alternatives no preference can be stated, since the diagram shows no connection between the two (indicating a lack of comparability).

Assessment of the method

PROMETHEE (like the other outranking methods) can deal with a lack of comparability and incomplete information. In addition, critical values for preferences and preference intensities can be included in the profitability analysis.

The required computational effort is relatively low, and the data collection slightly simplified by the possibility of using generalised criteria. However, the preference functions, outcomes and weightings must be determined for each criterion. The measurements must be cardinal, which restricts the consideration of qualitative attributes.

The limitation to six generalised criteria, although not compulsory, might also be regarded as a problem. In general, there is doubt as to whether the preferences of the decision-maker can be encapsulated by generalised criteria, preference functions, and value differences (rather than absolute values). Again, the effects of uncertainty may be examined using sensitivity analysis.

In regard to the outranking relationship and the flow measures that form the basis of profitability assessments, it is assumed that target weightings can be assigned on a cardinal scale. The weighted means of all preference values (additive functions) as stated in the outranking relationship are purported to give an adequate comparison of alternatives. This also assumes – similar to the AHP and utility value analysis – that completely independent judgements are being made on each criterion. Using flow measures, it is assumed that preferences over other alternatives (outflow measures) as well as the 'domination' by other alternatives (inflow measures) will enable the formulation of a ranking. One weakness is that, as with the AHP, the pair comparisons depend upon the available alternatives and so the ranking obtained is unstable.

The inclusion of outflow and inflow measures is specific to the method. Due to the inclusion of inflow measures, PROMETHEE only allows limited compensation for unfavourable outcomes.

An order formed with PROMETHEE will reflect the preferences of the decision-maker only if the assumptions described above are fully met. Yet, such a preference statement is not the principal purpose of the procedure. Rather, and this is more important than with the other methods, decision support via preference and problem structuring is the main purpose of the PROMETHEE method.

To conclude the examination of multi-criteria methods, it should be pointed out that they share some similarities, in that they all operate by partitioning a problem. In each method the separate elements and target criteria must be determined and weighted, transformed into individual utility values or comparable values (partial utility values, local priorities, preference values) and, finally, summed taking the individual weightings into account.

Common features of utility value analysis and the AHP are primarily the step sequence and the additive total utility function. The AHP requires more effort, but has the advantage of examining the subjective estimates for consistency.

The MAUT differs from utility value analysis and the AHP in that it has a utility theory foundation and corresponding preconditions. Apart from that, the procedure is very similar to utility value analysis.

The PROMETHEE method has some similarity to the AHP, since it is based on the execution of pair comparisons. However, it offers decision support rather than a procedure for determining an optimum solution. In this regard, it differs from the other methods.

All procedures discussed in this chapter have specific advantages and disadvantages. It is therefore not possible to give a general recommendation for any one procedure; the choice of method depends on the problem being considered. A combination of methods, or elements of methods, may be useful – e.g. the target criteria weighting used with the AHP and MAUT may be applied within the framework of a utility value analysis.

Assessment Material Chapter 6

Exercise 6-1 (Utility Value Analysis)

The copiers in a department are due for renewal. There is a choice between two types of copier that have the same basic technical functions. A financial profitability analysis shows no significant difference between the two. Carry out a utility value analysis with the following list of target criteria:

Target criteria	Criteria weightings	
1. User-friendliness	30%	
1.1. Handling of the operating parts		10%
1.2. Handling of paper loading		10%
1.3. Frequency of faults		50%
1.4. Finding and remedying faults		30%
2. Service from supplier	30%	
2.1. Term of guarantee		30%
2.2. Distance from customer service		30%
2.3. Maintenance performance		40%
3. Quality of copies	40%	
3.1. Copies on paper		60%
3.2. Copies on slides		10%
3.3. Copies on paper when in constant use		30%

Over four weeks of testing, staff members obtain the following results:

Target criteria	Outcomes	
	Copier A	*Copier B*
1.1.	Simple	Simple
1.2.	Moderately simple	Simple
1.3.	3 faults per 1,000 copies	7 faults per 1,000 copies
1.4.	Complicated	Very simple
2.1.	6 months	1 year
2.2.	200 km	10 km
2.3.	Very good	Good
3.1.	Very good	Good
3.2.	Good	Good
3.3.	Satisfactory	Good

Use the following tables to transform the results into partial utility values:

For criteria 1.1, 1.2 and 1.4:

Result	Partial utility values
Very simple	1.00
Simple	0.80
Moderately simple	0.60
Moderately complicated	0.40
Complicated	0.20
Very complicated	0.00

For criterion 1.3:

Result	Partial utility values
Up to 1 fault	1.00
2 – 4 faults	0.80
5 – 4 faults	0.60
9 – 15 faults	0.40
16 – 30 faults	0.20
More than 30 faults	0.00
(per 1,000 copies)	

For criterion 2.1:

Result	Partial utility values
6 months	0.00
1 year	0.50
2 years	1.00

For criterion 2.2:

Result	Partial utility values
0 – 50 km	1.00
51 – 250 km	0.50
More than 250 km	0.00

For criteria 2.3, 3.1, 3.2 and 3.3:

Result	Partial utility values
Unsatisfactory	0.00
Sufficient	0.25
Satisfactory	0.50
Good	0.75
Very good	1.00

a) Prepare the decision using utility value analysis.

b) Describe briefly the various steps of a utility value analysis.

c) What are the assumptions underlying a utility value analysis?

Exercise 6-2 (Analytical Hierarchy Process)

A company would like to use the analytical hierarchy process in planning its strategic investments. There are three strategies (alternatives) to choose from: Strategy A (growth), B (growth combined with a strategic alliance) and C (consolidation). The system of targets consists of three targets: 'company growth' (CG), 'securing the company's independence' (SI) and 'long-term profit maximisation' (LP). It is assumed here that these suffice to meet the requirements demanded of a system of targets within the scope of the AHP (see also Section 6.3).

The decision-makers have given the following assessments, using pair comparisons, of the relative importance of (a) the target criteria and (b) the alternatives:

	SG	**SI**	**LP**
SG	1	1	1/3
SI	1	1	1/3
LP	3	3	1

Tab. 6-5: Pair comparisons for the target criteria

Pair comparisons for the alternative strategies in relation to each target criterion:

	A	B	C
A	1	1	5
B	1	1	5
C	1/5	1/5	1

Tab. 6-6: 'Company growth'

	A	B	C
A	1	3	1/3
B	1/3	1	1/6
C	3	6	1

Tab. 6-7: 'Securing independence'

	A	B	C
A	1	1/3	1
B	3	1	2
C	1	1/2	1

Tab. 6-8: 'Long-term profit maximisation'

a) Determine the weighting vectors of the pair comparison matrices. Are the assessments sufficiently consistent?

b) Calculate the global priority of the alternatives and assess their relative profitability.

c) Assess the AHP in regard to the assumptions made in connection with its application.

Exercise 6-3 (Multi Attribute Utility Theory)

Now, the investment issue in Exercise 6-2 is reconsidered. It is assumed that it is possible to measure 'company growth' in terms of the number of employees (NE), and 'securing independence' in terms of the amount of outside capital required (OC). For these items and for the long-term profit (LP) it is assumed that preferences are mutually preferential independent and that the following data for the three Alternatives A, B and C can be forecasted with certainty.

Alternative	Criterion 1 (NE)	Criterion 2 (OC [€])	Criterion 3 (LP [€ p.a.])
A	15,000	5,000,000	3,000,000
B	12,000	2,500,000	4,000,000
C	10,000	1,000,000	3,200,000

Tab. 6-9: Data for alternatives A, B and C

The following individual utility values were determined for these outcomes of the target criteria:

u_1 (10,000) = 0	u_1 (15,000) = 1
u_2 (5,000,000) = 0	u_2 (1,000,000) = 1
u_3 (3,000,000) = 0	u_3 (4,000,000) = 1

Then, the following indifference assessments were made, in order to ascertain the relevant additional points for each of the functions u_1, u_2 und u_3:

Function u_1:

To determine $o_1^{0.5}$ using the third criterion:

(10,000; 3,200,000) ~ (12,000; 3,000,000)

(12,000; 3,200,000) ~ (15,000; 3,000,000)

Function u_2:

To determine $o_2^{0.5}$ using the third criterion:

(5,000,000; 3,400,000) ~ (3,000,000; 3,000,000)

(3,000,000; 3,400,000) ~ (1,000,000; 3,000,000)

Assume that the function u_2 is linear for the interval $[o_2^{0.5}, o_2^1]$.

Function u_3:

To determine $o_3^{0.5}$ using the first criterion:

(15,000; 3,000,000) ~ (10,000; 3,400,000)

(15,000; 3,400,000) ~ (10,000; 4,000,000)

Once again, assume linearity, here for the interval $[o_3^0, o_3^{0.5}]$.

a) Calculate the total utilities of each of the three alternatives and assess their relative profitability.

b) Discuss the advantages and disadvantages of MAUT.

Exercise 6-4 (PROMETHEE)

Look again at the strategic investment issue in Exercises 6-2 and 6-3. This time, use the PROMETHEE method for decision support. Take as valid all of the alternatives, target criteria and outcomes from Exercise 6-3. Instead of the indifference judgements from 6-3, the following generalised criteria and preference function parameters for the target criteria should be used in decision-making with PROMETHEE.

Number of employees (NE):
Criterion with linear preference, parameter: s = 3,000

Outside capital (OC):
Step-criterion with parameters q = 1,000,000 and s = 2,000,000

Long-term profit (LP):
Step-criterion with parameters q = 100,000 and s = 800,000

a) Determine the preference functions for the criteria.
b) Calculate the outranking relationship, as well as the inflow and outflow measures. In so doing, assume the following weightings: NE: 1/5; OC: 1/5; LP: 3/5.
c) Formulate an order of preference for the alternatives.
d) Discuss the advantages and disadvantages of PROMETHEE.

Chapter 7: Simultaneous Decision-Making Models

Decisions about investment programmes often involve simultaneous choices about types and numbers of investment projects. Additionally, models used for simultaneous decision-making might need to accommodate choices within a range of company areas such as financing, production, sales, human resources and tax policy. In this chapter, the finance and production areas – because of their relevance and close connections with investment decisions – are selected to illustrate ways of supporting investment decision-making in a broader sense than has been discussed previously. In the following sections some models are presented in detail, their practical relevance is discussed, and problems with their practical application are analysed.

First DEAN's model is illustrated, which is used to make a simultaneous choice between various investment and finance projects within a single time period. Thus, it is a *static model*, and it is also *single-tiered*, in that alternatives can be realised at only one point in time (normally the beginning of the planning period). Obviously, these characteristics limit the model's utility as a stand-alone decision support tool. Consequently, a model developed by HAX (1964) and WEINGARTNER (1963): a *multi-tier model* for simultaneous investment and finance decisions spanning multiple periods is also analysed. Concluding the chapter, the (multi-tier) extended model of FÖRSTNER and HENN (1957) is presented as an example of simultaneous investment and production decision-making support.

7.1 Static Model for Simultaneous Investment and Financing Decisions (DEAN Model)

Description of the model

A simultaneous analysis of investment and financing alternatives is usually precipitated by interdependencies between them: i.e. the availability and quality of financing choices might determine the feasibility and profitability of investment projects, and vice versa. Such interdependencies are taken into account in models of simultaneous investment and finance decision-making. Although the static model developed by DEAN is relatively simplistic and, because only one period is considered, of limited applicability in real life investment decision-making, it is explored here as a good illustration of the basic interdependencies between investment and financing decisions, and as a transparent introduction to simultaneous decision-making.

The simultaneous investment and finance decision-making models of DEAN, HAX and WEINGARTNER and others are based on the assumptions that:

- Certainty exists.
- A limited number of investment and financing alternatives are available.
- The investment and financing projects are not mutually exclusive and can be undertaken independently (although indirect relations might exist, for example, in regard to competition for finance).
- Only monetary effects of the investment and financing alternatives are relevant.
- All relevant effects of the investment and financing projects may be assigned to the separate projects as cash inflows and cash outflows, and to periods of discrete and identical time spans.
- Liquidity is a requirement for all the points in time under consideration.
- Tax payments do not affect the profitability of the alternatives.
- The economic life of the investment projects, or the term of the financing projects, is pre-defined.

In addition to these general assumptions, DEAN's model pre-supposes the following:

- The investment and financing projects involve only one time period, with cash flows at the beginning and at the end.
- All projects are completely divisible and may be undertaken in full, or in part up to a predetermined limit.

The objective considered in the model is to maximise the compound value of the total investment and finance programme (consisting of cash inflows from the investment activities less cash outflows from the financing projects) as at the end of the planning period. It is assumed that investment projects have cash inflows (surpluses) at the end of this period while, due to interest and redemption payments, financing projects have cash outflows (negative net cash flows).

At the beginning of the period, funds necessary to execute the investment projects (i.e. the total initial investment outlays) must be supplied by appropriate financing projects, including internal funds (Such funds can be included without explicit interest claims, i.e. using an interest rate of 0%, or using an interest rate derived from the appropriate opportunity cost.).

Mathematically, the model can be formulated using the variables and parameters specified below, as follows:

Variables:

x_j	=	Extent of realising the investment project j (j = 1...,J)
y_i	=	Extent of realising the financing project i (i = 1...,I)

Parameters:		
a_{jt}	=	Net cash flow per unit of the investment project j for the point in time t (t = 0,1)
d_{it}	=	Net cash flow per unit of the financing project i for the point in time t (t = 0,1)

Objective function (related to t = 1):

$$\sum_{j=1}^{J} a_{j1} \cdot x_j \quad + \quad \sum_{i=1}^{I} d_{i1} \cdot y_i \quad \Rightarrow \quad \max! \qquad (7.1)$$

Net cash flows of the investment projects — *Net cash flows of the financing projects*

The sum of the net cash flows resulting from the investment and financing projects is maximised.

The constraints are:

Financing constraint (related to t = 0):

$$\sum_{j=1}^{J} a_{j0} \cdot x_j \quad + \quad \sum_{i=1}^{I} d_{i0} \cdot y_i \quad = \quad 0 \qquad (7.2)$$

Net cash flows of the investment projects — *Net cash flows of the financing projects*

Project constraints:

$0 \le x_j \le 1, \quad$ for j = 1,...,J

$0 \le y_i \le 1, \quad$ for i = 1,...,I

The financing of cash outflows (initial investment outlay for the investment projects) is required at the beginning of the first (and only) period, when the sum of net cash flows from both investment and financing projects must be zero. Limits set, such as the maximum number of investment projects or loans (maximum number of financing projects), must be considered as well. The investment and financing projects can be undertaken in arbitrary fractions of their maxima ($x_j = 1$ or $y_i = 1$).

One way to find the optimum solution of this model is to use a graphical procedure. For this, capital demand and capital supply functions are illustrated in a diagram. The capital demand function indicates, for all available investment projects, the capital required as a function of the cost of capital. Analogously, the capital supply function shows the available capital as a function of interest rates. The point of intersection of the capital supply and capital demand curves indicates the optimum investment and finance programme. Also, the interest rate that is the hurdle rate for both investment and financing projects can be determined – i.e. the model's endogenous interest rate.

Where investments are *not* completely divisible, the optimum solution cannot be determined graphically. If only a limited number of projects is available the solution may be found using an enumeration procedure, otherwise integer linear optimisation methods must be used. The following example illustrates the optimisation for both completely divisible and discrete investment projects.

Example 7-1

Four completely divisible investment and financing projects are available. They are characterised by the following net cash flows (in €'000) a_{jt} or d_{it}:

	Data		**Intermediate results**		
Investment projects	a_{j0}	a_{j1}	**Interest rate (in %)**	**Priority**	**Accumulated capital demand**
IP1	–100.0	113.0	13.0	2	150
IP2	–60.0	66.0	10.0	4	240
IP3	–50.0	58.0	16.0	1	50
IP4	–30.0	33.6	12.0	3	180
Financing projects	d_{i0}	d_{i1}	**Interest rate (in %)**	**Priority**	**Accumulated capital supply**
FP1	25.0	–27.0	8.0	3	105
FP2	60.0	–64.0	$6.\bar{6}$	2	80
FP3	100.0	–120.0	20.0	4	205
FP4	20.0	–21.0	5.0	1	20

Tab. 7-1: Characterisations of the investment and financing projects

The optimisation problem is then expressed as:

Objective function:

$$113\,x_1 + 66\,x_2 + 58\,x_3 + 33{,}6\,x_4 - 27\,y_1 - 64\,y_2 - 120\,y_3 - 21\,y_4 \Rightarrow \max!$$

Constraints:

Financing constraint:

$$-100\,x_1 - 60\,x_2 - 50\,x_3 - 30\,x_4 + 25\,y_1 + 60\,y_2 + 100\,y_3 + 20\,y_4 = 0$$

Project constraints:

$$0 \le x_j \le 1,\ \text{for } j = 1,\dots,4$$
$$0 \le y_i \le 1,\ \text{for } i = 1,\dots,4$$

First, the graphical solution is illustrated. In preparation, the internal rates of return (IRRs) of the investment projects and the effective rates of interest for the financing projects must be calculated, using the following formula:

$$r_j = \left|\frac{a_{j1}}{a_{j0}}\right| - 1 \quad \text{or} \quad r_i = \left|\frac{d_{i1}}{d_{i0}}\right| - 1 \qquad (7.3)$$

Because all projects are divisible, a ranking according to profitability may be derived from the interest rates calculated. With rising interest rates, the profitability of financing projects decreases and that of investment projects increases: i.e. the most profitable financing project is the one with the lowest interest rate, and the most profitable investment project is the one with the highest rate. The internal rates of return and effective rates, as well as the resultant priority rankings, are shown in Table 7-1 above.

This table also shows total capital demand and supply as a function of interest rates. The priority rankings of the investment projects can be used, together with their maximum initial investment outlay, to determine their total capital demand as a function of interest rates. At any loan interest rate greater than 16%, no level of capital demand would be considered, because that rate exceeds the interest potentially receivable from the investments. At a rate of 16%, the decision-maker would be indifferent between investing and not investing in project 3, the most profitable one, because the financing cost equals the rate receivable. With a smaller interest rate, this project would be undertaken. Below an interest rate of 16%, the cumulative capital demand is currently €50,000, which corresponds to the maximum initial investment outlay of investment project 3, since the other investment projects would be rejected. The second priority investment project (project 1) earns an interest rate of 13%, so at this interest rate the total capital demand increases by the initial outlay required to undertake this investment project (€100,000). The cumulative capital demand then becomes €150,000. The other investment projects shape capital demand as a function of interest rates in the same way, and the resulting series can be represented in the capital demand curve shown in Figure 7-1.

By analogy, a curve of capital supply as a function of interest rates can be derived using the maximum loan amounts and effective rates of interest for the financing projects. The capital supply curve obtained in this example is also shown in Figure 7-1.

The optimum investment and financing programme balances capital demand and capital supply. In order to take the priorities of both investment and financing projects into account, investment projects – beginning with the highest priority project – are included in the optimum programme step by step (ranked by priority) as long as their IRRs exceed the interest rates of the financing projects necessary to finance their initial outlays.

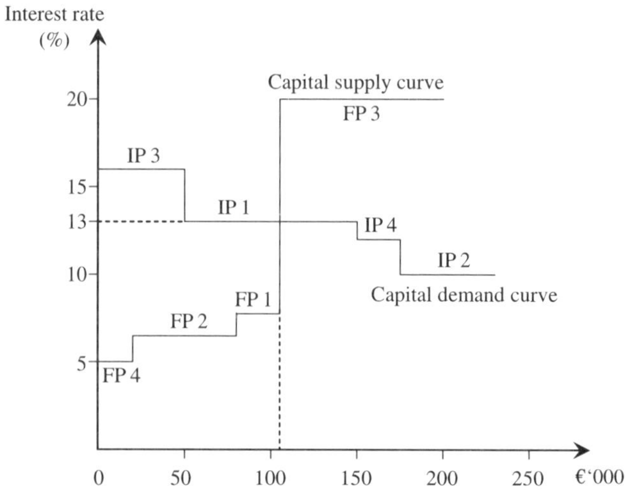

Fig. 7-1: Graphical solution using the DEAN model

This is the case up to the point where the capital supply and demand curves intersect, so the optimum investment programme and financing programme can be determined from this intersection. All investment and financing projects to the left of the intersection can be realised although, commonly, one project – investment or financing – can be undertaken only partially.

In the example given, financing projects 4, 2 and 1, investment project 3, and part of investment project 1 (55/100 or 11/20) comprise the optimum programme. The compound value (CV) of this programme is obtained from the cash flow surpluses of the optimum investment projects less the interest and redemption of the optimum financing projects (at time t = 1) and amounts to (in €'000):

$$CV = \underset{\text{IP 3}}{58} + \underset{\text{IP 1}}{11/20 \cdot 113} - \underset{\text{FP 4}}{21} - \underset{\text{FP 2}}{64} - \underset{\text{FP 1}}{27} = 8.15$$

The interest rate at which the capital demand and supply curves meet can be determined from the diagram: in the example it is 13%. This is the endogenous, or critical, interest rate, which may be used to generate the following rules:

a) Investment projects (financing projects) are undertaken wholly if their interest rates are higher (lower) than the endogenous rate.
b) Investment projects (financing projects) are undertaken partially if their interest rates equal the endogenous rate.
c) Investment projects (financing projects) are not undertaken if their interest rates are lower (higher) than the endogenous rate.

Provided the endogenous rate is known in advance, the optimum programme of financing and investment projects may be derived either from the stated conditions, or by using the net present value (NPV) method. Using the endogenous interest rate as a uniform discount rate, the projects may be assigned to the groups listed above regarding their calculated NPVs. The NPV will be either greater than zero (a), equal to zero (b), or less than zero (c). Incidentally, this example also demonstrates the suitability of the NPV method for decision-making in imperfect capital markets, provided the 'correct' interest rate is known. However, the endogenous interest rate is known only after an optimisation procedure and, therefore, can be used only for assessing additional projects once the original programme has been decided upon.

The assumption of complete divisibility will not be realistic for many investment projects. When projects are necessarily discrete and the graphically determined 'optimum' programme contains a partial investment project, as is the case in the example (investment project 1), this programme cannot be realised. In that case, neither undertaking project 1 in its entirety nor rejecting it will produce an optimal solution. This is because the rate of return of the investment projects, which was used for priority ordering, is no longer the only relevant criterion for programme optimisation. The size of the investment outlay also matters. It might be more profitable to favour an investment project with a lower capital demand over one with a higher rate of return.

As previously noted, the optimum programme may also be determined using either a complete or a limited enumeration. With a limited enumeration, all possible investment programmes, except for those that are obviously unprofitable, are analysed in the following way. For each combination of investment projects, the optimum financing programme is determined on the basis of the previous rank order, such that the sum of inflows and outflows at t = 0 is zero. The total compound value of each combination at t = 1 is then calculated. The programme with the maximum total compound value is optimal. This is illustrated in the following example, which is a continuation of the previous one. Obviously unprofitable investment programmes are ignored. Table 7-2 shows the results of the required calculations.

Investment programme	**Capital demand (€'000)**	**Financing programme**	**Compound value (€'000)**
IP3	50	FP4, 0.5 FP2	5.0
IP1	100	FP4, FP2, 0.8 FP1	6.4
IP3, IP1	150	FP4, FP2, FP1, 0.45 FP3	5.0
IP3, IP4	**80**	**FP4, FP2**	**6.6**
IP3, IP2	110	FP4, FP2, FP1, 0.05 FP3	6.0
IP3, IP4, IP1	180	FP4, FP2, FP1, 0.75 FP3	2.6
IP4, IP1	130	FP4, FP2, FP1, 0.25 FP3	4.6

Tab. 7-2: Compound values of the investment and financing programmes

The optimum in this example, with a compound-value of €6,600, is the combination of investment projects 3 and 4 financed by financing projects 2 and 4.

Assessment of the model

DEAN's model for simultaneous investment and financing decision-making is a relatively simple one and presents no special difficulties for data collection and model solution.

To assess the method's practicability, the reader should refer to comments made on the NPV method (see Chapter 3), with the proviso that the DEAN model does not assume a perfect capital market. However, the fundamental objections to combining 'imperfect capital market' and 'certainty' assumptions expressed in Chapter 4 (concerning the VoFI method) should again be emphasised.

Consumption decisions are largely ignored in this model. If no internal funds are available, or if they are included without interest claims and are, therefore, used to finance investments, the level of consumption is defined at the beginning of the planning period. If, however, interest rates are derived from opportunity costs, the available investment opportunities and alternative financing opportunities determine whether internal funds will be used. Then, assuming the opportunity costs reflect a time preference with regard to consumption, the inclusion of internal funds can be interpreted as a (simplified) integration of the consumption decision into the model.

The assumption that investment and financing projects are independent, and the limitation of a single-period time span, are also problematic. The time span limitation is particularly so, as investments are typically long-term and usually show long-term effects. Differences in the economic life of the investment and financing projects often occur, and misleading rankings can result. Moreover, future investment and financing opportunities are completely ignored where only a single term is considered. A more accurate solution to the simultaneous decision-making problem may be achieved using the following dynamic model.

7.2 Multi-Tier Model of Simultaneous Investment and Financing Decisions (HAX and WEINGARTNER Model)

Description of the model

The multi-tier model for simultaneous investment and financing decisions described in this section was developed by both HAX and WEINGARTNER independently, in almost identical form. Most of the assumptions underlying DEAN's model apply to this model also. However, unlike DEAN's model, the HAX and WEINGARTNER model is *multi-tier* in that the investment and financing projects considered may commence at different times.

The objective included in the model is, again, to maximise the compound value of the total investment and financing programme. It is assumed that any investment project surpluses earned before the end of the planning period are reinvested in a one-year financial investment at a given interest rate. Thus, a uniform discount rate is not required in this model. At the beginning of each time period within the planning period, a liquidity constraint is formulated to ensure that cash inflows and outflows are balanced. In addition, it is assumed that investment and financing projects can be executed repeatedly, but that investment projects are indivisible, or discrete. The cash flow profiles of the investment and financing projects are assumed to be independent of their size, i.e. the interest rate for a loan (financing project) is independent of the total sum borrowed.

The HAX and WEINGARTNER model can be expressed in mathematical form using the variables and parameters specified below. Investment and financing projects are sequentially numbered, but without index references to periods. An exception to this is the short term financial investment which is labelled Jt.

Variables:		
x_j	=	Number of units of investment project type j (j = 1,...,J–1)
x_{Jt}	=	Amount of the short term financial investment (in €) at time t (t = 0,…,T–1 or T)
y_i	=	Extent of financing project type i (in €) for i = 1,...,I
Parameters:		
a_{jt}	=	Cash outflow surplus per unit of the investment project j (j = 1,...,J–1) at time t (t = 0,1,...,T)
d_{it}	=	Cash outflow surplus per unit (€) of the financing project i at time t
IF_t	=	Internal funds at time t
X_j	=	Maximum number of units of investment project j (j = 1,...,J–1)
Y_i	=	Maximum amount of financing project i (i = 1,...,I)
c	=	Interest rate for the short term financial investment

The objective 'maximisation of the compound value (CV)' may be incorporated into the model in different ways. In the following formula, the cash flows of the last period constitute the objective function explicitly.

$$CV = \underbrace{IF_T}_{\text{Internal funds}} - \underbrace{\sum_{j=1}^{J-1} a_{jT} \cdot x_j}_{\text{Cash outflow surpluses of the investment projects}} - \underbrace{\sum_{i=1}^{I} d_{iT} \cdot y_i}_{\text{Cash outflow surpluses of the financing projects}}$$

$$+ \underbrace{(1+c) \cdot x_{JT-1}}_{\text{Compounded short-term financial investment at the previous point in time}} \Rightarrow \max! \qquad (7.4)$$

The compound value represents the surplus at the end of the programme planning period. Cash inflow surpluses in earlier points in time are transformed into a short-term financial investment. Accordingly, the compound value may be interpreted as a hypothetical short-term financial investment at time T.

If a variable x_{JT} and a liquidity constraint at time T are integrated into the model, then the objective function can be formulated as follows:

$$CV = x_{JT} \Rightarrow \quad \max!$$

Constraints:

Liquidity constraints:

For t = 0:

$$\underbrace{\sum_{j=1}^{J-1} a_{j0} \cdot x_j}_{\textit{Cash outflow surpluses of the investment projects}} + \underbrace{\sum_{i=1}^{I} d_{i0} \cdot y_i}_{\textit{Cash outflow surpluses of the financing projects}} + \underbrace{x_{J0}}_{\textit{Short-term financial investment}} = \underbrace{IF_0}_{\textit{Internal funds}} \qquad (7.5)$$

For t = 1,...,T:

$$\underbrace{\sum_{j=1}^{J-1} a_{jt} \cdot x_j}_{\textit{Cash outflow surpluses of the investment projects}} + \underbrace{\sum_{i=1}^{I} d_{it} \cdot y_i}_{\textit{Cash outflow surpluses of the financing projects}}$$

$$+ \underbrace{x_{Jt}}_{\textit{Short-term financial investment}} - \underbrace{(1+c) \cdot x_{JT-1}}_{\textit{Compounded short-term financial investment in the previous period}} = \underbrace{IF_t}_{\textit{Internal funds}} \qquad (7.6)$$

At t = 0, and throughout the planning period, cash outflow surpluses must at no time exceed the internal funds, i.e. illiquidity must be avoided. This is ensured by the mathematical formulation of the liquidity constraints and, additionally, by the further constraint that the short term financial investments must not be negative ($x_{Jt} \geq 0$). However, the balance of the internal financial funds (parameter IF_t) can become negative if the company managers intend to withdraw funds from the investment and financing programme (in order to make funds available for other parts of the company or the owners).

Project restrictions:

$$x_j \leq X_j, \qquad \text{for } j = 1,...,J-1$$

$$y_i \leq Y_i, \qquad \text{for } i = 1,...,I$$

$x_j \geq 0$ and integer, for j = 1,...,J–1
$x_{Jt} \geq 0,$ for t = 0,...,T–1
$y_i \geq 0,$ for i = 1,...,I

The number of units of investment projects j (j = 1,...,J–1) and the amounts of financing projects i (in €) may not be negative, nor may they exceed the (given) maximum limits. In addition, all investment projects are discrete, or indivisible.

The optimum solution of the HAX and WEINGARTNER model may be calculated using integer linear programming. Where investment projects are divisible, other useful information may be derived from the optimum solution in the form of endogenous interest rates. This is illustrated in the following example.

Example 7-2

The following table shows the cash flow profiles of investment projects 1–7 and financing projects 1–3. Two investment projects are started at time t = 1 (investment projects 6 and 7), i.e. this is a multi-tier example.

Investment projects may be undertaken up to the following maximum numbers: 5 (investment project 1), 4 (investment project 2), 2 (investment project 4), 3 (investment project 5), and 4 (investment project 6). Investment projects 3 and 7 are unrestricted. Maximum loans are €500,000 (financing project 1), €600,000 (financing project 2) and €100,000 (financing project 3), and the short term financial investment used for reinvesting surpluses earns an interest rate of 8% over the planning period.

	Net cash flows at times			
Investment projects	t = 0	t = 1	t = 2	t = 3
Investment project 1:	–90,000	45,000	40,000	40,000
Investment project 2:	–45,000	24,000	23,000	24,000
Investment project 3:	–80,000	35,000	35,000	40,000
Investment project 4:	–170,000	75,000	80,000	85,000
Investment project 5:	–100,000	40,000	50,000	50,000
Investment project 6:	0	–240,000	160,000	160,000
Investment project 7:	0	–160,000	92,000	96,000
Financing projects				
Financing project 1:	1	0	0	–1.481544
Financing project 2:	1	0	0	–1.404928
Financing project 3:	0	1	-0.12	–1.12

Tab. 7-3: Net cash flows of the investment and financing projects

The model for this example consists of:

Objective function:

$x_{83} \Rightarrow \max!$

Constraints:

Liquidity constraints:

t = 0: $90{,}000x_1 + 45{,}000x_2 + 80{,}000x_3 + 170{,}000x_4 + 100{,}000x_5 - y_1 - y_2 + x_{80} = 50{,}000$

t = 1: $-45{,}000x_1 - 24{,}000x_2 - 35{,}000x_3 - 75{,}000x_4 - 40{,}000x_5 + 240{,}000x_6 + 160{,}000x_7 - y_3 - 1.08x_{80} + x_{81} = 0$

t = 2: $-40{,}000x_1 - 23{,}000x_2 - 35{,}000x_3 - 80{,}000x_4 - 50{,}000x_5 - 160{,}000x_6 - 92{,}000x_7 + 0{,}12y_3 - 1.08x_{81} + x_{82} = 0$

t = 3: $-40{,}000x_1 - 24{,}000x_2 - 40{,}000x_3 - 85{,}000x_4 - 50{,}000x_5 - 160{,}000x_6 - 96{,}000x_7 + 1.481544y_1 + 1.404928y_2 + 1.12y_3 - 1.08x_{82} + x_{83} = 0$

Project constraints:

$x_1 \leq 5$
$x_2 \leq 4$
$x_4 \leq 2$
$x_5 \leq 3$
$x_6 \leq 4$
$y_1 \leq 500{,}000$
$y_2 \leq 600{,}000$
$y_3 \leq 100{,}000$
$x_j \geq 0$ and integer, for $j = 1,\ldots,7$
$y_i \geq 0$, for $i = 1,2,3$
$x_{8t} \geq 0$, for $t = 0,1,2$

The optimum solution of the model is:

$x_1 = 5$	$x_2 = 4$	$x_3 = 0$	$x_4 = 2$	$x_5 = 0$	$x_6 = 3$	$x_7 = 0$
$x_{80} = 137{,}962.96$	$x_{81} = 0$	$x_{82} = 920{,}000$	$x_{83} = 306{,}150.92$			
$y_1 = 457{,}962.96$	$y_2 = 600{,}000$	$y_3 = 100{,}000$				

This resulting optimum solution is, therefore, to invest in five units of investment project 1, four units of investment project 2, two units of investment project 4 and three units of investment project 6. Loans 1, 2 and 3 should be taken out in the following amounts: €457,962.96, €600,000 and €100,000 (i.e. loans 2 and 3 are used to their maximum value). At times $t = 0$, $t = 2$ and $t = 3$ short-term financial investments are recommended in the amounts of €137,962.96, €920,000 and €306,150.92 respectively. The financial investment at $t = 3$ (x_{83}) is identical to the objective function, i.e. the compound value that is maximised in the optimum programme.

In the following calculation, the liquidity constraint at $t = 0$ is presented with the various outcomes of the optimum solution. The cash flow surplus is invested at this point as a short-term financial investment:

$$t = 0: \quad 90{,}000 \cdot 5 + 45{,}000 \cdot 4 + 80{,}000 \cdot 0 + 170{,}000 \cdot 2 + 100{,}000 \cdot 0 - 457{,}962.96 - 600{,}000 + x_{80} = 50{,}000$$

$$\Rightarrow x_{80} = 137{,}962.96$$

At time $t = 1$ there is a particularly high capital demand owing to the initial investment outlays for three investment projects of type $j = 3$. Thus, the short-term financial investment realised is relinquished and an excessive loan is taken out at the beginning of the planning period (identifiable from the positive value of the short-term financial investment at $t = 0$).

Where investment projects are divisible, the optimum solution of a HAX and WEINGARTNER model allows the derivation of endogenous interest rates. In this example, the following optimum solution is obtained:

$x_1 = 5$	$x_2 = 4$	$x_3 = 0$	$x_4 = 2$	$x_5 = 1.8$	$x_6 = 2.68$	$x_7 = 0$
$x_{80} = 0$	$x_{81} = 0$		$x_{82} = 958{,}666.70$		$x_{83} = 324{,}297.87$	
$y_1 = 500{,}000$		$y_2 = 600{,}000$			$y_3 = 100{,}000$	

In decision problems involving divisible investment projects, useful information about scarce resources may be gained from the optimum solution. Opportunity costs or shadow prices can be identified that indicate changes in the objective function caused by easing the constraints. With the HAX and WEINGARTNER model, the shadow prices of liquidity constraints are particularly interesting.

Key Concept:

The shadow price of the liquidity constraint at time t indicates the increase in the value of the objective function (i.e. the compound value) that would result from an additional unit of financing (from internal funds) becoming available.

This value may be interpreted as an endogenous compounding factor indicating how an additional monetary unit, made available at time t, yields interest up to time T.

The value of the model endogenous compounding factor depends on the alternatives considered in the model and their effects. In the example, the model endogenous compounding factors q_t^* are:

$$q_0^* = 1.5947, \quad q_1^* = 1.3867, \quad q_2^* = 1.08 \quad \text{and} \quad q_3^* = 1$$

From these model endogenous compounding factors, model endogenous interest rates may be derived, which indicate the endogenous rates of interest for each period. The relationships between the model endogenous compounding factors q_t^* and the model endogenous interest rates i_t^* for the current example are illustrated as follows:

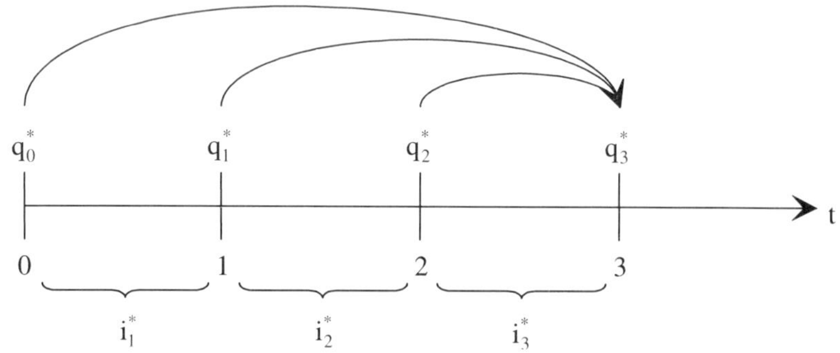

Fig. 7-2: Relationships between the model endogenous compounding factors and the model endogenous interest rates

The model endogenous compounding factor at time t is the product of all model endogenous compounding factors related to the individual periods from time t to the end of the planning period. The compounding factor relevant to a period is the sum of 1 plus the model endogenous interest rate for that period. Therefore, for the model endogenous compounding factor q_t^*, the following applies:

$$q_t^* = \prod_{\tau=t+1}^{T} (1+i_\tau^*) \tag{7.7}$$

Model endogenous compounding factors are derived from optimum solutions of linear optimisation problems. From these factors, the model endogenous interest rates may be calculated by changing the equation above. This is demonstrated for the example given in the following:

$$q_2^* = 1 + i_3^* \qquad \Rightarrow \qquad i_3^* = q_2^* - 1 = 0.08$$

$$q_1^* = (1+i_2^*)\cdot(1+i_3^*) = (1+i_2^*)\cdot q_2^* \qquad \Rightarrow \qquad i_2^* = \frac{q_1^*}{q_2^*} - 1 = 0.2840$$

$$q_0^* = (1+i_1^*)\cdot(1+i_2^*)\cdot(1+i_3^*) = (1+i_1^*)\cdot q_1^* \qquad \Rightarrow \qquad i_1^* = \frac{q_0^*}{q_1^*} - 1 = 0.15$$

The interest rate in the second period (28.4%) is particularly high: this is the result of high demands from the investment projects at time t = 1, as discussed above for the model stipulating investment project indivisibility. The endogenous interest rate for the third period (8%) equals the interest rate of the short-term financial investment, because at t = 2 no other investment opportunities exist.

Model endogenous interest rates may be used to assess single investment and financing projects separately. If these interest rates are used as uniform discount rates for calculating the NPVs of the separate projects (as in the DEAN model), the following relationships may be stated:

a) Investment or financing projects with an NPV greater than zero are undertaken to their maxima in an optimum programme.
b) Investment or financing projects with an NPV of zero are usually undertaken only partially in an optimum programme, i.e. not to their maxima.
c) Investment or financing projects with an NPV of less than zero are not included in an optimum programme.

If the endogenous interest rates were known, no optimisation of a simultaneous model would be needed. However, they are derived only as the result of an optimisation and, therefore, the application of endogenous interest rates (as uniform discount rates) is useful only for assessing additional projects considered once the optimum programme has already been determined.

In the example, it is now assumed that an additional investment project 9 becomes available. It has the following cash flow profile:

Times	t = 0	t = 1	t = 2	t = 3
Net cash flows	–10,000	4,000	4,500	5,000

Tab. 7-4: Cash flow profile for investment project 9

Utilising the endogenous interest rates determined above as uniform discount rates, the NPV of this additional investment project can be calculated:

$$c_9 = -€10{,}000 + \frac{€4{,}000}{1.15} + \frac{€4{,}500}{1.15 \cdot 1.284} + \frac{€5{,}000}{1.15 \cdot 1.284 \cdot 1.08}$$

$$c_9 = -€338.87$$

Because of its negative NPV, investment project 9 should not be included in the programme; the calculated optimum would be unaffected by this additional investment opportunity.

Additionally, the guidelines given in Section 3.6, for determining upper and lower bounds for the interest rates of investment and financing opportunities, can also be applied to assessing investment and financing projects separately within a simultaneous investment and financing decision process. It should be possible to define an interval within which the endogenous interest (or discount) rate falls, so that a range of possible NPV results for investment and financing projects can be calculated. Using this approach, it is easy to identify investment and financing projects which are definitely profitable (positive NPV at the upper limit for an investment and at the lower limit for a financing project) or definitely unprofitable (negative NPV at the opposite limits). Only the remaining projects would then require a model for simultaneous decision-making.

Model assessment and model extensions

The HAX and WEINGARTNER model requires the collection of data on forecasted project cash flow profiles, maximum numbers of projects, and internal funds.

Determining the optimum solution may – depending on the number of variables and periods under consideration – be difficult, particularly where the investment projects are indivisible. This has motivated the development of heuristic solution procedures for simultaneous investment and financing decisions; these also rely in part on knowing endogenous interest rates. While heuristic procedures might not always determine the optimum result, they will usually find acceptable solutions with relatively little computational effort. Nevertheless, improvements in computer resources have greatly improved the potential for solving integer linear optimisation problems.

A fundamental criticism of the HAX and WEINGARTNER model that should be emphasised is the combination of 'imperfect capital market' and 'certainty' assumptions.

Because of the model's multi-tier structure, interdependencies between investment and financing opportunities in different periods may be included in the analysis. Therefore, the optimum investment timing may be determined using the model.

Short-term financial investments that yield different rates of interest in different periods (or an interest rate of 0%, i.e. keeping surpluses as cash) may also be included. Alternative short- or long-term investments with divergent interest rates, and alternative short-term loans, can be accommodated as well.

Withdrawals may be interpreted as payments the company receives from the investment and financing programme. They can be included either as nominated amounts of (negative) internal funds, or as periodic withdrawals from the investment and financing programme that must be maximised. This approach requires a pre-set level for both the compound value and the desired cash withdrawal pattern. The objective then consists of the one variable to be maximised – the withdrawal level. The desired cash withdrawal pattern is taken into account by multiplying time-specific factors (which express the demand for cash at a specific point in time) by the withdrawal level, and integrating the products into the liquidity constraints.

Thus, consumption decisions can be integrated into the model (in a simplified form) either by nominating withdrawal amounts, or by maximising the withdrawal flow.

To accommodate more realistic scenarios, the project conditions might need to be modified, e.g. where multiple iterations of a project are not possible and/or investment projects (particularly financial investment projects) are divisible.

The analyses in this chapter have assumed that the last relevant cash flows occur at the end of the planning period. However, defining the planning period itself represents an additional decision problem for the analyst. This problem is exacerbated if a project's cash flows occur in the relatively distant future, in which case the planning period must be extended to incorporate the last cash flow. An alternative approach would be to choose a shorter planning period and discount the cash flows that arise beyond it. In that case, the following objective function is maximised:

$$x_{JT} - \sum_{t=T+1}^{\hat{T}} \left(\sum_{j=1}^{J-1} a_{jt} \cdot x_j + \sum_{i=1}^{I} d_{it} \cdot y_i \right) \cdot q^{-t+T} \Rightarrow \max! \qquad (7.8)$$

With:

q^{-t+T} = Discounting factor for time t

$\hat{T}$ = The time at which the last cash flow occurs

As with all models of simultaneous investment and financing decisions, the assumptions indicated above (certainty of the model data, independence of the projects, exclusion of non-monetary effects, the ability to allocate the effects to specific projects and periods, irrelevance of tax payments, nominated production programme and economic life etc.) may not apply in reality. Also questionable is the assumption that the cash flow profiles of investment and financing projects are independent of the number of projects undertaken. In addition, since cash flows are allocated at the beginning or end of each period, liquidity can only be assured for those points in time, and not for in-between periods. Therefore some financing decisions, despite their connections to decisions illustrated here, must be made outside the model. In practice, it is advisable to check the extent to which such divergences between reality and the model's assumptions might impact on the profitability of projects.

Some of the assumptions of the model can be avoided by modifying its formulation. This would make it possible, for example:

- To allow project interdependence.
- To accommodate balance sheet structures.
- To integrate tax payments into the model.
- To include different economic lives for investment projects and/or terms for financing projects within the model.

At this point, it should be noted that the model assumes centralised decision-making about investment and financing projects. However, the complexity resulting from centralised decision-making, together with possible problems with information transfer and the motivation of managers in decentralised company units, may create the need to decentralise decision-making processes. With decentralisation, the use of mathematical decomposition procedures, transfer prices and investment budgeting may become necessary in order to coordinate investment and financing activities. Also, managers in decentralised units might not, owing to goal conflicts or to asymmetric distribution of information, make decisions that are in the best interests of the company. To deal with this problem, incentive systems are often used.

Up to this point, production decisions have been assumed to be a given. In the following section this premise is discarded in order to consider decisions about production alongside investment programme decisions.

7.3 Multi-Tier Model of Simultaneous Investment and Production Decisions (Extended FÖRSTNER and HENN Model)

Description of the model

Models for simultaneous investment and production decisions analyse the following types of interdependency:

- The profitability of investment projects as a function of the production programme (i.e. the types and numbers of products produced).
- Investment in increased production capacity as an essential condition for a production programme decision.

To consider these interdependencies, product variables that indicate how many units of a product type will be produced are now introduced. Cash flows are also allocated to these variables, and the capacity used by the variables (or the products they represent) is incorporated into capacity constraint formulae.

The extended FÖRSTNER and HENN model described in this section is a linear optimisation model. Similar to the models for simultaneous investment and financing decisions, the following assumptions apply:

- There is no uncertainty concerning the model data.
- A limited number of suitable investment and production alternatives is available.
- The investment and production alternatives are not mutually exclusive and each may be undertaken independently (although indirect relationships might exist – for example, investment projects might compete with each other for scarce funds, or they might be designed to increase production capacity).
- Only the monetary effects of the investment and production alternatives are relevant.

- All effects relevant to the investment and production alternatives can be assigned to the relevant projects as cash inflows and outflows, and to the relevant periods (which are discrete and of identical length). All relevant effects from other areas of the company are recorded in these cash inflows.
- All relationships between variables and their effects are linear (for example, cash inflows are proportionate to the levels of production).
- A production process with more than one production step is assumed, and Capacity demands per unit can be allocated to products at every production step.
- The order in which products are manufactured has no influence on cash outflows and capacity demands.
- No storage is necessary, i.e. production volumes correspond to sales volumes.
- Solvency must be maintained for all periods under consideration.
- The financing programme is pre-set.

The FÖRSTNER and HENN model for making simultaneous investment and production decisions is derived from the basic model for a production programme decision. This is described briefly next. The specific production situation is illustrated in Figure 7-3 assuming the existence of two product types and three production facilities (i.e. machines).

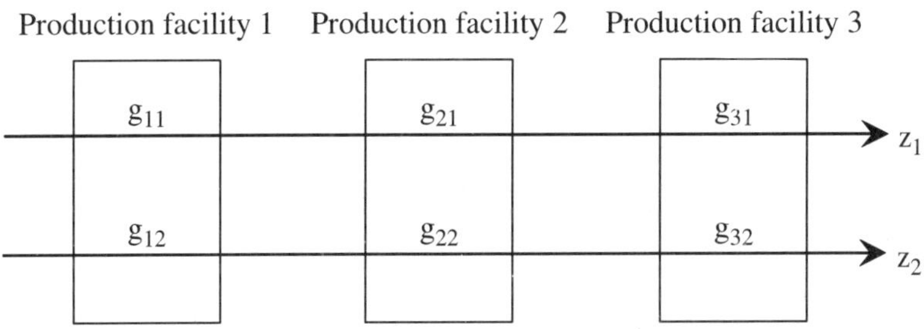

Fig. 7-3: Production structure in the basic model for a production programme decision

Products pass through three production facilities j (j = 1,2,3), and for every unit of a product k (k = 1,2) there is a specific and constant capacity requirement g_{jk}. This unit-related capacity requirement, the so-called production coefficient, is known. Also known are: the available capacity (in units) for each machine; the per unit variable costs for each product; and product prices (which are independent of sales volumes). The production volumes z_k are identical to the sales volumes – i.e. products are not stored.

The basic model is a static one, and the ultimate objective is to maximise profits. Restrictions result from machine capacity limits and, for obvious reasons, production volumes cannot be negative.

The FÖRSTNER and HENN model extends this basic model by removing one of its crucial assumptions: the fixed capacity of the production machines or facilities. Investment variables are introduced to indicate the extent to which the capacity can be raised.

In this Section 7.3, an extended version of the FÖRSTNER and HENN model is described. In contrast to the original model, it incorporates cash flows from product sales within the liquidity constraints. Moreover, cash outflows resulting from the investment projects are included.

The objective is to maximise compound value. Surpluses from a period may be reinvested in unlimited amounts as short-term, single-period financial investments, as in the HAX and WEINGARTNER model. Thus, a uniform discount rate is unnecessary. It is assumed that the economic lives of the investment projects purchased (here, production machines) are fixed. Liquidation values are taken into account at the end of the economic life and/or planning period.

In a multi-tier model, decisions (about investment and production) and the consequences resulting from them (cash inflows and outflows, creation and use of capacities) must be assigned to specific points in time. The following model assumes that:

- Investment projects' initial outlays, resultant cash flows and capacity increases occur at time t exactly (i.e. the beginning of period t + 1).
- Production and sales volumes for the period t + 1 are assigned at time t. The associated machine capacity demand occurs at time t, but production and sales do not result in product-related cash inflows and outflows until time t + 1.
- The liquidation values of investment projects become payable at either the end of the economic life, or the end of the planning period (if the end of the economic life is not reached within the planning period).

In formulating the model, the following variables and parameters are used:

Variables:

x_{jt}	=	Number of production machines of type j (j = 1,...,J–1), purchased at time t (t = 0,…,T–1)
z_{kt}	=	Production volume of product k (k = 1,...,K), assigned at time t (t = 0,...,T–1)
x_{Jt}	=	Short term financial investment at time t (t = 0,...,T–1)

Parameters:

p_{kt}	=	Price of a unit of product k, produced at time t
a_{vkt}	=	Variable cash outflow per unit of product k, produced at time t
$I_{fjt\tau}$	=	Fixed cash outflow at time t for production machine of type j, purchased at the point in time τ ($\tau = -T^*, -T^*+1, \ldots, 0, \ldots, T$) (If a machine of this type exists at the beginning of the planning period, $-T^*$ is the time at which the oldest machine was purchased.)

$x_{j\tau}$	=	Number of machines of type j purchased at time τ, for $\tau < 0$ (this data is known with certainty when formulating the model)
X_{jt}	=	Maximum number of machines of type j that can be purchased at time t
I_{0jt}	=	Initial investment outlay for a machine of type j bought at time t
$\hat{L}_{jt}$	=	Liquidation value per machine of type j bought at time t, which is received at the end of the planning period
$L_{j\tau}$	=	Liquidation value for one machine of type j purchased at time τ at the end of its economic life
$u_{jt\tau}$	=	Parameter indicating whether a machine of type j purchased at time τ has reached the end of its economic life at time t. If so, the parameter has the value of one; otherwise its value is zero
c	=	Interest rate for the short term financial investment
g_{jkt}	=	Capacity demand of machine j per unit of product k whose production is assigned at time t
$G_{jt\tau}$	=	Capacity of a machine of type j purchased at time τ related to time t
Z_{kt}	=	Maximum sales volume of the product k related to time t
IF_t	=	Available internal funds at time t

The model can be formulated as follows:

Objective function (related to the point in time T): (7.9)

$$x_{JT-1} \cdot (1+c) \quad + \quad \sum_{k=1}^{K} z_{kT-1} \cdot (p_{kT-1} - a_{vkT-1}) + \sum_{j=1}^{J-1} \sum_{\tau=-T^*}^{T-1} \hat{L}_{j\tau} \cdot x_{j\tau} \Rightarrow \max!$$

Compounded short-term financial investment of the previous period — *Cash inflow surpluses due to product-related payments* — *Cash inflows due to the liquidation of equipment at the end of the planning period*

Liquidity constraints: (7.10)

$$\sum_{j=1}^{J-1} x_{jt} \cdot I_{0jt} \quad + \quad \sum_{j=1}^{J-1} \sum_{\tau=-T^*}^{t} I_{fjt\tau} \cdot x_{j\tau} \quad - \sum_{k=1}^{K} z_{kt-1} \cdot (p_{kt-1} - a_{vkt-1})$$

Initial investment outlays — *Equipment-dependent cash outflows* — *Cash inflow surpluses due to product-related payments*

$$- \sum_{j=1}^{J-1} \sum_{\tau=-T^*}^{t-1} L_{j\tau} \cdot x_{j\tau} \cdot u_{jt\tau} \quad - \quad x_{Jt-1} \cdot (1+c) \quad + \quad x_{Jt} \quad = \quad IF_t$$

Cash inflows due to the liquidation of equipment, that has reached the end of its economic life — *Compounded short-term financial investment of the previous period* — *Short-term financial investment* — *Available internal funds*

At all times t (t = 0,...,T-1) the company must remain solvent.

Capacity constraints:

$$\underbrace{\sum_{k=1}^{K} g_{jkt} \cdot z_{kt}}_{\textit{Use of capacity}} \leq \underbrace{\sum_{\tau=-T^*}^{t} G_{jt\tau} \cdot x_{j\tau}}_{\textit{Available capacity}} \qquad (7.11)$$

Capacity demands on all investment projects j (j = 1,...,J-1) and at all times t (t = 0,...,T-1) must not exceed their available capacities.

Sales constraints:

$$\underbrace{z_{kt}}_{\textit{Volume of sales}} \leq \underbrace{Z_{kt}}_{\textit{Maximum volume of sales}} \qquad (7.12)$$

At all times t (t = 0,...,T–1) and for all products k (k = 1,...,K) the maximum sales volumes must not be exceeded.

Project constraints:

$x_{jt} \leq X_{jt}$, for j = 1,...,J–1; t = 0,...,T–1

$x_{jt} \geq 0$ and integer, for j = 1,...,J–1; t = 0,...,T–1

$x_{Jt} \geq 0$, for t = 0,...,T–1

$z_{kt} \geq 0$, for k = 1,...,K; t = 0,...,T–1

Example 7-3

In the following example, a simultaneous investment and production programme decision is required to cover three periods. The company produces three product types k (k = 1,2,3). For these product types, the following differences between prices and variable cash outflows per unit have been estimated (these are assumed to remain constant throughout the three years):

$p_1 - a_{v1}$ = €1.40 per unit

$p_2 - a_{v2}$ = €1.35 per unit

$p_3 - a_{v3}$ = €1.00 per unit

In each period, the maximum market demand for products of type k is indicated by the following parameters Z_k:

Z_1 = 8,000 units $\quad$ Z_2 = 6,000 units $\quad$ Z_3 = 5,000 units

Three machines j (j = 1,2,3) are required to produce each of the three products. The following matrix shows the production coefficients, e.g. the requirement of capacities of the three machines j per unit of the products k (in time units). These capacities are also assumed to be constant throughout the three periods:

Product	Machine 1	Machine 2	Machine 3
1	3	3	3
2	4	3	2
3	5	2	4

Tab. 7-5: Production coefficients for the three machines j and the products k

Initially, two machines of types 1 and 2 and four of type 3 are already in use. All have a remaining economic life of one period. Their capacities, relevant cash outflows and liquidation values are the same as for newly purchased machines, described next.

New machines can be purchased at the beginning of each period, without limit. The economic lives of the projects are three periods each and, if the machines are acquired at the beginning of period 1 (at time $t = 0$), their initial investment outlays (in €), capacities (in time units), and cash outflows (in €/machine) are:

Machine	Initial investment outlay	Capacity	Cash operating outflows
1	1,000	5,000	195
2	960	4,000	185
3	880	3,500	225

Tab. 7-6: Data for the machines

By acquiring the machines at $t = 1$ or $t = 2$, the initial investment outlays, the outflows and the production coefficients remain unchanged, but the capacities increase by 10% each period. The liquidation value at the end of the economic life is 10% of the initial investment outlay. The decline in investment project liquidation value occurs continuously over all periods of the economic life, starting from the initial investment outlay.

The following internal funds are available:

$t = 0$: €25,000 and $t = 1$: €5,000.

The interest rate on the short-term financial investment is 6%. The objective is to maximise the compound value.

For this decision problem, a simultaneous model must be formulated. The temporal structure of the liquidity, capacity and sales restrictions (R) as well as the objective function (OF) are shown in the following chart:

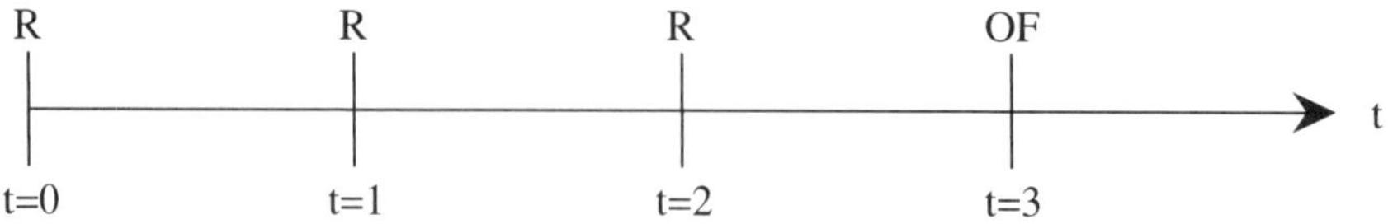

Fig. 7-4: Temporal structure of the liquidity, capacity and sales restrictions and the objective function

Objective function (related to t = 3):

$$x_{42} \cdot 1.06 + 0.1 \cdot (1{,}000x_{10} + 960x_{20} + 880x_{30}) + 0.4 \cdot (1{,}000x_{11} + 960x_{21} + 880x_{31}) + 0.7 \cdot (1{,}000x_{12} + 960x_{22} + 880x_{32}) + 1.4z_{12} + 1.35z_{22} + z_{32} \quad \Rightarrow \text{max!}$$

The objective function refers to the end of the last period. At this time, the short-term financial investment initiated at the beginning of that period is recouped (including interest), and the liquidation values of the investments made at different points in time, as well as the cash flow surpluses of the products produced at time $t = 2$, are included. The liquidation values amount to 10%, 40% or 70% of the respective initial investment outlays, according to the age of the investment projects.

Liquidity constraints:

$t = 0$:

$$1{,}000x_{10} + 960x_{20} + 880x_{30} + 195\,(2 + x_{10}) + 185\,(2 + x_{20}) + 225\,(4 + x_{30}) + x_{40} = 25{,}000$$

The liquidity constraint for $t = 0$ includes the initial investment outlays for the machines purchased at the beginning of the first period and the cash outflows for both new and existing machines. The short-term financial investment is also included. In keeping with the assumptions of the model, all cash outflows must be financed using available funds.

$t = 1$:

$$-1.4z_{10} - 1.35z_{20} - z_{30} + 1{,}000x_{11} + 960x_{21} + 880x_{31} + 195\,(x_{10} + x_{11}) + 185\,(x_{20} + x_{21}) + 225\,(x_{30} + x_{31}) - 2 \cdot 0.1 \cdot 1{,}000 - 2 \cdot 0.1 \cdot 960 - 4 \cdot 0.1 \cdot 880 - 1.06 \cdot x_{40} + x_{41} = 5{,}000$$

The liquidity restriction for $t = 1$ includes the initial investment outlays of the machines acquired at the beginning of the second period, the operating cash outflows for the machines purchased at $t = 0$ and $t = 1$, and the short-term financial investment. Cash inflows result from liquidation values, from the balance of the relevant cash inflows and outflows for products produced in the first period (assigned at $t = 0$), and from the compounded short-term financial investment undertaken in the time $t = 0$.

$t = 2$:

$$-1.4z_{11} - 1.35z_{21} - z_{31} + 1{,}000x_{12} + 960x_{22} + 880x_{32} + 195\,(x_{10} + x_{11} + x_{12})$$
$$+ 185\,(x_{20} + x_{21} + x_{22}) + 225\,(x_{30} + x_{31} + x_{32}) - 1{,}06 \cdot x_{41} + x_{42} = 0$$

Capacity constraints:

$t = 0$:

$$3z_{10} + 4z_{20} + 5z_{30} \leq 10{,}000 + 5{,}000x_{10}$$
$$3z_{10} + 3z_{20} + 2z_{30} \leq 8{,}000 + 4{,}000x_{20}$$
$$3z_{10} + 2z_{20} + 4z_{30} \leq 14{,}000 + 3{,}500x_{30}$$

$t = 1$:

$$3z_{11} + 4z_{21} + 5z_{31} \leq 5{,}000\,x_{10} + 5{,}500\,x_{11}$$
$$3z_{11} + 3z_{21} + 2z_{31} \leq 4{,}000\,x_{20} + 4{,}400\,x_{21}$$
$$3z_{11} + 2z_{21} + 4z_{31} \leq 3{,}500\,x_{30} + 3{,}850\,x_{31}$$

$t = 2$:

$$3z_{12} + 4z_{22} + 5z_{32} \leq 5{,}000\,x_{10} + 5{,}500\,x_{11} + 6{,}050\,x_{12}$$
$$3z_{12} + 3z_{22} + 2z_{32} \leq 4{,}000\,x_{20} + 4{,}400\,x_{21} + 4{,}840\,x_{22}$$
$$3z_{12} + 2z_{22} + 4z_{32} \leq 3{,}500\,x_{30} + 3{,}850\,x_{31} + 4{,}235\,x_{32}$$

Sales constraints:

$$z_{1t} \leq 8{,}000, \qquad \text{for } t = 0,1,2$$
$$z_{2t} \leq 6{,}000, \qquad \text{for } t = 0,1,2$$
$$z_{3t} \leq 5{,}000, \qquad \text{for } t = 0,1,2$$

Project constraints:

$$x_{jt} \geq 0 \text{ and integer}, \qquad \text{for } j = 1,2,3;\ t = 0,1,2$$
$$x_{4t} \geq 0, \qquad \text{for } t = 0,1,2$$
$$z_{kt} \geq 0, \qquad \text{for } k = 1,2,3;\ t = 0,1,2$$

The optimum solution of the model is:

$x_{10} = 6$	$x_{20} = 7$	$x_{30} = 5$	$x_{11} = 3$	$x_{21} = 3$	$x_{31} = 5$	$x_{12} = 0$	$x_{22} = 0$	$x_{32} = 0$
$x_{40} = 2{,}630.00$			$x_{41} = 8{,}867.63$			$x_{42} = 22{,}338.44$		
$z_{10} = 7{,}666.67$			$z_{11} = 8{,}000$			$z_{12} = 8{,}000$		
$z_{20} = 4{,}250$			$z_{21} = 5{,}625$			$z_{22} = 5{,}625$		
$z_{30} = 0$			$z_{31} = 0$			$z_{32} = 0$		

This optimum solution recommends that six units of machine 1, seven units of machine 2 and five units of machine 3 should be purchased at the beginning of the planning period; as well as three units of machines 1 and 2 and five units of machine 3 at time $t = 1$. The production and sales volumes of the products are: in the first period (i.e. at $t = 0$): 7,666.67 units of product 1 and 4,250 units of product 2. Short-term financial investments should be made at the beginning of the planning period (amount = €2,630.00) and at times $t = 2$ and $t = 3$ (amounts = €8,867.63 and €22,338.44 respectively). The objective function value (i.e. maximum compound value) is €48,296.50.

Assessment of the model

The model presented here captures the interdependencies between investment and production decisions relatively well by including product variables, investment variables, and their linkage via the capacity constraints. Thus, it also circumvents the assumption that a cash inflow must be allocated to a specific investment project – a potentially problematic assumption that is common to all other models discussed so far.

Difficulties may arise from the optimum determination process (particularly if the projects must be discrete) and from the processes of data collection. Moreover, deviations between the real environment and the ‘model-world’ may apply to all the assumptions mentioned. The assumption about available internal funds is one example; financing decisions remain outside the model, apart from short-term financial investments (although financing can be integrated into the model by introducing financing variables). Decisions about *how* to produce products are not part of the model, and the economic lives of the investment projects are assumed to be known. These and other weaknesses of the model can, however, be largely eliminated by extending the model further. Yet, extensions inevitably increase the complexities of data collection and calculation.

Although this and other models for simultaneous investment and production programme decision-making represent planning problems relatively well, they are rarely applied in company practice, for various reasons. One problem is that such generalised theoretical models must be adapted to the specific company situation.

The most crucial barriers to applying this sort of model are the challenging planning requirements and the effort involved in data acquisition and model solution. Difficulties are primarily due to the high complexity of these models including the requirement for projects to be discrete. This requirement may result in problems within the optimum solution calculation process, despite recent progress in computer technology. The model may also lead to data procurement problems, since a huge amount of data might need to be collected from across a company. In addition, the data relates almost exclusively to future periods, so must be forecasted. It is, therefore, highly uncertain, thus reducing the reliability of the model. The considerable influence that investment model data uncertainties have on the profitability of investment objects is considered in the following chapters.

Assessment Material Chapter 7

Exercise 7-1 (DEAN Model for Simultaneous Financing and Investment Decisions)

The choice is between the investment and finance projects below, each with their given cash flows, a_{jt} or d_{it} (in €'000):

Investment projects j	1	2	3	4	5
a_{j0} (€'000)	–120	–160	–70	–60	–30
a_{j1} (€'000)	+144	+170	+77	+78	+36

Tab. 7-7: Cash flows for the investment projects

Financing projects i	A	B	C	D
d_{i0} (€'000)	+50	+70	+160	+80
d_{i1} (€'000)	–54	–78	–200	–84

Tab. 7-8: Cash flows of for financing projects

a) For each project, calculate the internal rate of return (IRR) or the effective rate of interest. From this, deduce the capital supply and capital demand curves and draw these on a graph. Determine the optimum investment and financing programme as well as the endogenous rate of interest. What is the maximum compound value?

b) Take another look at the choice of investment and financing projects in part a) of the exercise. Assume all the investment projects must be realised in full (i.e. they are indivisible). Ascertain the optimum investment and financing programme and calculate the maximum compound value.

c) State the assumptions made by the DEAN model.

Exercise 7-2 (Multi-Tier Model for Simultaneous Financing and Investment Decisions)

A company faces the task of planning its investment and financing programme. It must choose between three investment projects (x_1, x_2, x_3). At any point in time, excess funds may be invested in the short term (x_{4t}). Interest on such short-term investments is 5%. The investment projects are characterised by the following net cash flows (€'000):

Time t	x_1	x_2	x_3
0	–100	0	–120
1	50	–80	60
2	50	55	40
3	50	55	40

Tab. 7-9: Net cash flows for the investment projects

There are also two financing projects available to the company (y_1, y_2) with the following net cash flows (€'000):

Time t	y_1	y_2
0	100	0
1	–10	100
2	–10	0
3	–115	–118

Tab. 7-10: Net cash flows for the financing projects

Each loan can be drawn down for up to €600,000 and divided up at will. Each investment project may be undertaken up to five times, but must be realised in full each time (i.e. the projects are indivisible).
The company invests internal funds as follows: €200,000 at the beginning of the first period and €100,000 each at the beginning of the second and third periods.
Formulate a multi-tier model for the simultaneous planning of an investment and financing programme appropriate to the problem described above.

Exercise 7-3 (Multi-Tier Model for Simultaneous Financing and Investment Decisions)

A company is faced with two investment projects (x_1, x_2) and two forms of long-term financial investment (x_3, x_4) plus one short-term financial investment (x_{5t}) in each period. The company may take up two loans (y_1, y_2) of up to €1,000,000 each.
For the available investment projects and loans, the following monetary consequences are expected (€'000):

Time t	x_1	x_2	x_3	x_4	x_{50}	x_{51}	x_{52}	x_{53}	y_1	y_2
0	100	80	50	100	100	0	0	0	–100	–100
1	–60	–50	0	–10	–105	100	0	0	0	0
2	–60	–50	0	–10	0	–105	100	0	0	0
3	–50	–40	–90	–120	0	0	–105	100	140	130

Tab. 7-11: Net cash outflows per unit of the variables (projects)

There are no internal funds available.

a) Formulate a multi-tier model for maximising the compound value of the investment and financing programme.

b) The following programmes are proposed:
i) $x_1 = 1.5$; $x_2 = 1$; $x_3 = 1$; $y_1 = 1$; $y_2 = 1$
ii) $x_1 = 1$; $x_2 = 1$; $y_1 = 1$; $y_2 = 1$
(The values of the variables x_{5t} are not given here but may be deduced from the other variables.)
Are the programmes feasible and, if so, optimal? Briefly outline the reasons for this.

c) How does the model change if additional cash inflows in the amount of €10,000 are expected for each unit of investment project 1 at each of the times t = 4 and t = 5, and 10% is the rate of interest for calculation purposes?

d) In optimising a HAX and WEINGARTNER model, the following endogenous compounding factors q_t^* where determined for the times t:

$q_0^* = 1.93908$; $q_1^* = 1.4916$; $q_2^* = 1.243$; $q_3^* = 1.1$; $q_4^* = 1$

Determine the endogenous rates of interest for periods 1-4, and assess the profitability of an additional project with the following cash flow profile:

Time t	**0**	**1**	**2**	**3**	**4**
Cash flows (€'000)	–300	120	120	120	110

Tab. 7-12: Cash flow profile of the additional project

Exercise 7-4 (Static and Multi-Tier Models for Simultaneous Financing and Investment Decisions)

a) A choice must be made between the investment and finance projects below, each with their forecasted cash flows, a_{jt} or d_{it} (in €'000).

Investment project	**A**	**B**	**C**	**D**
a_{j0}	–60	–70	–40	–100
a_{j1}	78	87.5	45	124

Tab. 7-13: Cash flows of the investment projects

Financing project	1	2	3
d_{i0}	100	100	100
d_{i1}	–110	–120	–132

Tab. 7-14: Cash flows of the financing projects

a1) Determine the optimum investment and financing programme when the investment and finance projects may all be divided at will.
What is the maximum compound value?

a2) Ascertain the optimum investment and finance programme assuming the investment projects cannot be divided.
What is the maximum compound value?

a3) Which programme is optimal if neither the finance projects nor the investment projects can be divided?
What is the maximum compound value?

b) A company wishes to plan its investment and financing programme simultaneously. There are four investment projects to choose from, A-D (investment variables x_A–x_D), with the following net cash flows (€'000):

Time t	A	B	C	D
0	–100	–150	–80	–50
1	40	40	25	15
2	40	50	25	20
3	40	55	25	15
4	40	55	25	10

Tab. 7-15: Net cash flows for the four investment projects

Investment projects A and C may be realised a maximum of three times. Internal funds available at t = 1 amount to €80,000. The investment projects A and B may also be realised at t = 1 (investment variables x_E, x_F), and an upper limit of 3 applies to the realisation of investment project A also at this time.

The following information on the financing projects 1-3 (financial variables y_1-y_3) is available:

- If the first financing project is realised, 60% of the cash inflows will be received at t = 0 and 40% at t = 1. At each time, interest at a rate of 10% is payable on the capital borrowed, which is to be repaid at t = 4.
- A payment of the full nominal amount of the second financing project will be received at t = 0 if this project is realised. 50% of the capital is to be repaid at t = 3, and the remaining 50% at t = 4. At each time, interest at a rate of 9% is also payable on capital previously received and not yet repaid.

- The third financing project generates only one positive payment at $t = 0$. Payments of interest and compound interest, as well as capital repayments, are due at times $t = 1$ to $t = 4$. The total amounts payable stay the same and the applicable rate of interest is 6%.
- For each of the financing projects the maximum amount is €200,000.

At each time, a short-term, single-period financial investment may be made, yielding interest at 3% (investment variables x_{Gt}, $t = 0,1,2,3,4$).
Also at each time (except $t = 4$), a short-term, single-period loan may be accessed bearing interest at 7% (financial variables y_{4t}, $t = 0,1,2,3$), while the maximum amount available at each time is, as for the other financing projects, €200,000.
Formulate a multi-tier model for this problem. Relate the objective function to $t = 4$ and assume a discount rate of 5% for period 5.

c) The models formulated in a), and b) aim to decide simultaneously on an investment and financing programme. Work out the differences between the models and, in so doing, state the differing assumptions involved.

Exercise 7-5 (Extended FÖRSTNER and HENN Model)

The head of a company's planning department wishes to decide about production and investments simultaneously. The following data are available: The company produces two kinds of products, k (k = 1,2). For each unit of product, it achieves a price p_k and has to pay variable cash outflows of a_{vk} resulting from the production process. It can sell maximum amounts of Z_k.

k	p_k (€ per unit)	Z_k (unit)	a_{vk} (€ per unit)
1	12.00	1,000	8.00
2	18.00	16,000	10.00

Tab. 7-16: Data for the two kinds of products

Both products are produced on three machines, j (j = 1,2,3). The utilisation of these machines j for each unit of the product k is given below (in units of capacity).

	Machine j		
Product k	1	2	3
1	3	4	6
2	2	5	7

Tab. 7-17: Utilisation of the machines

At the beginning of the planning period there is an initial stock of machinery with the capacity given below in time units:

Machine j	Capacity
1	300
2	400
3	800

Tab. 7-18: Existing capacity of the machines

Identical machines may be acquired at the beginning of each period. For each type of machine j, I_{0j} represents the initial investment outlays (in €), and G_j the relevant expansion in capacity (in time units).

Machine j	I_{0j}	G_j
1	1700	60
2	1400	80
3	3200	100

Tab. 7-19: Data for the machines

The liquidation value at the end of the economic life is 20% of the initial investment outlay for each machine. The decrease in liquidation value occurs evenly throughout all periods of the economic life.

In each case, the total economic life of the existing machine is two years and all existing machines have a remaining economic life of one year. The cash outflows to acquire these existing machines were equal to those for the machines available for purchase at t = 0.

a) Formulate a two-period model with the objective 'maximising the compound value'. In so doing, assume that the data given here – with the exception of the cash outflows for the aggregates acquired at t = 1 (which rise by 10% compared with the figures given) – are also valid for the second period. Note that the company must remain liquid at all times. Interest on the short-term financial investment is 10%. €10,000 of internal funds are available at t = 0 and again at t = 1.

b) What problems might be expected in setting up and solving such a model in a real business environment?

Exercise 7-6 (Extended FÖRSTNER and HENN Model)

Prepare a simultaneous investment and production decision using the following underlying data.

A company produces two kinds of product, k (k = 1,2). It has a monopoly position in the market and achieves prices p_k according to the following formulae. The maximum volumes it can sell, Z_k, and the variable cash outflows per unit, cof_{vk}, are also given below (with z_k = production amount and sales volume).

k	p_k (€ per unit)	Z_k (unit)	cof_{vk} (€ per unit)
1	$120 - 0.2 \cdot z_1$	600	50
2	$180 - 0.1 \cdot z_2$	1,800	100

Tab. 7-20: Data for the two products

Both products are manufactured on the machines j (j = 1,2) and take up the following time units per unit of product on these machines.

	Machine j	
Product k	1	2
1	4	6
2	5	5

Tab. 7-21: Data for the machines

At the beginning of the planning period, machine 1 has a capacity of 360 time units and a remaining economic life of one period. Its further characteristics are equal to those given below for new type 1 machines.

New type 1 and type 2 machines can be acquired at the beginning of each period. Their economic life is four periods and the liquidation value at the end of the economic life amounts to 20% of the initial investment outlay. The decrease in their liquidation value occurs linearly throughout all periods of their economic life.

Regardless of the date of acquisition, the cash outflows are €2,000 for the acquisition of machine 1, and €2,500 for machine 2. Each new machine purchased expands capacity by 90 time units (machine 1) and 100 time units (machine 2).

The rate of interest for short-term financial investments is 10%; there is €40,000 of internal funds available at t = 0.

Given the above, formulate a dynamic two-period model for determining an optimum investment and production programme with the objective of maximising the compound value. In so doing, assume that the data given – with the exception of the variable cash outflows per unit, which rises by 10% – are valid for both periods. Bear in mind that the company must remain liquid throughout both periods.

Further Reading Part IV

Belton, V. 1986. A Comparison of the Analytic Hierarchy Process and a Simple Multi-Attribute Value Function. *European Journal of Operational Research* 26 (1):7-21.

Bernroider, E., and V. Stix. 2007. A Method Using Weight Restrictions in Data Envelopment Analysis for Ranking and Validity Issues in Decision Making. *Computers & Operations Research* 34 (9):2637-2647.

Blohm, H., K. Lüder, and C. Schaefer. 2006. *Investition: Schwachstellenanalyse des Investitionsbereichs und Investitionsrechnung*. 9 ed. München: Vahlen.

Brans, J. P., and B. Mareschal. 1990. The PROMETHEE Methods for MCDM; The PROMCALC, GAIA and BANKADVISER Software. In *Readings in Multiple Criteria Decision Aid*, edited by C. A. Bana e Costa. Berlin et al.: Springer, 216-252.

———. 1992. PROMETHEE V: MCDM Problems with Segmentation Constraints. *INFOR* 30 (2):85-96.

Brans, J. P., and P. Vincke. 1985. A Preference Ranking Organisation Method. *Management Sciences* 31 (6):647-656.

Brans, J. P., P. Vincke, and B. Mareschal. 1986. How to Select and How to Rank Projects: The PROMETHEE method. *European Journal of Operational Research* 24 (2):228-238.

Charnes, A., W. W. Cooper, and M. H. Miller. 1959. Application of "Linear Programming" to Financial Budgeting and the Costing of Funds. *Journal of Business* 32 (1):20-46.

Dantzig, G. B. 1956. Recent Advances in Linear Programming. *Management Science* 2 (2):131-144.

Dean, J. 1950. Capital Budgeting and the Firm's Demand for Capital. *Zeitschrift für Ökonometrie* 1 (2):3-23.

———. 1954. Measuring the Productivity of Capital. *Harvard Business Review* 32 (1):120-130.

———. 1978. *Capital Budgeting*. 9 ed. New York, London: Columbia University Press.

Dyer, J. S. 1990. Remarks on the Analytic Hierarchy Process. *Management Science* 36 (3):249-258.

Dyer, J. S., P. C. Fishburn, R. E. Steuer, J. Wallenius, and S. Zionts. 1992. Multiple Criteria Decision Making, Multiattribute Utilility Theory: The Next Ten Years. *Management Science* 38 (5):645-654.

Ehrgott, M., K. Klamroth, and C. Schwehm. 2004. An MCDM approach to portfolio optimization. *European Journal of Operational Research* 155 (3):752-770.

Farquhar, P. H. 1977. A Survey of Multiattribute Utility Theory and Applications. *Multiple Criteria Decision Making*, edited by M. K. Starr and M. Zeleny. Amsterdam et al.: North-Holland, 59-89.

Fernandez-Castro, A. S., and M. Jiménez. 2005. PROMETHEE: an extension through fuzzy mathematical programming. *Journal of the Operational Research Society* 56 (1):119-122.

Förstner, K., and R. Henn. 1957. *Dynamische Produktions-Theorie und Lineare Programmierung*. Meisenheim/Glan: Hain.

French, S., T. Bedford, and E. Atherton. 2005. Supporting ALARP decision making by cost benefit analysis and multiattribute utility theory. *Journal of Risk Research* 8 (3):207-223.

Götze, U. 2006. *Investitionsrechnung*. 5 ed. Berlin et al.: Springer.

Harker, P. T. 1989. The Art and Science of Decision Making: The Analytic Hierarchy Process. In *The Analytic Hierarchy Process. Applications and Studies*, edited by B. L. Golden, E. A. Wasil and P. T. Harker. Berlin et al.: Springer, 3-36.

Hax, H. 1964. Investitions- und Finanzplanung mit Hilfe der linearen Programmierung. *Schmalenbachs Zeitschrift für betriebswirtschaftliche Foschung* 16 (7/8):430-446.

Hwang, C. L., and K. Yoon. 1981, Multiple Attribute Decision Making; Methods and Applications. Berlin et al.: Springer.

Jaquet-Lagréze, E. 1985. Basic Concepts for Multicriteria Decision Support. In *Multiple Criteria Decision Methods and Applications*, edited by G. Fandel and J. Spronk. Berlin et al.: Springer, 11-26.

Kruschwitz, L. 2007. *Investitionsrechnung*, 11 ed. München, Wien: Oldenbourg.

Millet, I., and T. A. Saaty. 2000. On the Relativity of Relative Measures - Accomodating Both Rank Preservations and Rank Reversals in the AHP. *European Journal of Operational Research* 121 (1):205-212.

Myers, S. C. 1974. Interactions of Corporate Financing and Investment Decisons - Implications for Capital Budgeting. *Journal of Finance* 29 (1):1-25.

Ozernoy, V. M. 1992. Choosing the "Best" Multiple Criteria Decision-making Method. *INFOR* 30 (2):159-171.

Pastijn, H., and J. Leysen. 1989. Constructing an Outranking Relation with ORESTE. *Mathematical Computing Modelling* 12:1255-1268.

Robichek, A. A., and D. Teichroew. 1965. Optimal Short Term Financing Decisions. *Management Science* 12 (1):1-36.

Roubens, M. 1982. Preference Relations on Actions and Criterions in Multicriteria Decision Making. *European Journal of Operational Research* 10 (1):51-55.

Roy, B. 1990. The Outranking Approach and the Foundations of ELECTRE Methods. In *Readings in Multiple Criteria Decision Aid, Berlin*, edited by C. A. Bana e Costa. Berlin et al.: Springer, 155-183.

Saaty, T. L. 1980. *The Analytic Hierarchy Process: Planning, Priority Setting, Resource Allocation*. New York et al.: McGraw-Hill.

———. 1990. How to Make a Decision: The Analytic Hierarchy Process. *European Journal of Operational Research* 48 (1):9-26.

———. 2006. *The Analytic Network Process - Dependence and Feedback in Decison-Making: Theory and Validation Examples*. Hershley, PA. et al.: Idea Group.

Saaty, T. L., and L. G. Vargas. 2006. *Decision Making with the Analytic Network Process*. Boston: Springer Science+Business Media.

Schneeweiß, C. 1991. *Planung, Bd. 1: Systemanalytische und entscheidungstheoretische Grundlagen*. Berlin et al.: Springer.

Siskos, J., G. WÃ¡scher, and H.-M. Winkels. 1984. Outranking approaches versus MAUT in MCDM. *European Journal of Operational Research* 16 (2):270-271.

Spronk, J., R. E. Steuer, and C. Zopounidis. 2005. *Multicriteria Decision Aid/Analysis in Finance*. New York et al.: Springer.

Teichroew, D., A. A. Robichek, and M. Montalbano. 1965a. Mathematical Analysis of Rates of Return under Certainty. *Management Science* 11 (3):393-403.

———. 1965b. An Analysis of Criteria for Investment and Financing Decisions under Certainty. *Management Science* 12 (3):151-179.

Van-Nam, H., Y. Nakamori, H. Tu-Bao, and T. Murai. 2006. Multiple-Attribute Decision Making Under Uncertainty: The Evidential Reasoning Approach Revisited. *IEEE Transactions on Systems, Man & Cybernetics: Part A* 36 (4):804-822.

Wang, C.-L., and A. S. M. Masud. 1979. *Multiple Objective Decision Making. Methods and Applications*. Berlin et al.: Springer.

Wang, C.-L., and B. K. Yoon. 1981. *Multiple Attribute Decision Making. Methods and Applications*. Berlin et al.: Springer.

Weingartner, H. M. 1963. *Mathematical Programming and the Analysis of Capital Budgeting Problems*. Englewood Cliffs, N.J.: Prentice Hall.

———. 1966a. Capital Budgeting of Interrelated Projects: Survey and Synthesis. *Management Science* 12 (7):485-516.

———. 1966b. Criteria for Programming Investment Project Selection. *Journal of Industrial Economics* 15 (1):65-76.

Weingartner, H. M., and D. N. Ness. 1967. Methods for the Solution of the Multi-Dimensional 0/1 Knapsack Problem. *Operations Research* 15 (1):83-103.

Wolf, J. 1988. *Lineare Fuzzy-Modelle zur Unterstützung der Investitionsplanung*. Frankfurt am Main et al.: Lang.

Xu, Z. S. 2007. Models for Multiple Attribute Decision Making With Intuitionistic Fuzzy Information. *International Journal of Uncertainty, Fuzziness & Knowledge-Based Systems* 15 (3):285-297.

Zanakis, S. H., A. Solomon, N. Wishart, and S. Dublish. 1998. Multi-attribute decision making: A simulation comparison of select methods. *European Journal of Operational Research* 107 (3):507-529.

Zimmermann, H.-J., and L. Gutsche. 1991. *Multi-Criteria-Analyse*. Berlin et al.: Springer.

Part V

Methods and Models that Incorporate Uncertainty

Chapter 8: Methods and Models for Appraising Investment Projects under Uncertainty

An investing company expects to achieve positive results from an investment project in regard to technologies, revenues, costs and/or cash flows. Under known or predictable conditions, i.e. under certainty, these results can be determined unambiguously. However, in reality, most investment conditions must be considered uncertain.

For example, goods produced on a new machine might not achieve sales at the levels expected; expected profits from a foreign investment might not be achieved; or a rationalisation or modernisation investment might take an unexpectedly long time to impact on efficiency. This uncertainty might be caused by customer, competitor or employee behaviour, or by technical processes and cyclical declines. All uncertainties create risks concerning the target measures reached by investments and the decisions based on investment appraisal. A risk can be understood as the danger of making a wrong decision that leads to failing the targets set. A more comprehensive interpretation, which is used in this chapter, is that risk captures the possibility that the realised target values might deviate from the expected targets with either negative or positive consequences.

Because company and environmental structures are complex and fast-changing, many investment decisions involve substantial uncertainty and, consequently, high risks. These should be considered in investment decision-making, in order to protect the company and ensure its long-term development.

There are several ways of incorporating uncertainty into planning. Through information gathering and processing, data may be obtained that helps to reduce uncertainty or assists in analysing its causes or effects. Analysis and forecasting techniques (such as the scenario method) allow the causes, forms and effects of uncertainty to be clarified. Also, specific investment appraisal models and methods can be used to determine how changing company or environmental conditions may cause variations in target measures. The results of investment decisions can then be predicted for a range of expectations. Additionally, the relative significance of various company and environmental conditions can be estimated in order to determine the value of further information-gathering and processing activities.

If several alternative environmental and/or company conditions are possible, different target measures will apply to each. When no one alternative dominates over the rest, a decision problem can be solved by means of decision-theory rules or criteria. Such rules and criteria are outlined in Section 8.1. The following sections present and discuss the following methods that incorporate uncertainty and are suitable for making decisions about single investment projects:

- Risk adjusted analysis
- Sensitivity analysis
- Risk analysis
- The decision-tree method
- Options pricing models

8.1 Decision Theory

Decision theory rules and criteria may be applied when alternative scenarios for uncertain environmental and company conditions are included in a model. This helps to consider the effects of uncertainty in the project appraisal and reveals the expected outcome of each project alternative under the various scenarios. Usually, only limited numbers of alternatives and scenarios are considered, each involving a distinct set of input data. The decision situation can be illustrated with the help of a decision matrix, as shown in Figure 8-1, which assumes that:

- A function can be formulated that assigns an unambiguous net present value (NPV) to every investment alternative under each scenario.
- The NPV is the only relevant target measure (an assumption that is valid for most of Chapters 8 and 9 – i.e. problems of multi-criteria decision-making are not taken into account).

In the decision matrix, the symbols A_j (j = 1,...,J) represent the alternatives, while the expected future scenarios are symbolised by S_u (u = 1,...,U). The matrix elements NPV_{ju} indicate the net present value of an alternative j for the scenario u.

Based on the matrix (NPV_{ju}), an investor can select an alternative with the help of decision rules. Some of these are described briefly in the following.

Scenario / **Alternatives**	S_1	...	S_u	...	S_U
A_1	NPV_{11}	...	NPV_{1u}	...	NPV_{1U}
⋮	⋮		⋮		⋮
A_j	NPV_{j1}	...	NPV_{ju}	...	NPV_{jU}
⋮	⋮		⋮		⋮
A_J	NPV_{J1}	...	NPV_{Ju}	...	NPV_{JU}

Fig. 8-1: Decision matrix

Decision Rules in Situations of Unknown Probabilities

If no probabilities can be estimated for the scenarios being considered, the following rules may be applied.

WALD or Maximin rule

According to the WALD or Maximin rule, the investment alternative selected from the set A_j is the one with the maximum NPV_{ju} in the least beneficial scenario S_u. To identify this alternative, the minimum NPV is identified for every line of the decision matrix (i.e. for every alternative) and the alternative A^* with the maximum value among these minima is selected. The optimum alternative A^* is therefore defined as:

$$A^* = \{ A_j \mid \max_j \min_u NPV_{ju} \} \tag{8.1}$$

An investor using this approach is typically highly risk averse. He or she assumes that environmental and company conditions will be extremely negative, resulting in the worst outcome scenario for each of the investment alternatives. The consistent application of this decision rule will result in many investment opportunities being rejected because they carry the danger of a loss situation. Chances will not be appropriately taken into account and, in the extreme case, only risk-free investment projects will be considered, in direct contrast to any notion of entrepreneurship.

For the following decision matrix, presenting net present values NPV_{ju} related to four investment alternatives A_j $(j = 1,...,4)$ and five possible scenarios S_u $(u = 1,...,5)$, the selection would be made in the way described above:

	S_1	S_2	S_3	S_4	S_5	Min u
A_1	180	120	110	130	125	110
A_2	160	135	120	115	145	115*
A_3	120	90	70	100	110	70
A_4	80	0	60	50	70	0

Tab. 8-1: Example of a matrix for the Maximin rule

The minimum NPV value for each line is listed in the column 'Min u'. The maximum of these minima is NPV_{24} (= 115), i.e. the NPV achieved by the second investment alternative A_2 under its least favourable scenario. Thus, investment project A_2 would be selected ($A^* = A_2$).

Maximax rule

An optimistic investor might use the Maximax rule, choosing the investment alternative that promises the highest possible NPV. This approach would completely disregard the risk associated with unfavourable conditions. The optimum alternative A^* is defined as:

$$A^* = \{ A_j \mid \max_j \max_u NPV_{ju} \} \tag{8.2}$$

This situation is illustrated in the following matrix:

	S_1	S_2	S_3	S_4	S_5	Max u
A_1	180	120	110	130	125	180*
A_2	160	135	120	115	145	160
A_3	120	90	70	100	110	120
A_4	80	0	60	50	70	80

Tab. 8-2: Example of a matrix for thc Maximax rule

With this rule, the line maxima are determined and the maximum of these is selected: the chosen alternative in this example is A_1 ($A^* = A_1$). Note that, because the Maximax and Maximin rules consider only one scenario, they both neglect much available information.

HURWICZ rule

The HURWICZ rule incorporates both the Maximin and Maximax rules, using a convex linear combination of the maximum of the minima and the maximum of the maxima. It constitutes, therefore, an optimism-pessimism rule. According to this rule, the optimum alternative A^* is:

$$A^* = \{ A_j \mid \max_j [(1-\alpha) \cdot \min_u NPV_{ju} + \alpha \cdot \max_u NPV_{ju}] \} \tag{8.3}$$

The α represents an optimism coefficient, with values between 0 and 1. For $\alpha = 1$, the Maximax rule is used, for $\alpha = 0$ the Maximin rule. A slightly risk-averse investor might choose, for instance, $\alpha = 0.4$. Then, for the example given above, the matrix will be:

	S_1	S_2	S_3	S_4	S_5	$(1-0.4) \cdot NPV_{ju}$	$0.4 \cdot NPV_{ju}$	$(1-0.4) \cdot \text{Min u } NPV_{ju} + 0.4 \cdot \text{Max u } NPV_{ju}$
A_1	180	120	110	130	125	66	72	138*
A_2	160	135	120	115	145	69	64	133
A_3	120	90	70	100	110	42	48	90
A_4	80	0	60	50	70	0	32	32

Tab. 8-3: Example of a matrix for the HURWICZ rule

The last column of the matrix records the measures determined for each investment alternative according to the HURWICZ rule. Alternative A_1 has the highest value and is therefore considered the most profitable (i.e. $A^* = A_1$).

The HURWICZ rule includes more information than the Maximin and the Maximax rules, yet not all available information is utilised. Generally, the omission of information represents a crucial disadvantage of these and similar rules for decision-making under uncertainty. By modifying the HURWICZ rule, other elements of the matrix could be included in the linear combination, but this requires the determination of several coefficients so that the expected results can be weighted.

Decision Rules and Criteria in Situations with Estimated Probabilities

Where the probabilities p_u for possible scenarios S_u can be estimated, other rules and criteria are applicable.

BAYES rule

One of these rules is BAYES rule, which uses the expected value E_j of an alternative j as the crucial criterion. This expected value is calculated for each alternative j by multiplying the net present value expected for each of the scenarios u (i.e. NPV_{ju}) by its probability p_u, and then adding all the resultant products together. The optimum alternative A^* is therefore:

$$A^* = \{ A_j \mid \max_j \sum_{u=1}^{U} NPV_{ju} \cdot p_u \} \quad (8.4)$$

For example, if the probabilities of five environmental conditions (S_1 to S_5) are:

$p_1 = 0.1, p_2 = 0.2, p_3 = 0.3, p_4 = 0.2, p_5 = 0.2$

Then the following expected net present values ($ENPV_j$) result:

	s_1	s_2	s_3	s_4	s_5	$ENPV_j$
A_1	180	120	110	130	125	126
A_2	160	135	120	115	145	115*
A_3	120	90	70	100	110	70
A_4	80	0	60	50	70	0

Tab. 8-4: Example of a matrix for the BAYES rule

Using BAYES rule, the alternative A_2 represents the optimum ($A^* = A_2$), because it has the highest expected NPV.

This rule implies that the matrix elements NPV_{ju} reflect the utilities of the investment outcomes, i.e. that the utility is proportional to the NPV and variations in possible NPVs have no influence on expected utility. Accordingly, a risk-neutral attitude is assumed.

μ-σ criterion (expected value-standard deviation criterion)

Other attitudes towards risk can be considered by using the μ-σ criterion (expected value-standard deviation criterion). The standard deviation indicates the possible deviation of the target measure from its expected value. The risk associated with a decision is assumed to be larger the higher the value of the standard deviation.

The utility of decision alternatives, the so-called risk utility, depends on the expected value and the standard deviation. The relationship between the risk utility on the one hand, and the expected value and standard deviation on the other hand, is expressed in the form of a risk preference function. The shape of the risk preference function is determined by the risk attitude of an investor: risk-friendly, risk-neutral or risk-averse. A risk-averse investor, for instance, prefers the investment alternative with the lowest standard deviation if the expected values are equal.

Using this μ-σ criterion, the total probability distribution for the possible NPVs of an investment alternative is omitted from the analysis: only the expected value and its standard deviation are considered. Thus, there is some loss of information when using this criterion. Determining the risk preference function is another problem. The μ-σ criterion is utilised by the capital asset pricing model as described in Section 8.2 as well as by the portfolio selection models discussed in Section 9.2.

BERNOULLI criterion

According to BERNOULLI, the expected values and risk measures can be replaced by expected utilities of target measures (e.g. NPVs). Thus, monetary target measures are replaced by the expected utilities that decision-makers associate with them, taking into account individual risk attitudes.

It is assumed that a decision-maker is able to determine the utility of investment alternatives. He or she then searches for the maximum of the 'moral expectation' (EM) which, according to BERNOULLI, is defined with respect to the target measure of the NPV as follows:

$$EM = \sum_{u=1}^{U} f(NPV_u) \cdot p_u \qquad \text{with:} \quad \sum_{u=1}^{U} p_u = 1 \tag{8.5}$$

Parameters:

$f(NPV_u)$ = Values of a degressively rising utility function
NPV_u = Net present value for scenario u
p_u = Probability that scenario u occurs

Using BERNOULLI's utility theory, a risk utility function for uncertain outcomes, for example NPVs, can be determined by estimating the so-called *certainty equivalent*, which is taken to be the equivalent of two uncertain results weighted by their associated probabilities. The risk-utility function expresses the risk attitude of the decision-maker:

- With a risk-neutral attitude, the certainty equivalent is identical to the expected value of the outcome.
- With a risk-friendly attitude, the certainty equivalent is higher than the expected value of the outcome.
- With a risk-averse attitude, the certainty equivalent is lower than the expected value of the outcome.

With the help of the utility function, expected utility values can be determined and used to assess the profitability of alternatives. In contrast to the μ-σ criterion, all possible results are transformed into utility measures. The optimum alternative is the one with the maximum expected value of the utility. For a risk-neutral attitude, this criterion corresponds to the BAYES rule.

The BERNOULLI utility theory is based on a system of specific axioms, which may be criticised because the question arises as to what extent they reflect human decision behaviour under uncertainty.

All models that explicitly consider several environmental conditions experience the problem of forecasting scenarios and their respective values and probabilities. Often, this can be done only by subjective estimation. Further, assuming only a limited number of potential scenarios is a simplification of reality, and it cannot be guaranteed that any of these scenarios will match the actual future outcome. Rather, there exists 'uncertainty about the uncertainty' – this refers to the probability of a scenario occurring, to forecasted target values, and to the range of company activities taken into account.

Knowledge about rules and criteria from decision theory underlies some of the procedures described in the remainder of this chapter. Most of the models used can also be interpreted as specific forms of models with several scenarios.

8.2 Risk-Adjusted Analysis

Correction procedure

This method adjusts the data, i.e. the probable or expected values of the input measures used for investment appraisal, to incorporate the risks involved. For example, NPV calculations might be adjusted by raising the uniform discount rate or the cash outflows, or by shortening the economic life. This increases the probability that the project will achieve the calculated NPV result.

A correction procedure has the disadvantage that only overall uncertainty is recognised – uncertainty is not identified with regard to specific data inputs. Thus, data might be corrected that are not (particularly) uncertain. Also, determining the extent of the corrections is subjective. Corrections are limited to negative effects and, where carried out by different personnel, such effects might accumulate. Therefore, the reliability of the calculated target value (e.g. NPV) must be considered relatively low. False evaluations of absolute and relative probability may result, and the effects of uncertainty cannot be shown.

Because of these methodological weaknesses, the correction procedure is deemed unsuitable for appraising uncertain investment decisions. The approaches outlined next also involve data correction, but mostly on a more theoretically sound basis.

Risk-adjusted discount rates

Various suggestions have been made as to how uncertainty and risk can be incorporated into determining a suitable uniform discount rate. A surcharge might be added to the uniform discount rate based on subjective personal risk attitudes, or derived from risk premiums observed in the market. The approach described next is derived from the capital asset pricing model and relates to the capital market. The concept that follows from it, the *adjusted present value approach*, may be deployed from either a subjective or a capital market perspective.

The first approach is to *adjust the uniform discount rate using the capital asset pricing model (CAPM)*. Based on portfolio theory, this model was primarily developed by SHARPE (1964), LINTNER (1965) and MOSSIN (1966), and originally served to explain prices or yields of risky capital market securities. However, it is also helpful for determining uniform discount rates that include uncertainty. Important assumptions of the CAPM are:

- There is only one relevant period.
- The investors are risk-averse and act rationally in this respect by holding portfolios that are efficient in regard to yield and risk (measured on the basis of the expected value and standard deviation of the portfolio's yield).
- Unlimited sums may be invested without risk for a 'risk-free' interest rate.
- The relevant capital markets are perfect, so (among other things): all securities are divisible; no market access limitations, taxes or transaction costs apply; and all investors have homogeneous expectations regarding the possible yields for traded securities and their probabilities (i.e. of their expected values and standard deviations).

In an equilibrium-based analysis it can be determined that all investors, independent of their personal risk attitude, acquire the same portfolio of risky securities by utilising the diversification opportunities of the market (TOBIN separation theorem). Moreover, this combination of securities comprises the market portfolio, which contains all risky securities traded in the market. Under these assumptions, for every risky security j traded in the capital market an expected equilibrium yield ($E(r_j)$) exists. It consists of the risk-free interest rate r_f plus a risk premium which is independent of the investor. This risk premium is formed by multiplying the 'market price of the risk' with the covariance of the yield relative to that of the market portfolio ($Cov(r_j, r_M)$):

$$E(r_j) = r_f + \underbrace{\frac{E(r_M) - r_f}{Var(r_M)}}_{\substack{\text{Market price}\\ \text{of the risk}}} \cdot Cov(r_j, r_M) \tag{8.6}$$

The market price of the risk includes the expected yield of the total capital market ($E(r_M)$) and the variance of this yield ($Var(r_M)$). The covariance of the yield relative to that of the market portfolio reflects how the yield changes if a change occurs in the market yield – i.e. it represents the relative risk contribution of a security j. Alternatively, the equilibrium yield can be expressed as follows:

$$E(r_j) = r_f + (E(r_M) - r_f) \cdot \beta_j, \qquad \text{with } \beta_j = \frac{Cov(r_j, r_M)}{Var(r_M)} \tag{8.7}$$

$E(r_M) - r_f$ indicates the premium yield, and β_j is the *beta factor* of the security which represents the non-diversifiable, or *systematic risk*. The equilibrium yield can now be used to determine an appropriate uniform discount rate for evaluating risky investments. It is assumed that the cost of capital assigned to an investment project corresponds to the expected yield achievable on the capital market for an investment project with identical risk. Thus, the uniform discount rate i_u that should be applied to take the risk resulting from uncertainty into account is:

$$i_u = r_f + (E(r_M) - r_f) \cdot \beta_u \tag{8.8}$$

A market-oriented assessment of risky investment projects can now be made by using this rate as the discount rate in calculating the present value of the future cash flow (EN_1) and the net present value of the investment (assuming an investment of one period's length):

$$NPV = -I_0 + EN_1 \cdot (1 + i_u)^{-1} \tag{8.9}$$

The present value of the uncertain cash flow(s) then can be interpreted as a market value, if it is higher than the initial investment outlay and, thus, the NPV is positive, an investment is absolutely profitable. It must be emphasised that the risk-dependent interest rate arises from the covariance, and not from an isolated risk premium. Therefore, an investment having highly uncertain cash flows may, nevertheless, have a positive effect on the overall risk position of a company, due to the effects of diversification.

Up until now, it has been assumed that only a company's internal financial funds are used. However, a risk-adjusted interest rate, determined as described above, may also be combined with an interest rate on external funds to calculate the *weighted average cost of capital* for use as a uniform discount rate. This approach may be appropriate, particularly if tax effects are relevant to the investment appraisal, and is often recommended, for example, for determining shareholder value by the discounted cash flow method. But in this case, another problem arises: the uniform discount rate now depends on the capital structure of the company, which is itself affected by the uniform discount rate (and the investment being appraised), i.e. there is a circularity problem.

One crucial aspect of using this market-oriented approach is collecting the necessary data. Often, the risk-free interest rate is derived from yields on government or mortgage bonds with similar terms. The premium yield equals the long-term difference between the average yield of risky investment projects (determined by analysing the long-term development of stock market indices), and the risk-free interest rate. The project-specific beta factor, indicating systematic risk, may be derived from the beta factors of comparable companies in the stock market. In the case of a diversification project, for example, the beta factor should relate to the risk of the targeted business, using the beta factor of a company in this same business (the analogy method). However, it should be kept in mind that this transforms a company-related beta factor into a project-specific one.

In evaluating this approach to investment appraisal under uncertainty, it should also be noted that the risk premium is derived from the market price of the risk and the covariance of the yield relative to that of the market portfolio only. Other influences – such as the index of industrial production, short-term real interest rates, short- and long-term inflation rates and the loan-loss risks – are not considered. In this respect, arbitrage pricing theory represents an extension of the CAPM, because it considers several measures of influence on risk premiums and, according to empirical research, explains them better.

Additionally, the market portfolio and its parameters, all assumed to be given, may be affected by the investment project under appraisal. The CAPM in its basic form spans one period only, while investments are typically evaluated using models that consider more than one time period. Where a constant uniform discount rate derived from the CAPM is used in such a dynamic model, this implies that risk rises from year to year as specified by the formulae. Therefore, it makes more sense to discount a net cash flow with a risk-adjusted uniform discount rate for only one period, to produce a certainty equivalent value related to the previous point in time. The risk-free interest rate can then be used for the remainder of the planning period. In this case the NPV is:

$$NPV = -I_0 + \sum_{t=1}^{T} EN_t \cdot (1+i_u)^{-1} \cdot (1+r_f)^{-t+1} \qquad (8.10)$$

One data collection problem of this approach lies in determining the investment-specific beta factors. Also, the fact that uncertainties are not reflected directly in the cash flows – even though cash flow is the measure most affected by most causes of uncertainty – together with the concentration on systematic risk, raises the danger that a project's risk is not fully captured and receives insufficient attention. Assessing the relative profitability of investments with different risks (and thus different uniform discount rates) is also problematic, because capital tie-up differences cannot be conclusively balanced (as with the internal rate of return method). To sum up, using the CAPM to determine a risk-adjusted discount rate does not facilitate an accurate and 'safe' assessment of risky investments. However, it provides theoretically supported indications of the 'correct' uniform discount rate, while also indicating relevant measures for defining the market-oriented risk premiums needed to adapt the uniform discount rate.

The *adjusted present value approach* (APV) is another approach to considering risks in uniform discount rates. With this method, a project's basic NPV is calculated first – namely, the NPV that arises when only internal funds are used and cash flows are discounted using the appropriate project-specific cost of capital. Then, this value is adapted to include the side effects of the investment (e.g. debt-financing) by calculating the incremental side effect NPVs and adding them to the basic NPV. Thus, all cash flows are discounted by uniform discount rates appropriate to their associated risks.

The APV approach gives results identical to a NPV calculation using a weighted average cost of capital (including taxes), if identical assumptions are made in both approaches. The approach can take into account not only risk-adjusted uniform discount rates, but also various forms of financing and, thus, an imperfect capital market. Because separate NPV components are added together, it is very transparent.

Yet, uncertainty is not reflected at the level of cash flow surpluses, so uncertainty effects on individual cash flow components are not differentiated. As with the CAPM approach, the derivation of specific discount rates creates problems.

Risk adjustment of cash flows

Instead of modifying the discount rate, uncertainty can also be included by adjusting a project's cash flows. Different approaches exist and usually assume that a finite number of potential cash flow surpluses can be forecasted for the various periods of the economic life. Two such approaches are briefly described in this section: the certainty equivalent method and the time state preference model.

The *certainty equivalent method* accounts for uncertain cash flows in the form of certainty equivalents, which represent the certain result that the decision-maker - given his specific risk preference – regards as being equivalent to the uncertain distribution of potential results. Using the net present value model, the results are represented by cash flows. Accordingly, the decision-maker determines period-specific certainty equivalents CE_t for the distributions of potential cash flows, discounts them with the risk-free interest rate r_f to the beginning of the planning period, and includes them in the NPV calculation:

$$NPV = \sum_{t=0}^{T} CE_t \cdot (1 + r_f)^{-t} \qquad (8.11)$$

The NPV now takes into account the distributions of potential results as well as the risk preference of the decision-maker, and can be applied as though the cash flows were certain.

Certainty equivalents can be determined in various ways, such as allocating certainty equivalents 'intuitively' to cash flows, deriving them from the decision-maker's risk-utility function, or basing them on a market assessment (for example using the CAPM). Conversely, it is also possible to determine a risk-adjusted discount rate based on a (personal) certainty equivalent. Given the same assumptions, the NPV is identical whether discounting *certainty equivalent* cash flows with the risk-free interest rate, or discounting *expected* cash flows with a risk-adjusted interest rate.

A key strength of this approach is its consistent inclusion of the uncertainty of future developments and the risk preferences of the decision-maker. In contrast to the adjustment of discount rates, the uncertainty is related directly to the uncertain measures. Moreover, this approach avoids the assumption of rising risk that is implicit in the constant risk-adjusted discount rate. However, only a (limited) number of potential results are assumed possible, and forecasting these results itself entails uncertainty. Also, it might be difficult for the decision-maker to determine the certainty equivalents or the underlying risk-utility functions. Finally, the uncertainty is accounted for (at least in the basic form of this procedure) at the level of aggregated cash flow surpluses in particular periods, so the uncertainty of specific cash flow components is not differentiated.

The *time state preference model* serves to explain the prices of claims that depend on states, i.e. these claims become cash flows only under certain conditions. These claims are also called ‘pure securities’, in contrast to usual securities for which claims arise under all environmental states. The assumptions of this model resemble those of the CAPM (i.e. certain initial assets of the investors in an economy, perfect capital markets, homogeneous expectations and rational behaviour of the market participants). The prices of pure securities are derived based on an equilibrium analysis of the decision behaviour of individual investors. The higher the probability of a state occurring, the lower the interest rate of risk-free investments, and/or the ‘poorer’ the national economy in that state, then the higher the price of a claim on a cash flow which is received (only) when that state occurs.

These state-dependent claims can also be applied to the appraisal of investments under uncertainty. If a market exists, which sets the prices of claims under every potential state in every period of the investment project, then these prices can be used for the investment appraisal. Each potential stream of cash flows can be interpreted as a bundle of state-dependent claims with associated current values that equal the market prices. The market value (MV) of the cash flows in relation to the beginning of the planning period (and therefore comparable to the NPV) can be stated as:

$$MV = \sum_{t=0}^{T} \sum_{s=1}^{S_t} p_{ts} \cdot NCF_{ts} \qquad (8.12)$$

Parameters and indices:

t	=	Time index
s	=	Index for a potential state at time t ($s = 1,...,S_t$)
p_{ts}	=	Price of the claim under state s at time t
NCF_{ts}	=	Net cash flow under state s at time t

This approach can be used, in the same way NPV is used under conditions of certainty, to decide whether to accept or reject an investment project under conditions of uncertainty.

Like the CAPM, the time state preference model works with restrictive assumptions and highly aggregated cash flows. Data procurement might be very difficult and will include a high level of uncertainty about the (uncertainty of) data, as is the case for the certainty equivalent method and decision-theoretical rules and criteria. The prices of pure securities or state-conditional claims can be determined only under a perfect capital market, implying that the number of traded securities must equal or exceed the number of possible states (although this assumption is unlikely to be fulfilled). However, the model does show that the risk premium depends on the distribution of cash flows under the different states, and on the correlation of this distribution with the results of the remaining investments: the higher the correlation (ceteris paribus), the more the investment under consideration increases the company's total investment risk and, therefore, the higher the risk premium should be. With a low correlation, a decrease in overall risk is possible, perhaps even justifying a reduction in the discount rate applied.

8.3 Sensitivity Analysis

Description of the method

Sensitivity analysis aims to investigate the relationships between the various data and the target values of an investment appraisal and, if possible, the profitability of alternatives as well. The following questions are addressed by sensitivity analysis:

- How does the target value change with given variations of an input measure or of several input measures? (type A analysis)
- Which critical values must an input measure, or a combination of several input measures, achieve to reach a given target value? (type B analysis)

The critical values addressed in the second question may reflect the maximal deviation from the original (expected or most likely) input measures that can occur without affecting the project's absolute or relative profitability.

The target value changes can be analysed in two ways: by starting with the original data and changing it by gradual increments, or by using different possible input values (e.g. one minimum, one mean, and one maximum value), each in a separate calculation. The execution of a sensitivity analysis is based on the construction of a decision model and the determination of its input data. The type and number of input measures are then determined and the time intervals are fixed. At this step, a number of options arise. For example, in determining the NPV of an investment to expand production to include a new product type, the following input data might be analysed:

- The initial investment outlay
- The product's sales price
- The sales or production volume
- The cash outflows dependent on production volumes
- The cash outflows independent of production volumes
- The economic life
- The uniform discount rate

In addition, it might be possible to disaggregate some of the input measures and to perform sensitivity analyses for the resulting components. Moreover, input measures can be analysed in isolation or in combination with other measures, and the analysis may be related to one, some, or all periods within the planning period. As a result, many variations of sensitivity analyses arise. Possible forms of sensitivity analyses are illustrated in the following example.

Example 8-1 (Sensitivity analysis and the net present value model)

In the following example, the differentiated NPV formula presented in Section 3.2 is re-presented, along with its assumptions. The two investment alternatives being appraised are characterised by the data given below (the periodic data is assumed to remain unchanged over the investment projects' economic lives):

Input measures	**Investment project I**	**Investment project II**
Initial investment outlay (I_0) (€)	100,000	60,000
Production and sales volume (x) (units)	1,000	1,000
Sales price (p) (€ per unit)	100	100
Cash outflow per unit (dependent on production volume) cof_v (€ per unit)	50	60
Cash outflow per period (independent of production volume) COF_f (€)	16,000	17,500
Liquidation value (L) (€)	0	0
Economic life (T) (years)	5	5
Uniform discount rate (i) (%)	10	10
Net present value (€)	28,886.74	25,292.69

Tab. 8-5: Data for the two investment projects

The NPVs were determined in accordance with the formula mentioned above:

$$NPV = -I_0 + \sum_{t=1}^{T} ((p - cof_v) \cdot x - COF_f) \cdot q^{-t} + L \cdot q^{-T} \qquad (8.13)$$

To start with, the first alternative I, and the effects of variations in each parameter, are examined. These may be determined by means of a type A sensitivity analysis, i.e. changing each input measure while holding the values of the others constant, and calculating the resulting effects on the target function value (here the NPV). Figure 8-2 shows these effects in graphical form.

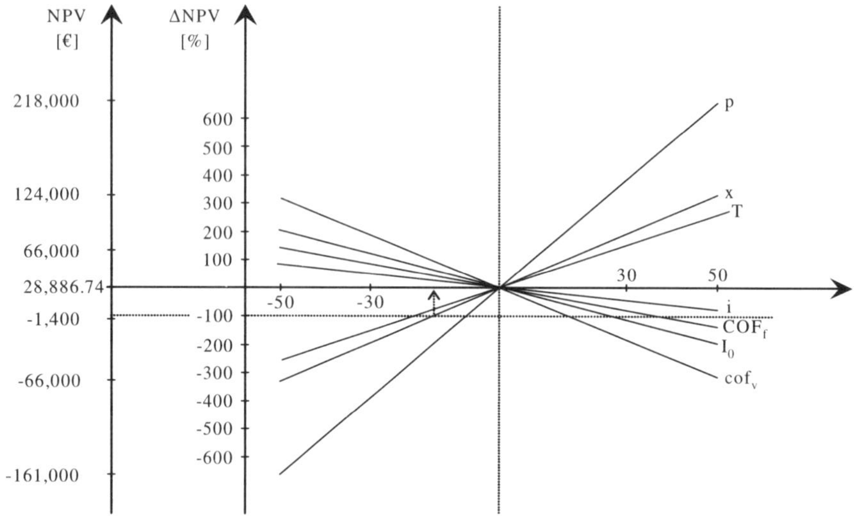

Fig. 8-2: Changes in the net present value with variations in individual input measures

In the example, linear representations of the NPV arise as functions of all input measures, with the exceptions of the uniform discount rate and economic life. The figure displays changes in the NPV as a function of changes in individual input measures. The steeper the NPV graph, the more sensitive the NPV is to variations in an input measure. In this example, p, x and cof_v have an especially strong influence on NPV.

With the help of this graph, the value of an input measure that leads to a minimum acceptable NPV can be estimated, i.e. critical values can be identified to form upper or lower limits. The difference between this critical value and the original estimated value, and the probability that this deviation might occur, are also useful inputs to decision-making.

The determination of critical values is the primary aim of a type B sensitivity analysis. For instance, the critical price p_{crit} that would achieve a NPV of zero may be determined with the help of the NPV formula (8.13):

$$NPV = -I_0 + \sum_{t=1}^{T} \left((p - cof_v) \cdot x - COF_f \right) \cdot q^{-t} + L \cdot q^{-T}$$

For NPV = 0, this may be transformed into:

$$0 = -I_0 + \sum_{t=1}^{T} ((p_{crit} - cof_v) \cdot x - COF_f) \cdot q^{-t} + L \cdot q^{-T} \qquad (8.14)$$

Or:

$$I_0 + \sum_{t=1}^{T} (cof_v \cdot x - COF_f) \cdot q^{-t} - L \cdot q^{-T} = p_{crit} \cdot x \cdot \sum_{t=1}^{T} q^{-t} \qquad (8.15)$$

And

$$\frac{I_0 + \sum_{t=1}^{T} (cof_v \cdot x + COF_f) \cdot q^{-t} - L \cdot q^{-T}}{x \cdot \sum_{t=1}^{T} q^{-t}} = p_{crit} \qquad (8.16)$$

Thus, for investment project I: p_{crit} = €92.38.

Similar calculations for the critical values of most other input measures are possible using appropriate formula transformations. These calculations are not viable for the uniform discount rate or the economic life, however, because these measures cannot be isolated in the NPV formula. The critical values of the uniform discount rate and the economic life are the results of the internal rate of return and dynamic payback period approaches; these calculations were discussed in Sections 3.4 and 3.5.

The following Figure 8-3 lists the critical values of investment project I for NPV = 0, together with the percentage deviations from the original values. These may be interpreted as a 'safety indicator'.

Input measure	Critical value	Deviation from original value
I_0	€128,886.74	28.89%
p	€92.38 per unit	7.62%
cof_v	€57.62 per unit	15.24%
x	847.60 units	15.24%
COF_f	€23,620.30	47.63%
i	20.76 %	107.60%
T	3.67 years	26.60%
L	–€46,522.38	–

Fig. 8-3: Critical values of individual input measures

A problem arises if changes are analysed for several periods over which the value of a measure varies. Then, the average allowable variation may be calculated with the help of a variation parameter.

If several input measures are examined simultaneously, the determination of critical value combinations results in a critical surface in the graphical illustration (the number of dimensions equals the number of analysed input measures -1). If, for example, the sales prices, and the sales and production volume are considered, the function for the critical combinations of prices and volumes for an NPV of zero is as follows:

$$p_{crit} = cof_v + \frac{I_0 + \sum_{t=1}^{T} COF_f \cdot q^{-t} - L \cdot q^{-T}}{x_{crit} \cdot \sum_{t=1}^{T} q^{-t}} \tag{8.17}$$

Figure 8-4 shows this function and the change in NPV caused by variations in sales prices and in sales and production volumes. This can be interpreted in the same way as when only one input measure varies.

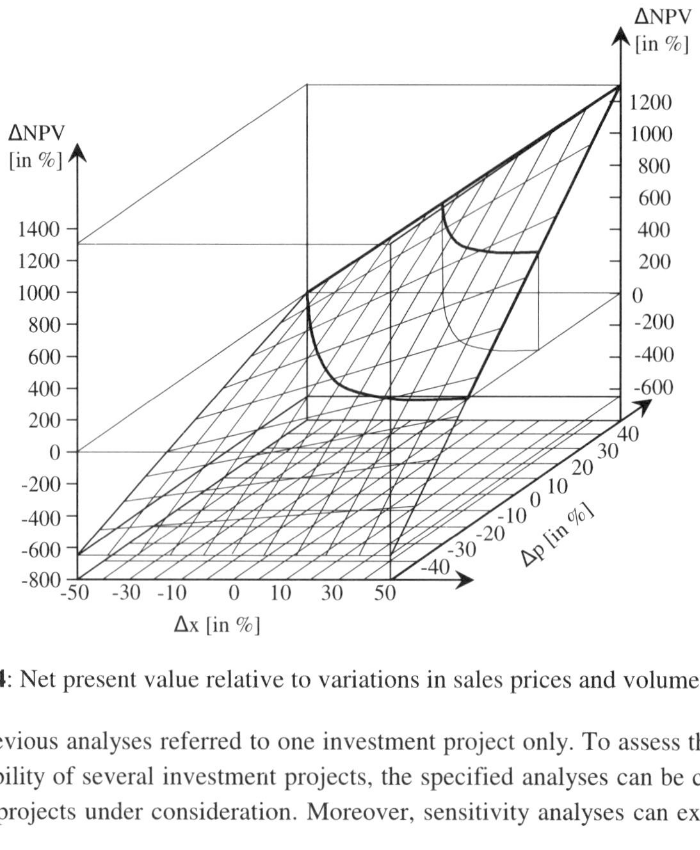

Fig. 8-4: Net present value relative to variations in sales prices and volumes

The previous analyses referred to one investment project only. To assess the relative profitability of several investment projects, the specified analyses can be carried out for all projects under consideration. Moreover, sensitivity analyses can examine the relative profitability of two investment projects directly. Different critical values then can be determined for every input measure. A special type of critical value arises if the values of a project's input measures are kept constant and the resultant target value (e.g. NPV) forms the starting point for determining critical values for another investment project (type (iii) as shown in Figure 8-5). This approach is particularly appropriate if an input measure affects the investment projects under consideration in different ways.

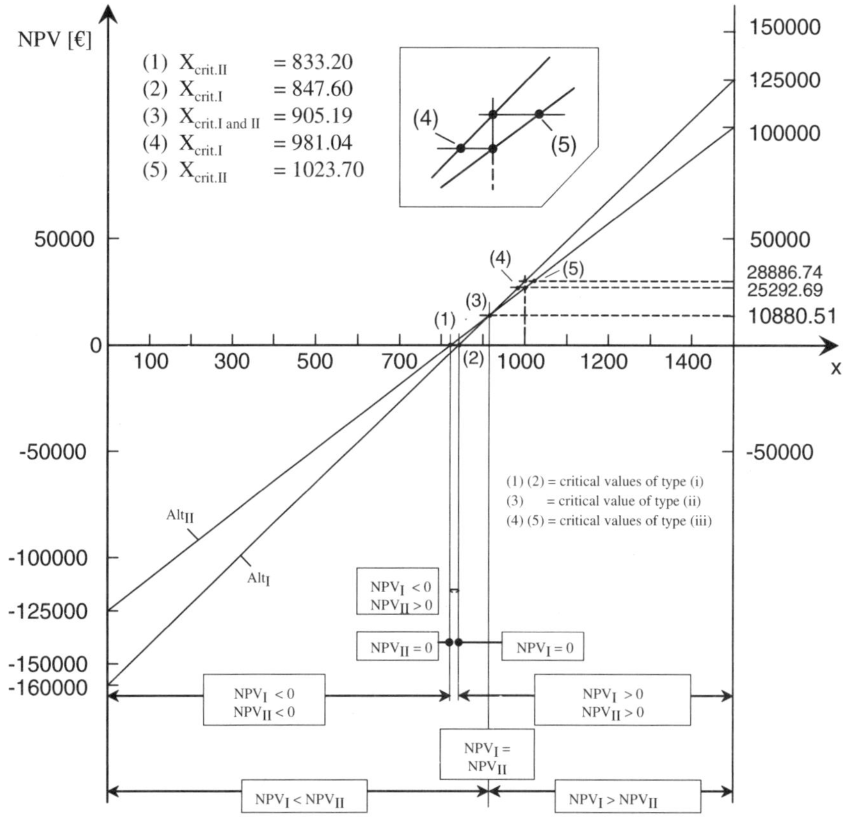

Fig. 8-5: Critical sales and production volumes for two investment alternatives

For uncertain measures that have an identical effect on both alternative projects (e.g. the sales or production volumes of a product generated by both projects), it is possible to determine a critical value at which both alternatives achieve identical target values (type (ii) in Figure 8-5). From this, areas of profitability can be pinpointed in regard to the input measures. This sort of critical value can be calculated by setting the NPV function of the fictitious differential investment to zero, and then deriving the critical value of the uncertain measure common to both projects. Figure 8-5 shows the critical values for the two investment projects in isolation from each other (type (i)) and in relation to each other (types (ii) and (iii)), using the example of production and sales volume variations. Using this approach, the influence of uncertain data on relative profitability may be readily determined for two investment projects, but with a high number of investment projects the calculations become very complicated.

Assessment of the method

Sensitivity analysis, as illustrated above, may be used in conjunction with any method for appraising a single investment project. For example, it can be applied to the visualisation of financial implications (VoFI) method, or to optimum economic life determinations. In addition, sensitivity analysis can also be applied to models that incorporate risk by adjusting the uniform discount rate or stream of cash flows (as discussed in Section 8.2).

The results of sensitivity analysis provide an insight into the structure of a model. Sensitivity analysis allows the examination of the effects of uncertain model data and violated assumptions on the model's results. It also contributes to project comparisons by showing how profitability depends on the data underlying a model's calculation. Yet, sensitivity analysis contains no decision rules, and it remains up to the decision-maker to select an investment alternative on the basis of the results generated.

With the help of sensitivity analysis, the relative importance of separate input measures can be ascertained and used to select alternatives and manage data procurement, planning and control activities. As sensitivity analysis requires little computational effort, it is a valuable instrument for investment decision-making under uncertainty.

A disadvantage of sensitivity analysis is that, for those measures not analysed, constancy is assumed. This assumption is often unrealistic, as input values seldom change independently. The simultaneous examination of changes in the values of two or more measures, though possible, leads to difficulties in interpretation. Other disadvantages are that only a few input values can be explicitly analysed, and no statements about the probability of their deviations are made. These disadvantages are avoided with risk analysis, as discussed next.

8.4 Risk Analysis

Description of the method

Risk analysis entails the representation of uncertain input measures as probability distributions. Taking into account the associations and interdependencies between input measures and between input and target measures, a probability distribution of possible values of a target measure is derived. This can be analysed to support decision-making under uncertainty.

Risk analysis comprises the following steps:

1. Formulation of a decision model.
2. Determination of the probability distributions for the input measures that are assumed to be uncertain.
3. Inclusion of dependencies between the uncertain input measures.
4. Calculation of a probability distribution for the target measure.
5. Interpretation of the results.

In contrast to sensitivity analysis, risk analysis covers not only the evaluation of a decision model, but other aspects of model analysis such as model construction and data procurement.

The initial formulation of a decision model involves, among other things, the selection of the input measures that are considered uncertain. The probability distributions for these input measures may be either discrete or continuous, like the (GAUSSIAN) normal distribution, the beta distribution, the triangular distribution, or the trapezoid distribution. Determining probability distributions is always problematic because, since all investment projects are unique, their estimation is likely to be subjective.

Another problem may arise from dependencies that exist between uncertain input measures. These are called 'stochastic dependencies', since the outcome of one uncertain input measure depends on the outcome of another uncertain input measure. They can be included in the analysis either with the help of correlation coefficients, or by defining a range of probability distributions for each (dependent) input measure that varies with another (independent) input measure. Then, for specific outcomes of the independent measure, a specific so-called *conditional* probability distribution of the dependent measure is determined and used in the calculations.

The fourth step of a risk analysis can involve either an analytic or a simulation approach. The analytic approach computes the distribution of the target function value from the distributions of the input measures. The application of this approach is constrained by certain assumptions, as it requires knowledge of the target value distribution. Since only a small number of input measures can be included, the analytical approach is not considered further here.

Using the simulation approach, multiple calculations are executed and, in every run, a random selection is made from the probability distributions of the input measures. The random choice of input measures must reflect their probabilities of occurring. A target value is then determined that incorporates both the uncertain input measures, taking their stochastic dependencies into account, and the known input measures. After multiple runs, a target value distribution is obtained. The number of simulation runs should be large enough to allow random numbers to be representative of the input measure probability distributions.

As a basis for the evaluation, the target values calculated in the multiple runs are assigned to different frequency classes. The absolute frequencies that arise for the separate classes can be translated into relative frequencies. These form the basis for determining a function that characterises the probability distribution (or density function), the distribution function, and/or the risk profile of the target measure. This procedure is demonstrated in the following example.

Example 8-2

Two investment projects A and B are under consideration. The following input measures are assumed to be uncertain: the sales prices, cash outflows (both dependent on and independent of production volumes), the liquidation values for both projects, and the production and sales volumes of alternative A. For all input measures, with the exception of the production and sales volumes of alternative A, the probability distribution is expected to remain unchanged in all periods. A triangular probability distribution is used and the distribution parameters (mean, minimum, and maximum value) are shown, along with the remaining relevant data, in Table 8-6. Stochastic dependencies between input measures and other distribution types remain unconsidered.

Input variable	**Alternative A**			**Alternative B**		
I_0		130,000			95,000	
i		0.1			0.1	
	Min. value	Mean value	Max. value	Min. value	Mean value	Max. value
L	0	20,000	50,000	0	12,000	30,000
p	92	100	105	92	100	105
cof_v	45	50	60	45	50	60
COF_f	15,000	16,000	17,000	11,500	12,500	13,500
X_t: t = 1	900	1,000	1,200	800	800	800
t = 2	950	1,050	1,150	800	800	800
t = 3	1,000	1,100	1,200	800	800	800
t = 4	950	1,050	1,150	800	800	800
t = 5	900	1,000	1,100	800	800	800

Tab. 8-6: Data for the two alternatives

In the following discussion, the risk analysis results are considered first with regard to investment project A. Figure 8-6 shows the NPV distribution function for this project.

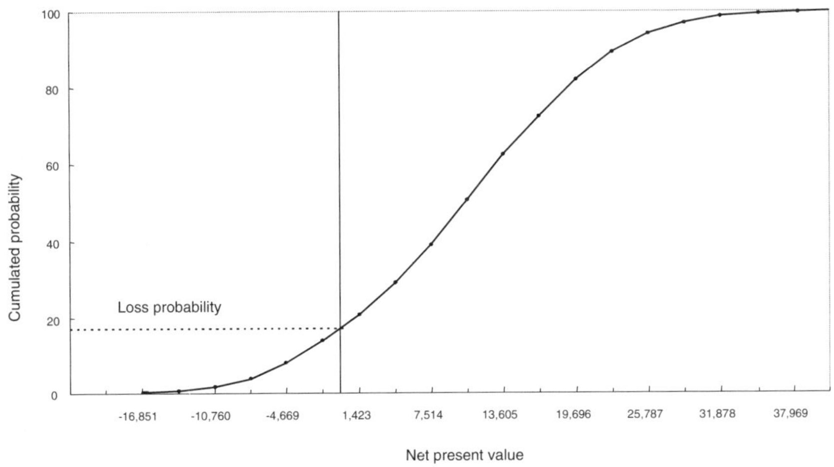

Fig. 8-6: Distribution function of the net present value of investment project A

Conclusions about the possible target value (NPV) outcomes can now be drawn from the position and shape of the distribution, or the distribution function. For example, the steeper the function, the smaller the variability in the target function values. Extreme values of the target measure become evident and significant ratios, such as expected values, standard deviations, variances, confidence intervals and loss probabilities can be determined. Also, the so-called value at risk, i.e. the maximum monetary loss with a given probability (confidence) level, can be derived from the distribution function (or the density function). In the example, the expected value of the NPV is €10,108; the standard deviation is €10,045 and the loss probability is approximately 18%.

The shape of the distribution function and the significant ratios are helpful for decision-making. They show the risk associated with an investment, and the probability of achieving a particular NPV outcome at best, can be derived for every point on the distribution function. When the NPV is zero, the corresponding probability indicates the likelihood that the project under consideration will be absolutely unprofitable. It can be interpreted as a loss probability and applied as an indicator of so-called *stochastic dominance* over the option to reject the project (it is a stochastic dominance because of the inclusion of uncertainties).

Key Concept:

When the loss probability is zero, accepting an investment project achieves stochastic dominance over the 'rejection' option because absolute profitability is achieved for each scenario of input measures taken into account.

Risk analysis can also be used to assess the relative profitability of investments. Using the approach outlined above, a probability distribution, distribution function and/or key ratios can be calculated for each alternative and used in decision-making. In the current example, the results of the risk analysis for project B (expected value of the NPV is €9,666; standard deviation is €6,676; loss probability is approximately 8%) can be compared with those of project A. Also, the distribution functions can be used to assess the relative profitability of alternatives. Stochastic dominance might also be identified from the distribution functions.

> *Key Concept:*
> Based on the comparison of distribution functions, a project exhibits first degree stochastic dominance over an alternative project if its NPV at least equals that of the alternative at every cumulative probability and exceeds it at least once.
> A project exhibits second degree stochastic dominance over an alternative if the area that is constituted by cumulating the differences between the distribution function of the project and that of the alternative is *either* always positive, *or* never negative and positive at least once.

Assuming the decision-maker is risk-averse, second degree stochastic dominance may suffice for decision-making in the absence of first degree dominance.

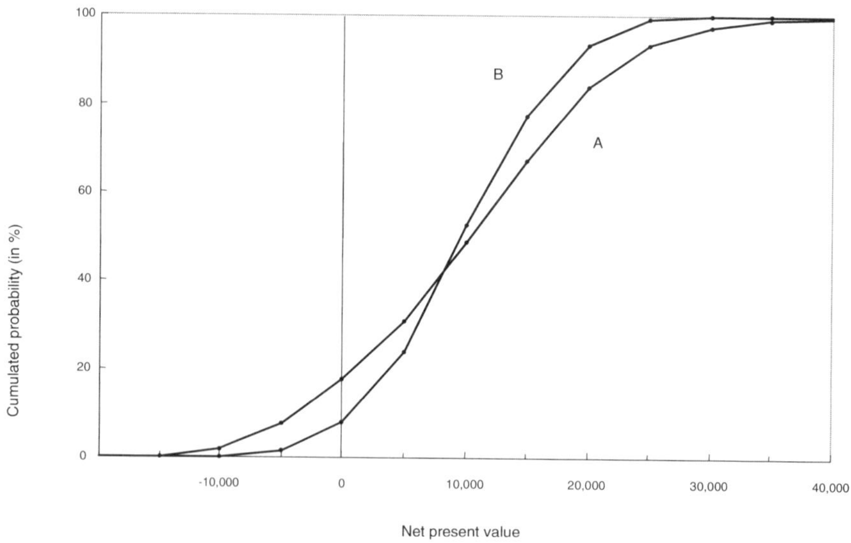

Fig. 8-7: Distribution function of the net present values of investment projects A and B

Figure 8-7 presents distribution functions for the NPVs of projects A and B. In this case no stochastic dominance is present. This is obvious in regard to first degree stochastic dominance because the distribution functions intersect. The absence of second degree dominance may be deduced either by constituting an area of cumulated differences as described before, or from the observation that alternative A has both a higher loss probability and a higher expected value. Thus, the sign of the function of cumulated differences must change and there can be no stochastic dominance.

The relative profitability of two investments may be better assessed using a simulation of the differential investment (worked out by comparing the cash flow profiles). The NPV of the differential investment then is re-calculated over multiple simulation runs, taking into account the probability distributions of any uncertain input measures.

Using a simulation of the NPV distribution for the differential investment, random influences can be included in the analysis either independently, or by considering that components of both projects' NPVs depend on some of the same factors. These components therefore undergo identical random movements for both investment projects in every simulation run. This is an advantage of a differential investment simulation over separate simulations for the two investment projects. Improved evaluation possibilities are another advantage. The results of differential investment simulation are similar to those for a single investment (described previously), so the probability of achieving specific NPV differences can be deduced directly from the distribution function of a differential investment. Accordingly, the probability of a particular relative profitability occurring can be also seen from the distribution function, at the point where NPV is zero. However, it should be noted that it is not possible to assess the absolute profitability of both projects under consideration, and multiple differential investments must be formed if several alternatives are being assessed.

Assessment of the method

As presented, risk analysis determines a probability distribution for an investment's outcome. It takes into account: a relatively large number of potential influences, different combinations of data, their probabilities and any stochastic dependencies between input measures. By showing the range of possible project outcomes, this procedure provides appropriate risk measures to support the assessment and selection of risky investment alternatives.

The method does not, however, supply a decision rule. In cases where the project acceptance decision fails to achieve stochastic dominance over the 'rejection' option (e.g. in the assessment of absolute profitability), or a project has no first degree stochastic dominance over an alternative investment (e.g. in the assessment of relative profitability), the choice must be based on the projects' data distributions and the decision-maker's personal preferences for certainty.

The application of risk analysis requires the use of specific computer software. Problems often occur with determining the input data, particularly the probability distributions and stochastic dependencies. The considerable effort needed to procure this data may be one reason for the limited use of risk analysis in practice. In addition, because many decision situations are unique and non-repeatable, figures are based on subjective estimations rather than statistical data. The uncertainty of data, and therefore of the results, tends to be particularly high in unique decision situations. Another disadvantage of risk analysis is that, in the form presented here, it cannot identify the influence of individual input measures on the result. However, by combining the last two methods described a 'sensitive risk analysis' can be undertaken.

8.5 Decision-Tree Method

Description of the method

The decision-tree method uses a dynamic model that includes several scenarios, their probabilities of occurring and the subsequent decisions that are contingent upon their occurrence. Since it is assumed that subsequent decisions will be based on these various scenarios and their differing expectations of the future, the impact of information access is also taken into account. The name of the method is derived from the undirected graph, the so-called *decision-tree* (see Figure 8-8), used to illustrate the decision problem. The models considered, as well as the planning procedure, are said to be *flexible*, since the procedure incorporates opportunities to react to new information. The branches and knots of the decision-tree can be described as follows:

D	–	Decision knot, i.e. a knot that characterises a decisive event
d	–	Branch that represents a decision alternative
S	–	Random knot, i.e. a knot that marks a random event
s	–	Branch that points to the scenario that results from a random event,
R	–	Result knot, i.e. a knot that characterises the consequences of a sequence of one or more decisions and scenarios
R/D	–	Knot that signifies when a result exists and a decision is to be made

The s branches are assigned probabilities to reflect the likelihood of the various scenarios occurring. The number of possible scenarios is assumed to be limited.

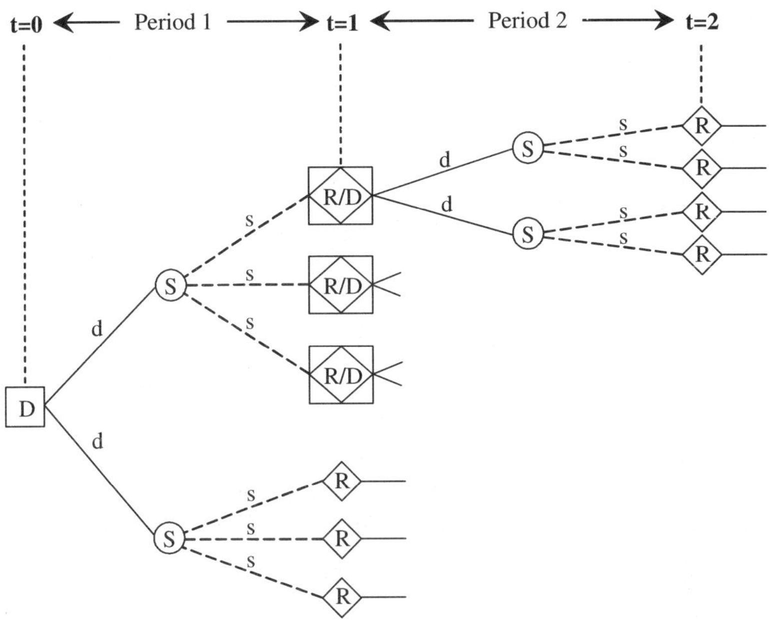

Fig. 8-8: Formal structure of a decision-tree

In the first step of the method the structure of the decision-tree is determined by defining the planning period, its different parts, the alternatives and the possible scenarios. Forecasting the other relevant decision-making data is the next step. If an NPV model, for example, is used to assess project profitability, the initial investment outlays, economic lives, liquidation values, sales and production volumes, prices and cash outflows must be forecast, and the probabilities of the scenarios and uniform discount rate must be estimated.

The target measure is usually the expected value of the NPV, so:

> *Key Concept:*
> The optimum outcome is achieved by pursuing the decision sequence that shows the highest expected NPV.

To determine this decision sequence, the rollback procedure of MAGEE (based on dynamic optimisation) can be used. This procedure first considers the last point in time at which decisions should be made. The decision choice faced at this point in time is characterised by a specific previous sequence of actions and scenarios that determines the current scope for action and expectations. Based on the data forecasted for potential scenarios, the alternative with the maximum expected NPV is selected, and only this option is examined further. Next, the optimum alternative is determined for the preceding decision knots, taking into account previously selected actions and their expected NPVs. The continuation of this procedure leads to the selection of the optimum alternative at the beginning of the planning period. This is illustrated in the following examples.

Example 8-3

The first example deals with *assessing profitability including subsequent decisions*. At the beginning of the planning period two investment alternatives A and B are available. By choosing alternative B the decision-maker is able to select one of two following investment projects that are under consideration (B_1, B_2) at the beginning of the next period. For simplicity, the planning period includes only two periods. Assume all cash outflows and sales prices are known, and that cash inflows and outflows occur at the ends of the periods. Certainty is also assumed for the initial investment outlay, the uniform discount rate and the liquidation values received at the end of the planning period when the investments end. The production and sales volumes are uncertain, and it is expected that favourable or unfavourable scenarios could occur in every period. The probabilities of the various production and sales volumes scenarios appear with the other relevant data in Table 8-7:

Input measures	**Alternatives**			
	A	**B**	**B_1**	**B_2**
Initial investment outlays (€)	1,000,000	500,000	550,000	300,000
Cash outflows (independent of production volumes) (€)	120,000	50,000	50,000	50,000
Cash outflows per unit (dependent on production volumes) (€ per unit)	50	50	50	50
Sales prices (€ per unit)	100	100	100	100
Liquidation values (€)	100,000	50,000	55,000	30,000
Production and sales volumes (units)				
t = 1:				
high demand (w = 0.6)	20,000	10,000	–	–
low demand (w = 0.4)	12,500	8,000	–	–
t = 2:				
if high demand at t = 1				
high demand (w = 0.6)	20,000	10,000	16,000	10,000
low demand (w = 0.4)	12,500	8,000	12,000	8,000
if low demand at t = 1				
high demand (w = 0.4)	20,000	10,000	16,000	10,000
low demand (w = 0.6)	12,500	8,000	12,000	8,000
Uniform discount rate (%)		10		

Tab. 8-7: Data for the alternatives

Figure 8-9 presents the decision-tree for this example. It contains three decision knots. Decisions must be made at t = 0 and t = 1, the latter under two potential scenarios (high demand (H) and low demand (L) in the first period). One of the subsequent investment projects, B_1 or B_2, may be realised or the decision-maker might refrain from investing; an alternative designated Ra.

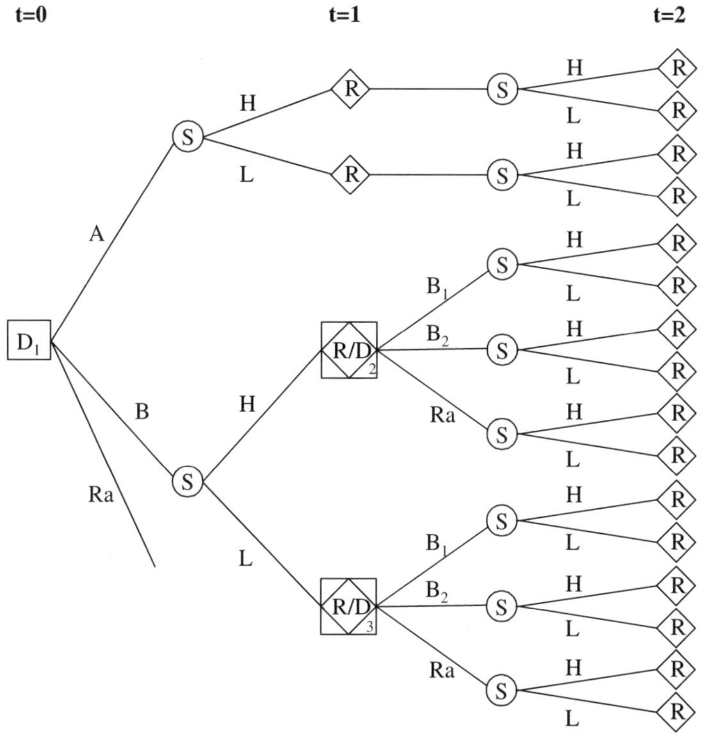

Fig. 8-9: Decision-tree of Example 8-3

Using the rollback procedure, the decision situation is analysed first for t = 1. Thus, knot R/D_2, which represents the case of an initial decision for B and a high demand in period 1, is considered. For the alternative B_1, the expected value of the NPV at t = 1 is:

$$ENPV_{B_1} = -550{,}000 + (0.6 \cdot 16{,}000 \cdot (100-50) + 0.4 \cdot 12{,}000 \cdot (100-50)) \cdot 1.1^{-1}$$

Initial investment outlay — *Surpluses of the cash inflows over the quantity-dependent cash outflows under the scenarios in t = 2, weighted by the probabilities of each scenario and discounted to t = 1*

$$- 50{,}000 \cdot 1.1^{-1} \quad + \quad 55{,}000 \cdot 1.1^{-1}$$

Discounted quantity-independent cash outflow — *Discounted liquidation value*

$$ENPV_{B_1} = €109{,}090.91$$

The expected NPV of alternative B_2 may be determined in the same way:

$$ENPV_{B_2} = €100{,}000$$

As the expected NPV of the 'refrain' alternative Ra is zero, alternative B_1 is the most profitable. Accordingly, given current information, B_1 would be selected if option B was chosen at the beginning of the first period and a high demand followed. Only this alternative, along with its associated expected NPV, is considered further in analysing the preceding decision (i.e. the initial decision at $t = 0$) and regarding the case of a positive scenario (high demand).

The knot R/D_3 is associated with an unfavourable environmental condition (low demand) after implementing B. For this knot, the expected NPVs of the alternative choices may be calculated as described above. They are:

$$ENPV_{B_1} = €72{,}727.27$$
$$ENPV_{B_2} = €81{,}818.18$$
$$ENPV_{Ra} = €0$$

Accordingly, if option B was selected at $t = 0$, then B_2 is the optimum choice at $t = 1$ if unfavourable conditions prevail. Only B_2 and its expected NPV is further considered, therefore.

Now, after all the $t = 1$ decision options have been analysed, the initial decision at $t = 0$ is considered. The expected NPVs for alternatives A and B must be determined and, in the case of B, the subsequent alternatives are considered. For alternative A the following expected NPV arises (as at $t = 0$):

$$ENPV_A = -1{,}000{,}000 - 120{,}000 \cdot 1{,}1^{-1} - 120{,}000 \cdot 1.1^{-1}$$

Initial investment outlay — *Present values of the quantity-independent cash outflows in t = 1 and t = 2*

$$+ (0.6 \cdot 20{,}000 \cdot (100 - 50) + 0.4 \cdot 12{,}500 \cdot (100 - 50)) \cdot 1.1^{-1}$$

Present values of the surpluses of the cash inflows over the quantity-dependent cash outflows in t=1, weighted by the probabilities of each scenario

$$+ \begin{pmatrix} (0.6 \cdot 0.6 + 0.4 \cdot 0.4) \cdot 20{,}000 \cdot (100 - 50) + \\ (0.6 \cdot 0.4 + 0.4 \cdot 0.6) \cdot 12{,}500 \cdot (100 - 50) \end{pmatrix} \cdot 1.1^{-2}$$

Present values of the surpluses of the cash inflows over the quantity-dependent cash outflows in t = 2, weighted by the probabilities of each scenario

$$+ 100{,}000 \cdot 1.1^{-2}$$

Present value of the liquidation value

$$ENPV_A = €324{,}793.32$$

Note, that the probability of a scenario involving several random events appears within this calculation as a product of the probabilities of the separate associated scenarios.

For alternative B the expected NPV can be determined (as at t = 0) in the following way:

$$ENPV_B = -500{,}000 \quad - 50{,}000 \cdot 1{,}1^{-1} - 50{,}000 \cdot 1.1^{-2}$$

Initial investment outlay — *Present values of the quantity-independent cash outflows in t = 1 and t = 2*

$$+ (0.6 \cdot 20{,}000 \cdot (100 - 50) + 0.4 \cdot 12{,}500 \cdot (100 - 50)) \cdot 1.1^{-1}$$

Present values of the surpluses of the cash inflows over the quantity-dependent cash outflows in t = 1, weighted by the probabilities of each scenario

$$+ \begin{pmatrix} (0.6 \cdot 0.6 + 0.4 \cdot 0.4) \cdot 10{,}000 \cdot (100 - 50) + \\ (0.6 \cdot 0.4 + 0.4 \cdot 0.6) \cdot 8{,}000 \cdot (100 - 50) \end{pmatrix} \cdot 1.1^{-2}$$

Present values of the surpluses of the cash inflows over the quantity-dependent cash outflows in t = 2, weighted by the probabilities of each scenario

$$+ 50{,}000 \cdot 1.1^{-2}$$

Present value of the liquidation value

$$+ 0.6 \cdot 109{,}090.91 \cdot 1.1^{-1} + 0.4 \cdot 81{,}818.18 \cdot 1.1^{-1}$$

Present values of the weighted expected NPVs of the optimal follow-up investments (weighted by the probabilities of each scenario)

$$ENPV_B = €335{,}537.14$$

The expected NPV of alternative B is higher than those of alternative A and the 'refrain' alternative Ra. Accordingly, the optimum decision sequence consists in first selecting alternative B and then – depending on the prevailing conditions – either alternative B_1 (in the case of high demand) or B_2 (in the case of low demand). However, it should be pointed out that this recommendation is based on the data available at the beginning of the planning period (t = 0). Any changes in these data may require renewed investment decision-making at t = 1.

Example 8-4

The second example deals with a *decision about investment timing*. A company can undertake an investment project immediately (i.e. at t = 0) or at the beginning of the following periods (t = 1 or t = 2). Whatever the start time is, an initial investment outlay of €100,000 is required. Uncertainty exists regarding future product demand. This means that, at the end of the first period (t = 1), there is an equal probability of achieving a cash flow surplus of either €14,000 (situation H) or €9,000 (situation L).

For the second period, the expected cash flow surplus (at t = 2) depends on that of the first period, and there is an equal probability that it will grow by 40% (H) or reduce by 10% (L). Furthermore, it is assumed, for simplicity, that the uncertainty is resolved at the end of the second period, and that perpetuity is achieved from t = 3 onwards, of an amount equalling the cash flow surplus at t = 2. The following decision-tree illustrates the problem situation.

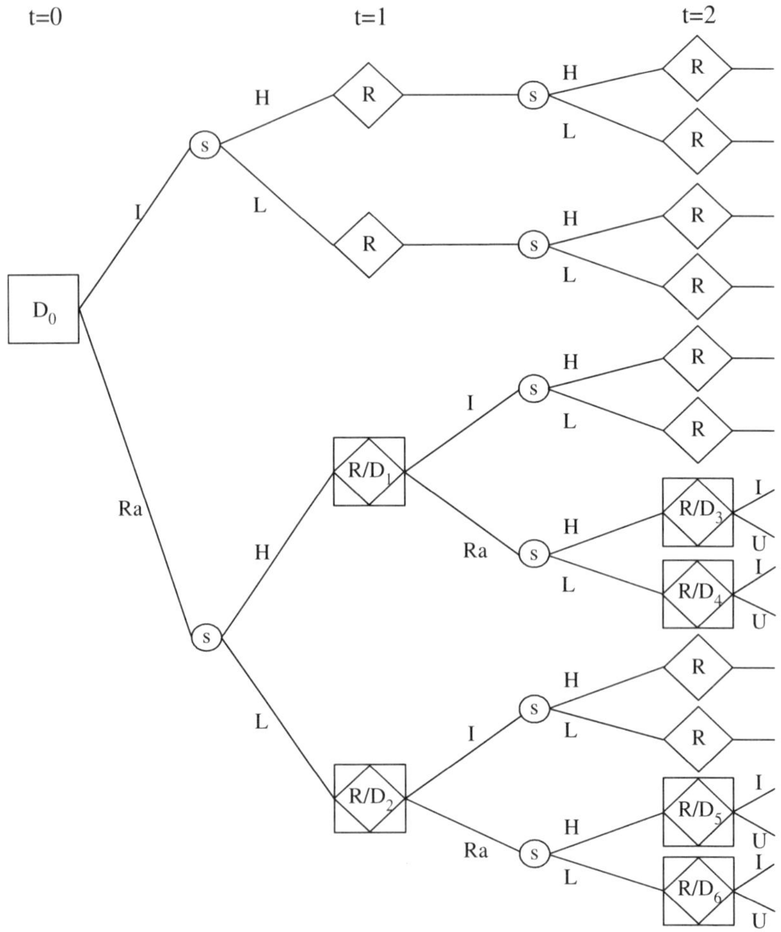

Fig. 8-10: Decision-tree for a decision about investment timing

Assuming a uniform discount rate of 12% and the aim of maximising the expected NPV, the optimum investment time (t = 0, 1 or 2) must be determined.

To solve this problem, the decision knots at t = 2 should be analysed first. At the decision knots R/D_j the following expected NPVs (in €) arise for the alternative 'investment' ($ENPV_{Ij}$):

$$ENPV_{I3} = -100{,}000 + \frac{19{,}600}{0.12} = 63{,}333.33$$

$$ENPV_{I4} = ENPV_{I5} = -100{,}000 + \frac{12{,}600}{0.12} = 5{,}000$$

$$ENPV_{I6} = -100{,}000 + \frac{8{,}100}{0.12} = -32{,}500$$

As the expected NPV of the 'refrain' alternative is zero in each case, it can be concluded that an investment should be undertaken at the decision knots R/D_3, R/D_4 and R/D_5, but at knot R/D_6 an investment should be rejected. In the latter situation, two unfavourable demand developments have rendered the investment's expected future prospects particularly negative (expressed as expected cash flows).

In the next step, conditional decisions should be made at t = 1. For knot R/D_1 the following expected NPVs ($ENPV_{I1}$ or $ENPV_{Ra1}$) are calculated (in €):

$$ENPV_{I1} = -100{,}000 + \frac{\left(0.5 \cdot \left(19{,}600 + \frac{19{,}600}{0.12}\right) + 0.5 \cdot \left(12{,}600 + \frac{12{,}600}{0.12}\right)\right)}{1.12} = 34{,}166.67$$

$$ENPV_{Ra1} = \left(\frac{0.5 \cdot 63{,}333.33 + 0.5 \cdot 5{,}000}{1.12}\right) = 30{,}505.95$$

Similarly, the expected values of $ENPV_{I2}$ or $ENPV_{Ra2}$ relating to knot R/D_2 are (in €):

$$ENPV_{I2} = -100{,}000 + \frac{\left(0.5 \cdot \left(12{,}600 + \frac{12{,}600}{0.12}\right) + 0.5 \cdot \left(8{,}100 + \frac{8{,}100}{0.12}\right)\right)}{1.12} = -13{,}750$$

$$ENPV_{Ra2} = \left(\frac{0.5 \cdot 5{,}000 + 0.5 \cdot 0}{1.12}\right) = 2{,}232.14$$

Because of the higher expected NPV at knot R/D_1, the investment should be made, while at knot R/D_2 the 'refrain' alternative should be chosen.

Finally, the options existing at the beginning of the planning period (knot D_0) can be assessed. The expected NPVs ($ENPV_{I0}$ and $ENPV_{Ra0}$) are (in €):

$$\mathrm{ENPV}_{I0} = -100{,}000 + \frac{0.5 \cdot 14{,}000 + 0.5 \cdot 9{,}000}{1.12}$$

$$+ \frac{0.5 \cdot \left(0.5 \cdot \left(19{,}600 + \frac{19{,}600}{0.12}\right) + 0.5 \cdot \left(12{,}600 + \frac{12{,}600}{0.12}\right)\right)}{1{,}12^2}$$

$$+ \frac{0.5 \cdot \left(0.5 \cdot \left(12{,}600 + \frac{12{,}600}{0.12}\right) + 0.5 \cdot \left(8{,}100 + \frac{8{,}100}{0.12}\right)\right)}{1.12^2} = 8{,}668.15$$

$$\mathrm{ENPV}_{Ra0} = \left(\frac{0.5 \cdot 34{,}166.67 + 0.5 \cdot 2{,}232.14}{1.12}\right) = 16{,}249.47$$

The results show that it is profitable:

- To reject any investment at t = 0.
- To invest at t = 1 after a positive scenario (high demand) in the first period.
- And, in the case of an unfavourable scenario (low demand) in the first period, to reject the investment at t = 1, but invest at t = 2 if a positive scenario follows in the second period.

The total expected NPV of this decision sequence is €16,249.47.

In the literature, the issue of information access is often neglected. Information access here is reflected in scenario-specific expectations about future developments, which are included within the likewise scenario-specific choice of subsequent investments. The benefit of information access depends on the degree of uncertainty: it rises ceteris paribus with growing uncertainty. In addition, the timing of information access (the earlier the better) and the quality of the additional information influence its impact on the investment outcome. The quality of the additional information depends on the number of possible environmental conditions in a period, and the extent to which the information differs between scenarios (i.e. on the probabilities of possible scenarios and the expected scenario-specific results).

Figure 8-11 shows differing potential future developments after information is accessed at t = 1 (for situations A, B and C). An assumed given number of scenarios at t = 1 and a given number of possible (and uncertain) future developments after t = 1 are symbolised by straight lines with a terminator point. The terminator point at t = T symbolises the expected value of the target values (e.g. NPVs) attainable at t = 1. For each, two positive and two negative target values (TV) could be obtained. The degree of uncertainty is documented only by the range of possible developments. As a simplification, the probabilities of these developments, which may also influence the degree of uncertainty, are not considered here.

Assess to additional information is particularly valuable if, as in situation A, only one development and one corresponding scenario can occur after t = 1. The information tends to have a higher (lower) value if the future developments can be described in a highly (less) differentiated way. In situation B, the additional information has moderate value because only two different future developments can occur after each of the scenarios at t = 1. If future developments after t = 1 are independent of the scenarios identified at t = 1, then additional information has no value (as in situation C).

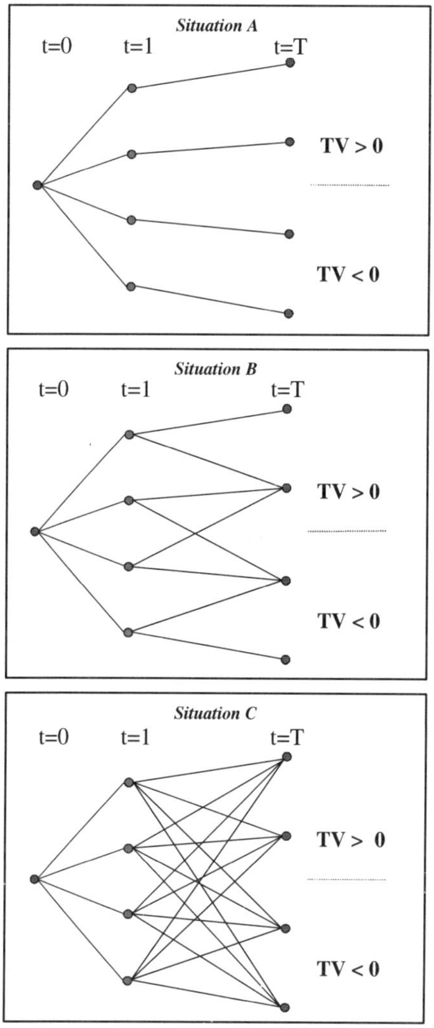

Fig. 8-11: Differentiated expectations about future developments

Assessment of the method

The decision-tree method is designed to evaluate flexible models. This form of analysis can greatly assist investment decision-making since the aspects it includes (potential scenarios and their probabilities of occurring, information access and scenario-specific subsequent alternatives, and the flexibility of alternatives) significantly affect the profitability of the investment options available at t = 0. The inclusion of expected future access to information is especially important for decisions about the timing of investments.

The rollback procedure, complete enumeration, dynamic optimisation and mixed-integer programming can all be used to determine optimum decision sequences for the model forms presented here. Problems arise with all these procedures, however, where high numbers of decisions, decision alternatives and possible scenarios are being considered, since the decision-tree becomes very complex, complicating data collection and the calculation of optimum solutions. Thus, it is necessary to limit the number of scenarios analysed. In the form presented here, the decision-tree method is feasible only if relatively few uncertain measures are incorporated. Furthermore, only a few developments of uncertain measures can be included and only one monetary target measure (e.g. NPV) is considered.

Another disadvantage is that only expected values enter into the decision, not potential deviations from these values. In accordance with the BERNOULLI principle, this implies risk-neutral decision-makers. Divergent risk attitudes can be included via risk utility functions or certainty equivalents in the decision-tree method, although this increases the complexity of the calculations. Additionally, risk-adjusted uniform discount rates may be used, though it should be noted that the risk structure varies according to the scenarios and the decisions made. Therefore, a single risk-adjusted discount rate cannot reflect risk accurately: scenario-specific interest rates are necessary. However, their determination is also problematic. A combination of the decision-tree method and sensitivity analysis offers an alternative means of including risk, as do market-based estimations of cash flows and the options pricing model. The latter will be described in the next section.

8.6 Options Pricing Models

Characteristics, types and value of real options

Companies can reduce the uncertainty associated with investments by exploiting their potential to adapt to future developments. For example, they might take an opportunity to delay an investment, change it, interrupt it temporarily, or abandon it altogether. Such scope for action, or project flexibility, can be called *real options* (as opposed to options on securities, which are financial options). Additionally, in a broader sense every investment can be understood as a real option – a chance (option) to achieve (uncertain) cash flow surpluses in the future from an initial investment outlay. However, in the following, the term *real option* is not used in this broad sense, but as an expression of the future scope for action associated with investment projects.

A real option enables the investor to carry out a particular action without obligation. A company will exercise the option only if it expects to receive an economic advantage from doing so and will reject it otherwise. Therefore, real options help to limit the danger of loss associated with investments, while at the same time enabling companies to exploit opportunities. Accordingly, their value is always higher than, or equal to, zero. The execution of an option represents an irreversible action, resulting in the loss of the option itself.

Real options can appear in many different forms. These include:

- *Waiting or delay options* (flexibility in the timing of an initial investment).
- *Closing options* (enabling an end to an investment).
- *Deactivation options* (enabling an interruption in the realisation, or use, of an investment project for a specific time).
- *Continuation options* (where an investment project is subdivided into parts and, after the end of a part, a new decision can be made).
- *Extension and restriction options* (a company can extend or diminish the capacities created by an investment).
- *Changeover options* (input factors used and products generated can be varied).
- *Innovation options* (investments in research and development that create the basis for developing new technologies, products and markets).

Moreover, options may be differentiated according to other characteristics. A *single option* can be carried out independently from others, while a *combined option* exists only in association with others. *Exclusive options* are reserved for a single company, which is not the case for *shared options*. *Call options* are related to buying decisions, whereas *put options* concern selling decisions. An *american option* can be carried out at any time during the project's life, while a *european option* can be exercised only at certain times (real options are usually american options).

The value of a real option is determined by several factors. *Uncertainty* about future developments is a key factor: with increasing uncertainty, the value of an option rises ceteris paribus. A positive correlation also exists, particularly in the case of delay options, between the length of the option's *life* and its value: the longer the option exists, the more time is available to observe environmental developments and adapt to them, so the higher the option value. Moreover, the *quality of additional information* is important, since the more the information reduces uncertainty the more valuable it is. Another factor is the *exclusiveness* of the option. When increasing numbers of companies can use an option its value drops, due to greater competition and the fact that its life tends to shorten because of the danger of another company utilising it. The value of financial options is essentially determined by their *settlement prices*. These correspond, in real options, with the initial cash outflows payable for the option (the 'exercise price'): the higher these cash outflows, the smaller the net value of the option.

Real options can significantly affect the profitability of investment projects: a factor that 'classical' investment appraisal methods (such as NPV) have been accused of disregarding. But, this criticism is valid only where models such as NPV assume certainty and, therefore, the potential value of options under conditions of uncertainty is overlooked. The criticism does *not* apply where revised procedures like the decision-tree method are combined with the NPV model, since the analysis then explicitly includes uncertainty, and subsequent decisions depending on scenarios as well as on future episodes of information access. The decision-tree method is designed to take real options, like delay or continuation options, into account. However, given the substantial effort needed to use the decision-tree model, alternative approaches that encompass both uncertainty and future scope for action should be considered. Since financial options encompass similar issues, the procedures developed by options pricing theory for the valuation of financial options might also have potential for assessing real options. The so-called *binomial model* seems particularly suitable for valuing real options. This model is presented and discussed next.

The binomial model

The binomial model was originally developed by COX, ROSS and RUBINSTEIN (1979) for valuing financial options. The model assumes it is possible to buy a portfolio of traded stocks that has identical cash flows to the option. In a perfect capital market (and, thus, a market free of arbitrage), this portfolio would have the same price as the option. It is, therefore, termed a *duplication* or *hedge portfolio*. The value of the option may be derived from the prices of the securities in the duplication portfolio: a procedure termed 'pricing by duplication'. Subjective risk preferences remain unconsidered in this valuation, since any risk premiums are implicit in the prices of the securities.

First, the value of options that entitle the holder to acquire one or more shares in a particular company is calculated. Using the binomial model, a duplication portfolio, comprising risk-free financial investments plus a number of these share options, is analysed for the period during which the option may be exercised. This period is subdivided into a limited number of equal intervals for purposes of analysis. All market participants are assumed to have homogeneous expectations of share price movements within each of these time intervals. These movements are specified in that, given a known value at the beginning of the period (time t), only two values (binomial process) are possible at the end of the period (time t + 1).

Based on the following arguments, a formula for the current value of an option with a term of one period can be derived. At the beginning of the option term, a share quotation S is given. At its end, the share price will have changed to either $u \cdot S$ (a favourable development) or $d \cdot S$ (an unfavourable development). The option holder may buy the share at the end of the option term for a certain price (K), the so-called settlement price. The decision to exercise the option will depend on the share price. If it is above the settlement price, the option will be exercised; otherwise the option will be allowed to lapse. Therefore, the option's value at the end of the term, which is called C_u or C_d depending on the change in the share price (u or d), equals either the difference between the share price and the settlement price (if this is greater than zero) or zero. To calculate the option value at the beginning of the term (symbolised by C), a duplication portfolio of Δ shares and a risk-free financial investment of an amount B and with an interest rate i (giving rise to a compounding factor $r = 1 + i$) is considered. The possible changes in the value of this duplication portfolio and the option value in the binomial model are presented in Figure 8-11, together with the underlying share prices and their probabilities q and $1 - q$.

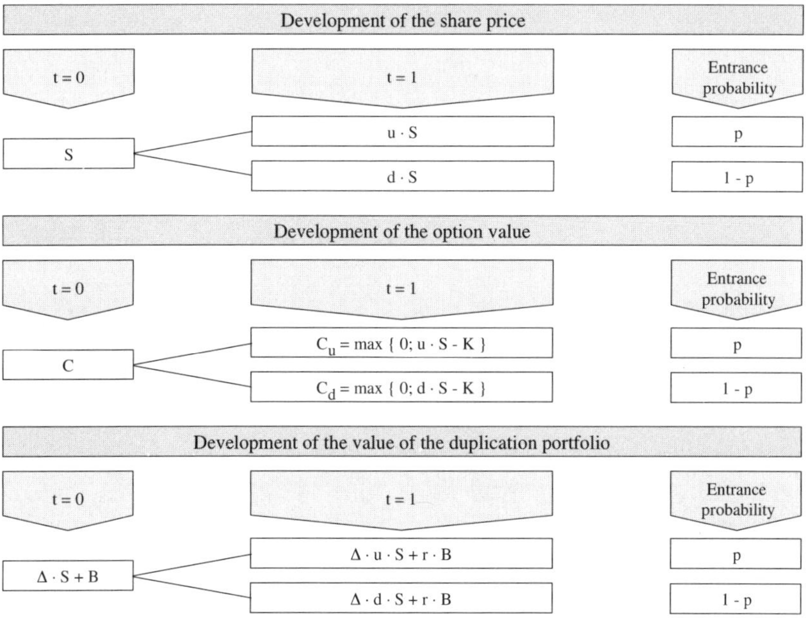

Fig. 8-12: Share prices, option values and value of the duplication portfolio in the binomial model

At the end of the option term, the value of the duplication portfolio and the option value are equal for both possible outcomes. This is expressed as:

$$\Delta \cdot u \cdot S + r \cdot B = C_u \quad \text{and} \tag{8.18}$$

$$\Delta \cdot d \cdot S + r \cdot B = C_d \tag{8.19}$$

The values for Δ and B can be derived from these equations using the following formula:

$$\Delta = \frac{C_u - C_d}{(u - d) \cdot S} \tag{8.20}$$

After transformation, B is:

$$B = \frac{u \cdot C_d - d \cdot C_u}{(u - d) \cdot r} \tag{8.21}$$

Since the option and the duplication portfolio are expected to have the same cash flows under the assumptions made (particularly the exclusion of arbitrage opportunities), they must also have the same price. Therefore:

$$C = \Delta \cdot S + B \tag{8.22}$$

And thus:

$$C = \frac{C_u - C_d}{u - d} + \frac{u \cdot C_d - d \cdot C_u}{(u - d) \cdot r} \tag{8.23}$$

As well as:

$$C = \frac{\left(\frac{r - d}{u - d}\right) \cdot C_u + \left(\frac{u - r}{u - d}\right) \cdot C_d}{r} \tag{8.24}$$

Using:

$$q = \frac{r - d}{u - d} \quad \text{and} \quad 1 - q = \frac{u - r}{u - d} \tag{8.25}$$

The current value of an option (of one period's length) becomes:

$$C = \frac{q \cdot C_u + (1 - q) \cdot C_d}{r} \tag{8.26}$$

The symbol q represents a so-called pseudo probability, as $0 < q < 1$ is valid, but q or $1 - q$ do not correspond with the actual probabilities of the respective share price occurring. This points to an interesting feature of the binomial model – the probabilities of the share price developments p and $1 - p$ are not included in the valuation formula for the option and, therefore, need not be estimated subjectively. Moreover, the value of the option is not affected directly by the risk preference of individual investors. Because of these circumstances, this form of option valuation can be described as 'preference free'. Finally, it is worth noting that the share price movement is the only uncertain measure that directly affects the value of the option. However, price movements in other securities, risk preferences of investors, or expectations about the probabilities of various share price changes can affect the measures used in the valuation formula (S, u, d, and r), thereby affecting the option value indirectly.

Up to this point, options of a single-period term have been considered. Multiple period options can be valued by calculating backwards using the previous formula. First, the value of the option at the beginning of its final period is determined and then, successively, the values at the preceding points in time are calculated. In the case of american options, the value of the unused option and the value that would result from exercising the option must be compared at each point in time, and the alternative with the higher value chosen. This determines the settlement strategy – it resembles the rollback procedures described for the decision-tree method in Section 8.5.

The use of the binomial model to value real options is discussed next. The first step is to construct a valuation model that incorporates all possible actions that could be taken. Then, the data required to value the option must be forecasted. For example, in the case of a buying or delaying option these are:

- The initial investment outlay (as the equivalent of the price K of the option settlement).
- The investment period corresponding to the term of the option.
- The expected cash flows or their NPV (as the equivalent of the current share price S).
- Information on the range of possible cash flows (or their NPV) as specified by the parameters u and d.
- The interest rate i that can be achieved by a risk-free financial investment.
- The cash flows lost by forgoing an immediate investment, or other monetary disadvantages (as the equivalent of dividend payments).

Once this information is gathered, the valuation formula outlined above can be used in a reverse calculation to value the real option.

The valuation of other types of options (i.e. other than buying and delaying options) involves similar steps that draw on their specific case data and, possibly, use different valuation formulae (e.g. for a sales option). In some cases complex models may be needed, for example when valuing combined options.

The valuation of a real option with the binomial model will now be illustrated using an example. The underlying assumptions are discussed in the concluding model assessment.

Example 8-5 (Binomial model)

The example of the decision-tree method (Example 8.4) is re-considered here. The company again has the option to undertake an investment immediately (t = 0) or at the beginning of one of the next two periods (t = 1 or t = 2). The appropriate investment time decision can be understood as a decision about utilising waiting (or delay) options. Therefore, to support its decision-making the company decides to evaluate these options using the binomial model, accepting its assumptions.

The cash flows are expected to be the same as in the original example. The initial investment outlay will be €100,000 regardless of the investment's start time. Uncertainty in demand will again lead to cash flows of either €9,000 or €14,000 (in accordance with a binomial process) at the end of the first period, and the cash flows at the end of the following period will be either 40% greater than the previous period's value, or will decrease by 10%. In addition, it is assumed (for simplicity) that, from t = 3 onwards, a perpetuity can be achieved of an amount equal to the cash flow at t = 2.

The interest rate of a risk-free investment project is 10%. A company share is available that is suitable for use in a duplication portfolio because it has the same probabilities of increasing by 40% or decreasing by 10%. Its price S is currently €1,000. Figure 8-13 shows the possible trends in share prices and the corresponding potential cash flows of the real investment, including the NPV of the perpetuity discounted to t = 2 using the risk-free interest rate.

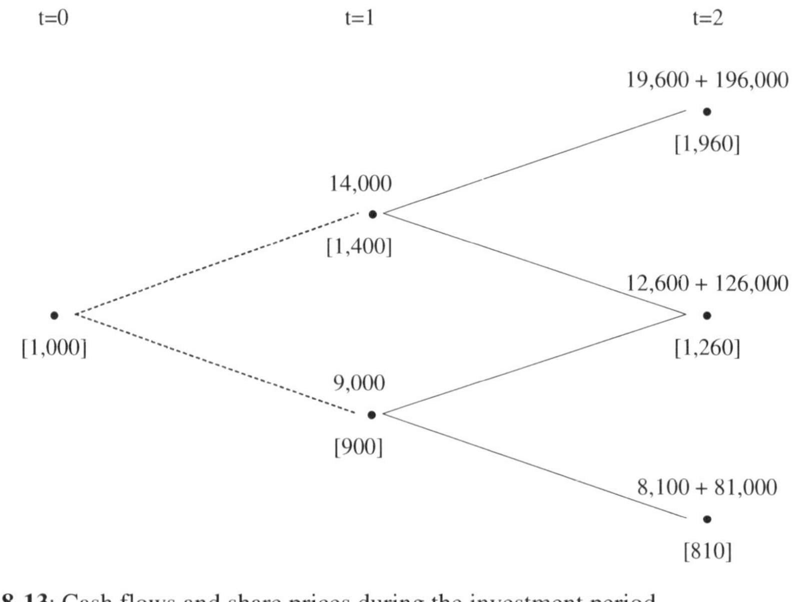

Fig. 8-13: Cash flows and share prices during the investment period

The binomial model is now used to decide whether to start or reject the investment at t = 2. For this option, values are determined for two years of positive development (C_{uu2}), one year each of positive and negative development (C_{ud2} and C_{du2}), and two years of negative development (C_{dd2}). Using the formula for the NPV of perpetuity and the risk-free interest rate, the following is obtained (in €):

$$C_{uu2} = \max\left\{-100{,}000 + \frac{19{,}600}{0.1}; 0\right\} = 96{,}000$$

$$C_{ud2} = C_{du2} = \max\left\{-100{,}000 + \frac{12{,}600}{0.1}; 0\right\} = 26{,}000$$

$$C_{dd2} = \max\left\{-100{,}000 + \frac{8{,}100}{0.1}; 0\right\} = 0$$

Concluding from these results the investment at t = 2 will be undertaken, provided that *at least one* of the previous two years experienced a positive demand change. Two years of negative demand (and cash flow) changes would lead to a decision to reject the investment.

To value the option of waiting to invest until time t = 2, a pseudo-probability q is required. It can be determined using u = 1.4, d = 0.9 and r = 1.1:

$$q = \frac{r-d}{u-d} \quad \Rightarrow \quad q = \frac{1.1-0.9}{1.4-0.9} = 0.4$$

Then, the value of the option to invest at t = 2 can be calculated as at time t = 1 for cases where favourable (C_{u2}) or unfavourable (C_{d2}) demand had developed in the first period (in €):

$$C_{u2} = \frac{0.4 \cdot 96{,}000 + 0.6 \cdot 26{,}000}{1.1} = 49{,}090.91$$

$$C_{d2} = \frac{0.4 \cdot 26{,}000 + 0.6 \cdot 0}{1.1} = 9{,}454.55$$

For the case of C_{d2} it is shown, that the option value can also be determined using a duplication portfolio. This requires the calculation of S_{d1}, Δ_{d1} and B_{d1}, which arise at t = 1 after an unfavourable demand change in the first period. In the example:

$$\Delta_{d1} \cdot u \cdot S_{d1} + r \cdot B_{d1} = C_{du2} \qquad \Rightarrow \qquad \Delta_{d1} \cdot 1.4 \cdot 900 + 1.1 \cdot B_{d1} = €26{,}000$$

$$\Delta_{d1} \cdot d \cdot S_{d1} + r \cdot B_{d1} = C_{dd2} \qquad \Rightarrow \qquad \Delta_{d1} \cdot 0.9 \cdot 900 + 1.1 \cdot B_{d1} = €0$$

From this, the following are obtained: $\Delta_{d1} = 57.78$ and $B_{d1} = -42{,}545.45$. The negative sign shows that in this case, instead of the risk-free financial investment that was assumed to be undertaken in the general description of the binomial model, a financing project of €42,545.45 (as a counterpart of such an investment) is realised. Then, the value of the duplication portfolio at t = 1 (after an unfavourable demand change) is:

$$\Delta_{d1} \cdot S_{d1} + B_{d1} \quad \Rightarrow \quad 57.78 \cdot 900 + (-42{,}545.45) = €9{,}454.55$$

Once the future option values are known, the final step is to calculate the value of the option to invest at t = 2 as at the beginning of the planning period (t = 0). This value (C_2) is calculated as follows:

$$C_2 = \frac{0.4 \cdot 49{,}090.91 + 0.6 \cdot 9{,}454.55}{1.1} = €23{,}008.27$$

This current value of the real option to invest at t = 2 is based on the cash flows expected after at least one year of favourable demand changes, and the fact that the investment can be rejected if two unfavourable demand years occur. However, this value is not necessarily directly relevant for decision-making, as there is also an opportunity to invest at t = 1. This alternative may be more profitable, since cash flows can be achieved earlier.

The decision whether to invest at t = 1 will also depend on demand changes. A scenario-specific choice must be made between (i) exercising the investment option at t = 1, or (ii) not exercising it then, but possibly exercising it later. First, consider the case where a favourable demand change has occurred in the first period. The option value C_{u1} takes into account the settlement price, the scenario-specific NPV of the perpetuity, and the expected cash flows at t = 2. In calculating the option value, it is assumed that pseudo-probabilities can be used to derive certainty equivalents of future cash flows, and that the risk-free interest rate can be used as a discount rate:

$$C_{u1} = \max\left\{-100{,}000 + \frac{0.4 \cdot \left(\frac{19{,}600}{0.1} + 19{,}600\right) + 0.6 \cdot \left(\frac{12{,}600}{0.1} + 12{,}600\right)}{1.1}; 0\right\} = €54{,}000$$

Comparing this result with the value of the option at t = 2 (€49,090.91), realising the option at t = 1 is shown to be more profitable (assuming a positive demand change in the first period). Next, the case of an unfavourable demand change in the first period (C_{d1}) should be considered in the same way:

$$C_{d1} = \max\left\{-100{,}000 + \frac{0.4 \cdot \left(\frac{12{,}600}{0.1} + 12{,}600\right) + 0.6 \cdot \left(\frac{8{,}100}{0.1} + 8{,}100\right)}{1.1}; 0\right\} = €0$$

In this case, the option should not be exercised at time t = 1. Now, the value of the option to wait for future investment possibilities at t = 1 and t = 2 related to the beginning of the planning period (C_{1+2}) can be derived from the previous results:

$$C_{1+2} = \frac{0.4 \cdot 54{,}000 + 0.6 \cdot 9{,}454.55}{1.1} = €24{,}793.39$$

In conclusion, the value of an immediate investment (C_0) is calculated in order to find the optimum investment time. Again, it is assumed that certainty equivalents of future cash flows can be determined using pseudo-probabilities. Then, the optimum investment time is found by weighting the different scenarios' expected cash flows and the scenario-specific NPVs of the perpetuity by these pseudo-probabilities, and discounting them using the risk-free interest rate:

$$C_0 = -100{,}000 + \frac{0.4 \cdot 14{,}000 + 0.6 \cdot 9{,}000}{1.1}$$
$$+0.4 \cdot \left(\frac{0.4 \cdot \left(\frac{19{,}600}{0.1} + 19{,}600 \right) + 0.6 \cdot \left(\frac{12{,}600}{0.1} + 12{,}600 \right)}{1.1^2} \right)$$
$$+0.6 \cdot \left(\frac{0.4 \cdot \left(\frac{12{,}600}{0.1} + 12{,}600 \right) + 0.6 \cdot \left(\frac{8{,}100}{0.1} + 8{,}100 \right)}{1.1^2} \right) = €20{,}000$$

Because the value is lower than that of the 'wait' option, the investment should not go ahead at the beginning of the planning period. Then, the optimum decision is to undertake the investment at t = 1 given a favourable demand change during the first period, or at t = 2 after successive unfavourable, then favourable, demand changes. If two unfavourable years occur, the investment should be rejected. The value of the investment opportunity with this decision sequence is €24,793.39.

The optimum decision sequence is identical to the one found using the decision-tree method. Yet, different target values (i.e. NPVs) arise, due to differences in the valuation approach. While the decision-tree method used subjective probabilities and a uniform discount rate of 12%, the option model valuation uses pseudo-probabilities derived from u and d and a risk-free uniform discount rate.

Additionally, it should be noted that the results determined using the option pricing theory binomial model can also be also found in another way. If identical assumptions are made, the same valuations of real options can be generated from a decision-tree model by using scenario-specific, risk-adjusted uniform discount rates and a scenario-dependent valuation of cash flows. This can be shown for the example of the investment time determination (Example 8-4). Here, from $t = 2$ onwards a risk-free interest rate of 10% is assumed, while for the previous periods specifically adapted uniform discount rates must be used. As an example, the case of a favourable demand change in the first period and the option of investing at $t = 2$ is regarded (with the expected net present value $ENPV_U$ in the decision-tree model and the value C_{u2} in the real options (binomial) model). Using the risk-free interest rate from $t = 2$ onwards, both the real options and decision-tree models produce expected NPVs or option values at $t = 2$ of either €96,000 or €26,000, depending on demand changes. As shown below, using the decision-tree method (i.e. weighting with subjective probabilities and discounting with a corresponding risk-adjusted uniform discount rate) achieves identical results to an option pricing analysis (i.e. using pseudo-probabilities and the risk-free interest rate):

$$\frac{0.5 \cdot 96{,}000 + 0.5 \cdot 26{,}000}{1.242592593} = \frac{0.4 \cdot 96{,}000 + 0.6 \cdot 26{,}000}{1.1} = €49{,}090.91$$

From this equation, it can also be deduced that the corresponding risk-adjusted uniform discount rate (0.242592593) depends on the risk-free interest rate (0.1), and the relation between the expected value (€61,000) and the certainty equivalent produced using pseudo-probabilities (€54,000).

Assessment of the binomial model and the options pricing models approach

The binomial model and other option pricing theory models or procedures are suitable for investment decision-making under uncertainty where some scope for differing actions (i.e. real options) exists. Compared with the classic decision-tree method, these models have the advantage that neither subjectively estimated probabilities nor subjective risk preferences contribute directly to the decision-making process. Instead, a valuation is made based on a 'preference free' market-oriented evaluation.

Yet options pricing models in general and the binomial model in particular, involve assumptions that can substantially limit the applicability and precision of the results. For instance, it is assumed in the binomial model that future changes in uncertain measures (e.g. share price, value of the option) occur as a discrete but random process. Therefore only two values, at multiples (u, d) of the original value, are permitted for each scenario, severely limiting the binomial model's ability to take account of future developments. The decision-tree method offers a greater degree of freedom in this respect.

Other option pricing theory models (such as the pioneering BLACK and SCHOLES model (1973), developed for the valuation of european options) assume different random processes. However, BLACK and SCHOLES' original model, despite being suggested for the valuation of real options, can produce only approximate valuations.

Moreover, the following assumptions of the binomial and other option pricing models reduce their empirical validity: the capital market is perfect and free of arbitrage; market participants share homogeneous expectations about future share price movements; and, in particular, the parameters u and d, which considerably affect the option value, are known.

Additionally, real options have some peculiarities compared to financial options, such as: the (usual) non-tradability of the investment projects; the problems of determining a duplication portfolio of securities that correlate with the real option; the stronger associations between various options; and influences from competition. These effects can be approximated in more complex, and thus more demanding, valuation models.

Furthermore, as already discussed, the results of a binomial option price model can also be produced using risk-adjusted interest rates or scenario-specific valuations of cash flows, provided identical assumptions are made. The last approach is closely related to options pricing theory as regards the assumptions made about capital markets. Greater differences might arise compared with the risk-adjusted uniform discount rate approach. Although it is difficult to determine risk-adjusted uniform discount rates using subjective estimates or capital market theory approaches (e.g. CAPM), and there are challenges in determining subjective probabilities for scenarios, the alternative of applying options pricing theory models might also be problematic.

Their similar range of applications, and the possibility of generating identical results, point to a close relationship between options pricing theory approaches and the decision-tree method. The binomial model also shows common characteristics in the way it illustrates the decision-situation and presents a solution (rollback) procedure, so in these respects it can be seen as a variation on a 'flexible planning' or decision-tree method.

Taking into account these arguments, general superiority cannot be claimed for the options pricing theory models. In fact, some literature rejects the view that options pricing theory is suitable for quantitative investment appraisal at all, because of the issues discussed above. It is generally agreed, however, that the formal (or even informal) consideration of the options dimensions in investments might result in qualitative insights that increase decision-makers' attention to factors affecting the flexibility and value of options (e.g. uncertainty, terms, the quality of additional information, exclusivity and settlement prices). This is likely to strengthen the analysis and management of flexibility-creating investments.

Assessment Material Chapter 8

Exercise 8-1 (Sensitivity Analysis)

A company plans to purchase a machine. The price is €50,000. A volume of 1,000 units of product X can be manufactured and sold per period using the machine. Cash outflows dependent on the production volume total €40 per unit, and a sales price of €100 per unit can be achieved. The economic life of the machine is expected to be three periods. Cash outflows independent of the production volume total €25,000 in the first period and rise by 10% in each subsequent period. The interest rate is assumed to be 9%.

The investment decision should be made using the NPV method, and a sensitivity analysis should provide additional information.

a) Calculate the NPV of the investment project using the formula

$$NPV = -I_0 + \sum_{t=1}^{T} \left((p - cof_v) \cdot x - COF_{ft} \right) \cdot q^{-t}$$

Parameters:

NPV	=	Net present value
x	=	Expected annual sales and production volume
p	=	Sales price of the product X
cof_v	=	Cash outflows dependent on the production volume (per unit)
COF_{ft}	=	Cash outflows independent of the production volume at time t
I_0	=	Initial investment outlay
q^{-t}	=	$\frac{1}{q^t} = \frac{1}{(1+i)^t}$ = Discounting factor in t
t	=	Time index
T	=	Economic life of the project

b) Determine NPVs assuming that sales prices of €60, €80, €120 or €140 (each per unit) can be achieved.

c) Use sensitivity analysis to determine critical values for the:
- Initial investment outlay
- Sales price
- Sales and production volumes
- Production volume-dependent cash outflows
- Production volume-independent cash outflows
- Liquidation value
- Economic life
- Uniform discount rate

Exercise 8-2 (Sensitivity Analysis)

A company plans to acquire a new machine to manufacture a product. The forecasted data are:

Initial investment outlay:	€120,000
Economic life:	4 years
Liquidation value:	€10,000
Uniform discount rate:	10%
Sales price:	€48 per unit
Cash outflows dependent on production volume:	€42 per unit

t	1	2	3	4
Sales and production volume (units)	10,000	12,000	14,000	12,000
Cash outflows independent of production volume (€)	30,000	30,000	35,000	35,000

Tab. 8-8: Production volume and output-independent cash outflows

Assume that production and sales volumes are always identical. Tax and transfer payments can be ignored. The initial investment outlay occurs at $t = 0$, the liquidation value at the end of the economic life, and current cash flows at the end of each period. The expected NPV of the investment project is €10,899.53.

Use sensitivity analysis to find the following critical values at which NPV = 0:

a) The critical value of the initial investment outlay.
b) The critical value of the economic life.
c) The critical value of the liquidation value.
d) The critical value of the uniform discount rate.
e) The critical value of the sales price.
f) The critical value of the production volume-dependent cash outflows.
g) The critical level of the sales and production volumes.
h) The critical level of the production volume-independent cash outflows.
i) The critical values of the sales and production volumes at $t = 1$.

Exercise 8-3 (Sensitivity Analysis)

In the following exercise, the investment problem in Exercise 5-5 should be reconsidered using a sensitivity analysis.

a) Assume that investment projects A and B are pursued until the end of their technical lives ($t = 4$ or $t = 3$). Applying the NPV criterion, determine for each project in isolation (without considering subsequent projects):
   a1) The critical liquidation value.

a2) The critical level of the annual cash flow surpluses which result in a change in absolute profitability.

b) Based on Exercise 5-5, consider the possibility of prolonging the economic lives of projects A and B up to the end of their technical lives. Determine, by what percentage the liquidation values of both projects (i.e. A & B jointly) must increase at the end of the technical life so that the technical and optimum economic lives are identical, assuming:
   b1) A single substitution of machine A by machine B (Exercise 5-5, a)).
   b2) An unlimited chain of A and B, one after another (Exercise 5-5, b)).

Exercise 8-4 (Decision-Tree Method)

A company is, at $t = 0$, considering an investment to extend production capacity. This investment requires an initial outlay of €40,000 and raises capacity by 5,000 to 20,000 product units, with variable cash outflows unchanged at €12 per unit. The sales price is constant and independent of the sales volume, at €20 per unit. The planning period consists of two periods and the uniform discount rate is set at 10%.
The sales volume will be 20,000 units at time $t = 1$ if there is a favourable development (H: high demand), which has an expected probability (p) of 0.5. In the case of an unfavourable development (L: low demand) (probability $p = 0.5$), the sales volume will be 17,000 units.
At the end of period 1 the company may execute the same extension investment with an initial investment outlay of €30,000, if it has not invested at $t = 0$. The variable cash outflows and the sales price remain unchanged.
If there is high demand in period 1, the probability p of having further demand growth (sales volume: 20,000 units) in period 2 is $p = 0.75$. If there is low demand in period 1, this probability reduces to $p = 0.25$. Further low demand in period 2 would result in sales of only 17,000 units in that period.

a) Illustrate the decision problem by means of a decision-tree.

b) Determine the optimum decision sequence, assuming that the company wants to maximise its expected NPV.

c) What risk attitude does an investor who maximises the expected NPV have?

Exercise 8-5 (Decision-Tree Method)

A company is planning for an investment decision under uncertainty with a two-year planning period.

At t = 0, three alternatives exist:

I: Big investment (initial investment outlay: €22,000 / maximum attainable cash inflow surplus: €100,000)

II: Small investment (€12,000 / €80,000)

III: Refrain alternative (no investment) (€0 / €60,000)

Then at t = 1 the following possibilities exist:

Provided that I was executed:

I a: No subsequent investment opportunity (€0 / €100,000)

Provided that II was undertaken:

II a: Extension investment (€13,000 / €100,000)

II b: No subsequent investment (€0 / €80,000)

Provided that III was undertaken:

III a, III b, III c according to the options at t = 0

Demand in the second period will be either high (H: maximum attainable cash flow surplus €100,000) or low (L: maximum attainable surplus €60,000).
In the first period, the expected probabilities are: H: p = 0.1 and L: p = 0.9. In the second period, the probability of H is 0.8, provided that period 1 also had high demand, or p = 0.4 otherwise.

a) Illustrate the decision problem with the help of a decision-tree.

b) Determine the optimum decision sequence for the investor using a uniform discount rate of 10%.

Exercise 8-6 (Decision-Tree Method)

a) A company must decide between two mutually exclusive strategic investment projects, A and B, at t = 0. This company uses the scenario method, and three scenarios (optimistic, most likely, pessimistic) are formulated. The occurrence of the optimistic scenario (opt) has a probability of 0.3, the most likely scenario (mlike) has a probability of 0.5, and the pessimistic scenario (pess) has a probability of 0.2. The cash flows from the investment projects are dependent on the occurrence of these scenarios, with the following data forecasted:

Strategy	Scenario	Expected market size at t = 1 (€)	Expected market growth (% per period related to the preceding period)	Expected market share of the company (%)
A	Opt	1,200,000	20	25
	Mlike	1,200,000	10	25
	Pess	1,200,000	–5	25
B	Opt	1,200,000	20	20
	Mlike	1,200,000	10	20
	Pess	1,200,000	–5	25

Strategy	Scenario	Initial investment outlay at t = 0 (€)	Expected liquidation value at t = 5 (€)	Expected cash outflows at t = 1 (€)	Expected change in current cash outflows (as % of the preceding period's cash outflows)
A	Opt	400,000	100,000	200,000	5
	Mlike	400,000	100,000	200,000	10
	Pess	400,000	50,000	200,000	10
B	Opt	250,000	50,000	180,000	5
	Mlike	250,000	50,000	180,000	10
	Pess	250,000	50,000	180,000	10

Tab. 8-9: Data for the strategies A and B

The planning period spans 5 periods, the uniform discount rate is set at 10%. Prepare a suitable form of investment appraisal to help with this decision. Discuss briefly which project is preferable.

b) It is further assumed that project B may be extended at time t = 2. The cash flows associated with it are forecasted as follows (in €):

Scenario	Initial investment outlay at t = 2	Current cash outflows at t = 3	Liquidation value at t = 5
Opt	100,000	35,000	10,000
Mlike	90,000	40,000	10,000
Pess	90,000	40,000	10,000

Tab. 8-10: Cash flows of the three scenarios

For the extended investment project, an economic life of 3 periods is assumed. If the extension project goes ahead, the market share will increase by 5% of the market size under all three scenarios. Apart from that, the remaining data are unchanged.

b1) Illustrate the decision problem in graphical form.
b2) What decisions should be taken at t = 2?
How does this change the decision situation at t = 0?

Exercise 8-7 (Economic Life and Replacement Time Decisions using the Decision-Tree Method)

a) A company must determine the optimum economic life of a new machine A, characterised by the following data (€'000):

t_A	0	1	2	3	4	5	6	7
Net cash flows	0	150	140	130	120	110	100	90
Liquidation value	–	450	400	350	300	250	170	80

Tab. 8-11: Data for the new machine A

The uniform discount rate is 10% and the initial investment outlay is €550,000. Determine the optimum economic life of machine A, and the NPV that can be achieved when:

a1) There is no replacement.
a2) There is one identical replacement.
a3) The machines are replaced twice by identical machines.
a4) The machines are replaced an infinite number of times by identical machines.

b) Now, 5 years after starting to use machine A, the company is discussing its replacement. There is a rumour that the machine manufacturer may introduce a technically improved machine B, which serves the same function, onto the market within the next few years.
For B, an initial investment outlay of €600,000 and the following additional data are forecasted (€'000):

t_B	0	1	2	3	4	5	6
Cash inflows surpluses at t_B	0	190	180	170	160	150	140
Liquidation value at t_B	–	450	400	350	300	250	170

Tab. 8-12: Data for machine B

There is a 60% probability that B will be available at t = 1, and a 30% probability it will become available at t = 2. If not available by that time, B will not be offered at all. Technical progress exceeding that achieved by B is not expected for the next few years.

All data from a) concerning machine A remain unchanged.

When should the existing machine A be replaced and how (i.e. by another of type A or by machine B)?

Assume that, based on market trends, the product generated using the machine can be sold for only another 5 years. Therefore, the planning period will end at t = 5 and the existing machine will be sold at that time. Because of the poor future prospects for the product, the existing machine is to be replaced only once, or not at all.

Present a graphical illustration of this problem before solving it with appropriate calculations.

Exercise 8-8 (Decision-Tree Method)

At t = 0, a company has the choice between making an investment or rejecting it (refrain alternative). The investment creates a production capacity of 20,000 units after an initial investment outlay of €350,000.

If the investment is undertaken, no others are possible. If it is rejected at t = 0, then another investment may be undertaken at t = 1 with an initial investment outlay of €300,000 and a capacity of 17,000 units. No other investment projects are possible in later years.

The planning period totals three periods. With regard to future developments, two input measures are assumed to be uncertain. In the first period, maximum sales volume is expected to be either 15,000 units (probability 40%) or 20,000 units (probability 60%). The cash outflow per unit for the first period is estimated at either €12 (probability 50%) or €10 (probability 50%). It is assumed that the (random) developments that influence the sales volumes and cash outflows per unit are independent.

In all periods, the sales price will be €20 (this is certain). It is further assumed that the per unit cash outflows experienced in the first period will remain unchanged in subsequent periods.

If in the first period the maximum sales volume amounts to of 20,000 units, it will either remain at this level (probability 60%), or rise to 22,000 units (probability 40%) in the final two periods.

In the case of a maximum sales volume of 15,000 units in the first period, the maximum sales volume is forecasted to either stay the same (probability 50%) or to rise to 18,000 units (probability 50%) in the final two periods.

Other cash outflows need not be considered. The liquidation values at the end of the planning period are either €30,000 with investment at t = 0, or €40,000 with investment at t = 1. The uniform discount rate is 10%.

a) Illustrate the decision problem in the form of a decision-tree.

b) Determine the optimum decision sequence and the maximum expected NPV.

Exercise 8-9 (Decision-tree method)

At t = 0, an investor must decide whether to use €510,000 to either make a direct investment in Genetic Engineering Inc., a young genetic technologies company, or to invest in the capital market earning a yield of 8% per year.
The shares in Genetic Engineering Inc. are traded at the present time (t = 0) on the stock exchange at €500 per share. Their nominal value is €100 per share. The medium-term trend in the price of these shares is influenced by various factors.
During the next year, tests will be done on the newest product developed by Genetic Engineering Inc., the results of which are expected to be available at the end of the year (t = 1). With positive results (probability 40%), the share price is expected to increase by €100; with negative results, the share price is expected to decline by €50.
The legislative body has announced that a decision on guaranteeing patent protection for gene-technology products will take effect in the second year. Patent protection is expected with 50% probability. In the case of favourable test results, this patent protection will result in a share price rise at t = 2 of €250; in the case of negative test results, the share price rise will be only €100. A refusal of patent protection is expected to result in a fall in share prices of €100.
Other factors influencing the share price (e.g. general share price index changes and other investor transactions) and tax payments should be ignored.
The investor is considering purchasing the shares at t = 0 or t = 1. After having purchased in t = 0 it will be possible to sell the shares at t = 1 or to hold them until t = 2. His aim is to maximise his expected assets – consisting of shares and/or cash – as at t = 2. The share will be valued at t = 2 at its current market price (future sales expenses are ignored).
The investor assumes that any funds not invested in the shares can be invested elsewhere at 8% per period. Purchase and sales expenses for any share transaction are estimated at 2% of the share price. At the end of a period, and independently of how the company develops, he expects to receive a dividend of 10% on the nominal value of the shares. The dividend payments are made before the purchase or sales transactions. Any dividend the investor receives at t = 1 is reinvested for one period at 8%.

Illustrate this decision problem with the help of a decision-tree, and determine the optimum investment strategy, taking into account the investor's *compound value maximisation* target, and using the rollback procedure.

Chapter 9: Analysing Investment Programmes under Uncertainty

9.1 Overview

Uncertainty plays a significant role in all investment decision-making. In the previous chapter the analysis of single investment projects under conditions of uncertainty was discussed. In this chapter analogous methods and models for analysing investment programmes under uncertainty will be considered. When investment programmes are planned, often many (or even an infinite number of) investment alternatives exist, considerably complicating analytical models and/or evaluations that attempt to take account of uncertainty. Limitations on the ranges of uncertain conditions or investment alternatives then become necessary.

The most useful analytical models for these circumstances are:

- Sensitivity analysis
- Chance-constrained programming
- Simulation
- Fuzzy set models
- Portfolio selection models
- Flexible planning.

The portfolio selection and flexible planning models are discussed in detail in Sections 9.2 and 9.3. The discussion of flexible planning is supplemented with some observations about chance-constrained programming. The following discussion outlines the other models less detailed.

There are various ways that sensitivity analysis can be used to support investment programme decisions. A *local sensitivity analysis* examines the extent to which certain key data (model coefficients) can be changed without affecting the optimum solution. A *global sensitivity analysis* considers the entire range of possible values for one or more coefficients, to determine the alternative optimum solutions that result from various values of the coefficients. This global form of sensitivity analysis is also called parametric programming.

Local and global sensitivity analyses reveal the extent to which the investment recommendation depends on the input data, and the significance of each of the different coefficients for the investment outcome. However, these analyses can only be undertaken in isolation for a small number of input data, and, moreover, problems arise when integrity assumptions are necessary (i.e. when the investments must be accepted in total rather than in part).

A *simulation* uses a simulative risk analysis procedure to support investment programme decisions. This can be done in various ways. One option is to carry out simulation experiments for selected investment programmes in order to calculate a probability distribution of a target measure (e.g. NPV) for each programme. Then, based on the probability distributions, one programme is selected. Alternatively, possible future developments can be simulated so that a combination of circumstances can be considered, with an optimisation carried out for each resultant scenario. A distribution of optimum investment programmes and an investment recommendation can then be derived. The first approach has the disadvantage that only a limited number of investment programmes can be included, so it is likely that some promising programmes will be overlooked. The second approach requires considerable calculative effort and, moreover, a single 'over-all optimum' programme cannot be derived from a distribution of 'optimum' programmes; using heuristic rules, only a 'good' programme can be found.

With the help of *fuzzy set models*, fuzziness – a specific form of uncertainty – can be included in the analysis of investment programme decisions (see also Section 1.2.3). So far, uncertainty has been considered only in regard to the occurrence of particular events or states (uncertainty or risk situations) and it has been assumed that this set of possible events or states can be defined unambiguously. In fuzzy set models this assumption is no longer valid, and there is no clear distinction between the set of elements to which a statement about a particular fact applies and the set to which the statement does not apply. Fuzziness can appear in the following forms:

- *Fuzzy relations* are relations that are not unambiguously true or false (for instance 'a little bit larger than' or 'much better than').
- *Fuzzy descriptions* of phenomena result from articulations of individual assessments (intrinsic fuzziness), as in the statement 'achieving an acceptable return', or from attempts to summarise complex circumstances (informational fuzziness), as when defining a 'strategic investment'.

Fuzzy relations or descriptions exist in many investment problems. They can be included in the analysis by using *fuzzy sets*.

In fuzzy set theory, there is no strict separation between an element's membership (value 1) or non-membership (value 0) of a set. Instead, fuzzy logic describes an element's (x) membership of the set (A) using values between zero and one. The degree of an element x's membership to a fuzzy set A is described by a membership function $f_A(x)$, which assigns a value between zero and one to the element x:

$$f_A(x): x \rightarrow [0,1] \tag{9.1}$$

Many models for investment programme planning are linear optimisation models. It is possible to introduce fuzzy sets into the restriction limits, the restriction coefficients and/or the target function coefficients of these models. In the following the inclusion of fuzzy sets in simultaneous planning models is illustrated using the example of a sales restriction.

In decision models under conditions of certainty, a sales restriction limits the sales volume to an exact amount. With the help of fuzzy set models, it is possible to incorporate a sales limit that is not known exactly. If only an interval can be determined for it, this can be included in a model using fuzzy logic by allowing a 'violation of the restriction' of the following form:

> 'Try to include sales volumes at or near the lower limit and exclude sales volumes identical to or exceeding the upper limit.'

The extent to which such a restriction is met can be represented by a linear membership function, as shown in Figure 9-1.

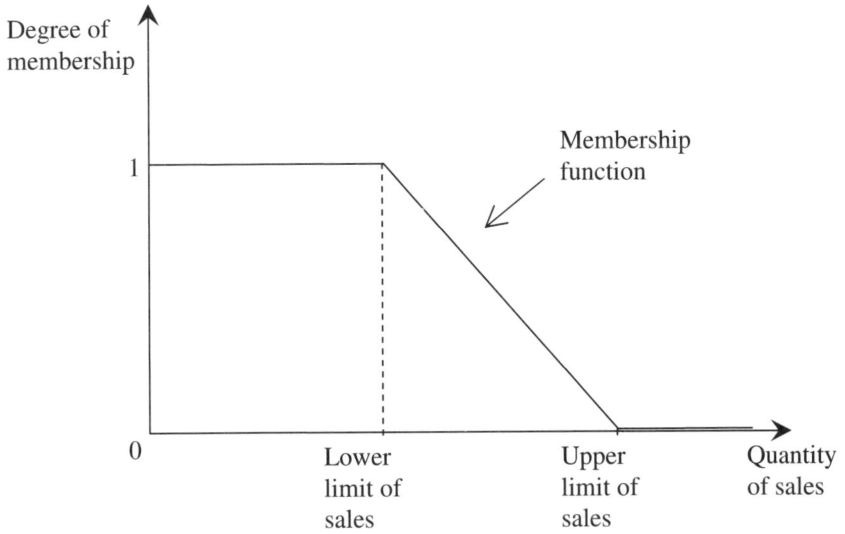

Fig. 9-1: Linear membership function for a sales restriction

Now it is assumed that the investor wants to deviate from the lower limit restriction as little as possible. Thus, fuzzy target functions can be derived from the original restrictions. A multi-criteria optimisation problem then arises, with the aim of satisfying each of the fuzzy target functions as much as possible. The level of satisfaction is measured by the value of the membership function, with a higher value indicating less deviation from the lower limit.

The original target function, for instance compound value or NPV maximisation, must also be included in such fuzzy, multi-criteria optimisations. But this target function (measured in €) is not comparable with the fuzzy target function (measured as relative membership satisfaction) without being adapted. To solve this problem, the target function can be transformed into a membership function that reflects the level of satisfaction with different target function outcomes. Two target function values are needed to construct this membership function: the minimum value that must be reached in all cases (membership value zero), and the maximum attainable value (membership value one). They can be calculated by considering all lower and upper limit values in the original deterministic model and then determining the optimum solutions.

Having completed this step, a number of fuzzy target functions are known. To link these target functions, the so-called *minimum operator* can be used. Generally, this combines two membership functions $f_A(x)$ and $f_B(x)$ into a function $f_C(x)$. It does so by assigning to every value x the *minimum* value produced for x by one of the two membership functions $f_A(x)$ and $f_B(x)$. That is:

$$f_C(x) = f_A(x) \cap f_B(x) = \min[f_A(x), f_B(x)] \tag{9.2}$$

If the minimum operator is applied to solving the described multi-criteria optimisation problem, the target is to maximise the minimum membership value that arises for one of the membership functions. A linear optimisation model can be formulated to do this (the form of such a model is not considered here).

The advantage of the fuzzy set approach is that it allows fuzzy statements to be included in the model analysis. Also, fuzzy restriction coefficients and fuzzy target function coefficients can be considered within linear optimisation models. However, problems arise with determining the membership functions and interpreting the degree of 'satisfaction' achieved within the imposed restrictions. When using the minimum operator to construct a linear optimisation model, the most unfavourable developments become the focus of the analysis, so that other information is lost. In place of the minimum operator, other operators can be used which may better correspond with human behaviour in the decision-making process. However, this means that no linear optimisation model can be formulated, and the model becomes more complex.

9.2 Portfolio Selection

Description of the model

Portfolio selection models are often used to analyse financial investments, such as purchases of shares, bonds or other titles in the capital market. The expected returns from financial investments arise from dividends and/or capital market price increases. However, these returns are not certain and depend on economic influences and, possibly, price movements for other securities. In some cases it is possible to estimate risk measures for the expected returns and correlation measures for the mutual dependencies between the returns of different financial investments. A portfolio of several securities or financial investments can then be described by different combinations of the expected return and risk of the securities. An efficient portfolio shows the lowest possible degree of risk for a given expected return, or the maximum expected return for a given level of risk.

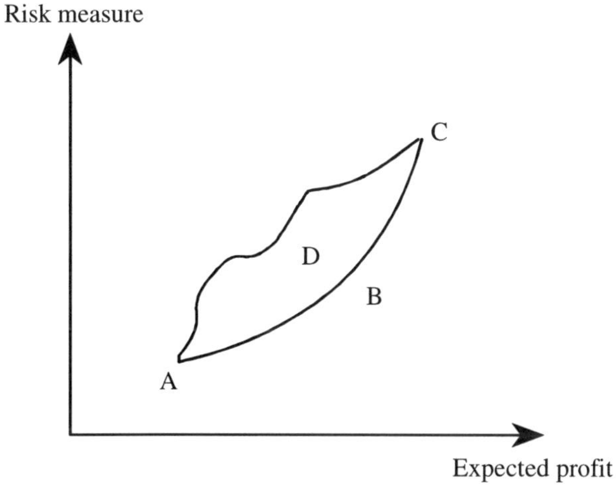

Fig. 9-2: Expected profit and risk measures of portfolios

In Figure 9-2, the profit-risk combinations lying on the curve ABC represent efficient portfolios, while combinations in the area D are inefficient.

In MARKOWITZ's portfolio models, the variances and covariances of securities and portfolios are used as risk measures. The model formulation is based on the following considerations (MARKOWITZ, 1952).

The return from a security, as mentioned, is affected by two components: the payments (dividends or interest) received, and price movements. As a relative measure, the return on a security of type j can be described as follows:

$$r_{Gj1} = \frac{k_{j1} - k_{j0}}{k_{j0}} \cdot 100 + \frac{d_{j1}}{k_{j0}} \cdot 100 \qquad (9.3)$$

With:

r_{Gj1} = Gross return on the security j at the end of the planning period (t = 1)
k_{j0} = Starting price at the beginning of the planning period (t = 0)
k_{j1} = Final price at time t = 1
d_{j1} = Dividend (or interest) received at the end of the planning period (t = 1)

The inclusion of purchase and sales charges (commission, brokerage etc.) and taxes on market profits, dividends and interest received – assuming constant charges and tax rates – leads to the following net return r_{Nj1}:

$$r_{Nj1} = \frac{(k_{j1} \cdot (1 - r_s) - k_{j0} \cdot (1 + r_p)) \cdot (1 - r_{t1})}{k_{j0} \cdot (1 + r_p)} \cdot 100 + \frac{d_{j1} \cdot (1 - r_{t2})}{k_{j0} \cdot (1 + r_p)} \cdot 100 \qquad (9.4)$$

With:

r_{Nj1} = Net return on the security j at the end of the planning period (t = 1)
r_{t1} = Rate of taxation on market profits
r_{t2} = Rate of taxation on dividends and interest
r_s = Rate of sales charges
r_p = Rate of purchase charges

In the subsequent discussions, the net return r_{Nj1} is represented by the symbol r_j. The return r_j can be stated for a prior period. For example, over a period of time share A_1 may have earned the return r_{1t} while share A_2 earned the return r_{2t}, as shown in Figure 9-3.

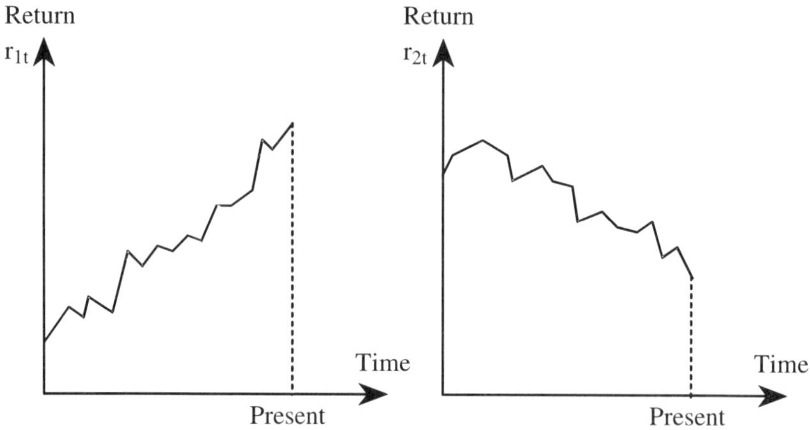

Fig. 9-3: Development of share returns

Future returns are affected by a number of different factors whose effects cannot be forecasted accurately. Notably, the final price at a future point in time t = 1 and the dividend to be received are crucial to a security's expected future return, but are highly uncertain. The investor may consider several prices possible and, under some circumstances, may be able to estimate a probability for each of them.

In the following discussion, r_{jl} is defined as a random variable affecting the future return. This random variable can take the outcomes $r_{j1}, r_{j2}, \ldots, r_{jL}$ and for every outcome r_{jl} a subjective probability p_{jl} is estimated. The sum of the probabilities must equal 1.

The expected return (e_j) of security j can be calculated as the sum of the possible returns r_{jl} weighted by their probabilities. That is:

$$e_j = \sum_{l=1}^{L} p_{jl} \cdot r_{jl} \qquad \text{with:} \qquad \sum_{l=1}^{L} p_{jl} = 1 \tag{9.5}$$

Figure 9-4 shows two possible returns distributions. For simplicity, they are assumed to have a normal distribution. The expected return on the first security is lower than the expected return on the second security and has a narrower range of possible outcomes.

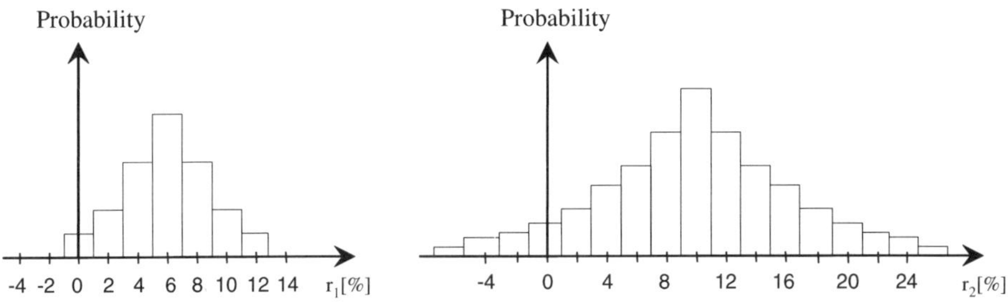

Fig. 9-4: Distribution of security returns

As Figure 9-4 shows, the uncertain conditions mean that several different returns with different probabilities may occur, and either positive or negative variations could occur around the expected return. The variance vj can be used as a risk measure for security j:

$$v_j = \sum_{l=1}^{L} p_{jl} \cdot (r_{jl} - e_j)^2, \qquad \text{with:} \qquad j = 1,...,J \tag{9.6}$$

Thus, for every security j, the expected return (e_j) and the risk measure (v_j), which are the target measures relevant for combining financial investments within portfolios can be described. Now, the expected return (E) and the variance (V) must be defined for a portfolio of several securities j.

The proportion of a portfolio made up of security j is represented by the variable x_j. It is:

$$0 \le x_j \le 1 \qquad \text{and} \qquad \sum_{j=1}^{J} x_j = 1 \tag{9.7}$$

Then, the expected value of the portfolio return is:

$$E = \sum_{j=1}^{J} e_j \cdot x_j \tag{9.8}$$

To determine the portfolio's variance V, the covariances c_{ji} of the returns are considered:

$$c_{ji} = K_{ji} \cdot \sqrt{v_j \cdot v_i} \qquad \text{with:} \quad j \neq I \tag{9.9}$$

And:

K_{ji} = Correlation coefficient for the returns of securities j and i

The variance V is:

$$V = \sum_{j=1}^{J} \sum_{i=1}^{J} c_{ji} \cdot x_j \cdot x_i \qquad \text{with:} \quad c_{jj} = v_j \tag{9.10}$$

Or, alternatively:

$$V = \sum_{j=1}^{J} c_{jj} \cdot x_j^2 + 2 \cdot \sum_{j=1}^{J-1} \sum_{i>j}^{J} c_{ji} \cdot x_j \cdot x_i \tag{9.11}$$

For portfolios comprising two or three securities, feasible and efficient combinations can be presented graphically. With three securities the variance can be expressed as:

$$\begin{aligned} V = {} & c_{11} \cdot x_1^2 + \bar{c}_{12} \cdot x_1 \cdot x_2 + \bar{c}_{13} \cdot x_1 \cdot x_3 + c_{22} \cdot x_2^2 \\ & + \bar{c}_{23} \cdot x_2 \cdot x_3 + c_{33} \cdot x_3^2 \quad \Rightarrow \min! \end{aligned} \tag{9.12}$$

Note: for simplification, $\bar{c}_{ji}$ is used for $2c_{ji}$, where $2c_{ji}$ results from $c_{ji} = c_{ji.}$

Furthermore, the sum of the portfolio proportions must amount to one, that is:

$$x_1 + x_2 + x_3 = 1 \tag{9.13}$$

Using this relationship, a variable x_j can be substituted in the variance formula. Consider the example of variable x_3. Using:

$$x_3 = 1 - x_1 - x_2 \tag{9.14}$$

Variable x_3 can be substituted into equation 9.12 to obtain the following:

$$\begin{aligned} V = {} & (c_{11} - \bar{c}_{13} + c_{33}) \cdot x_1^2 + (c_{22} - \bar{c}_{23} + c_{33}) \cdot x_2^2 \\ & + (\bar{c}_{12} - \bar{c}_{13} - \bar{c}_{23} + 2c_{33}) \cdot x_1 \cdot x_2 + (\bar{c}_{13} - 2c_{33}) \cdot x_1 \\ & + (\bar{c}_{23} - 2c_{33}) \cdot x_2 + c_{33} \quad \Rightarrow \min! \end{aligned} \tag{9.15}$$

This is a square function for the x_1 versus x_2 diagram. The lines of identical variances with higher values than the minimum variance form ellipses (iso-variance-ellipses), as shown in Figure 9-5.

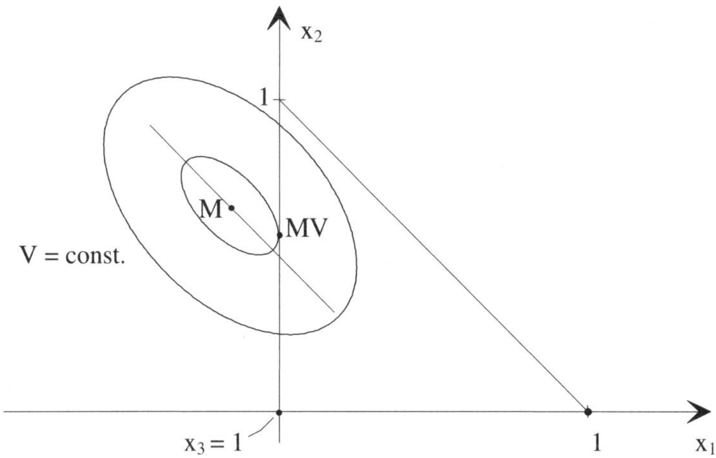

Fig. 9-5: Iso-variance-ellipses

The pole of the x_1x_2-diagram is at $x_3 = 1$. At any point on the straight line between $x_1 = 1$ and $x_2 = 1$, x_3 is equal to 0.

The absolute (arithmetic) minimum M of the variances lies in the common centre of the iso-variance-ellipses; this point is not a feasible security combination (since $x_1 < 0$).

The minimum variance (V_m) of all feasible portfolio combinations is the point MV in Figure 9-5. At this point it is: $x_1 = 0$, $x_2 > 0$ and $x_3 > 0$, i.e. securities 2 and 3 are combined (in the proportions x_2 and x_3) to achieve the minimum variance (point MV).

For the expected return (E) of the portfolio, a function dependent on x_1 and x_2 can be formed. The starting point is:

$$E = e_1 \cdot x_1 + e_2 \cdot x_2 + e_3 \cdot x_3 \tag{9.16}$$

Since the sum of the portfolio proportions must equal 1, and so $x_3 = 1 - x_1 - x_2$, it follows that:

$$E = (e_1 - e_3) \cdot x_1 + (e_2 - e_3) \cdot x_2 + e_3 \tag{9.17}$$

For constant values of E (e.g. E_1 to E_5), straight lines arise in the x_1x_2 diagram as shown in Figure 9-6.

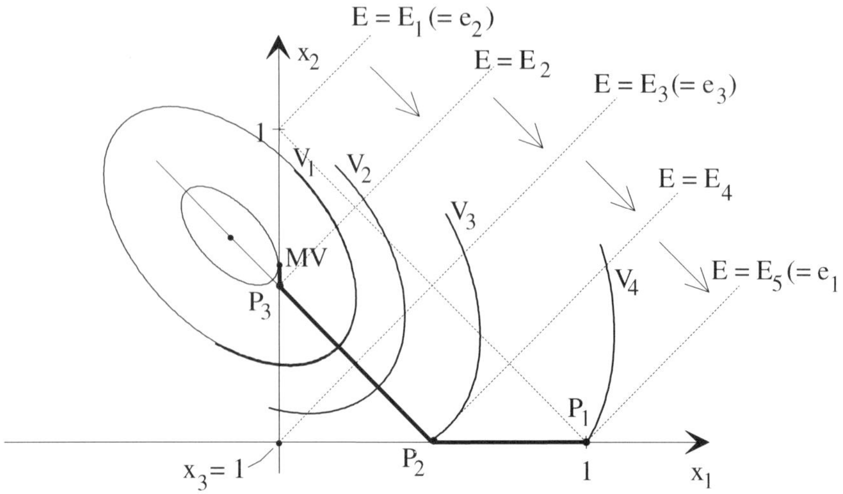

Fig. 9-6: Iso-variance-ellipses, expected returns and efficient portfolios

It can be seen from Figure 9-6 that:

$$E_5 > E_4 > E_3 > E_2 > E_1 \tag{9.18}$$

And:

$$V_4 > V_3 > V_2 > V_1 > V_m \tag{9.19}$$

All efficient portfolios have a minimum variance V for any given expected return. Accordingly, efficient portfolios lie on the line $P_1 - P_2 - P_3 - MV$. In the graphical example (Figure 9-6) the expected value E_5 corresponds to a portfolio that consists only of security type 1. As variances reduce, combinations of x_1 and x_3 display efficiencies initially (from $P_1 - P_2$). Between P_2 and P_3 combinations of the three securities are efficient, and between P_3 and MV the variables x_2 and x_3 are combined.

The combination of the critical line $P_1 - P_2 - P_3 - MV$ can also be represented in a return-variance (E-V) diagram (as shown in Figure 9-7).

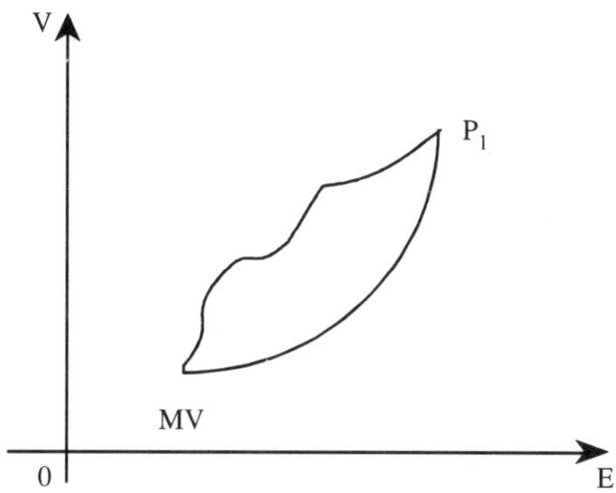

Fig. 9-7: Efficient portfolios in the return-variance diagram

With more than three securities, efficient portfolios cannot be illustrated graphically and must be determined numerically. Either E can be maximised for a given V, or V minimised for a given E. It seems helpful to formulate portfolio selection problems as variance minimisation models rather than return maximisation models, because more algorithms are available for this. The optimum solution of the resultant convex quadratic optimisation problem can be found using quadratic optimisation procedures such as those developed by WOLFE (1959) and ROSEN (1960) (1961).

An optimum can be selected from the efficient portfolios taking into account the risk attitude of the investor. Both V and E should be included in a target function and one of them should be weighted with a parameter (ν), which indicates the investor's preference for expected returns in relation to risk. Then the optimisation problem can be formulated as a minimisation task, as follows:

Objective function:

$$K(X) = V(X) - \nu \cdot E(X) \quad \Rightarrow \text{min!} \tag{9.20}$$

Constraints:

$$\sum_{j=1}^{J} x_j = 1 \tag{9.21}$$

$$x_j \geq 0, \qquad j = 1,\ldots,J \tag{9.22}$$

This represents a problem of convex square optimisation with linear constraints. The following example illustrates this approach.

Example 9-1

A portfolio is being constructed from a combination of three securities. Their proportions (to be determined) are x_1, x_2 and x_3. The expected returns e_i and the variances and covariances c_{ij} of the returns have already been estimated. They are:

$$e_1 = 0.3 \qquad e_2 = 0.1 \qquad e_3 = 0.2$$

$$C = (c_{ij}) = \begin{pmatrix} 0.04 & 0.0032 & 0.008 \\ 0.0032 & 0.0004 & -0.0004 \\ 0.008 & -0.0004 & 0.01 \end{pmatrix}$$

Assuming that the parameter ν equals 1, the optimisation problem can be specified as follows:

Objective function:

$$\begin{aligned} K(X) = \; & 0.04\,x_1^2 + 0.0004\,x_2^2 + 0.01\,x_3^2 + 0.0064x_1x_2 \\ & + 0.016x_1x_3 - 0.0008x_2x_3 - 1 \cdot (0.3x_1 + 0.1x_2 + 0.2x_3) \quad \Rightarrow \min! \end{aligned}$$

Constraints:

$$x_1 + x_2 + x_3 = 1$$

$$x_j \geq 0, \qquad j = 1,2,3$$

The resultant optimum solution, which can be found with one of the procedures mentioned above, is:

$$x_1 = 1 \qquad x_2 = 0 \qquad x_3 = 0$$

That is, only security type 1 is purchased and comprises 100% of the 'portfolio'.

Assessment of the model

Portfolio selection models illustrate the risk and probability structures of financial investment returns, and assist in the determination of efficient or optimum portfolios (within the model's assumptions).

However, the collection of data and the calculation of efficient or optimum portfolios can be problematic. The analysis requires forecasts of the expected values, variances and covariances of the investment returns. Also, the calculation of efficient or optimum portfolios relies on solving non-linear optimisation problems. This can be difficult, particularly when a large range of securities is available.

Additionally, it should be noted that portfolio selection models are based on the μ-σ criterion (as described in Section 8.1). Thus, criticisms that this criterion results in a loss of information also apply here.

However, portfolio selection theory not only lends support to programme decisions concerning financial investments. It also supplies a theoretical basis for general diversification and for other capital market theory models, including the capital asset pricing model (CAPM, see Section 8.2).

9.3 Flexible Planning

Description of the method/model

Flexible planning models are multi-tier decision models. They consider various possible environmental states and their probabilities of occurring, together with subsequent decisions made in the event of particular environmental states, and an expected information access. In this regard, the models considered here are similar to those for the decision-tree method discussed in Section 8.5. However, the decision-tree method analyses single decisions while the flexible planning method deals with investment programme decisions.

Flexible planning principles can be applied to all multi-tier, simultaneous planning models. In the following discussion, a flexible model is formulated based on the model described in Section 7.2 for simultaneous investment and financing decisions (the HAX and WEINGARTNER model). All assumptions described in Section 7.2, with the exception of data certainty, still apply.

As a basis for constructing such a model, the different possible environmental states and their probabilities must first be forecasted. These can be illustrated in a *stochastic tree* as shown in Figure 9-8.

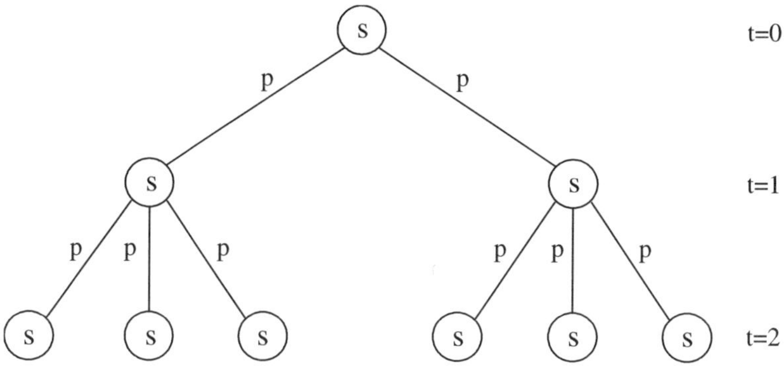

Fig. 9-8: Stochastic tree

In the stochastic tree, a knot s represents an environmental state: often a random event. The various developments that may result from these random events are represented by the lines (branches) of the tree, and probabilities (p) are assigned to them.

After identifying the relevant environmental states, the next step is determining which investment and financing projects can be undertaken under these different states. Then, the appropriate cash flow profiles of all projects must be determined for each possible environmental state.

A flexible model for simultaneous investment and financing decisions is presented below, first in general form. The following variables and parameters are used:

Variables:

x_j = Number of units of investment project j ($j = 1,...,J-1$)

x_{Js} = Amount of the short term financial investment (in €) under state s ($s \in S$)

x_{Jsp} = Amount of the short term financial investment under state sp preceding state s ($sp, s \in S$)

y_i = Extent of the financial project i (in €) for $i = 1,...,I$

Parameters:

a_{js} = Cash outflow surplus per unit of the investment project j ($j = 1,...,J-1$) under state s ($s \in S$)

d_{is} = Cash outflow surplus per unit (in €) of the financial project i under state s

IF_s = Internal funds provided under state s

X_j = Maximum number of units of investment project j ($j = 1,...,J-1$)

Y_i = Maximum extent of financial project I ($i = 1,...,I$)

c = Interest rate payable for the short term financial investment

p_s = Probability of state s occurring, assigned to the end of the planning period ($s \in S_T$)

Sets of indices:

S = Set of all states s

S_T = Set of all states s at time T

The expected compound value (ECV) can be used as a target measure for a flexible model for simultaneous investment and financial decision-making. This comprises the sum of the compound values, weighted by the probabilities of all possible states, at the end of the planning period. The compound value under state s (with $s \in S_T$) can be represented by the short-term financial investment x_{Js}. The objective function then becomes:

$$ECV = \sum_{\forall s \in S_T} p_s \cdot x_{Js} \quad \Rightarrow \max! \tag{9.23}$$

It is assumed that the solvency of the company is assured throughout the planning period and under all states s ($s \in S$). That is, the cash outflow surpluses of all investment and financial projects, under every state, must not exceed the internal funds, and the short-term finance investments must never become negative.

Liquidity constraints:

For the initial state s = 1 in t = 0:

$$\sum_{j=1}^{J-1} a_{j1} \cdot x_j \quad + \quad \sum_{i=1}^{I} d_{i1} \cdot y_i \quad + \quad x_{J1} \quad = \quad IF_1$$

Cash outflow surpluses of the investment projects	*Cash outflow surpluses of the financing projects*	*Short-term financial investment*	*Internal financial funds*

For all other $s \in S$:

$$\sum_{j=1}^{J-1} a_{js} \cdot x_j \quad + \quad \sum_{i=1}^{I} d_{is} \cdot y_i \quad + \quad x_{Js} \quad - \quad (1+c) \cdot x_{Jsp} \quad = \quad IF_s$$

Cash outflow surpluses of the investment projects	*Cash outflow surpluses of the financing projects*	*Short-term financial investment*	*Compounded short-term financial investment of the preceding state*	*Internal financial funds*

Additionally, the following project constraints must be noted:

Project constraints:

$x_j \leq X_j$	and integer,	for $j = 1,\dots,J-1$
$y_i \leq Y_i$,		for $i = 1,\dots,I$
$x_j \geq 0$,		for $j = 1,\dots,J-1$
$x_{Js} \geq 0$,		for all $s \in S$
$y_i \geq 0$,		for $i = 1,\dots,I$

The model formulated here is a linear model whose optimum solution can be determined using integer linear optimisation procedures.

Example 9-2

A planning horizon of three periods is assumed for this decision problem. For each environmental state, a random event is followed by two possible subsequent states. Therefore, fifteen environmental states are considered in total. The stochastic tree in Figure 9-9 shows these environmental states, the probabilities that future developments will lead to their occurrence, and the terminal probabilities (i.e. the probabilities of each state prevailing at the end of the third period).

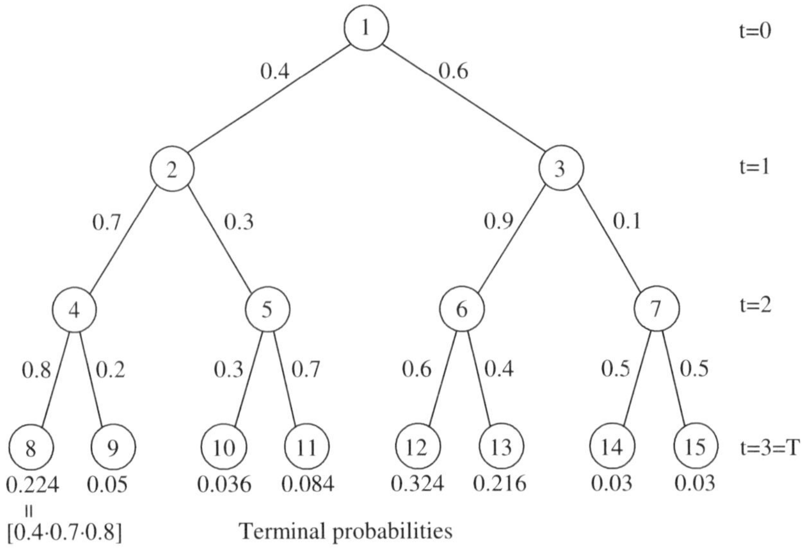

Fig. 9-9: Stochastic tree for the example model

Five different long-term investment projects are available. Projects 1, 2 and 3 can be realised at the beginning of the planning period under state 1 (variables x_1, x_2 and x_3). The other two projects (4 and 5) can be carried out at time t = 1 under both states 2 and 3. Since it has to be decided whether to invest in these projects under either state, two variables are introduced in each case. Variable x_4 represents the number of project type 4 investments that should be made if state 2 occurs. Variable x_5 is the number of these projects that should be invested in if state 3 occurs instead. Variables x_6 and x_7 are the appropriate numbers of type 5 investment projects under states 2 and 3 respectively. No upper limits exist for any of these investment projects.

Three financial projects are available to finance the investment projects. Loans 1 and 2 can be taken out at the beginning of the planning period (variables y_1 and y_2). Loan 3 can be taken out at time t = 1 under both states 2 and 3 (variables y_3 and y_4). The maximum loan amount is € 200,000 for loans 1 and 2 and € 225,000 for loan 3.

The net cash flows of the investment projects (IP) and financial projects (FP) (each in €'000s) at the different points in time, and under the different possible states, are shown in the following table.

Net cash flows (in €'000s)															
Point in time	**0**	**1**		**2**				**3**							
State	**1**	**2**	**3**	**4**	**5**	**6**	**7**	**8**	**9**	**10**	**11**	**12**	**13**	**14**	**15**
IP 1	-40	50	30	40	35	30	25	60	55	50	45	40	35	30	25
IP 2	-60	45	25	45	40	35	30	55	50	45	40	35	30	25	20
IP 3	-60	35	15	35	30	25	20	45	40	35	30	25	20	15	10
IP 4	-	-80	-	60	55	-	-	90	85	80	75	-	-	-	-
IP 5	-	-	-80	-	-	50	45	-	-	-	-	70	65	60	55
IP 6	-	-100	-	90	85	-	-	60	55	50	45	-	-	-	-
IP 7	-	-	-100	-	-	80	75	-	-	-	-	40	35	30	25
FP 1	100	-10	-10	-10	-10	-10	-10	-140	-140	-140	-140	-140	-140	-140	-140
FP 2	100	-	-	-	-	-	-	-180	-180	-180	-180	-180	-180	-180	-180
FP 3	-	150	-	-40	-40	-	-	-160	-160	-160	-160	-	-	-	-
FP 4	-	-	150	-	-	-40	-40	-	-	-	-	-160	-160	-160	-160

Tab. 9-1: Net cash flows of the investment and financial projects

Note also that at every time (and under every state) a short term financial investment (variable x_{8s}, with s = 1,...,15) can be made with an interest rate of 5% (c = 0.05).

The following flexible model can be formulated for this decision problem:

Objective function:

$$ECV = 0.224x_{8,8} + 0.056x_{8,9} + 0.036x_{8,10} + 0.084x_{8,11} + 0.324x_{8,12} + 0.216x_{8,13} + 0.03x_{8,14} + 0.03x_{8,15} \Rightarrow \max!$$

Liquidity constraints:

s = 1:

$$40x_1 + 60x_2 + 60x_3 - 100y_1 - 100y_2 + x_{8,1} = 0$$

s = 2:

$$-50x_1 - 45x_2 - 35x_3 + 80x_4 + 100x_6 + 10y_1 - 150y_3 - 1.05x_{8,1} + x_{8,2} = 0$$

s = 3:

$$-30x_1 - 25x_2 - 15x_3 + 80x_5 + 100x_7 + 10y_1 - 150y_4 - 1.05x_{8,1} + x_{8,3} = 0$$

s = 4:

$$-40x_1 - 45x_2 - 35x_3 - 60x_4 - 90x_6 + 10y_1 + 40y_3 - 1.05x_{8,2} + x_{8,4} = 0$$

s = 5:

$$-35x_1 - 40x_2 - 30x_3 - 55x_4 - 85x_6 + 10y_1 + 40y_3 - 1.05x_{8,2} + x_{8,5} = 0$$

s = 6:

$$-30x_1 - 35x_2 - 25x_3 - 50x_5 - 80x_7 + 10y_1 + 40y_4 - 1.05x_{8,3} + x_{8,6} = 0$$

s = 7:
$$-25x_1 - 30x_2 - 20x_3 - 45x_5 - 75x_7 + 10y_1 + 40y_4 - 1.05x_{8,3} + x_{8,7} = 0$$
s = 8:
$$-60x_1 - 55x_2 - 45x_3 - 90x_4 - 60x_6 + 140y_1 + 180y_2 + 160y_3 - 1.05x_{8,4} + x_{8,8} = 0$$
s = 9:
$$-55x_1 - 50x_2 - 40x_3 - 85x_4 - 55x_6 + 140y_1 + 180y_2 + 160y_3 - 1.05x_{8,4} + x_{8,9} = 0$$
s = 10:
$$-50x_1 - 45x_2 - 35x_3 - 80x_4 - 50x_6 + 140y_1 + 180y_2 + 160y_3 - 1.05x_{8,5} + x_{8,10} = 0$$
s = 11:
$$-45x_1 - 40x_2 - 30x_3 - 75x_4 - 45x_6 + 140y_1 + 180y_2 + 160y_3 - 1.05x_{8,5} + x_{8,11} = 0$$
s = 12:
$$-40x_1 - 35x_2 - 25x_3 - 70x_5 - 40x_7 + 140y_1 + 180y_2 + 160y_4 - 1.05x_{8,6} + x_{8,12} = 0$$
s = 13:
$$-35x_1 - 30x_2 - 20x_3 - 65x_5 - 35x_7 + 140y_1 + 180y_2 + 160y_4 - 1.05x_{8,6} + x_{8,13} = 0$$
s = 14:
$$-30x_1 - 25x_2 - 15x_3 - 60x_5 - 30x_7 + 140y_1 + 180y_2 + 160y_4 - 1.05x_{8,7} + x_{8,14} = 0$$
s = 15:
$$-25x_1 - 20x_2 - 10x_3 - 55x_5 - 25x_7 + 140y_1 + 180y_2 + 160y_4 - 1.05x_{8,7} + x_{8,15} = 0$$

Project constraints:

$x_j \geq 0$ and integer, for j = 1,...,7

$x_{8s} \geq 0$, for s = 1,...,15

$y_i \leq 2$, for i = 1, 2

$y_i \leq 1.5$, for i = 3, 4

$y_i \geq 0$, for i = 1,...,4

The optimum solution for the model (calculated using integer linear programming procedures) is:

$X_1 = 10$	$x_2 = 0$	$x_3 = 0$	$x_4 = 8$	$x_5 = 6$	$x_6 = 0$	$x_7 = 0$

$X_{8,1} = 0$	$x_{8,2} = 0$	$x_{8,3} = 0$	$x_{8,4} = 817.33$	$x_{8,5} = 727.33$
$x_{8,6} = 526.67$	$x_{8,7} = 446.67$	$x_{8,8} = 1{,}367.53$	$x_{8,9} = 1{,}277.53$	$x_{8,10} = 1{,}093.03$
$x_{8,11} = 1{,}003.03$	$x_{8,12} = 519.67$	$x_{8,13} = 439.67$	$x_{8,14} = 275.67$	$x_{8,15} = 195.67$

$y_1 = 2$	$y_2 = 2$	$y_3 = 1.07$	$y_4 = 1.33$

Accordingly, the recommendation is to invest in 10 units of project 1 at the beginning of the planning period (t = 0) at a total expense of €400,000. Loans 1 and 2 should be taken up at the same time to their maximum amounts (i.e. 2 units of

€100,000 each, corresponding to a total amount of €200,000). A short-term financial investment is not made at t = 0.

At time t = 1, 8 units of investment project 4 will be bought if state 2 occurs, at a total expense of €640,000. Loan 3 should be used to finance this (i.e. 1.07 units of loan 3 or €160.500 (= 150,000 · 1.07)) and, again, no short-term financial investment is made. In contrast, if state 3 occurs, only 6 units of investment project 4 should be bought. Due to the lower cash flows, 1.33 units of loan 3 would be required and, again, no short-term financial investment is recommended.

In the third and final time period, the values of the short-term financial investment differ in each case. Weighting these values by their terminal probabilities at time t = 3, the maximum expected value for the compound value of the programme can be calculated at €778,950.

Assessment of the method/model

Flexible planning models allow the analysis of programme decision problems taking into account: different environmental states and their probabilities; subsequent decisions; and an expected information access. It should be noted that the model assumes the decision maker is risk neutral, as evidenced by its use of 'maximise the expected compound value' as the objective. The inclusion of other risk attitudes is possible, but it leads to non-linear optimisation models whose optimum solutions are difficult to determine, especially if only numerically discrete outcomes are allowable.

Another problem is the requirement that liquidity must be guaranteed under every environmental state. This restriction considerably limits the scope of permissible investment programmes. In reality, it may be acceptable for an investor to violate this liquidity requirement for a situation that has a low probability of occurring. Using *chance constrained programming* models, this can be introduced by modifying the formulation of the liquidity restrictions. Using this approach, coefficients used in the liquidity restrictions, such as the cash flows assigned to the investment and financing variables, are regarded as random variables. These coefficients can take various values with related probabilities. The cash flows resulting from the random developments must meet a specified minimum probability to ensure that the liquidity constraints are not violated. However, one problem with this approach, besides the optimum solution determination itself, lies in defining this minimum probability.

Generally, for all flexible planning models the collection of data and the determination of the optimum solution are extremely difficult. The relevant data must be determined for all possible environmental states and for all investment and financing projects. The optimisation can also be complicated depending on the number and types of variables and constraints, due to the large range of the models and to constraints imposed by the need for numerically discrete variables. Therefore, flexible planning models are practicable only when there is a relatively low number of possible environmental states and investment alternatives.

Determining the appropriate degree of complexity is a fundamental issue when formulating and evaluating investment analysis models. The demand for realism tends to lead to complex models. Yet, practical problems in collecting data, calculating optimum solutions, and interpreting the results suggest it might sometimes be advisable to favour less realistic but more 'useable' models.

Further Reading Part V

Abdel-Kader, M. G., and D. Dugdale. 2001. Evaluating Investments in Advanced Manufacturing Technology: A Fuzzy Set Theory Approach. *British Accounting Review* 33 (4):455-489.

Alesii, G. 2006. Payback Period and Internal Rate of Return in Real Options Analysis. *Engineering Economist* 51 (3):237-257.

Arrow, K. J. 1963. The Role of Securities in the Optimal Allocation of Risk-Bearing. In *Collected Papers*. Cambridge, Mass.: Belknap Press of Harvard University Press, 46-57.

Black, F., and M. Scholes. 1973. The Pricing of Options and Corporate Liabilities. *Journal of Political Economy* 81 (3):637-654.

Blohm, H., K. Lüder, and C. Schaefer, C. 2006. *Investition: Schwachstellenanalyse des Investitionsbereichs und Investitionsrechnung*. 9 ed. München: Vahlen.

Bogue, M. C., and R. Roll. 1974. Capital Budgeting of Risky Projects With 'Imperfect' Markets for Physical Capital. *Journal of Finance* 29 (2):601-613.

Breuer, W. 2001. *Investition II. Entscheidungen bei Risiko*. Wiesbaden: Gabler.

Charnes, A., and W. W. Cooper. 1959. Chance-Constrained Programming. *Management Sciences* 6 (1):73-79.

Cox, J. C., S. A. Ross, and M. Rubinstein. 1979. Option Pricing: A Simplified Approach. *Journal of Financial Economics* 7 (3):229-263.

Dixit, A. K., and R. S. Pindyck. 1994. *Investment Under Uncertainty*. Princeton, N.J.: Princeton University Press.

Epstein, L. G., and S. M. Turnbull. 1980. Capital Asset Prices and the Temporal Resolution of Uncertainty. *Journal of Finance* 35 (3):627-643.

Fama, E. F. 1977. Risk-Adjusted Discount Rates and Capital Budgeting Under Uncertainty. *Journal of Financial Economics* 5 (1):3-24.

———. 1996. Discounting under uncertainty. *Journal of Business* 69 (4):415-428.

Fama, E. F., and K. R. French. 1996. The CAPM is Wanted, Dead or Alive. *Journal of Finance* 51 (5):1947-1958.

———. 2004. The Capital Asset Pricing Model: Theory and Evidence. *Journal of Economic Perspectives* 18 (3):25-46.

———. 2006. The Value Premium and the CAPM. *Journal of Finance* 61 (5):2163-2185.

———. 2007. Disagreement, tastes, and asset prices. *Journal of Financial Economics* 83 (3):667-689.

Franke, G., and H. Hax. 2008: *Finanzwirtschaft des Unternehmens und Kapitalmarkt,* 6 ed. Berlin: Springer.

French, S. 1986. *Decision Theory - An Introduction to the Mathematics of Rationality*. Chichester: Ellis Horwood.

Götze, U. 2006. *Investitionsrechnung*. 5 ed. Berlin et al.: Springer.

Hax, H., and H. Laux. 1972: Flexible Planung - Verfahrensregeln und Entscheidungsmodelle für die Planung bei Ungewissheit. *Zeitschrift für betriebswirtschaftliche Forschung*. 24:318 – 340

Hertz, D. B. 1964. Risk Analysis in Capital Investment. *Harvard Business Review* 42 (1):95-106.

Hespos, R. F., and P. A. Strassmann. 1965. Stochastic Decision Trees for the Analysis of Investment Decisions. *Management Science* 10 (10):B244-B259.

Hillier, F. S. 1963. The Derivation of Probabilistic Information for the Evaluation of Risky Investments. *Management Science* 9 (3):443-457.

Hirshleifer, J. 1964. Efficient Allocation of Capital in an Uncertain World. *American Economic Review* 54 (3):77-85.

———. 1965. Investment Decision Under Uncertainty: Choice-Theoretic Approaches. *Quarterly Journal of Economics* 79 (4):509-536.

———. 1966. Investment Decision Under Uncertainty: Applications of the State-Preference Approach. *Quarterly Journal of Economics* 80 (2):252-277.

Kayali, M. M. 2006. Real Options as a Tool for Making Strategic Investment Decisions. *Journal of American Academy of Business, Cambridge* 8 (1):282-286.

Kruschwitz, L. 2007. *Investitionsrechnung*, 11 ed. München, Wien: Oldenbourg

Lintner, J. 1965. The Valuation of Risk Assets and the Selection of Risky Investment in Stock Portfolios and Capital Budgets. *Review of Economics and Statistics* 47 (1):13-17.

———. 1969. The Valuation of Risk Assets and the Selection of Risky Investment in Stock Portfolios and Capital Budgets: A Reply. *Review of Economics and Statistics* 51 (2):222-224.

Liu, K. F. R. 2007. A High-level Fuzzy Petri Nets Model for Integrating Quantitative and Qualitative Decision-making. *International Journal of Uncertainty, Fuzziness & Knowledge-Based Systems* 15 (3):253-284.

Magee, J. F. 1964a. Decision Trees for Decision Making. *Harvard Business Review* 42 (4):126-138.

———. 1964b. How to Use Decision Trees in Capital Investment. *Harvard Business Review* 42 (5):79-96.

Markowitz, H. M. 1952. Portfolio Selection. *Journal of Finance* 7 (1):77-91.

———. 1959. *Portfolio Selection: Efficient Diversification of Investments*. New York et al.: Wiley.

Merton, R. C. 1969. Lifetime Portfolio Selection Under Uncertainty: The Continuous-time Case. *Review of Economics & Statistics* 51 (3):247-257.

———. 1972. An Analytic Derivation of the Efficient Portfolio Frontier. *Journal of Financial & Quantitative Analysis* 7 (4):1851-1872.

———. 1973. An Intertemporal Capital Asset Pricing Model. *Econometrica* 41 (5):867-887.

———. 1974. On the Pricing of Corporate Debt: The Risk Structure of Interest Rates. *Journal of Finance* 29 (2):449-470.

———. 1978. On the Cost of Deposit Insurance When There Are Surveillance Costs. *Journal of Business* 51 (3):439-452.

———. 1981. On Market Timing and Investment Performance. I. An Equilibrium Theory of Value for Market Forecasts. *Journal of Business* 54 (3):363-406.

———. 1987. A Simple Model of Capital Market Equilibrium with Incomplete Information. *Journal of Finance* 42 (3):483-510.

Modigliani, F. 1988. MM - Past, Present, Future. *Journal of Economic Perspectives* 2 (4):149-158.

Mossin, J. 1966. Equilibrium in a Capital Asset Pricing Market. *Econometrica* 34 (4):768-783.

Roll, R., and S. A. Ross. 1980. An Empirical Investigation of the Arbitrage Pricing Theory. *Journal of Finance* 35 (5):1073-1103.

Rosen, J. B. 1960. The Gradient Projection Method for Nonlinear Programming, Part I: Linear Constraints. *SIAM, Journal of Applied Mathematics* 8 (1):181-217.

———. 1961. The Gradient Projection Method for Nonlinear Programming, Part II: Nonlinear Constraints. *SIAM, Journal of Applied Mathematics* 9 (4):514-532.

Ross, S. A. 1976. The Arbitrage Theory of Capital Asset Pricing. *Journal of Economic Theory* 13 (3):341-360.

———. 1977. The Interrelations of Finance and Economics: Theoretical Perspectives. *American Economic Review* 77 (2):29-34.

———. 1978. A Simple Approach to the Valuation of Risky Streams. *Journal of Business* 51 (3):453-475.

Rubinstein, M. 1976. The Valuation of Uncertain Income Streams and the Pricing of Options. *Bell Journal of Economics* 7 (2):407-425.

———. 2002. Markowitz's "Portfolio Selection": A Fifty-Year Retrospective. *Journal of Finance* 57 (3):1041-1045.

———. 2005. Great Moments in Financial Economics: IV. The Fundamental Theorem (PART I). *Journal of Investment Management* 3 (4):87-103.

———. 2006. Great Moments in Financial Economics: IV. The Fundamental Theorem (PART II). *Journal of Investment Management* 4 (1):22-30.

Rubinstein, M., and P. Stephens. 2001. Rational Markets: Yes or No? The Affirmative Case. *Financial Analysts Journal* 57 (3):15-29.

Rudd, A., and B. Rosenberg. 1980. The "Market Model" In Investment Management. *Journal of Finance* 35 (2):597-607.

Schubert, W., and L. Barenbaum. 2007. Real Options and Public Sector Capital Project Decision-making. *Journal of Public Budgeting, Accounting & Financial Management* 19 (2):139-152.

Sharpe, W. F. 1964. Capital Asset Prices: A Theory of Market Equilibrium under Conditions of Risk. *Journal of Finance* 19 (3):425-442.

Terborgh, G. 1949. *Dynamic Equipment Policy*. New York et al.: McGraw-Hill.

Wolf, J. 1988. *Lineare Fuzzy-Modelle zur Unterstützung der Investitionsplanung*. Frankfurt am Main et al.: Lang.

Wolfe, P. 1959. The Simplex Method for Quadratic Programming. *Econometrica* 27 (3):382-298.

Zadeh, L. A. 1965. Fuzzy Sets. *Information and Control* 8 (3):338-353.

Solutions

Solutions

2-1

a) C_A = €68,750 per year; C_B = €66,000 per year; C_C = €60,000 per year
⇒ Alternative C is relatively profitable

b) C_A = €87,083.33 per year; C_B = €90,000 per year; C_C = €100,000 per year
⇒ Alternative A is relatively profitable

c) and d) See Section 2.1

2-2

a) $C = C_f + C_v$ with: C_f = fixed costs; C_v = variable costs

$$C_A = 2{,}400 - \frac{8}{100{,}000}x^2 + 1.7x$$

$$C_B = 2{,}966.67 + 0.8x$$

$$C_C = 1.5x$$

b) b1) C_A = €7,920 per year; C_B = €6,166.67 per year; C_C = €6,000 per year
⇒ Alternative C is relatively profitable

b2) C_A = €10,880 per year; C_B = €9,366.67 per year; C_C = €12.000 per year
⇒ Alternative B is relatively profitable

b3) C_A = €11,400 per year; C_B = €12,366.67 per year (2,000 units are to be bought in from another company, because the required volume exceeds the maximum capacity of 8,000 units); C_C = €15,000 per year
⇒ Alternative A is relatively profitable

2-3

a) P_A = 160,000 – 130,580 = €29,420 per year;
P_B = 192,000 – 167,930 = €24,070 per year
⇒ Alternative A is relatively profitable

b) ARR_A = 30.93 %; ARR_B = 22.83 %
⇒ Alternative A is relatively profitable

c) PP_A = 4.01 years; PP_B = 4.84 years
⇒ Alternative A is relatively profitable

3-1

a) NPV = €22,892.31; NPV > 0
⇒ The project is absolutely profitable

b) EV = €156,845.19

c) Ann = €5,287.55; Ann > 0
⇒ The project is absolutely profitable

3-2

a) NPV_A = €8,231.55; NPV_B = €20,347.59; NPV_C = €4,551.66
$NPV_B > NPV_A > NPV_C$
⇒ Project B is relatively profitable

b) $r_A \approx 11.25\%$; $r_B \approx 12.65\%$; $r_C \approx 10.50\%$

3-3

a) NPV_I = €3,641.81; NPV_{II} = €5,476.84
Ann_I = €1,051; Ann_{II} = €1,580.57
$r_I \approx 7.46\%$; $r_{II} \approx 7.59\%$
PP_I = 3.88 years; PP_{II} = 3.78 years (PP: dynamic payback period)
Net present value method: $NPV_{II} > NPV_I$
⇒ Project II is relatively profitable
Annuity method: $Ann_{II} > Ann_I$
⇒ Project II is relatively profitable
Internal rate of return method: $r_{II} > r_I$
⇒ Project II is relatively profitable
Dynamic payback period method: $PP_{II} < PP_I$
⇒ Project II is relatively profitable

b) See Sections 3.2 and 3.4.

c) See Sections 3.2 – 3.5.

4-1

a) Mandatory account balancing: (CV = Compound value)
CV_{7I} = €98,322.72; CV_{7II} = €124,017.86;
$CV_{7II} > CV_{7I}$ ⇒ Project II is relatively profitable
Prohibited account balancing:
Project I: CV_{7I}^{+} = €1,125,989.65; CV_{7I}^{-} = €–1,089,230.56;
CV_{7I} = €36,759.09
Project II: CV_{5II}^{+} = €1,146,611.50; CV_{5II}^{-} = €–1,116,689.34;
CV_{5II} = €29,922.16
CV_{7II} = €32,989.18
$CV_{7I} > CV_{7II}$
⇒ Project I is relatively profitable

b) Mandatory account balancing:
$d_{cI} \approx 9.88\%$; $d_{cII} \approx 12.27\%$
Prohibited account balancing:
$d_{cI} \approx 8.52\%$; $d_{cII} \approx 8.57\%$

c) See Section 4.1

d)

	t=0	t=1	t=2	t=3	t=4	t=5
Series of net cash flows	-760,000	240,000	320,000	180,000	120,000	160,000
Internal funds						
– Withdrawal of capital						
+ Contribution of capital	152,000					
Instalment loan						
+ Borrowing						
– Redemption						
– Debt interest						
Loan with final redemption						
+ Borrowing	228,000					
– Redemption						-240,000
– Debt interest		-16,800	-16,800	-16,800	-16,800	-16,800
Annuity loan						
+ Borrowing	228,000					
– Redemption		-38,864.07	-41,973.20	-45,331.05	-48,957.54	-52,874.14
– Debt interest		-18,240	-15,130.87	-11,773.02	-8,146.53	-4,229.93
Current account loan						
+ Borrowing	152,000					
– Redemption		-150,895.93	-1,104.07	0		
– Debt interest		-15,200	-110.41	0		
Financial investment						
– Reinvestment			-244,881.45	-118,340	-64,257	
+ Disinvestment						132,530.15
+ Credit interest				12,244.07	18,161.07	21,373.92
Financial balance	0	0	0	0	0	0
Balances						
Loans:						
Instalment loan						
Loan with final redemption	240,000	240,000	240,000	240,000	240,000	0
Annuity loan	228,000	189,135.93	147,162.73	101,831.68	52,874.14	0
Current account loan	152,000	1,104.07	0	0	0	0
Financial investment			244,881.45	363,221.45	427,478.45	294,948.30
Net balance	-620,000	-430,240	-142,281.28	21,389.77	134,604.31	**294,948.30**

The compound value amounts to €294,948.30.

The opportunity income value amounts to €152,000 · 1.06^5 = €203,410.29

⇒ Project II is absolutely profitable

e)

	t=0	t=1	t=2	t=3	t=4	t=5
Series of net cash flows	-760,000	240,000	320,000	180,000	120,000	160,000
Internal funds						
– Withdrawal of capital		**-52,824.87**	**-52,824.87**	**-52,824.87**	**-52,824.87**	**-52,824.87**
+ Contribution of capital	152,000					
Instalment loan						
+ Borrowing						
– Redemption						
– Debt interest						
Loan with final redemption						
+ Borrowing	228,000					
– Redemption						-240,000
– Debt interest		-16,800	-16,800	-16,800	-16,800	-16,800
Annuity loan						
+ Borrowing	228,000					
– Redemption		-38,864.07	-41,973.20	-45,331.05	-48,957.54	-52,874.14
– Debt interest		-18,240	-15,130.87	-11,773.02	-8,146.53	-4,229.93
Current account loan						
+ Borrowing	152,000					
– Redemption		-98,071.06	-53,928.94	0	0	0
– Debt interest		-15,200	-5,392.89	0	0	0
Financial investment						
– Reinvestment			-133,949.23	-59,968.52	-2,966.95	
+ Disinvestment						196,884.70
+ Credit interest				6,697.46	9,695.89	9,844.24
Financial balance	0	0	0	0	0	0
Balances						
Loans:						
Instalment loan						
Loan with final redemption	240,000	240,000	240,000	240,000	240,000	0
Annuity loan	228,000	189,135.93	147,162.73	101,831.68	52,874.14	0
Current account loan	152,000	53,928.94	0	0	0	0
Financial investment			133,949.23	193,917.75	196,884.70	0
Net balance	-620,000	-483,064.87	-253,213.50	-147,913.93	-95,989.44	0

Annual withdrawal: €52,824.87

4-2

a) NPV_I = €931.63; NPV_{II} = €1,136.40

$NPV_{II} > NPV_I$

⇒ Project II is relatively profitable

NPV_{diff} = €204.77

b) $r_I \approx 15.66\%$; $r_{II} \approx 13.86\%$; $r_D \approx 11.55\%$

⇒ Project I is relatively profitable

For the net present value curves see Section 3.4

c) $PP_I = 2.59$ years; $PP_{II} = 3.72$ years

d) d1) Mandatory account balancing:

CV_{4I} = €888.54; CV_{4II} = €830.15

$CV_{4I} > CV_{4II}$ ⇒ Project I is relatively profitable

d2) Prohibited account balancing:

Project I: $CV_{3I}^{+} = €14{,}232$; $CV_{3I}^{-} = €-14{,}049.28$

$CV_{3I} = €182.72$; $CV_{4I} = €197.34$

Project II: $CV_{4II}^{+} = €18{,}764.74$; $CV_{4II}^{-} = €-18{,}882.23$

$CV_{4II} = €-117.49$

$CV_{4I} > CV_{4II} \Rightarrow$ Project I is relatively profitable

e) e1) Mandatory account balancing:

$s_{kI} \approx 15.66\%$; $s_{kII} \approx 13.86\%$

e2) Prohibited account balancing:

$s_{kI} \approx 12.48\%$; $s_{kII} \approx 11.83\%$

f) Project I

	t=0	t=1	t=2	t=3
Series of net cash flows	-10,000	5,000	5,000	3,000
Internal funds				
– Withdrawal of capital				
+ Contribution of capital	5,000			
Instalment loan				
+ Borrowing	4,000			
– Redemption		-1,333.33	-1,333.33	-1,333.34
– Debt interest		-440	-293.33	-146.67
Current account loan				
+ Borrowing	1,000			
– Redemption		-1,000		
– Debt interest		-130		
Financial investment				
– Reinvestment		-2,096.67	-3,520.11	-1,913.16
+ Disinvestment				
+ Credit interest			146.77	393.17
Financial balance	0	0	0	0
Balances				
Loans:				
Instalment loan	4,000	2,666.67	1,333.34	0
Current account loan	1,000	0	0	0
Financial investment		2,096.67	5,616.78	7,529.94
Net balance	-5,000	-570	4,283.44	**7,529.94**

The compound value amounts to €7,529.94.

The opportunity income value amounts to €6,475.15 (= $5{,}000 \cdot 1.09^3$).

$\Rightarrow$ Project I is absolutely profitable

Project II

	t=0	t=1	t=2	t=3	t=4
Series of net cash flows	-12,000	3,000	4,000	4,000	6,000
Internal funds					
– Withdrawal of capital					
+ Contribution of capital	5,000				
Instalment purchase loan					
+ Borrowing	4,000				
– Redemption		-1,000	-1,000	-1,000	-1,000
– Debt interest		-440	-330	-220	-110
Loan with final redemption					
+ Borrowing	2,000				
– Redemption					-2,000
– Debt interest		-200	-200	-200	-200
Current account loan					
+ Borrowing	1,000				
– Redemption		-1,000			
– Debt interest		-130			
Financial investment					
– Reinvestment		-230	-2,496.10	-2,770.13	-3,074.04
+ Disinvestment					
+ Credit interest			16.10	190.13	384.04
Financial balance	0	0	0	0	0
Balances					
Loans:					
Installment loan	4,000	3,000	2,000	1,000	0
Loan with final redemption	2,000	2,000	2,000	2,000	0
Current account loan	1,000	0	0	0	0
Financial investment		230	2,716.10	5,486.23	8,560.27
Net balance	-7,000	-4,770	-1,283.90	2,486.23	**8,560.27**

The compound value of object II amounts to €8,560.27 and exceeds the opportunity income value (€7,057.91 = $5{,}000 \cdot 1.09^4$) as well as the compound value of project I related to t = 4
(€8,207.63 = $7{,}529.94 \cdot 1.09$).

⇒ Project II is absolutely and relatively profitable.

5-1

a) $NPV_I^* = €575.51$; $NPV_{II}^* = €858.85$

b)

	t = 0	t = 1	t = 2	t = 3	t = 4
Series of net cash flows	-12,000.00	3,000.00	4,000.00	4,000.00	6,000.00
Internal funds					
– Withdrawal of capital					
+ Contribution of capital	5,000.00				
Instalment loan					
+ Borrowing	4,000.00				
– Redemption		-1,000.00	-1,000.00	-1,000.00	-1,000.00
– Debt interest		-440.00	-330.00	-220.00	-110.00
Loan with final redemption					
+ Borrowing	2,000.00				
– Redemption					-2,000.00
– Debt interest		-200.00	-200.00	-200.00	-200.00
Current account loan					
+ Borrowing	1,000.00				
– Redemption		-1,000.00			
– Debt interest		-130.00			
Financial investment					
– Reinvestment		-538.00	-2,304.60	-2,467.39	-1,837.02
+ Disinvestment					
+ Credit interest			37.66	198.98	371.70
Taxes					
– Tax payments			-203.06	-311.59	-1,224.68
+ Tax refund		308.00			
Financial balance	0	0	0	0	0
Balances					
Loans:					
Instalment loan	4,000.00	3,000.00	2,000.00	1,000.00	0
Loan with final redemption	2,000.00	2,000.00	2,000.00	2,000.00	0
Current account loan	1,000.00	0	0	0	0
Financial investment	0	538.00	2,842.60	5,309.99	7,147.01
Net balance	-7,000.00	-4,462.00	-1,157.40	2,309.99	**7,147.01**

	t = 1	t = 2	t = 3	t = 4
Net cash flow	3,000.00	4,000.00	4,000.00	6,000.00
– Depreciation	-3,000.00	-3,000.00	-3,000.00	-3,000.00
– Gain of liquidation	0	0	0	0
– Interest expenses	-770.00	-530.00	-420.00	-310.00
+ Interest income	0	37.66	198.98	371.70
= Change of profit	-770.00	507.66	778.98	3,061.70
Change of tax payment (tax rate 40%)	-308.00	203.06	311.59	1,224.68

The opportunity income value amounts to €6,170.67 (= $5{,}000 \cdot 1.054^4$).

⇒ Project II is absolutely profitable

5-2

a) NPV = €63,570.69

b) b1) n_{opt} (Optimum economic life) = 7; NPV_{max} = €65,669.97

b2) $n_{1opt} = 6$; NPV_{Cmax} = €100,173.17

b3) $n_{1opt} = 5$; NPV_{Cmax} = €119,659.10

b4) $n_{opt} = 4$; Ann_{max} = €15,188.54; NPV_{∞} = €151,885.37

c) See Section 5.3.

5-3

a) NPV = €8,479.39

b) b1) $n_{opt} = 7$; NPV_{max} = €9,726.24

b2) $n_{1opt} = 6$; NPV_{Cmax} = €15,088.16

b3) $n_{opt} = 4$; Ann_{max} = €2,349.41; NPV_{∞} = €23,494.10

5-4

a) a1) $n_{opt} = 7$; NPV_{max} = €143,589.65

a2) $n_{opt} = 6$; NPV_{max} = €220,537

a3) $n_{opt} = 6$; NPV_{max} = €263,971.77

a4) $n_{opt} = 6$; NPV_{max} = €320,266.65

b) $n_{opt} = 1$; NPV_{max} = €330,000; Ann_{max} = €33,000

replacement at: 31 December 2009 or 31 December 2010

c) The two-year old machine will be used for three years.
Ann_{max} = €38,296.07; NPV_{max} = €382,960.70

replacement at: 31 December 2009

5-5

a) $n_{Bopt} = 2$, NPV_{Bmax} = (€'000) 2,235.54

$n_{Aopt} = 3$, $P_{3A} = 870 > i \cdot NPV_{Bmax} = 223.55$, $P_{4A} = 110 < 223.55$

NPV_{A3} = (€'000) 1,628.85

NPV_{Cmax} = (€'000) 3,308.44

b) $NPV_{1,1}$ = (€'000) 1,553.72, $Ann_{1,1}$ = (€'000) 895.23
$NPV_{1,2}$ = (€'000) 2,305.04, $Ann_{1,2}$ = (€'000) 926.89 => $n_{Aopt} = 1$, $n_{Bopt} = 2$
$NPV_{2,1}$ = (€'000) 2,139.75, $Ann_{2,1}$ = (€'000) 860.43
$NPV_{2,2}$ = (€'000) 2,822.76, $Ann_{2,2}$ = (€'000) 890.50
$NPV_{3,1}$ = (€'000) 2,687.52, $Ann_{3,1}$ = (€'000) 847.83
$NPV_{3,2}$ = (€'000) 3,308.44, $Ann_{3,2}$ = (€'000) 872.76

5-6

a) a1)

n or t	$-I_0$ resp. NCF_t	$-I_0$ resp. $NCF_t \cdot q^{-t}$	$-I_0 + \sum_{t=1}^{n} NCF_t \cdot q^{-t}$	$L_n \cdot q^{-n}$	NPV_n
0	–580,000.00	–580,000.00	–580,000.00		
1	180,000.00	163,636.36	–416,363.64	445,454.55	29,090.91
2	150,000.00	123,966.94	–292,396.69	338,842.98	46,446.29
3	150,000.00	112,697.22	–179,699.47	232,907.59	53,208.12
4	140,000.00	95,621.88	–84,077.59	170,753.36	86,675.77
5	140,000.00	86,928.99	2,851.39	130,393.48	133,244.87
6	85,000.00	47,980.28	50,831.68	84,671.09	**135,502.77**

⇒ The optimum economic life is 6 years, NPV_{max} = €135,502.77.

a2)

n_1	$NPVn_1$	$NPV_{2max} \cdot q^{-n1}$	NPV_C
0	0	135,502.77	135,502.77
1	29,090.91	123,184.34	152,275.25
2	46,446.29	111,985.76	158,432.05
3	53,208.12	101,805.24	155,013.36
4	86,675.77	92,550.22	179,225.99
5	133,244.87	84,136.56	**217,381.43**
6	135,502.77	76,487.78	211,990.55

⇒ The optimum economic life of the first project is 5 years, that of the subsequent project 6 years. NPV_{Cmax} = €217,381.43.

a3) See Section 5.3.3.

b) b1)

n	1	2	3	4	5	6
r_n [%]	15.52	15.00	14.33	15.86	17.78	17.47

⇒ The optimum economic life is 5 years.

b2)

⇒ The optimum economic lives of the first and the subsequent project are 5 years each (no chain effect).

c)

t	N_t	I_t	ΔV_t	V_t	L_t	CV_t	$CV_t \cdot 1.08^{6-t}$
0	–580,000.00			–580,000.00			
1	180,000.00	–69,600.00	110,400.00	–469,600.00	490,000.00	20,400.00	29,974.29
2	150,000.00	–56,352.00	93,648.00	–375,952.00	410,000.00	34,048.00	46,321.93
3	150,000.00	–45,114.24	104,885.76	–271,066.24	310,000.00	38,933.76	49,045.32
4	140,000.00	–32,527.95	107,472.05	–163,594.19	250,000.00	86,405.81	100,783.74
5	140,000.00	–19,631.30	120,368.70	–43,225.49	210,000.00	166,774.51	180,116.47
6	85,000.00	–5,187.06	79,812.94	36,587.45	150,000.00	186,587.45	**186,587.45**

⇒ The optimum economic life is 6 years, CV_{max} = €186,587.45.

5-7

a) $NPV_A = 4{,}228.54$ absolutely profitable

$NPV_B = -2{,}786.01$ absolutely not profitable

⇒ Project A is relatively profitable

b) b1) NPV of investment B at t = 1:

$$NPV_{B1} = -175{,}000 + \frac{50{,}000}{1.1} + \frac{55{,}000}{1.1^2} + \frac{60{,}000}{1.1^3} + \frac{75{,}000}{1.1^4} = 12{,}213.99$$

NPV of investment B at t = 0:

$$NPV_{B0} = NPV_{B1} \cdot 1.1^{-1} = 11{,}103.63$$

⇒ As $NPV_{B0} > NPV_A$, the investment at t = 0 should be renounced in favour of the investment in B at t = 1.

b2) Future investments will not yield at the relevant uniform discount rate

b3) Calculate and compare compound values at t = 5 (for B_1: invest internal funds from t = 0 to t = 1, then determine CV at t = 5; compound CV_A and CV_{B0} from t = 4 to t = 5; calculate the opportunity income value)

6-1

a) $U(\text{Utility value})_A = 0.675$; $U_B = 0.753$; $U_B > U_A$ ⇒ Copier B is relatively profitable.

b) and c) see Section 6.2.

6-2

a) Weighting vector of target criteria:

(0.2; 0.2; 0.6)

Value of consistency = 0

Weighting vector for the alternatives concerning the criterion "SG":

(0.4545; 0.4545; 0.090909)

Value of consistency = 0

Weighting vector for the alternatives concerning the criterion "SI":

(0.249855; 0.095337; 0.654806)

Value of consistency: 0.015771

Weighting vector for the alternatives concerning the criterion "LP":

(0.209843; 0.549945; 0.240210)

Value of consistency = 0.015771

b) Global priorities

Alternative A: 0.2668

Alternative B: 0.4399

Alternative C: 0.2933

⇒ Alternative B is relatively profitable.

c) See Section 6.3.

6-3

a) $U_{MA} = 0.2 \cdot 1 + 0.4 \cdot 0.0 + 0.4 \cdot 0 = 0.2$
$U_{MB} = 0.2 \cdot 0.5 + 0.4 \cdot 0.625 + 0.4 \cdot 1 = 0.75$
$U_{MC} = 0.2 \cdot 0 + 0.4 \cdot 1 + 0.4 \cdot 0.25 = 0.5$
$\Rightarrow$ Alternative B is relatively profitable.

b) See Section 6.4.

6-4

a)

$$p_1(d_1) = \begin{cases} 0, & \text{for } d_1 \leq 0 \\ \dfrac{d_1}{3{,}000}, & \text{for } 0 < d_1 \leq 3{,}000 \\ 1, & \text{for } d_1 > 3{,}000 \end{cases}$$

$$p_2(d_2) = \begin{cases} 0, & \text{for } d_2 \leq 1{,}000{,}000 \\ 0.5, & \text{for } 1{,}000{,}000 < d_2 \leq 2{,}000{,}000 \\ 1, & \text{for } d_2 > 2{,}000{,}000 \end{cases}$$

$$p_3(d_3) = \begin{cases} 0, & \text{for } d_3 \leq 100{,}000 \\ 0.5, & \text{for } 100{,}000 < d_3 \leq 800{,}000 \\ 1, & \text{for } d_3 > 800{,}000 \end{cases}$$

b) Outranking relationship, inflow and outflow measures

	A	**B**	**C**	F^+
A	0	0.2	0.2	0.4
B	0.8	0	0.43	1.23
C	0.5	0.1	0	0.6
F^-	1.3	0.3	0.63	

c)

	A	**B**	**C**
A	x	–	–
B	BPA	x	BPC
C	CPA	–	x

Alternative B is preferable to A and C; C is preferable to A.

d) See Section 6.5.

7-1

a)

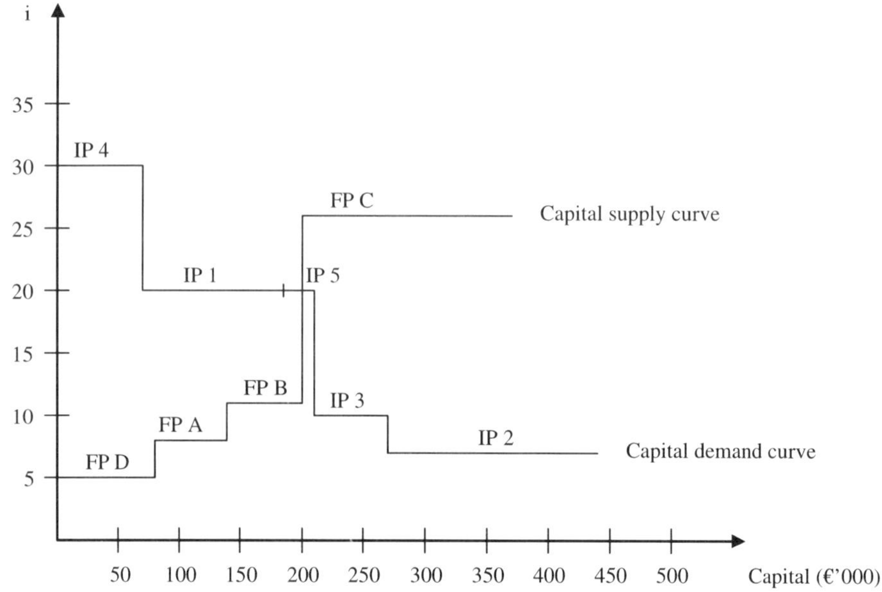

Optimum investment and financing programme:

Investment projects: IP 4, IP 1, 2/3 IP 5 or IP 4, IP 5, 11/12 IP 1 or other combinations with all IP 4 and IP 1 as well as parts of IP 5

Financing projects: FP D, FP A, FP B

Endogenous interest rate: 20%

Maximum compound value: (€'000) 30

Optimum investment and financing programme:

Investment projects: IP 4, IP 1, IP 5

Financing projects: FP D, FP A, FP B, 1/16 FP C

Maximum compound value: (€'000) 29.5

b) See Section 7.1.

7-2

Objective function: $x_{43} \Rightarrow \max!$

Liquidity constraints:

t = 0: $100x_1 + 120x_3 - 100y_1 + x_{40} = 200$

t = 1: $-50x_1 + 80x_2 - 60x_3 + 10y_1 - 100y_2 - (1+0.05)x_{40} + x_{41} = 100$

t = 2: $-50x_1 - 55x_2 - 40x_3 + 10y_1 - (1+0.05)x_{41} + x_{42} = 100$

t = 3: $-50x_1 - 55x_2 - 40x_3 + 115y_1 + 118y_2 - (1+0.05)x_{42} + x_{43} = 0$

Project constraints:

$xj \leq 5, \quad j = 1,2,3$

$yi \leq 6, \quad i = 1,2$

$x_j \geq 0$ and integer, $j = 1,2,3$

$y_i \geq 0, \quad i = 1,2$
$x_{4t} \geq 0, \quad t = 0,1,2$

7-3

a) Objective function:

$x_{53} \Rightarrow \max!$

Liquidity constraints:

$t = 0: \quad 100x_1 + 80x_2 + 50x_3 + 100x_4 - 100y_1 - 100y_2 + 100x_{50} = 0$
$t = 1: \quad -60x_1 - 50x_2 - 0x_3 - 10x_4 - 105x_{50} + 100x_{51} = 0$
$t = 2: \quad -60x_1 - 50x_2 - 0x_3 - 10x_4 - 105x_{51} + 100x_{52} = 0$
$t = 3: \quad -50x_1 - 40x_2 - 90x_3 - 120x_4 + 140y_1 + 130y_2 - 105x_{52} + 100x_{53} = 0$

Project constraints:

$y_i \leq 10, \quad i = 1,2$
$x_j \geq 0, \quad j = 1,2,3,4$ and integer for $j = 1,2$
$y_i \geq 0, \quad i = 1,2$
$x_{5t} \geq 0, \quad t = 0,1,2$

b) Programme 1:
The programme is inadmissible as:
i) investment project 1 is not divisible
ii) liquidity constraints violated at t = 0:

$$100 \cdot 1.5 + 80 \cdot 1 + 50 \cdot 1 + 100 \cdot 0 - 100 \cdot 1 - 100 \cdot 1 + 100 \cdot x_{50} = 0$$
$$\Leftrightarrow \quad x_{50} = -0.8$$

Programme 2:
The programme is feasible as all constraints are fulfilled.
It is not optimal as loan 1 is used before the (cheaper) loan 2 is fully utilised

c) Under inclusion of cash flows in t > T (discounted to T) the following objective function arises:

$x_{53} + 10 \cdot (1+0.1)^{-1} \cdot x_1 + 10 \cdot (1+0.1)^{-2} \cdot x_1 \Rightarrow \max!$

d) $i_4^* = 0.1;\ i_3^* = 0.13;\ i_2^* = 0.2;\ i_1^* = 0.3$

NPV = –5.96778 $\Rightarrow$ the additional project is not profitable.

7-4

a) a1) Optimum programme:
Investment projects: A, B, D (70%)
Financing projects: 1, 2
Maximum compound value: (€'000) 22.30

a2) Optimum programme:
Investment projects: A, D
Financing projects: 1, 2 (60%)
Maximum compound value: (€'000) 20

a3) Optimum programme:
Investment projects: A, C, D
Financing projects: 1, 2
Maximum compound value: (€'000) 17

b) Objective function:

$$x_{G4} + 40 \cdot 1.05^{-1} x_E + 55 \cdot 1.05^{-1} x_F \Rightarrow \max!$$

Liquidity constraints:

$$t = 0: \quad 100x_A + 150x_B + 80x_C + 50x_D - 0.6y_1 - y_2 - y_3 - y_{40} + x_{G0} = 0$$

$$t = 1: \quad -40x_A - 40x_B - 25x_C - 15x_D + 100x_E + 150x_F - 0.34y_1 + 0.09y_2 + 0.2886y_3 + 1.07y_{40} - y_{41} - 1.03x_{G0} + x_{G1} = 80$$

$$t = 2: \quad -40x_A - 50x_B - 25x_C - 20x_D - 40x_E - 40x_F + 0.1y_1 + 0.09y_2 + 0.2886y_3 + 1.07y_{41} - y_{42} - 1.03x_{G1} + x_{G2} = 0$$

$$t = 3: \quad -40x_A - 55x_B - 25x_C - 15x_D - 40x_E - 50x_F + 0.1y_1 + 0.59y_2 + 0.2886y_3 + 1.07y_{42} - y_{43} - 1.03x_{G2} + x_{G3} = 0$$

$$t = 4: \quad -40x_A - 55x_B - 25x_C - 10x_D - 40x_E - 55x_F + 1.1y_1 + 0.545y_2 + 0.2886y_3 + 1.07y_{43} - 1.03x_{G3} + x_{G4} = 0$$

Project constraints:

$x_A \leq 3$, $x_C \leq 3$, $x_E \leq 3$

$y_i \leq 200$, $i = 1,2,3$

$x_j \geq 0$, $j = A,B,C,D,E,F$

$y_i \geq 0$, $i = 1,2,3$

x_j integer, $j = A,B,C,D,E,F$

$x_{Gt} \geq 0$, $t = 0,1,2,3,4$

$y_{4t} \geq 0$, $t = 0,1,2,3$

$y_{4t} \leq 200$, $t = 0,1,2,3$

c) See Sections 7.1, 7.2

7-5

a) Objective function:

$$x_{41} \cdot 1.1 + 0.2 \cdot 1{,}700x_{10} + 0.2 \cdot 1{,}400x_{20} + 0.2 \cdot 3{,}200x_{30} + 0.6 \cdot 1{,}870x_{11} + 0.6 \cdot 1{,}540x_{21} + 0.6 \cdot 3{,}520x_{31} + 4z_{11} + 8z_{21} \Rightarrow \max!$$

Capacity constraints:

$$t = 0: \quad 3z_{10} + 2z_{20} \leq 300 + 60x_{10}$$
$$4z_{10} + 5z_{20} \leq 400 + 80x_{20}$$
$$6z_{10} + 7z_{20} \leq 800 + 100x_{30}$$

$$t = 1: \quad 3z_{11} + 2z_{21} \leq 60(x_{10} + x_{11})$$
$$4z_{11} + 5z_{21} \leq 80(x_{20} + x_{21})$$
$$6z_{11} + 7z_{21} \leq 100(x_{30} + x_{31})$$

Sales constraints:

$z_{1t} \leq 1{,}000$ for $t = 0, 1$; $z_{2t} \leq 16{,}000$ for $t = 0, 1$

Liquidity constraints:

$t = 0$: $1{,}700x_{10} + 1{,}400x_{20} + 3{,}200x_{30} + x_{40} = 10{,}000$

$t = 1$: $-4z_{10} - 8z_{20} + 1{,}870x_{11} + 1{,}540x_{21} + 3{,}520x_{31} - 1.1 \cdot x_{40}$
$- 0.2 \cdot (1{,}700 \cdot 5 + 1{,}400 \cdot 5 + 3{,}200 \cdot 8) + x_{41} = 10{,}000$

Product variable: $z_{kt} \geq 0$ for $k = 1, 2; t = 0, 1$

Investment variable: $x_{jt} \geq 0$ and integer for $j=1, 2, 3; t = 0, 1$
$x_{4t} \geq 0$ for $t = 0, 1$

b) See Section 7.3.

7-6

Objective function:

$$1.1x_{31} + 0.8 \cdot 2{,}000 \cdot x_{11} + 0.8 \cdot 2{,}500 \cdot x_{21} + 0.6 \cdot 2{,}000 \cdot x_{10} + 0.6 \cdot 2{,}500 \cdot x_{20} + (120 - 0.2 \cdot z_{11}) \cdot z_{11} + (180 - 0.1 \cdot z_{21}) \cdot z_{21} - 55z_{11} - 110z_{21} \Rightarrow \max!$$

Capacity constraints:

$t = 0$: $4z_{10} + 5z_{20} \leq 360 + 90x_{10}$
$6z_{10} + 5z_{20} \leq 100x_{20}$

$t = 1$: $4z_{11} + 5z_{21} \leq 90(x_{10} + x_{11})$
$6z_{11} + 5z_{21} \leq 100(x_{20} + x_{21})$

Liquidity constraints:

$t = 0$: $2{,}000x_{10} + 2{,}500x_{20} + x_{30} = 40{,}000$

$t = 1$: $-(120 - 0.2z_{10})z_{10} + 50z_{10} - (180 - 0.1z_{20})z_{20} + 100z_{20} + 2{,}000x_{11}$
$+ 2{,}500x_{21} - 1{,}600 - 1.1x_{30} + x_{31} = 0$

Sales constraints:

$t = 0$: $z_{10} \leq 600$; $z_{20} \leq 1{,}800$, $t = 1$: $z_{11} \leq 600$; $z_{21} \leq 1{,}800$

Non-negativity and integrity:

$x_{jt} \geq 0$ and integer for $j = 1,2; t = 0,1$

$x_{30} \geq 0, x_{31} \geq 0$

$z_{kt} \geq 0$ for $k = 1,2; t = 0,1$

8-1

a) NPV = €32,437.15

b)

p [€]	NPV [€]
60	–68,814.64
80	–18,188.74
120	83,063.04
140	133,688.94

c) Initial investment outlay: I0crit = €82,437.15
Sales price: p_{crit} = €87.19
Sales and production volume: x_{crit} = 786.43 units

Production volume-dependent cash outflows: cof_{vcrit} = €52.80

Production volume-independent cash outflows: α_{crit} = 146.71%;

(with α_{crit} = critical level of volume-independent cash outflows)

Liquidation value: L_{crit} = €–42,007.05

Economic life: Payback period ≈ 1.65 years

Uniform discount rate: Internal rate of return ≈ 43.95%

8-2

a) $I_{0crit} = €130{,}899.53$

b) $PP \approx 3.66$ years

c) $L_{crit} = € -5{,}958$

d) $r \approx 0.13827$

e) $p_{crit} = €47.71$

f) $cof_{vcrit} = €42.29$

g) $\alpha_{crit} = 0.9518$

h) $\alpha_{crit} = 1.1066$

i) $x_{crit} = 8001.75$ units

8-3

a) a₁) ΔNPV_A=€–1,703.98 ΔNPV_B=€–2,197.97

$$L_{crit_A} = 1{,}200 - 1{,}703.98 \cdot 1.1^4 \quad L_{crit_B} = 1{,}400 - 2{,}197.97 \cdot 1.1^3$$

$$L_{crit_A} = € -1{,}294.80 \quad L_{crit_B} = € -1{,}525.50$$

a₂) critical level of annual cash flow surpluses:

$\alpha_{critA} = 78.39\%$, $\alpha_{critB} = 61.07\%$

b) b₁) $NPV_{opt} = €3{,}308.44$

$$3{,}308.44 = -7{,}000 + \frac{3{,}500}{1.1} + \frac{3{,}500}{1.1^2} + \frac{1{,}500}{1.1^3} + \frac{1{,}000}{1.1^4} + \frac{1{,}200\alpha}{1.1^4} - \frac{4{,}500}{1.1^4} + \frac{3{,}500}{1.1^5} + \frac{1{,}800}{1.1^6} + \frac{1{,}300}{1.1^7} + \frac{1{,}400\alpha}{1.1^7}$$

$\alpha_{crit} = 6.71\%$

b₂) necessary $NPV_{\text{technical economic life}} = 926.88 : 0.205405499 = €4{,}512.44$

$$4{,}512.44 = -7{,}000 + \frac{3{,}500}{1.1} + \frac{3{,}500}{1.1^2} + \frac{1{,}500}{1.1^3} + \frac{1{,}000}{1.1^4} + \frac{1{,}200\alpha}{1.1^4} - \frac{4{,}500}{1.1^4} + \frac{3{,}500}{1.1^5} + \frac{1{,}800}{1.1^6} + \frac{1{,}300}{1.1^7} + \frac{1{,}400\alpha}{1.1^7}$$

$\alpha_{crit} = 84.99\%$

8-4

a) See figure on the following page.

b) Calculations for the decision knots at t = 1 (knot 2, 3):

Knot 2: (no investment at t = 0 and high demand)

- investment at t = 1:

$$ENPV = -30{,}000 + 8 \cdot (0.75 \cdot 5{,}000 + 0.25 \cdot 2{,}000) \cdot 1.1^{-1} = €909.09$$

- no investment at t = 1: ENPV = €0

=> investment at t = 1 is preferred.

Knot 3: (no investment at t = 0 and low demand)

- investment at t = 1:

$$ENPV = -30{,}000 + 8 \cdot (0.25 \cdot 5{,}000 + 0.75 \cdot 2{,}000) \cdot 1.1^{-1} = €-10{,}000$$

- no investment at t = 1:

$$ENPV = €0$$

=> refrain alternative/no investment at t = 1 is preferred.

Calculations for the decision knots at t = 0 (knot 1):

- investment at t = 0:

$$ENPV = -40{,}000 + 8 \cdot (0.5 \cdot 5{,}000 + 0.5 \cdot 2{,}000) \cdot 1.1^{-1} + 8 \cdot (0.75 \cdot 0.5 \cdot 5{,}000 + 0.25 \cdot 0.5 \cdot 2{,}000 + 0.25 \cdot 0.5 \cdot 5{,}000 + 0.75 \cdot 0.5 \cdot 2{,}000) \cdot 1.1^{-2}$$
$$= €8{,}595.04$$

- no investment at t = 0:

$$ENPV = 0 + 0.5 \cdot 909.09 \cdot 1.1^{-1} + 0 = €413.22$$

=> optimum investment strategy: investment at t = 0.

Expected net present value: €8,595.04

To a) Decision tree:

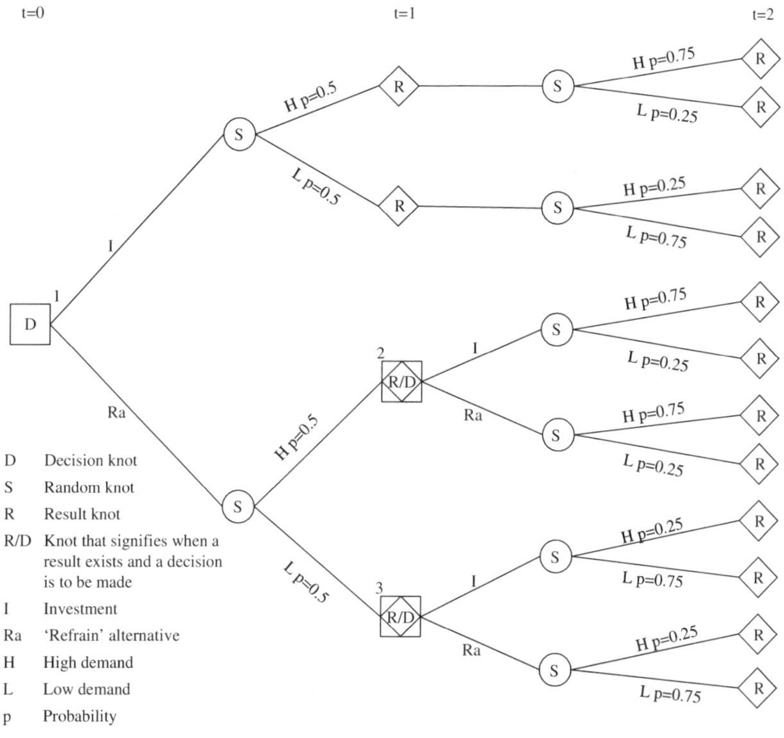

c) See Section 8.5

8-5

a) Decision tree:

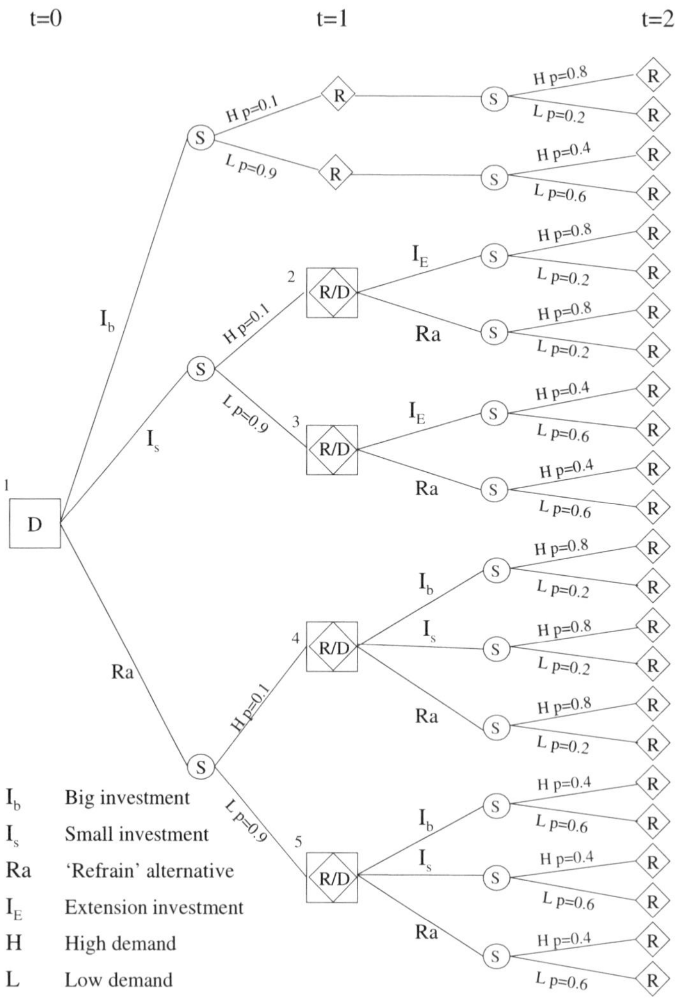

b) Calculations for the decision knots at t = 1:

Knot 2: (small investment at t = 0 and high demand)

- investment at t = 1:

$$ENPV = -13{,}000 + (0.8 \cdot 20{,}000 + 0.2 \cdot 0) \cdot 1.1^{-1} = €1{,}545.45$$

- no investment at t = 1:

$$ENPV = €0$$

=> investment at t = 1 is preferred.

Knot 3: (small investment at t = 0 and low demand)

- investment at t = 1:

$$ENPV = -13,000 + (0.4 \cdot 20,000 + 0.6 \cdot 0) \cdot 1.1^{-1} = €-5,727.27$$

- no investment at t = 1:

$$ENPV = €0$$

=> refrain alternative/no investment at t = 1 is preferred.

Knot 4: (no investment at t = 0 and high demand)

- at t = 1 big investment:

$$ENPV = -22,000 + (0.8 \cdot 40,000 + 0.2 \cdot 0) \cdot 1.1^{-1} = €7,090.91$$

- at t = 1 small investment:

$$ENPV = -12,000 + (0.8 \cdot 20,000 + 0.2 \cdot 0) \cdot 1.1^{-1} = €2,545.45$$

- at t = 1 no investment:

$$ENPV = €0$$

=> big investment at t = 1 is preferred.

Knot 5: (no investment at t = 0 and low demand)

- at t = 1 big investment:

$$ENPV = -22,000 + (0.4 \cdot 40,000 + 0.6 \cdot 0) \cdot 1.1^{-1} = €-7,454.55$$

- at t = 1 small investment:

$$ENPV = -12,000 + (0.4 \cdot 20,000 + 0.6 \cdot 0) \cdot 1.1^{-1} = €-4,727.27$$

- at t = 1 no investment:

$$ENPV = €0$$

=> refrain alternative/no investment at t = 1 is preferred.

Calculations for the decision knot 1 at t = 0:

- at t = 0 big investment:

$$ENPV = -22,000 + (0.1 \cdot 40,000 + 0.9 \cdot 0) \cdot 1.1^{-1} + (0.8 \cdot 0.1 \cdot 40,000 + 0.2 \cdot 0.1 \cdot 0 + 0.4 \cdot 0.9 \cdot 40,000 + 0.6 \cdot 0.9 \cdot 0) \cdot 1.1^{-2} = €-3,818.18$$

- at t = 0 small investment:

$$ENPV = -12,000 + (0.1 \cdot 20,000 + 0.9 \cdot 0) \cdot 1.1^{-1} + (0.1 \cdot 1,545.45 + 0.9 \cdot 0) \cdot 1.1^{-1} + (0.1 \cdot 0.8 \cdot 20,000 + 0.9 \cdot 0.4 \cdot 20,000) \cdot 1.1^{-2} = €-2,768.59$$

- at t = 0 no investment:

$$ENPV = 0 + (0.1 \cdot 0 + 0.9 \cdot 0) \cdot 1.1^{-1} + (0.1 \cdot 7,090.91 + 0.9 \cdot 0)1.1^{-1} = €644.63$$

Optimum investment strategy:

Refrain alternative/no investment at t = 0 followed at t = 1 by:

- big investment in case of high demand at t = 0 and
- no investment in case of low demand at t = 0.

Expected net present value = €644.63.

8-6

a) Cash flow profiles

t	A_{opt}	A_{mlike}	A_{pess}
0	–400,000	–400,000	–400,000
1	100,000	100,000	100,000
2	150,000	110,000	65,000
3	211,500	121,000	28,750
4	286,875	133,100	–8,987.50
5	478,978.75	246,410	1,531.88

t	B_{opt}	B_{mlike}	B_{pess}
0	–250,000	–250,000	–250,000
1	60,000	60,000	120,000
2	99,000	66,000	87,000
3	147,150	72,600	52,950
4	206,347.50	79,860	17,632.50
5	328,872.88	137,846	30,813.88

Net present values of the combinations of strategies and scenarios:

NPV_{Aopt} = €467,126.72; NPV_{Amlike} = €116,637.59; NPV_{Apess} = €–238,959.01

NPV_{Bopt} = €342,061.91; NPV_{Bmlike} = €53,773.34; NPV_{Bpess} = €1,950.08

Resulting expected net present values:

$ENPV_A$ = €150,665.01

$ENPV_B$ = €129,895.26

⇒ A is relatively profitable (risk neutral decision maker).

b) b1) See figure on the following page

b2) Calculations for the decision knot 1 at t = 2:

Net present value at t = 2:

$$NPV_I = -100{,}000 + (86{,}400 - 35{,}000)\cdot 1.1^{-1} + (103{,}680 - 36{,}750)\cdot 1.1^{-2} + (124{,}416 - 38{,}587.50 + 10{,}000)\cdot 1.1^{-3}$$
$$= €74{,}038.69$$

NPV_{Ra} = €0

⇒ investment!

Calculations for the decision knot 2 at t = 2:

Net present value at t = 2:

$$NPV_I = -90{,}000 + (72{,}600 - 40{,}000)\cdot 1.1^{-1} + (79{,}860 - 44{,}000)\cdot 1.1^{-2} + (87{,}846 - 48{,}400 + 10{,}000)\cdot 1.1^{-3}$$
$$= €6{,}422.24$$

NPV_{Ra} = €0

⇒ investment!

Calculations for the decision knot 3 at t = 2:

Net present value at t = 2:

$$NPV_I = -90{,}000 + (54{,}150 - 40{,}000) \cdot 1.1^{-1} + (51{,}442.50 - 44{,}000) \cdot 1.1^{-2} + (48{,}870.38 - 48{,}400 + 10{,}000) \cdot 1.1^{-3}$$
$$= €-63{,}118.98$$

⇒ no investment!

Expected net present value at t = 0:

$$ENPV = 129{,}895.26 + 0.3 \cdot 74{,}038.69 \cdot 1.1^{-2} + 0.5 \cdot 6{,}422.24 \cdot 1.1^{-2} + 0.2 \cdot 0 \cdot 1.1^{-2}$$
$$= €150{,}905.78$$

⇒ B is relatively profitable (risk neutral decision maker).

To b1) Decision tree:

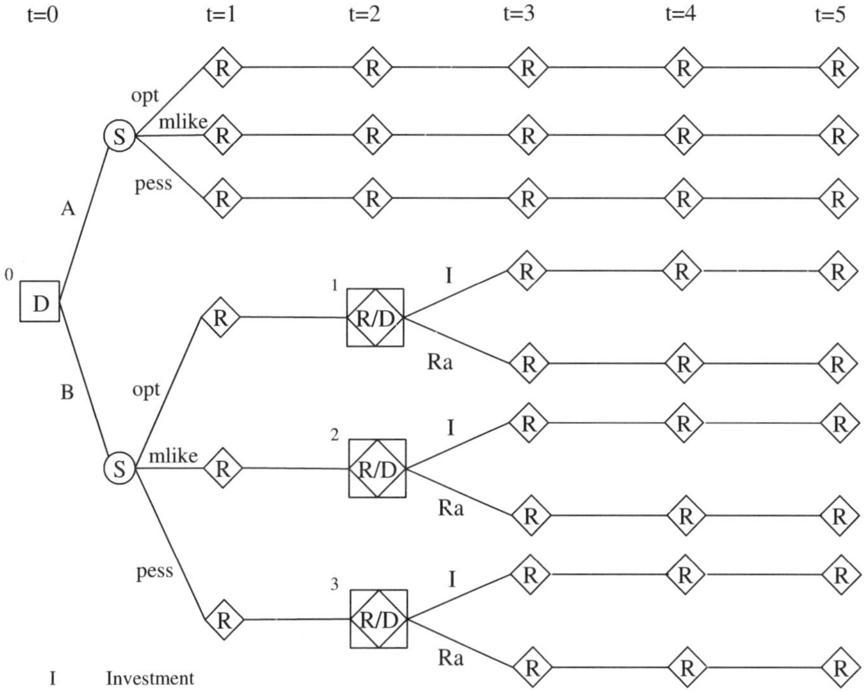

I Investment

Ra 'Refrain' alternative

8-7

a) a1) Optimum economic life $n_{opt} = 5$;
Net present value NPV_{opt} = € 105,230.30

a2) $n_{opt} = 5$; NPV_{opt} = €170,570.03

a3) $n_{opt} = 5$; NPV_{opt} = €211,140.85

a4) $n_{opt} = 5$; NPV_{opt} = €277,594.80

b) Decision tree:

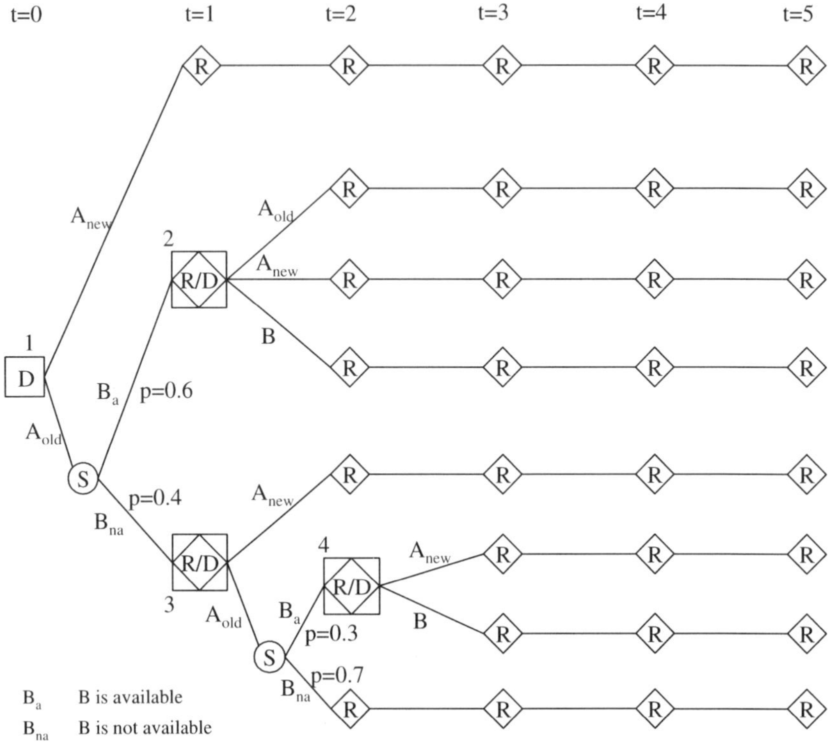

Net present values B				
t	**1**	**2**	**3**	**4**
NPV_t	–18,181.82	52,066.21	112,171.29	163,397.29

For the decision knot at t = 2 (knot 4) by comparison of the net present values of machine A and machine B with economic life of three years the result arises to prefer machine B.

At knot 2 in t = 1 B is also preferred against a new machine type A (higher net present value with economic life of four years). The old machine type A should be immediately replaced by a machine type B as it has already passed its optimum economic life and because the net present value of B for four years is higher than for three years economic life.

Knot 3:

Alternative A_{new}:

$$ENPV = \underbrace{170{,}000}_{\substack{\text{Liq.value} \\ A_{old} \text{ at } t=1}} + \underbrace{86{,}602.66}_{\substack{\text{NPV } A_{new} \\ \text{with } t_{NA}=4}} = €256{,}602.66$$

With t_{NA}: economic life of machine A

Alternative: A_{old}

$$ENPV = (\underbrace{80{,}000}_{\substack{\text{Liqu.value} \\ \text{at } t=2}} + \underbrace{90{,}000}_{\substack{\text{Net cashflow} \\ A_{old} \text{ at } t=2}} + \underbrace{0.3 \cdot 112{,}171.29}_{\substack{NPV_B \text{ with} \\ t_{NB}=3\ (p=0.3)}} + \underbrace{0.7 \cdot 62{,}697.20}_{\substack{NPV_{Anew} \text{ with } t_{NA}=3 \\ (p=0.7)}}) \cdot 1.1^{-1}$$

$$= €225{,}035.83$$

with t_{NB}: Economic life of machine B

$\Rightarrow$ Replacement of A_{old} by A_{new} at t = 1

Decision at t = 0 (Knot 1)

Alternative: A_{new}

$$ENPV = \underbrace{250{,}000}_{\substack{\text{Liqu.value} \\ A_{old} \text{ at } t=0}} + \underbrace{105{,}230.30}_{\substack{NPV_{Anew} \\ \text{with } t_{NA}=5}} = €355{,}230.30$$

Alternative: A_{old}

$$ENPV = 0.6 \cdot (\underbrace{163{,}397.29}_{\substack{NPV_B \\ \text{with } t_{NB}=4}} + \underbrace{170{,}000}_{\substack{\text{Liqu.value} \\ A_{old} \text{ at } t=1}}) \cdot 1.1^{-1} + 0.4 \cdot \underbrace{256{,}602.66}_{\substack{\text{conditional NPV} \\ \text{Knot 3}}} \cdot 1.1^{-1} + \underbrace{100{,}000}_{\text{cash flow } A_{old}} \cdot 1.1^{-1}$$

$$= €366{,}072.25$$

$\Rightarrow$ Decision: t = 0 no investment, t = 1 A or B depending on future development

8-8

a) See figure on the following page.

b) Decision at t = 1

Knot 1:

- investment at t = 1:

$$ENPV = -300{,}000 + 17{,}000 \cdot 10 \cdot 1.1^{-1} + 17{,}000 \cdot 10 \cdot 1.1^{-2} + 40{,}000 \cdot 1.1^{-2}$$
$$= €28{,}099.17$$

- no investment at t = 1:

$ENPV = €0$ $\Rightarrow$ no investment at t = 1 is preferred.

Knot 2:

- investment at t = 1:

$$ENPV = -300{,}000 + 17{,}000 \cdot 8 \cdot 1.1^{-1} + 17{,}000 \cdot 8 \cdot 1.1^{-2} + 40{,}000 \cdot 1.1^{-2}$$
$$= €{-30{,}909.09}$$

- no investment at t = 1:

$ENPV = €0$ $\Rightarrow$ no investment at t = 1 is preferred.

Knot 3:

- investment at t = 1:

$$ENPV = -300{,}000 + 0.5 \cdot 17{,}000 \cdot 10 \cdot 1.1^{-1} + 0.5 \cdot 15{,}000 \cdot 10 \cdot 1.1^{-1} + 0.5 \cdot 17{,}000 \cdot 10 \cdot 1.1^{-2} + 0.5 \cdot 15{,}000 \cdot 10 \cdot 1.1^{-2} + 40{,}000 \cdot 1.1^{-2}$$
$$= €10{,}743.80$$

- no investment at t = 1:

  ENPV = €0 ⇒ investment at t = 1 is preferred.

Knot 4:

- investment at t = 1:

$$\begin{aligned}\text{ENPV} &= -300{,}000 + 0.5 \cdot 17{,}000 \cdot 8 \cdot 1.1^{-1} + 0.5 \cdot 15{,}000 \cdot 8 \cdot 1.1^{-1} \\ &\quad + 0.5 \cdot 17{,}000 \cdot 8 \cdot 1.1^{-2} + 0.5 \cdot 15{,}000 \cdot 8 \cdot 1.1^{-2} \\ &\quad + 40{,}000 \cdot 1.1^{-2} \\ &= €-44{,}793.39\end{aligned}$$

- no investment at t = 1:

  ENPV = €0 ⇒ no investment at t = 1 is preferred.

To a) Decision tree

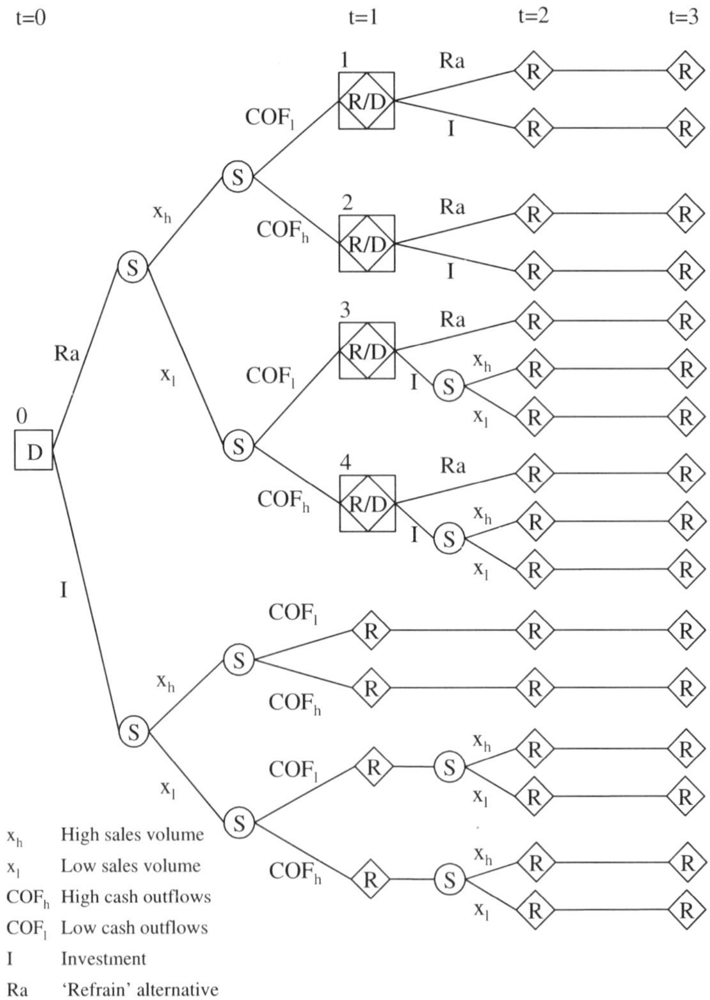

Decision at t = 0

- investment at t = 0:

$$
\begin{aligned}
ENPV &= -350{,}000 + 0.5 \cdot 10 \cdot (0.6 \cdot 20{,}000 + 0.4 \cdot 15{,}000) \cdot 1.1^{-1} \\
&\quad + 0.5 \cdot 8 \cdot (0.6 \cdot 20{,}000 + 0.4 \cdot 15{,}000) \cdot 1.1^{-1} \\
&\quad + 0.5 \cdot 10 \cdot (0.6 \cdot 20{,}000 + 0.4 \cdot (0.5 \cdot 18{,}000 + 0.5 \cdot 15{,}000)) \\
&\quad \cdot (1.1^{-2} + 1.1^{-3}) \\
&\quad + 0.5 \cdot 8 \cdot (0.6 \cdot 20{,}000 + 0.4 \cdot (0.5 \cdot 18{,}000 + 0.5 \cdot 15{,}000)) \\
&\quad \cdot (1.1^{-2} + 1.1^{-3}) + 30{,}000 \cdot 1.1^{-3} \\
&= €83{,}929.38
\end{aligned}
$$

- no investment at t = 0:

$$
\begin{aligned}
ENPV &= 0.6 \cdot 0.5 \cdot 28{,}099.17 \cdot 1.1^{-1} + 0.4 \cdot 0.5 \cdot 10{,}743.80 \cdot 1.1^{-1} \\
&= €9{,}616.83
\end{aligned}
$$

$\Rightarrow$ investment at t = 0 is preferred.

8-9

Decision tree:

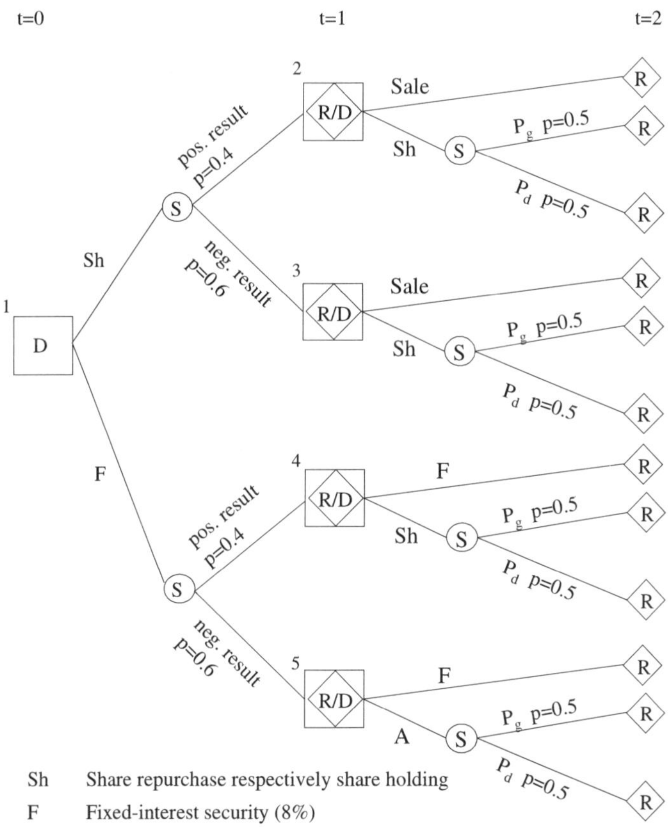

Sh	Share repurchase respectively share holding
F	Fixed-interest security (8%)
P_g	Patent protection granted
P_d	Patent protection denied

Knot 5:

Financial funds: $510{,}000 \cdot 1.08 = €550{,}800$

- Fixed-interest security: $ECV = 550{,}800 \cdot 1.08 =$ **€594,864**
- Investment of 1,200 shares at 450 each $(550{,}800 : 459\ (= 450 \cdot 1.02) = 1{,}200)$

  $ECV = 0.5 \cdot 550 \cdot 1{,}200 + 0.5 \cdot 350 \cdot 1{,}200 + 1{,}200 \cdot 10$ (dividends)

  $= €552{,}000$

Conditional decision: fixed-interest security

Knot 4:

Financial funds: $510{,}000 \cdot 1.08 = €550{,}800$

- Fixed-interest security: $ECV = 550{,}800 \cdot 1.08 = €594{,}864$
- Investment of 900 shares at 600 each $(550{,}800 : 612\ (= 600 \cdot 1.02) = 900)$

  $ECV = 0.5 \cdot 850 \cdot 900 + 0.5 \cdot 500 \cdot 900 + 900 \cdot 10 =$ **€616,500**

Conditional decision: investment in shares

Knot 3:

Financial funds: $1{,}000 \cdot 450$ (shares) $+ 10{,}000$ (dividends) $= €460{,}000$

- Sales of shares: $ECV = (460{,}000 - 9{,}000$ (sales costs)$) \cdot 1.08 =$ **€487,080**
- Holding of shares: $ECV = 0.5 \cdot 550 \cdot 1{,}000 + 0.5 \cdot 350 \cdot 1{,}000$

  $+ 10{,}000 \cdot 1.08 + 10{,}000 = €470{,}800$

Conditional decision: selling of shares

Knot 2:

Financial funds: $1{,}000 \cdot 600$ (shares) $+ 10{,}000$ (dividends) $= €610{,}000$

- Sales of shares: $ECV = (610{,}000 - 12{,}000$ (sales costs)$) \cdot 1.08 = €645{,}840$
- Holding of shares: $ECV = 0.5 \cdot 850 \cdot 1{,}000 + 0.5 \cdot 500 \cdot 1{,}000$

  $+ 10{,}000 \cdot 1.08 + 10{,}000 =$ **€695,800**

Conditional decision: holding of shares

Knot 1:

- at $t = 0$ no investment in shares

  $ECV = 0.6 \cdot 594{,}864 + 0.4 \cdot 616{,}500 =$ **€603,518.40**
- at $t = 0$ investment in shares

  $ECV = 0.6 \cdot 487{,}080 + 0.4 \cdot 695{,}800 = €570{,}568$

Optimum investment strategy:

At $t = 0$ financial funds should be investment for 8% p.a.

In case of positive test results an investment in the shares of the company should be made at $t = 1$, while in case of negative results this should be neglected.

References

References

Abdel-Kader, M. G., and D. Dugdale. 2001. Evaluating Investments in Advanced Manufacturing Technology: A Fuzzy Set Theory Approach. *British Accounting Review* 33 (4):455-489.

Alesii, G. 2006. Payback Period and Internal Rate of Return in Real Options Analysis. *Engineering Economist* 51 (3):237-257.

Ang, J. S., J. H. Chua, and R. Sellers. 1979. Generating Cash Flow Estimates: An Actual Study Using the Delphi Technique. *Financial Management* 8 (1):64-67.

Arrow, K. J. 1963. The Role of Securities in the Optimal Allocation of Risk-Bearing. In *Collected Papers*. Cambridge, Mass.: Belknap Press of Harvard University Press, 46-57.

Bacon, P. W. 1977. The Evaluation of Mutually Exclusive Investments. *Financial Management* 6 (2):55-58.

Baldwin, C. Y. 1982. Optimal Sequential Investment When Capital is Not Readily Reversible. *Journal of Finance* 37 (3):763-782.

Baldwin, C. Y., and R. S. Ruback. 1986. Inflation, Uncertainty, and Investment. *Journal of Finance* 41 (3):657-669.

Baldwin, R. H. 1959. How to Assess Investment Proposals. *Harvard Business Review* 37 (3):98-105.

Baron, D. P. 1979. Investment Policy, Optimality, and the Mean-Variance Model. *Journal of Finance* 34 (1):207-232.

Baumol, W. J., and R. E. Quandt. 1965. Investment and Discount Rates Under Capital Rationing - a Programming Approach. *Economic Journal* 75 (298):317-329.

Belton, V. 1986. A Comparison of the Analytic Hierarchy Process and a Simple Multi-Attribute Value Function. *European Journal of Operational Research* 26 (1):7-21.

Berkovitch, E., and R. Israel. 2004. Why the NPV Criterion does not Maximize NPV. *Review of Financial Studies* 17 (1):239-255.

Bernroider, E., and V. Stix. 2007. A Method Using Weight Restrictions in Data Envelopment Analysis for Ranking and Validity Issues in Decision Making. *Computers & Operations Research* 34 (9):2637-2647.

Black, F., and M. Scholes. 1973. The Pricing of Options and Corporate Liabilities. *Journal of Political Economy* 81 (3):637-654.

Block, S. 2005. Are There Differences in Capital Budgeting Procedures Between Industries? An Empirical Study. *Engineering Economist* 50 (1):55-67.

Blohm, H., K. Lüder, and C. Schaefer. 2006. *Investition: Schwachstellenanalyse des Investitionsbereichs und Investitionsrechnung*. 9 ed. München: Vahlen.

Bogue, M. C., and R. Roll. 1974. Capital Budgeting of Risky Projects With 'Imperfect' Markets for Physical Capital. *Journal of Finance* 29 (2):601-613.

Boulding, K. E. 1936. Time and Investment. *Economica* 3 (12):196-214.

Boyle, G., and G. Guthrie. 2006. Payback without apology. *Accounting & Finance* 46 (1):1-10.

Brans, J. P., and B. Mareschal. 1990. The PROMETHEE Methods for MCDM; The PROMCALC, GAIA and BANKADVISER Software. In *Readings in Multiple Criteria Decision Aid*, edited by C. A. Bana e Costa. Berlin et al.: Springer, 216-252.

———. 1992. PROMETHEE V: MCDM Problems with Segmentation Constraints. *INFOR* 30 (2):85-96.

Brans, J. P., and P. Vincke. 1985. A Preference Ranking Organisation Method. *Management Sciences* 31 (6):647-656.

Brans, J. P., P. Vincke, and B. Mareschal. 1986. How to Select and How to Rank Projects: The PROMETHEE method. *European Journal of Operational Research* 24 (2):228-238.

Brealey, R. A., S. C. Myers, and F. Allen. 2007. *Principles of Corporate Finance*. 9 ed. Boston et al.: McGraw-Hill/Irwin.

Breuer, W. 2001. *Investition II. Entscheidungen bei Risiko*. Wiesbaden: Gabler.

———. 2007. *Investition I. Entscheidungen bei Sicherheit*. 3 ed. Wiesbaden: Gabler.

Brown, R. J. 2006. Sins of the IRR. *Journal of Real Estate Portfolio Management* 12 (2):195-199.

Burton, R. M., and W. W. Damon. 1974. On the Existence of a Cost of Capital Under Pure Capital Rationing. *Journal of Finance* 29 (4):1165-1173.

Charnes, A., and W. W. Cooper. 1959. Chance-Constrained Programming. *Management Sciences* 6 (1):73-79.

Charnes, A., W. W. Cooper, and M. H. Miller. 1959. Application of "Linear Programming" to Financial Budgeting and the Costing of Funds. *Journal of Business* 32 (1):20-46.

Cooper, W. D., R. G. Morgan, A. Redman, and M. Smith. 2001. Capital Budgeting Models: Theory vs. Practice. *Business Forum* 26 (1/2):15-19.

Copeland, T. E., J. F. Weston, and K. Shastri. 2005. *Financial Theory and Corporate Policy*. 4 ed. Boston: Addison Wesley.

Cox, J. C., S. A. Ross, and M. Rubinstein. 1979. Option Pricing: A Simplified Approach. *Journal of Financial Economics* 7 (3):229-263.

Dantzig, G. B. 1956. Recent Advances in Linear Programming. *Management Science* 2 (2):131-144.

Dean, J. 1950. Capital Budgeting and the Firm's Demand for Capital. *Zeitschrift für Ökonometrie* 1 (2):3-23.

———. 1954. Measuring the Productivity of Capital. *Harvard Business Review* 32 (1):120-130.

———. 1978. *Capital Budgeting*. 9 ed. New York, London: Columbia University Press.

Derbes Jr, M. J. 1987. Economic Life Concepts. *Appraisal Journal* 55 (2):216-224.

Dixit, A. K., and R. S. Pindyck. 1994. *Investment Under Uncertainty*. Princeton, N.J.: Princeton University Press.

Doenges, R. C. 1972. The 'Reinvestment Problem' in a Practical Perspective. *Financial Management* 1 (1):85-91.

Dorfman, R. 1981. The Meaning of the Internal Rate of Return. *Journal of Finance* 36 (5):1011-1021.

Dyer, J. S. 1990. Remarks on the Analytic Hierarchy Process. *Management Science* 36 (3):249-258.

Dyer, J. S., P. C. Fishburn, R. E. Steuer, J. Wallenius, and S. Zionts. 1992. Multiple Criteria Decision Making, Multiattribute Utilility Theory: The Next Ten Years. *Management Science* 38 (5):645-654.

Ehrgott, M., K. Klamroth, and C. Schwehm. 2004. An MCDM approach to portfolio optimization. *European Journal of Operational Research* 155 (3):752-770.

Elton, E. J. 1970. Capital Rationing And External Discount Rates. *Journal of Finance* 25 (3):573-584.

Elton, E. J., and M. J. Gruber. 1971. Valuation and the Cost of Capital for Regulated Industries. *Journal of Finance* 26 (3):661-670.

Emery, G. W. 1982. Some Guidelines for Evaluating Capital Investment Alternatives with Unequal Lives. *Financial Management* 11 (1):14-19.

Epstein, L. G., and S. M. Turnbull. 1980. Capital Asset Prices and the Temporal Resolution of Uncertainty. *Journal of Finance* 35 (3):627-643.

Ewert, R., A. Wagenhofer, and P. Schuster. 2008. *Management Accounting*. Berlin et al.: Springer.

Fama, E. F. 1970. Efficient Capital Markets: A Review of Theory and Empirical Work. *Journal of Finance* 25 (2):383-417.

———. 1977. Risk-Adjusted Discount Rates and Capital Budgeting Under Uncertainty. *Journal of Financial Economics* 5 (1):3-24.

———. 1996. Discounting under uncertainty. *Journal of Business* 69 (4):415-428.

Fama, E. F., and K. R. French. 1996. The CAPM is Wanted, Dead or Alive. *Journal of Finance* 51 (5):1947-1958.

———. 1999. The corporate cost of capital and the return on corporate investment. *Journal of Finance* 54 (6):1939-1967.

———. 2002. The Equity Premium. *Journal of Finance* 57 (2):637-659.

———. 2004. The Capital Asset Pricing Model: Theory and Evidence. *Journal of Economic Perspectives* 18 (3):25-46.

———. 2006. The Value Premium and the CAPM. *Journal of Finance* 61 (5):2163-2185.

———. 2007. Disagreement, tastes, and asset prices. *Journal of Financial Economics* 83 (3):667-689.

Fama, E. F., and M. R. Gibbons. 1982. Inflation, Real Returns and Capital Investment. *Journal of Monetary Economics* 9 (3):297-323.

Fama, E. F., and A. B. Laffer. 1971. Information on Capital Markets. *Journal of Business* 44 (3):289-298.

Farquhar, P. H. 1977. A Survey of Multiattribute Utility Theory and Applications. *Multiple Criteria Decision Making*, edited by M. K. Starr and M. Zeleny. Amsterdam et al.: North-Holland, 59-89.

Fernández-Castro, A. S., and M. Jiménez. 2005. PROMETHEE: an extension through fuzzy mathematical programming. *Journal of the Operational Research Society* 56 (1):119-122.

Fisher, I. 1930. *Theory of Interest*. New York: Macmillan.

Förstner, K., and R. Henn. 1957. *Dynamische Produktions-Theorie und Lineare Programmierung*. Meisenheim/Glan: Hain.

Franke, G., and H. Hax. 2008: *Finanzwirtschaft des Unternehmens und Kapitalmarkt,* 6 ed. Berlin: Springer.

French, S. 1986. *Decision Theory - An Introduction to the Mathematics of Rationality*. Chichester: Ellis Horwood.

French, S., T. Bedford, and E. Atherton. 2005. Supporting ALARP decision making by cost benefit analysis and multiattribute utility theory. *Journal of Risk Research* 8 (3):207-223.

Gaddis, P. O. 1966. Analyzing Overseas Investment. *Harvard Business Review* 44 (3):115-122.

Götze, U. 2006. *Investitionsrechnung*. 5 ed. Berlin et al.: Springer.

Grob, H. L. 1993. *Capital Budgeting with Financial Plans: An Introduction.* Wiesbaden: Gabler.

Harker, P. T. 1989. The Art and Science of Decision Making: The Analytic Hierarchy Process. In *The Analytic Hierarchy Process. Applications and Studies*, edited by B. L. Golden, E. A. Wasil and P. T. Harker. Berlin et al.: Springer, 3-36.

Hax, H. 1964. Investitions- und Finanzplanung mit Hilfe der linearen Programmierung. *Schmalenbachs Zeitschrift für betriebswirtschaftliche Foschung* 16 (7/8):430-446.

Hax, H., and H. Laux. 1972: Flexible Planung - Verfahrensregeln und Entscheidungsmodelle für die Planung bei Ungewissheit. *Zeitschrift für betriebswirtschaftliche Forschung*. 24:318 – 340

Heister, M. 1962. *Rentabilitätsanalyse von Investitionen*. Köln et al.: Westdeutscher Verlag.

Hertz, D. B. 1964. Risk Analysis in Capital Investment. *Harvard Business Review* 42 (1):95-106.

Hespos, R. F., and P. A. Strassmann. 1965. Stochastic Decision Trees for the Analysis of Investment Decisions. *Management Science* 10 (10):B244-B259.

Hillier, F. S. 1963. The Derivation of Probabilistic Information for the Evaluation of Risky Investments. *Management Science* 9 (3):443-457.

Hirshleifer, J. 1958. On the Theory of Optimal Investment Decision. *The Journal of Political Economy* 66 (4):329-352.

———. 1961. Risk, the Discount Rate, and Investment Decisions. *American Economic Review* 51 (2):112-120.

———. 1964. Efficient Allocation of Capital in an Uncertain World. *American Economic Review* 54 (3):77-85.

———. 1965. Investment Decision Under Uncertainty: Choice-Theoretic Approaches. *Quarterly Journal of Economics* 79 (4):509-536.

———. 1966. Investment Decision Under Uncertainty: Applications of the State-Preference Approach. *Quarterly Journal of Economics* 80 (2):252-277.

Hwang, C. L., and K. Yoon. 1981, Multiple Attribute Decision Making; Methods and Applications. Berlin et al.: Springer.

Ingraham Jr, H. G. 1979. An Analysis of Two Cost Comparison Methods - Interest Adjusted Cost vs. Linton Yield. *CLU Journal* 33 (4):34-43.

Jääskeläinen, V. 1966. *Optimal Financing and Tax Policy of the Corporation.* Helsinki: Helsinki Research Institute for Business Economics.

Jaquet-Lagréze, E. 1985. Basic Concepts for Multicriteria Decision Support. In *Multiple Criteria Decision Methods and Applications*, edited by G. Fandel and J. Spronk. Berlin et al.: Springer, 11-26.

Kaplan, R. S., and D. P. Norton. 2001. Transforming the Balanced Scorecard from Performance Measurement to Strategic Management: Part I. *Accounting Horizons* 15 (1):87-104.

Kayali, M. M. 2006. Real Options as a Tool for Making Strategic Investment Decisions. *Journal of American Academy of Business, Cambridge* 8 (1):282-286.

Keane, S. M. 1979. The Internal Rate of Return and the Reinvestment Fallacy. *Abacus* 15 (1):48-55.

Keef, S. P., and M. L. Roush. 2001. Discounted cash flow methods and the fallacious reinvestment assumption: a review of recent texts. *Accounting Education* 10 (1):105-116.

Kelleher, J. C., and J. J. MacCormack. 2005. Internal rate of return: A cautionary tale. *McKinsey Quarterly*:70-75.

Kern, W. 1974. *Investitionsrechnung*. Stuttgart: Poeschel.

Kruschwitz, L. 2007. *Investitionsrechnung*, 11 ed. München, Wien: Oldenbourg.

Kruschwitz, L., and A. Loeffler. 2006. *Discounted Cash Flow: A Theory of the Valuation of Firms*. Chichester et al.: Wiley.

Lessard, D. R. 1985. Evaluating International Projects: an Adjusted Value Approach. In *International Financial Management. Theory and Application*, edited by D. R. Lessard. New York et al.: Wiley, 570-584.

Lewellen, W. G., H. P. Lanser, and J. J. McConnell. 1972. Payback Substitutes for Discounted Cash Flow. *Financial Management* 8 (2):195-206.

Lintner, J. 1965. The Valuation of Risk Assets and the Selection of Risky Investment in Stock Portfolios and Capital Budgets. *Review of Economics and Statistics* 47 (1):13-17.

———. 1969. The Valuation of Risk Assets and the Selection of Risky Investment in Stock Portfolios and Capital Budgets: A Reply. *Review of Economics and Statistics* 51 (2):222-224.

Little, J. D. C. 2004. Models and Managers: The Concept of a Decision Calculus. *Management Science* 50 (12):1841-1853.

Liu, K. F. R. 2007. A High-level Fuzzy Petri Nets Model for Integrating Quantitative and Qualitative Decision-making. *International Journal of Uncertainty, Fuzziness & Knowledge-Based Systems* 15 (3):253-284.

Longbottom, D. A., and L. Wiper. 1977. Capital Appraisal and the Case for Average Rate of Return. *Journal of Business Finance and Accounting* 4 (4):419-426.

———. 1979. Capital Appraisal and the Case for Average Rate of Return: A Reply. *Journal of Business Finance & Accounting* 6 (2):243-244.

Lücke, W. 1955. Investitionsrechnungen auf der Grundlage von Ausgaben oder Kosten? *Zeitschrift für handelswissenschaftliche Forschung, NF* 7:310-324.

———. 1991. *Investitionslexikon*. 2 ed. München: Vahlen.

Lutz, F. A., and V. Lutz. 1951. *The Theory of Investment of the Firm*. Princeton N.J.: Princeton University Press.

Magee, J. F. 1964a. Decision Trees for Decision Making. *Harvard Business Review* 42 (4):126-138.

———. 1964b. How to Use Decision Trees in Capital Investment. *Harvard Business Review* 42 (5):79-96.

Maloney, K. J., and T. I. Selling. 1985. Simplifying Tax Simplification: An Analysis of Its Impact on the Profitability of Capital Investment. *Financial Management* 14 (2):33-42.

Markowitz, H. M. 1952. Portfolio Selection. *Journal of Finance* 7 (1):77-91.

———. 1959. *Portfolio Selection: Efficient Diversification of Investments*. New York et al.: Wiley.

Merton, R. C. 1969. Lifetime Portfolio Selection Under Uncertainty: The Continuous-time Case. *Review of Economics & Statistics* 51 (3):247-257.

———. 1972. An Analytic Derivation of the Efficient Portfolio Frontier. *Journal of Financial & Quantitative Analysis* 7 (4):1851-1872.

———. 1973. An Intertemporal Capital Asset Pricing Model. *Econometrica* 41 (5):867-887.

———. 1974. On the Pricing of Corporate Debt: The Risk Structure of Interest Rates. *Journal of Finance* 29 (2):449-470.

———. 1978. On the Cost of Deposit Insurance When There Are Surveillance Costs. *Journal of Business* 51 (3):439-452.

———. 1981. On Market Timing and Investment Performance. I. An Equilibrium Theory of Value for Market Forecasts. *Journal of Business* 54 (3):363-406.

———. 1987. A Simple Model of Capital Market Equilibrium with Incomplete Information. *Journal of Finance* 42 (3):483-510.

Meyer, R. L. 1979. A Note on Capital Budgeting Techniques and the Reinvestment Rate. *Journal of Finance* 34 (5):1251-1254.

Miller, M. H. 1977. Debt and Taxes. *Journal of Finance* 32 (2):261-275.

Miller, M. H., and F. Modigliani. 1966. Some Estimates of the Cost of Capital to the Electric Utility Industry, 1954-57. *American Economic Review* 56 (3):333-392.

———. 1967. Some Estimates of the Cost of Capital to the Electric Utility Industry: 1954-57: Reply. *American Economic Review* 57 (5):1288-1300.

Millet, I., and T. L. Saaty. 2000. On the Relativity of Relative Measures - Accomodating Both Rank Preservations and Rank Reversals in the AHP. *European Journal of Operational Research* 121 (1):205-212.

Modigliani, F. 1982. Debt, Dividend Policy, Taxes, Inflation and Market Valuation. *Journal of Finance* 37 (2):255-274.

———. 1983. Debt, Dividend Policy, Taxes, Inflation, and Market Valuation: Erratum. *Journal of Finance* 38(3):1041-1042.

———. 1988. MM - Past, Present, Future. *Journal of Economic Perspectives* 2 (4):149-158.

Modigliani, F., and M. H. Miller. 1958. The Cost of Capital, Corporation Finance and the Theory of Investment. *American Economic Review* 48 (3):261-297.

———. 1959. The Cost of Capital, Corporation Finance, and the Theory of Investment: Reply. *American Economic Review* 49 (4):655-669.

———. 1963. Corporate Income Taxes and the Cost of Capital: A Correction. *American Economic Review* 53 (3):433-443.

Modigliani, F., and R. Sutch. 1966. Innovations in Interest Rate Policy. *American Economic Review* 56 (2):178-197.

Modigliani, F., and H. M. Weingartner. 1958. Forecasting Uses of Anticipatory Data on Investment and Sales. *Quarterly Journal of Economics* 72 (1):23-54.

Mossin, J. 1966. Equilibrium in a Capital Asset Pricing Market. *Econometrica* 34 (4):768-783.

Myers, S. C. 1974. Interactions of Corporate Financing and Investment Decisons - Implications for Capital Budgeting. *Journal of Finance* 29 (1):1-25.

Nicol, D. J. 1981. A Note on Capital Budgeting Techniques and the Reinvestment Rate: Comment. *Journal of Finance* 36 (1):193-195.

Ozernoy, V. M. 1992. Choosing the "Best" Multiple Criteria Decision-making Method. *INFOR* 30 (2):159-171.

Pastijn, H., and J. Leysen. 1989. Constructing an Outranking Relation with ORESTE. *Mathematical Computing Modelling* 12:1255-1268.

Perridon, L., and M. Steiner, M. 2007. *Finanzwirtschaft der Unternehmung*. 14 ed. München: Vahlen.

Pogue, M. 2004. Investment appraisal: A new Approach. *Managerial Auditing Journal* 19 (4):565-569.

Pratt, J. W., and J. S. Hammond III. 1979. Evaluating and Comparing Projects: Simple Detection of False Alarms. *Journal of Finance* 34 (5):1231-1241.

Preinreich, G. A. D. 1937. Valuation and Amortization. *The Accounting Review* 12 (3):209-226.

———. 1940. The Economic Life of Industrial Equipment. *Econometrica* 8 (1):12-44.

Remer, D. S., and A. P. Nieto. 1995a. A Compendium and Comparison of 25 Project Evaluation Techniques.: Part 1: Net Present Value and Rate of Return Methods. *International Journal of Production Economics* 42 (1):79-96.

———. 1995b. A Compendium and Comparison of 25 Project Evaluation Techniques. Part 2: Ratio, Payback, and Accounting Methods. *International Journal of Production Economics* 42 (2):101-129.

Robichek, A. A., and D. Teichroew. 1965. Optimal Short Term Financing Decisions. *Management Science* 12 (1):1-36.

Roll, R., and S. A. Ross. 1980. An Empirical Investigation of the Arbitrage Pricing Theory. *Journal of Finance* 35 (5):1073-1103.

Rosen, J. B. 1960. The Gradient Projection Method for Nonlinear Programming, Part I: Linear Constraints. *SIAM, Journal of Applied Mathematics* 8 (1):181-217.

———. 1961. The Gradient Projection Method for Nonlinear Programming, Part II: Nonlinear Constraints. *SIAM, Journal of Applied Mathematics* 9 (4):514-532.

Ross, S. A. 1976. The Arbitrage Theory of Capital Asset Pricing. *Journal of Economic Theory* 13 (3):341-360.

———. 1977. The Interrelations of Finance and Economics: Theoretical Perspectives. *American Economic Review* 77 (2):29-34.

———. 1978. A Simple Approach to the Valuation of Risky Streams. *Journal of Business* 51 (3):453-475.

Ross, S. A., R. W. Westerfield, J. F. Jaffe, and D. J. Bradford. 2007. *Corporate Finance: Core Principles & Applications*. 6 ed. Boston, Mass. et al.: McGraw-Hill/Irwin.

Roubens, M. 1982. Preference Relations on Actions and Criterions in Multicriteria Decision Making. *European Journal of Operational Research* 10 (1):51-55.

Roy, B. 1990. The Outranking Approach and the Foundations of ELECTRE Methods. In *Readings in Multiple Criteria Decision Aid, Berlin*, edited by C. A. Bana e Costa. Berlin et al.: Springer, 155-183.

Rubinstein, M. 1976. The Valuation of Uncertain Income Streams and the Pricing of Options. *Bell Journal of Economics* 7 (2):407-425.

———. 2002. Markowitz's "Portfolio Selection": A Fifty-Year Retrospective. *Journal of Finance* 57 (3):1041-1045.

———. 2005. Great Moments in Financial Economics: IV. The Fundamental Theorem (PART I). *Journal of Investment Management* 3 (4):87-103.

———. 2006. Great Moments in Financial Economics: IV. The Fundamental Theorem (PART II). *Journal of Investment Management* 4 (1):22-30.

Rubinstein, M., and P. Stephens. 2001. Rational Markets: Yes or No? The Affirmative Case. *Financial Analysts Journal* 57 (3):15-29.

Rudd, A., and B. Rosenberg. 1980. The "Market Model" In Investment Management. *Journal of Finance* 35 (2):597-607.

Saaty, T. L. 1980. *The Analytic Hierarchy Process: Planning, Priority Setting, Resource Allocation*. New York et al.: McGraw-Hill.

———. 1990. How to Make a Decision: The Analytic Hierarchy Process. *European Journal of Operational Research* 48 (1):9-26.

———. 2006. *The Analytic Network Process - Dependence and Feedback in Decison-Making: Theory and Validation Examples*. Hershley, PA. et al.: Idea Group.

Saaty, T. L., and L. G. Vargas. 2006. *Decision Making with the Analytic Network Process*. Boston: Springer Science+Business Media.

Scarf, P. A., and M. H. Hashem. 1997. On the Application of an Economic Life Model with a Fixed Planning Horizon. *International Transactions in Operational Research* 4 (2):139-150.

Schneeweiß, C. 1991. *Planung, Bd. 1: Systemanalytische und entscheidungstheoretische Grundlagen*. Berlin et al.: Springer.

Schubert, W., and L. Barenbaum. 2007. Real Options and Public Sector Capital Project Decision-making. *Journal of Public Budgeting, Accounting & Financial Management* 19 (2):139-152.

Shank, J. K., and V. Govindarajan. 1992. Strategic Cost Analysis of Technological Investments. *SLOAN Management Review* 34 (1):39-51.

Sharpe, W. F. 1964. Capital Asset Prices: A Theory of Market Equilibrium under Conditions of Risk. *Journal of Finance* 19 (3):425-442.

Siskos, J., G. Wäscher, and H.-M. Winkels. 1984. Outranking approaches versus MAUT in MCDM. *European Journal of Operational Research* 16 (2):270-271.

Spronk, J., R. E. Steuer, and C. Zopounidis. 2005. *Multicriteria Decision Aid/Analysis in Finance*. New York et al.: Springer.

Teichroew, D., A. A. Robichek and M. Montalbano. 1965a. Mathematical Analysis of Rates of Return under Certainty. *Management Science* 11 (3):393-403.

———. 1965b. An Analysis of Criteria for Investment and Financing Decisions under Certainty. *Management Science* 12 (3):151-179.

Terborgh, G. 1949. *Dynamic Equipment Policy*. New York et al.: McGraw-Hill.

Van-Nam, H., Y. Nakamori, H. Tu-Bao, and T. Murai. 2006. Multiple-Attribute Decision Making Under Uncertainty: The Evidential Reasoning Approach Revisited. *IEEE Transactions on Systems, Man & Cybernetics: Part A* 36 (4):804-822.

Wang, C.-L., and A. S. M. Masud. 1979. *Multiple Objective Decision Making. Methods and Applications*. Berlin et al.: Springer.

Wang, C.-L., and B. K. Yoon. 1981. *Multiple Attribute Decision Making. Methods and Applications*. Berlin et al.: Springer.

Weingartner, H. M. 1963. *Mathematical Programming and the Analysis of Capital Budgeting Problems*. Englewood Cliffs, N.J.: Prentice Hall.

———. 1966a. Capital Budgeting of Interrelated Projects: Survey and Synthesis. *Management Science* 12 (7):485-516.

———. 1966b. Criteria for Programming Investment Project Selection. *Journal of Industrial Economics* 15 (1):65-76.

———. 1969. Some New Views on the Payback Period and Capital Budgeting. *Management Science* 15 (2):594-607.

Weingartner, H. M., and D. N. Ness. 1967. Methods for the Solution of the Multi-Dimensional 0/1 Knapsack Problem. *Operations Research* 15 (1):83-103.

Wolf, J. 1988. *Lineare Fuzzy-Modelle zur Unterstützung der Investitionsplanung*. Frankfurt am Main et al.: Lang.

Wolfe, P. 1959. The Simplex Method for Quadratic Programming. *Econometrica* 27 (3):382-298.

Xu, Z. S. 2007. Models for Multiple Attribute Decision Making With Intuitionistic Fuzzy Information. *International Journal of Uncertainty, Fuzziness & Knowledge-Based Systems* 15 (3):285-297.

Yu, Z., and I. Friend. 1986. The Effects of Different Taxes on Risky and Risk-Free Investment and on the Cost of Capital. *Journal of Finance* 41 (1):53-66.

Zadeh, L. A. 1965. Fuzzy Sets. *Information and Control* 8 (3):338-353.

Zanakis, S. H., A. Solomon, N. Wishart, and S. Dublish. 1998. Multi-attribute decision making: A simulation comparison of select methods. *European Journal of Operational Research* 107 (3):507-529.

Zimmermann, H.-J., and L. Gutsche. 1991. *Multi-Criteria-Analyse*. Berlin et al.: Springer.

Index

Index

Absolute scale 172
Adjusted present value approach 124, 271 f.
Analytic hierarchy process 23, 174, 179 ff., 213 f.
Annuity 52 f., 65 ff., 141 ff.
Annuity factor 53, 56, 65 ff., 143
Annuity method 53, 65 ff., 93, 141 ff.
Anti-symmetry 172 f.
Asymmetry 6
Average rate of return 41 ff.
Average rate of return method 41 ff.

Balanced scorecard 20 f.
BAYES rule 265 ff.
BERNOULLI criterion 266 ff., 296
Beta factor 269 ff.

Capital asset pricing model 266, 268 ff., 329
Capital budgeting 3, 7
Capital demand function 223 ff.
Capital supply function 223 ff.
Capital recovery factor 53, 65 ff., 143
Capital tie-up 35 ff., 41 ff., 61 ff., 67 ff., 81, 96 ff., 271
- Average capital tie-up 35 f., 41
Cardinal scale 172, 175, 213
Cash flow 3 ff., 38, 44 ff., 51 ff., 93 ff., 111 ff., 222 ff., 270 ff., 330 ff.
- Cash inflow 3, 31, 45, 51 ff., 78 f., 94 ff., 112 ff.
- Cash outflow 3, 31, 45, 51 ff., 78 f., 94 ff., 112 ff.
- Derivative cash flow 101
- Original cash flow 101
- Risk-adjusted cash flow 272 ff.
Chain effect 139
Completeness 172 f.
Compound value 93 ff., 101 ff., 116 ff., 129, 222 ff., 229 ff., 240 ff., 330 ff.
Compound value method 83, 93 ff.
Compounding 51 ff., 93 ff.

Compounding factor 51 f.
- Model endogenous compounding factor 233 f.
- Periodical compounding factor 52
Cost comparison method 32 ff.
Criterion 171 ff.
- Criterion with linear preference (and indifference) 205 ff.
- GAUSS-criterion 205 f.
- Generalised criterion 205 ff.
- Quasi-criterion 205 ff.
- Step-criterion 205 ff.
- Usual criterion 205 f.
Critical debt interest rate method 98 ff.

Decision-tree 286 ff.
Decision-tree method 286 ff., 298 ff., 305 ff., 329
Decision theory 262 ff.
- Decision matrix 262
- Decision theory rules 262 ff.
Depreciation 32 ff., 45, 112 ff.
Differential investment 56, 60, 74, 279 f., 285
Discount rate 51 ff., 97, 107, 112 ff., 122 ff., 154 f., 227, 229, 235, 268 ff.
- Risk-adjusted discount rate 268 ff., 296, 305 ff.
- Tax-adjusted discount rate 112 ff.
- Time-span dependent discount rate 81 ff.
Discounting 51 ff.
Discounting factor 51 f.
Discounted Cash Flow Method 51 ff., 270
Distribution function 282 ff.
Dynamic investment appraisal method 53, 93

Economic life 25, 31 ff., 51 ff., 61 f., 131 ff.
- Optimum economic life 25, 131 ff.
Economic life decision 131 ff.
Eigenvalue 183 ff.
Eigenvector 182 ff.
Enumeration 148 f., 224 ff., 296
Equilibrium yield 269

Exchange rate 119 ff.
Expected value-standard deviation criterion 266 f., 269, 320 ff.

Financial budget (and redemption) plan 58 f., 72 f.
Financial investment 4 ff., 58 ff., 68 ff., 78 ff., 93 ff., 119 ff., 298 ff., 320 ff.
- Short-term financial investment 101 ff., 229 ff., 240 ff., 330 f.
FISHER condition 83
- International FISHER condition 121 ff., 5.2.2
FISHER separation theorem 107, 121
Flexible planning 329 ff.
Flow measure 207 ff.
- Inflow measure 208 ff.
- Outflow measure 207 ff.
Foreign direct investment 118 ff.
- Foreign direct investments and the NPV method 122 ff.
- Foreign direct investments and the VoFI method 127 ff.
Fuzziness 318
- Fuzzy descriptions 318
- Fuzzy relations 318
Fuzzy set models 318 ff.
Fuzzy set theory 23 f., 318 ff.

Goal setting 7 f., 171

HURWICZ rule 264 f.

Index of consistency 184 ff.
Indifference curve 197
Inflation 83, 120 f.
Initial investment outlay 3, 33 ff., 53 ff., 78, 270, 275 ff.
Interest rate 13, 31 ff., 52 f., 80 ff., 93 ff., 116 ff., 121 f., 135 ff., 296 ff.
- Credit interest rate 53, 93 ff.
- Critical debt interest rate 98 ff.
- Critical interest rate 226
- Debt interest rate 53, 93 ff.
- Endogenous interest rate 226 f., 233 ff.
- Exchange-rate adjusted interest rate 121 ff.

Internal rate of return 67 ff., 99 f., 151, 277
Internal rate of return method 53, 67 ff., 93, 98 ff., 271, 277
Interpolation formula 71 f., 76 f., 98 ff.
Interpolation procedure 70 ff., 76 f., 98 ff., 103
Interval scale 171 f., 202 f.
Investment Decision-Making Process 8 ff.
Investment planning 6 ff.
Investment project 3 ff.
- Classification of investment projects 4 ff.
- Isolated investment project 68 ff., 98 f.
- Normal investment project 69
- Subsequent investment project 6, 61 ff., 78, 97, 132 ff., 153, 159, 288 ff.
Investment timing 25, 151 ff., 236, 291 ff.
Irreflexivity 172

Lifetime
- Life cycle 6
- Economic life 31 ff., 51 ff., 61 f., 65, 76, 78 ff., 93 ff., 121 ff., 222 ff., 268, 275 ff.
- Optimum economic life 25, 131 ff.
- Option's life 297
- Technical life 131
Liquidation value 33 ff., 55 ff., 80, 111 ff., 119 ff., 132 ff., 240 ff., 275 ff.
Loan 57 f., 64, 72 f., 75, 81 f., 94, 101 ff., 116 f., 122 ff., 223 ff., 229 ff., 270, 332 ff.

Mandatory account balancing 94 ff., 99 f.
Marginal profit 134 ff., 138 ff., 142 ff., 145 ff.
Maximax rule 264 f.
Maximin rule 263 ff.
Membership function 318 ff.
Model 10, 19, 23 ff.
- Binomial 298 ff.
- Dynamic 25, 51 ff., 93 ff., 111 ff., 228 ff., 286 ff., 329 ff.
- Flexible 286 ff., 329 ff.
- Multi-tier 25, 159 f., 228 ff., 286 ff., 329 ff.
- Single-tier 25, 31 ff., 51 ff., 93 ff., 171 ff., 221 ff.
- Static 25, 31 ff., 171 ff., 221 ff.
Model endogenous compounding factor 234

Model endogenous interest rate 226 f., 233 ff.
Multi-attribute decision-making 171 ff.
Multi-attribute utility theory 174, 193 ff., 214
Multi-criteria decision-making 171 ff.
Multi-objective decision-making 171

Net cash flow 55 ff., 78 f., 94 ff., 112 ff., 132 ff., 222 ff., 271 ff.
Net present value 19 f., 54 ff., 65 ff., 75 ff., 97, 113 ff., 122 ff., 132 ff., 152 ff., 176, 235 ff., 262 ff.
- Tax-adjusted net present value 111 ff.
Net present value method 53 ff., 65 ff., 75 ff., 93 f., 97 f., 106 ff., 111 ff., 132 ff., 152 ff., 155, 226 ff., 262 ff.
- considering foreign direct investments 122 ff.
- considering taxes 111 ff.
Nine-point scale 181 ff.
Nominal scale 171

Option 296 ff.
- Real option 296 ff.
Options pricing model 137, 152, 159, 262, 296 ff.
Ordinal scale 171

Payback period 14, 19, 32, 44 ff., 75 ff., 106 f.
Payback period method 32, 44 ff., 53, 75 ff., 93, 277
- Dynamic payback period method 53, 75 ff., 93, 277
- Static payback period method 32, 44 ff.
Portfolio selection 267, 320
Preference order 172 f.
- Indifference order 172 f.
- Strict preference order 173
- Weak preference order 173
Probability 263 ff., 318 ff.
- Conditional probability 281
Problem identification and analysis 7 f.
Production coefficient 239 ff.
Profit comparison method 32, 39 ff., 41 ff.

Profitability 3 ff., 24 f., 31 ff., 54 ff., 113, 118 ff., 132 ff., 144 f., 152, 175 ff., 221 ff., 262 ff., 287 ff.
- Absolute profitability 24 f., 31 ff., 54 ff., 132, 155, 175 ff., 262 ff., 274 ff., 283
- Relative profitability 25, 31 ff., 54 ff., 132, 175 ff., 262 ff., 278 f., 283 ff.
Programme decision 6, 9 ff., 24 ff., 221 ff., 318 ff.
Prohibited account balancing 94 ff., 99
Project chain 132 f., 137 ff.
- Infinite (or unlimited) chain 141 ff., 144 ff.
- Limited project chain 137 ff., 148 ff.
- Multi-project chain 138 f.
- Two-project chain 137 ff.
PROMETHEE 174, 203 ff.

Rate of return 13, 80 f.
- Average rate of return 41 ff.
- Internal rate of return 67 ff., 99 f., 151, 277
- Rate of return for the internal funds invested 103 ff.
Rate of taxation 112 ff.
Replacement time 132, 151
- Optimum replacement time 144 ff., 148 ff.
Replacement time decision 131 ff., 144 ff., 148 ff., 155 ff.
Reflexivity 172 f.
Relational scale 172, 180 f., 192
Risk 5 ff., 13 ff., 22 f., 44 ff., 77, 83, 119 ff., 124, 152, 261 ff., 317 ff.
- Systematic risk 269 ff.
Risk-adjusted analysis 13, 262, 268 ff.
Risk analysis 15, 20, 137, 180, 262, 280 ff., 317 f.
Risk measure 266, 285, 320 ff.
Risk preference 266 ff., 327, 335
Rollback procedure 287 ff., 301, 307

Safety indicator 277
Search for alternatives 7 f., 24
Sensitivity analysis 12, 25, 38, 46, 179, 193, 203, 262, 274 ff., 281, 296, 317
- Global sensitivity analysis 317
- Local sensitivity analysis 317
Shadow price 233

Simultaneous decision-making 26, 221 ff., 317 ff.
Simultaneous investment and finance decision-making 221 ff., 329 ff.
Simultaneous investment and production decision-making 238 ff.
Static analysis method 25 f., 31 ff.
Static payback period method 44 ff.
Stochastic dominance 283 ff.
Stochastic tree 329 ff.
Strategic cost management analysis 21 ff.
Subsequent investment projects 6, 61 ff., 78, 97, 132 ff., 153, 159, 288 ff.
Symmetry 172 f.

Target criterion 171 ff.
Taxes 111 ff., 119
- Taxes and the net present value method 111 ff.
- Taxes and the visualisation of financial implications method 116 ff.
Technology roadmapping 22 ff.
Time state preference model 273 f.
Timing decision 25, 151 ff., 236, 291 ff.
Transitiveness 172 f.

Uncertainty 5 ff., 13, 25 f., 261 ff., 317 ff.
Utility function 173, 179, 193 ff., 214, 272 f., 296
Utility value 175 ff.
- Partial utility value 176 ff.
Utility value analysis 174, 175 ff., 186, 192 ff., 202 f., 213 f.

Value of consistency 185 ff.
Visualisation of financial implications (VoFI) method 93, 100 ff., 116 ff., 127 ff., 160, 228
- Visualisation of financial implications (VoFI) method considering foreign direct investments 127 ff.
- Visualisation of financial implications (VoFI) method considering taxes 116 ff.
VoFI table 101 ff., 116 ff., 127 ff.

WALD rule 263 ff.
Weighted average cost of capital 270 f.

Printing: Krips bv, Meppel, The Netherlands
Binding: Stürtz, Würzburg, Germany